The Rites of the Catholic Church
as revised
by the Second Vatican Ecumenical Council

VOLUME IA, INITIATION

The Roman Ritual revised by
Decree of the Second Vatican Ecumenical Council
and published by authority
of Pope Paul VI

THE RITES
OF THE
CATHOLIC CHURCH

VOLUME IA, INITIATION

Prepared by the
International Commission on English in the Liturgy
A Joint Commission of
Catholic Bishops' Conferences

Approved for use in the
Dioceses of the United States of America by the
National Conference of Catholic Bishops
and confirmed
by the Apostolic See

STUDY EDITION

PUEBLO PUBLISHING COMPANY
New York

Concordat cum originali: John A. Gurrieri

Published by authority of the Bishops' Committee on the Liturgy, National Conference of Catholic Bishops.

Design: Frank Kacmarcik

Acknowledgements are on page xii.

ISBN: 0-916134-94-6

Printed in the United States of America

CONTENTS

PREFACE

The Roman Ritual has undergone numerous revisions since the edition of Pope Paul V, of 1614. In response to the directives of the Second Vatican Ecumenical Council, a total revision has been made by the Holy See. One of the animating principles that has guided the preparation of the new rites is to encourage the people of God to understand and participate more fully in these sacred celebrations.

The matter is clearly stated in the Instruction on the Proper Implementation of the Constitution on the Sacred Liturgy (*Inter Oecumenici*, September 26, 1964), no. 5:

"It is essential that everybody be persuaded that the scope of the Constitution on the Sacred Liturgy is not limited merely to the changing of liturgical rites and texts. Rather its aim is to foster the formation of the faithful and that pastoral activity of which the liturgy is the summit and source (see Const., Art. 10). The changes in the liturgy which have already been introduced or which will be introduced later, have this same end in view."

The Constitution on the Sacred Liturgy (*Sacrosanctum Concilium*) itself points out:

"Mother Church earnestly desires that all the faithful should be led to that full, conscious, and active participation in liturgical celebrations which is demanded by the very nature of the liturgy, and to which the Christian people, 'a chosen race, a royal priesthood, a holy nation, a redeemed people' (1 Pet. 2:9, 4-5) have a right and obligation by reason of their baptism.

"In the restoration and promotion of the sacred liturgy the full and active participation by all the people is the aim to be considered before all else, for it is the primary and indispensable source from which the faithful are to derive the true Christian spirit. Therefore, in all their apostolic activity, pastors of souls should energetically set about achieving it through the requisite pedagogy" (no. 14).[1]

The Constitution on the Sacred Liturgy goes on to point out the need for liturgical reforms along the following lines:

[1]Unless otherwise noted, the quotations are from the Constitution on the Sacred Liturgy (*Sacrosanctum Concilium*).

"In order that the Christian people may more certainly derive an abundance of graces from the sacred liturgy, holy Mother Church desires to undertake with great care a general restoration of the liturgy itself. For the liturgy is made up of unchangeable elements divinely instituted, and elements subject to change. These latter not only may be changed but ought to be changed with the passage of time, if they have suffered from the intrusion of anything out of harmony with the inner nature of the liturgy or have become less suitable. In this restoration both texts and rites should be drawn up so as to express more clearly the holy things which they signify. The Christian people, as far as is possible, should be able to understand them with ease and take part in them fully, actively, and as a community" (no. 21).

Although the liturgy "is principally the worship of the divine Majesty, it likewise contains much instruction for the faithful" (no. 33). Modern courses in religion from the elementary grades through college as well as advanced studies in seminaries and graduate schools are careful to give the study of liturgy a prominent place in the development of the spiritual and intellectual aspects of Christian life.

The purpose of this book is to bring together for the first time in one volume the rites of initiation. These texts are essential to the planning of liturgical celebrations, are studied and referred to in theology courses, and are of special concern to the laity in general. These rites are Christian Initiation, Rite of Christian Initiation of Adults, Rite of Baptism for Children, and Rite of Confirmation.

As a further aid to the study of these rites a comprehensive outline of each rite precedes the official text.

The following is a description of the general principles which guided the Fathers of Vatican II in the reforms of the liturgy: The Constitution on the Sacred Liturgy (*Sacrosanctum Concilium*) states:

"With the passage of time . . . there have crept into the rites of the sacraments and sacramentals certain features which have rendered their nature and purpose far from clear to the people of today. Hence some changes are necessary to adapt them to present-day needs" (no. 62).

The purpose and plan of revision of the liturgical books is closely allied to an enlarged view of the importance of sacred scripture as a source of the liturgy.

"Sacred Scripture is of the greatest importance in the celebration of the liturgy. For it is from it that lessons are read and explained in the homily, and psalms are sung. It is from the Scriptures that the prayers, collects, and hymns draw their inspiration and their force, and that actions derive their meaning. Hence in order to achieve the restoration, progress, and adaptation of the sacred liturgy it is essential to promote that sweet and living love for Sacred Scripture to which the venerable tradition of Eastern and Western rites gives testimony" (no. 24).

The Constitution closes its section on the general norms for liturgical reforms with a reiteration of its concern for popular participation:

"To promote active participation, the people should be encouraged to take part by means of acclamations, responses, psalms, antiphons, hymns, as well as by actions, gestures and bodily attitudes. And at the proper time a reverent silence should be observed" (no. 30). Also:

"When the liturgical books are being revised, the people's parts must be carefully indicated by the rubrics" (no. 31). The document gives further "Norms Based on the Educative and Pastoral Nature of the Liturgy." Thus:

". . . the visible signs which the sacred liturgy uses to signify invisible divine things have been chosen by Christ or by the Church. Thus not only when things are read 'which were written for our instruction' (Rom. 15:4), but also when the Church prays or sings or acts, the faith of those taking part is nourished, and their minds are raised to God so that they may offer him their spiritual homage and receive his grace more abundantly" (no. 33).

In accordance with the above principles the Council set forth the basic direction of the reform of specific rites—requirements which were further elaborated by certain post-Vatican II documents.

RITE OF BAPTISM

Certain rites which did not appear in the old ritual and yet stem from the usage of the early Church are restored. Such is the "catechumenate for adults, comprising several distinct steps" which is "to be restored and brought into in use at the discretion of the local ordinary. By this means the time of the catechumenate, which is intended as a period of suitable instruction, may be sanctified by sacred rites to be celebrated at successive intervals of time" (no. 64).

"Both rites for the baptism of adults are to be revised, not only the simpler rite but also, taking into consideration the restored catechumenate, the more solemn rite. A special Mass 'For the conferring of Baptism' is to be inserted into the Roman Missal" (no. 66).

The Constitution continues:

"The rite for the baptism of infants is to be revised, its revision taking into account the fact that those to be baptized are infants. The roles of parents and godparents, and also their duties, should be brought out more clearly in the rite itself" (no. 67).

"The baptismal rite should contain variants, to be used at the discretion of the local ordinary when a large number are to be baptized. Likewise a shorter rite is to be drawn up, especially for mission countries which catechists, and also the faithful in general, may use when there is danger of death and neither priest nor deacon is available (no. 68).

"In place of the rite called 'Rite for supplying what was omitted in the baptism of an infant' a new rite is to be drawn up for converts who have already been validly baptized. It should indicate that they are now admitted to communion with the Church" (no. 69).

"Baptismal water, outside of paschal time, may be blessed within the rite of Baptism itself by an approved shorter formula" (no. 70).

RITE OF CONFIRMATION

"Incorporated into the Church by Baptism, the faithful are appointed by their baptismal character to Christian religious worship; reborn as sons of God, they must profess before men the faith they have received from God through the Church. By the sacrament of Confirmation they are more perfectly bound to the Church and are endowed with the · special strength of the Holy Spirit. Hence they are, as true witnesses of Christ, more strictly obliged to spread the faith by word and deed" Dogmatic Constitution on the Church (*Lumen Gentium*), no. 11.

The reasons for the changes and adaptations of the rites of both baptism and confirmation lie in the close relationship between the two sacraments and their function in the Christian life. Thus:

"The rite of Confirmation is to be revised also so that the intimate connection of this sacrament with the whole of the Christian initiation may more clearly appear. For this reason the renewal of baptismal promises should fittingly precede the reception of this sacrament. Confirmation may be conferred within Mass when convenient. For conferring outside Mass, a formula introducing the rite should be drawn up" (no. 71).

ACKNOWLEDGMENTS

The English translation, original texts, additional notes, arrangement, and design of *Rite of Christian Initiation of Adults* © 1985, International Committee on English in the Liturgy, Inc. (ICEL), 1275 K Street, NW, Suite 1202, Washington, DC 20005-4097 USA; the English translation of the *Rite of Baptism for Children* © 1969, ICEL; the English translation of the *Rite of Reception of Baptized Christians into Full Communion with the Catholic Church* © 1974, ICEL; excerpts from the English translation of *The Roman Missal* ©1973, ICEL; excerpts from the English translation of *Rite of Penance* © 1974, ICEL; the English translation of the *Rite of Confirmation*, Second Edition © 1975, ICEL; excerpts from *Pastoral Care of the Sick: Rites of Anointing and Viaticum* © 1982, ICEL; excerpts from the English translation of *Documents on the Liturgy, 1963–1979: Conciliar, Papal, and Curial Texts* © 1982, ICEL. All rights reserved.

The English translation of the "Apostles' Creed" and the "Nicene Creed" by the International Consultation on English Texts (ICET).

The arrangement and various texts in "Sending of the Catechumens for Election" (nos. 106-117), the "Rite of Election or Enrollment of Names" for children of catechetical age (nos. 277-290), "Rite of Welcoming the Candidates" (nos. 411-433), "Rite of Sending the Candidates for Recognition by the Bishop and for the Call to Continuing Conversion" (nos. 434-445), "Rite of Calling the Candidates to Continuing Conversion" (nos. 446-458), "Penitential Rite (Scrutiny)" (nos. 459-472), "Celebration of the Rite of Acceptance into the Order of Catechumens and of the Rite of Welcoming Baptized but Previously Uncatechized Adults Who Are Preparing for Confirmation and/or Eucharist or Reception into the Full Communion of the Catholic Church" (nos. 505-529), "Parish Celebration Sending Catechumens for Election and Candidates for Recognition by the Bishop" (nos. 530-546), "Celebration of the Rite of Election of Catechumens and of the Call to Continuing Conversion of Candidates Who Are Preparing for Confirmation and/or Eucharist or Reception into the Full Communion of the Catholic Church" (nos. 547-561), "National Statutes for the Catechumenate" (Appendix III) © 1988, United States Catholic Conference (USCC), 1312 Massachusetts Avenue, NW, Washington, DC 20005-4105 USA. All rights reserved.

Excerpts from *Vatican Council II, the Conciliar and Post Conciliar Documents* copyright © 1975, Harry J. Costello and Rev. Austin Flannery, O.P.

Excerpts from the *Code of Canon Law: Latin-English Edition* © copyright 1983, Canon Law Society of America.

CHRISTIAN INITIATION

CHRISTIAN INITIATION,

GENERAL INTRODUCTION

1. In the sacraments of Christian initiation we are freed from the power of darkness and joined to Christ's death, burial, and resurrection. We receive the Spirit of filial adoption and are part of the entire people of God in the celebration of the memorial of the Lord's death and resurrection.[1]

2. Baptism incorporates us into Christ and forms us into God's people. This first sacrament pardons all our sins, rescues us from the power of darkness, and brings us to the dignity of adopted children,[2] a new creation through water and the Holy Spirit. Hence we are called and are indeed the children of God.[3]

By signing us with the gift of the Spirit, confirmation makes us more completely the image of the Lord and fills us with the Holy Spirit, so that we may bear witness to him before all the world and work to bring the Body of Christ to its fullness as soon as possible.[4]

Finally, coming to the table of the eucharist, we eat the flesh and drink the blood of the Son of Man so that we may have eternal life[5] and show forth the unity of God's people. By offering ourselves with Christ, we share in the universal sacrifice, that is, the entire community of the redeemed offered to God by their High Priest,[6] and we pray for a greater outpouring of the Holy Spirit, so that the whole human race may be brought into the unity of God's family.[7]

[1]See Vatican Council II, Decree on the Church's Missionary Activity *Ad gentes*, no. 14.
[2]See Colossians 1:13; Romans 8:15; Galatians 4:5. See also Council of Trent, sess. 6., *Decr. de iustificatione*, cap. 4: Denz.-Schön. 1524.
[3]See 1 John 3:1.
[4]See Vatican Council II, Decree on the Church's Missionary Activity *Ad gentes*, no. 36.
[5]See John 6:55.
[6]See Augustine, *De civitate Dei* 10,6: PL 41, 284. Vatican Council II, Dogmatic Constitution on the Church *Lumen gentium*, no. 11; Decree on the Ministry and Life of Priests *Presbyterorum Ordinis*, no. 2.
[7]See Vatican Council II, Dogmatic Constitution on the Church *Lumen gentium*, no. 28.

Thus the three sacraments of Christian initiation closely combine to bring us, the faithful of Christ, to his full stature and to enable us to carry out the mission of the entire people of God in the Church and in the world.[8]

DIGNITY OF BAPTISM

3. Baptism, the door to life and to the kingdom of God, is the first sacrament of the New Law, which Christ offered to all, that they might have eternal life.[9] He later entrusted this sacrament and the Gospel to his Church, when he told his apostles: "Go, make disciples of all nations, and baptize them in the name of the Father, and of the Son, and of the Holy Spirit."[10] Baptism is therefore, above all, the sacrament of that faith by which, enlightened by the grace of the Holy Spirit, we respond to the Gospel of Christ. That is why the Church believes that it is its most basic and necessary duty to inspire all, catechumens, parents of children still to be baptized, and godparents, to that true and living faith by which they hold fast to Christ and enter into or confirm their commitment to the New Covenant. In order to enliven such faith, the Church prescribes the pastoral instruction of catechumens, the preparation of the children's parents, the celebration of God's word, and the profession of faith at the celebration of baptism.

4. Further, baptism is the sacrament by which its recipients are incorporated into the Church and are built up together in the Spirit into a house where God lives,[11] into a holy nation and a royal priesthood.[12] Baptism is a sacramental bond of unity linking all who have been signed by it.[13] Because of that unchangeable effect (given expression in the Latin liturgy by the anointing of the baptized person with chrism in the presence of God's people), the rite of baptism is held in highest honor by all Christians. Once it has been validly celebrated, even if by Christians with whom we are not in full communion, it may never lawfully be repeated.

[8]See ibid., no. 31.
[9]See John 3:5.
[10]Matthew 28:19.
[11]See Ephesians 2:22.
[12]See 1 Peter 2:9.
[13]See Vatican Council II, Decree on Ecumenism *Unitatis redintegratio*, no. 22.

5. Baptism, the cleansing with water by the power of the living word,[14] washes away every stain of sin, original and personal, and makes us sharers in God's own life[15] and his adopted children.[16] As proclaimed in the prayers for the blessing of the water, baptism is a cleansing water of rebirth[17] that makes us God's children born from on high. The blessed Trinity is invoked over those who are to be baptized, so that all who are signed in this name are consecrated to the Trinity and enter into communion with the Father, the Son, and the Holy Spirit. They are prepared for this high dignity and led to it by the scriptural readings, the prayer of the community, and their own profession of belief in the Father, the Son, and the Holy Spirit.

6. Far superior to the purifications of the Old Law, baptism produces these effects by the power of the mystery of the Lord's passion and resurrection. Those who are baptized are united to Christ in a death like his;[18] buried with him in death, they are given life again with him, and with him they rise again.[19] For baptism recalls and makes present the paschal mystery itself, because in baptism we pass from the death of sin into life. The celebration of baptism should therefore reflect the joy of the resurrection, especially when the celebration takes place during the Easter Vigil or on a Sunday.

OFFICES AND MINISTRIES OF BAPTISM

7. The preparation for baptism and Christian instruction are both of vital concern to God's people, the Church, which hands on and nourishes the faith received from the apostles. Through the ministry of the Church, adults are called to the Gospel by the Holy Spirit and infants are baptized in the faith of the Church and brought up in that faith. Therefore it is most important that catechists and other laypersons should work with priests and deacons in the preparation for baptism. In the actual celebration, the people of God (represented not only by the parents, godparents, and relatives, but also, as far as possible, by friends, neighbors, and some members of the local Church) should

[14]See Ephesians 5:26.
[15]See 2 Peter 1:4.
[16]See Romans 8:15; Galatians 4:5.
[17]See Titus 3:5.
[18]See Romans 6:4–5.
[19]See Ephesians 2:5–6.

take an active part. Thus they will show their common faith and the shared joy with which the newly baptized are received into the community of the Church.

8. It is a very ancient custom of the Church that adults are not admitted to baptism without godparents, members of the Christian community who will assist the candidates at least in the final preparation for baptism and after baptism will help them persevere in the faith and in their lives as Christians. In the baptism of children, as well, godparents are to be present in order to represent both the expanded spiritual family of the one to be baptized and the role of the Church as a mother. As occasion offers, godparents help the parents so that children will come to profess the faith and live up to it.

9. At least in the later rites of the catechumenate and in the actual celebration of baptism, the part of godparents is to testify to the faith of adult candidates or, together with the parents, to profess the Church's faith, in which children are baptized.

10. Therefore godparents, chosen by the catechumens or by the families of children to be baptized, must, in the judgment of the parish priest (pastor), be qualified to carry out the proper liturgical functions mentioned in no. 9.

1. Godparents are persons, other than the parents of candidates, who are designated by the candidates themselves or by a candidate's parents or whoever stands in the place of parents, or, in the absence of these, by the pastor or the minister of baptism. Each candidate may have either a godmother or a godfather or both a godmother and a godfather.

2. Those designated must have the capability and intention of carrying out the responsibility of a godparent and be mature enough to do so. A person sixteen years of age is presumed to have the requisite maturity, but the diocesan bishop may have stipulated another age or the pastor or the minister may decide that there is a legitimate reason for allowing an exception.

3. Those designated as godparents must have received the three sacraments of initiation: baptism, confirmation, and eucharist, and be living a life consistent with faith and with the responsibility of a godparent.

4. Those designated as godparents must also be members of the Catholic Church and be canonically free to carry out this office. At the request of parents, a baptized and believing Christian not belonging to the Catholic Church may act as a Christian witness along with a Catholic godparent.[20] In the case of separated Eastern Christians with whom we do not have full communion the special discipline for the Eastern Churches is to be respected.

11. The ordinary ministers of baptism are bishops, priests, and deacons.

1. In every celebration of this sacrament they should be mindful that they act in the Church in the name of Christ and by the power of the Holy Spirit.

2. They should therefore be diligent in the ministry of the word of God and in the manner of celebrating the sacrament. They must avoid any action that the faithful could rightly regard as favoritism.[21]

3. Except in a case of necessity, these ministers are not to confer baptism outside their own territory, even on their own subjects, without the requisite permission.

12. Bishops are the chief stewards of the mysteries of God and leaders of the entire liturgical life in the Church committed to them.[22] This is why they direct the conferring of baptism, which brings to the recipient a share in the kingly priesthood of Christ.[23] Therefore bishops should personally celebrate baptism, especially at the Easter Vigil. They should have a particular concern for the preparation and baptism of adults.

13. It is the duty of pastors to assist the bishop in the instruction and baptism of the adults entrusted to their care, unless the bishop makes other provisions. Pastors, with the assistance of catechists or other qualified laypersons, have the duty of preparing the parents and godparents of

[20]See *Codex Iuris Canonici*, can. 873 and 874, §§ 1 and 2.
[21]See Vatican Council II, Constitution on the Liturgy *Sacrosanctum Concilium*, art. 32; Pastoral Constitution on the Church in the Modern World *Gaudium et spes*, no. 29.
[22]See Vatican Council II, Decree on the Pastoral Office of Bishops *Christus Dominus*, no. 15.
[23]See Vatican Council II, Dogmatic Constitution on the Church *Lumen gentium*, no. 26.

children through appropriate pastoral guidance and of baptizing the children.

14. Other priests and deacons, since they are co-workers in the ministry of bishops and pastors, also prepare candidates for baptism and, by the invitation or consent of the bishop or pastor, celebrate the sacrament.

15. The celebrant of baptism may be assisted by other priests and deacons and also by laypersons in those parts that pertain to them, especially if there are a large number to be baptized. Provision for this is made in various parts of the rituals for adults and for children.

16. In imminent danger of death and especially at the moment of death, when no priest or deacon is available, any member of the faithful, indeed anyone with the right intention, may and sometimes must administer baptism. In a case simply of danger of death the sacrament should be administered, if possible, by a member of the faithful according to one of the shorter rites provided for this situation.[24] Even in this case a small community should be formed to assist at the rite or, if possible, at least one or two witnesses should be present.

17. Since they belong to the priestly people, all laypersons, especially parents and, by reason of their work, catechists, midwives, family or social workers or nurses of the sick, as well as physicians and surgeons, should be thoroughly aware, according to their capacities, of the proper method of baptizing in case of emergency. They should be taught by pastors, deacons, and catechists. Bishops should provide appropriate means within their diocese for such instruction.

REQUIREMENTS FOR THE CELEBRATION OF BAPTISM

18. The water used in baptism should be true water and, both for the sake of authentic sacramental symbolism and for hygienic reasons, should be pure and clean.

---

[24]See *Rite of Christian Initiation of Adults*, nos. 351–375; *Rite of Baptism for Children*, nos. 157–164.

19. The baptismal font, or the vessel in which on occasion the water is prepared for celebration of the sacrament in the sanctuary, should be spotlessly clean and of pleasing design.

20. If the climate requires, provision should be made for the water to be heated beforehand.

21. Except in case of necessity, a priest or deacon is to use only water that has been blessed for the rite. The water blessed at the Easter Vigil should, if possible, be kept and used throughout the Easter season to signify more clearly the relationship between the sacrament of baptism and the paschal mystery. Outside the Easter season, it is desirable that the water be blessed for each occasion, in order that the words of blessing may explicitly express the mystery of salvation that the Church remembers and proclaims. If the baptistery is supplied with running water, the blessing is given as the water flows.

22. As the rite for baptizing, either immersion, which is more suitable as a symbol of participation in the death and resurrection of Christ, or pouring may lawfully be used.

23. The words for conferring baptism in the Latin Church are: I BAPTIZE YOU IN THE NAME OF THE FATHER, AND OF THE SON, AND OF THE HOLY SPIRIT.

24. For celebrating the liturgy of the word of God a suitable place should be provided in the baptistery or in the church.

25. The baptistery or the area where the baptismal font is located should be reserved for the sacrament of baptism and should be worthy to serve as the place where Christians are reborn in water and the Holy Spirit. The baptistery may be situated in a chapel either inside or outside the church or in some other part of the church easily seen by the faithful; it should be large enough to accommodate a good number of people. After the Easter season, the Easter candle should be kept reverently in the baptistery, in such a way that it can be lighted for the celebration of baptism and so that from it the candles for the newly baptized can easily be lighted.

26. In the celebration the parts of the rite that are to be celebrated outside the baptistery should be carried out in different areas of the church that most conveniently suit the size of the congregation and the several parts of the baptismal liturgy. When the baptistery cannot accommodate all the catechumens and the congregation, the parts of the rite that are customarily celebrated inside the baptistery may be transferred to some other suitable area of the church.

27. As far as possible, all recently born babies should be baptized at a common celebration on the same day. Except for a good reason, baptism should not be celebrated more than once on the same day in the same church.

28. Further details concerning the time for baptism of adults and of children will be found in the respective rituals. But at all times the celebration of the sacrament should have a markedly paschal character.

29. Pastors must carefully and without delay record in the baptismal register the names of those baptized, of the minister, parents, and godparents, as well as the place and date of baptism.

ADAPTATIONS BY THE CONFERENCES OF BISHOPS

30. According to the Constitution on the Liturgy (art. 63, b), it is within the competence of the conferences of bishops to compose for their local rituals a section corresponding to this one in the Roman Ritual, adapted to the needs of their respective regions. After it has been reviewed by the Apostolic See, it may be used in the regions for which it was prepared.

In this connection, it is the responsibility of each conference of bishops:

1. to decide on the adaptations mentioned in the Constitution on the Liturgy (art. 39);

2. carefully and prudently to weigh what elements of a people's distinctive traditions and culture may suitably be admitted into divine worship and so to propose to the Apostolic See other adaptations considered useful or necessary that will be introduced with its consent;

3. to retain distinctive elements of any existing local rituals, as long as they conform to the Constitution on the Liturgy and correspond to contemporary needs, or to modify such elements;

4. to prepare translations of the texts that genuinely reflect the characteristics of various languages and cultures and to add, whenever helpful, music suitable for singing;

5. to adapt and augment the Introductions contained in the Roman Ritual, so that the ministers may fully understand the meaning of the rites and carry them out effectively;

6. to arrange the material in the various editions of the liturgical books prepared under the guidance of the conference of bishops, so that these books may better suit pastoral use.

31. Taking into consideration especially the norms in the Constitution on the Liturgy (art. 37–40, 65), the conferences of bishops in mission countries have the responsibility of judging whether the elements of initiation in use among some peoples can be adapted for the rite of Christian baptism and of deciding whether such elements are to be incorporated into the rite.

32. When the Roman Ritual for baptism provides several optional formularies, local rituals may add other formularies of the same kind.

33. The celebration of baptism is greatly enhanced by the use of song, which stimulates in the participants a sense of their unity, fosters their praying together, and expresses the joy of Easter that should permeate the whole rite. The conference of bishops should therefore encourage and help specialists in music to compose settings for those liturgical texts particularly suited to congregational singing.

ADAPTATIONS BY THE MINISTER OF BAPTISM

34. Taking into account existing circumstances and other needs, as well as the wishes of the faithful, the minister should make full use of the various options allowed in the rite.

35. In addition to the adaptations that are provided in the Roman Ritual for the dialogue and blessings, the minister may make other adaptations for special circumstances. These adaptations will be indicated more fully in the Introductions to the rites of baptism for adults and for children

RITE OF CHRISTIAN INITIATION OF ADULTS

RITE OF CHRISTIAN INITIATION OF ADULTS

Decree
FOREWORD
Roman decree
Introduction (1–35)

PART I
CHRISTIAN INITIATION OF ADULTS
Outline for Christian Initiation of Adults

PERIOD OF EVANGELIZATION AND PRECATECHUMENATE (36–40)

FIRST STEP: ACCEPTANCE INTO THE ORDER OF CATECHUMENS (41–47)

Rite of Acceptance into the Order of Catechumens

Receiving the Candidates (48)
Greeting (49)
Opening Dialogue (50–51)
Candidates' First Acceptance of the Gospel (52)
Affirmation By the Sponsors and the Assembly (53)
Signing of the Candidates with the Cross (54)
1. Signing of the Forehead (55)
2. [Signing of the Other Senses] (56)
3. Concluding Prayer (57–59)
Invitation to the Celebration of the Word of God (60)

Liturgy of the Word
Instruction (61)
Readings (62)
Homily (63)
[Presentation of a Bible] (64)
Intercessions for the Catechumens (65)
Prayer over the Catechumens (66)
Dismissal of the Catechumens (67)

Liturgy of the Eucharist (68)

Optional Rites (69)
Exorcism and Renunciation of False Worship (70)
Exorcism (71)
Renunciation of False Worship (72)

Liturgy of the Eucharist (170) (See no. 156, above.)

Third Scrutiny
(Fifth Sunday of Lent)

Liturgy of the Word
Readings (171)
Homily (172)
Invitation to Silent Prayer (173) (See no. 152, above.)
Intercessions for the Elect (174)
Exorcism (175)
Dismissal of the Elect (176)

Liturgy of the Eucharist (177) (See no. 156, above)

Presentation of the Lord's Prayer (178)
(Fifth Week of Lent)

Liturgy of the Word
Readings (179)
Gospel Reading (Presentation of the Lord's Prayer) (180)
Homily (181)
Prayer over the Elect (182)
Dismissal of the Elect (183)

Liturgy of the Eucharist (184)

Preparation Rites on Holy Saturday (185–186)

Model for a Celebration of the Preparation Rites (187–192)
Recitation of the Creed (193)
Reading and Homily (194)
Prayer before the Recitation (195)
Recitation of the Creed (196)

Ephphetha Rite (197)
Reading and Instruction (198)
Ephphetha (199)

[Choosing a Baptismal Name] (200)
Reading and Instruction (201)
Naming of the Elect (202)

Concluding Rites (203)
Prayer of Blessing (204)
Dismissal (205)

Receiving the Children (262)
Greeting (263)
Opening Dialogue (264)
Affirmation by the Parents(Sponsors) and the Assembly (265)
Signing of the Candidates with the Cross (266)
Signing of the Forehead (267)
[Signing of the Other Senses] (268)
Invitation to the Celebration of the Word of God (269)

Liturgy of the Word
Instruction (270)
Readings (271)
Homily (272)
[Presentation of a Bible] (273)
Intercessions for the Children (274)
Prayer over the Children (275)
Dismissal (276)

RITE OF ELECTION OR ENROLLMENT OF NAMES
[OPTIONAL] (277–280)

Liturgy of the Word
Homily (281)
Presentation of the Children (282)
Affirmation by the (Parents,) Godparents [and the Assembly] (283)
Invitation and Enrollment of Names (284)
Act of Admission or Election (285)
[Recognition of the Godparent(s)] (286)
Intercessions for the Elect (287)
Prayer over the Elect (288)
Dismissal of the Elect (289)

Liturgy of the Eucharist (290)

SECOND STEP: PENITENTIAL RITES (SCRUTINIES)
(291–294)

Penitential Rite (Scrutiny)

Liturgy of the Word
Greeting and Introduction (295)
Prayer (296)
Readings (297)
Homily (298)
Intercessions (299)

Exorcism (300)
Anointing with the Oil of Catechumens [or Laying on of Hands] (301)
Dismissal of the Children (302)

Liturgy of Penance (303)

THIRD STEP: CELEBRATION OF THE SACRAMENTS
OF INITIATION (304–308)

Celebration of the Sacraments of Initiation

Liturgy of the Word (309)

Celebration of Baptism
Invitation to Prayer (310)
Prayer over the Water (311)
[Community's Profession of Faith] (312)
Children's Profession of Faith (313)
1. Renunciation of Sin (314)
2. [Anointing with the Oil of Catechumens] (315)
3. Profession of Faith (316)
Baptism (317)
Explanatory Rites (318) (See no. 227, above.)
1. [Anointing after Baptism] (319)
2. [Clothing with a Baptismal Garment] (320)
3. Presentation of a Lighted Candle (321)

Celebration of Confirmation (322–323)
Invitation (324)
Laying on of Hands (325) (See no. 234, above.)
Anointing with Chrism (326)

Liturgy of the Eucharist (327–329)

PERIOD OF POSTBAPTISMAL CATECHESIS OR
MYSTAGOGY (330)

2. CHRISTIAN INITIATION OF ADULTS IN
EXCEPTIONAL CIRCUMSTANCES (331–335)

Christian Initiation of Adults in Exceptional Circumstances
(Abbreviated Form) (336–339)

Receiving the Candidate (340)
Greeting (341)
Opening Dialogue (342)
Candidate's Declaration (343)

Affirmation by the Godparents (344)
Invitation to the Celebration of the Word of God (345)

Liturgy of the Word (346)
Readings (347)
Homily (348)
Intercessions for the Candidate (349)
[Penitential Rite] (350)
Prayer of Exorcism (351)
Anointing with the Oil of Catechumens or Laying on of
Hands (352)

Celebration of Baptism
Invitation to Prayer (353)
Prayer over the Water (354)
Profession of Faith (355) (See no. 223, above.)
1. Renunciation of Sin (356)
2. Profession of Faith (357)
Baptism (358)
Explanatory Rites (359)
1. [Clothing with a Baptismal Garment] (360) (See no. 229,
above.)
2. Presentation of a Lighted Candle (361)

Celebration of Confirmation (362–363)
Invitation (364)
Laying on of Hands (365)
Anointing with Chrism (366)

Liturgy of the Eucharist (367–369)

**3. CHRISTIAN INITIATION OF A PERSON IN
DANGER OF DEATH (370–374)**

Christian Initiation of a Person in Danger of Death (375–
376)

Introductory Rites
Opening Dialogue (377)
Affirmation by the Godparent and Witnesses (378)

Liturgy of the Word
Gospel Reading (379)
Intercessions for the Candidate (380)
Prayer over the Candidate (381)

Celebration of Baptism
Renunciation of Sin (382)
Profession of Faith (383)
Baptism (384)
[Anointing After Baptism] (385–387)

Celebration of Confirmation (388)
Invitation (389)
Laying on of Hands (390)
Anointing with Chrism (391–392)

Celebration of Viaticum (393)
Invitation to Prayer (394)
Communion As Viaticum (395)
Prayer After Communion (396)

Concluding Rites
Blessing (397)
Sign of Peace (398)

Alternate Concluding Rites (399)

4. PREPARATION OF UNCATECHIZED ADULTS FOR CONFIRMATION AND EUCHARIST (400–410)

OPTIONAL RITES FOR BAPTIZED BUT UNCATECHIZED ADULTS

4A. RITE OF WELCOMING THE CANDIDATES (411–415)

Welcoming the Candidates (416)
Greeting (417)
Opening Dialogue (418)
Candidates' Declaration of Intent (419)
Affirmation by the Sponsors and the Assembly (420)
Signing of the Candidates with the Cross (421)
1. Signing of the Forehead (422)
2. Signing of the Other Senses (423)
3. Concluding Prayer (424)

Liturgy of the Word
Instruction (425)
Reading (426)
Homily (427)
[Presentation of a Bible] (428)
Profession of Faith (429)
General Intercessions (430)

Prayer over the Candidates (431)
[Dismissal of the Assembly] (432)

Liturgy of the Eucharist (433)

4B. RITE OF SENDING THE CANDIDATES FOR RECOGNITION BY THE BISHOP AND FOR THE CALL TO CONTINUING CONVERSION (434–437)

Liturgy of the Word
Homily (438)
Presentation of the Candidates (439)
Affirmation by the Sponsors [and the Assembly] (440–441)
General Intercessions (442)
Prayer over the Candidates (443)
[Dismissal of the Assembly] (444)

Liturgy of the Eucharist (445)

4C. RITE OF CALLING THE CANDIDATES TO CONTINUING CONVERSION (446–449)

Liturgy of the Word
Homily (450)
Presentation of the Candidates for Confirmation and Eucharist (451)
Affirmation by the Sponsors [and the Assembly] (452–453)
Act of Recognition (454)
General Intercessions (455)
Prayer over the Candidates (456)
[Dismissal of the Assembly] (457)

Liturgy of the Eucharist (458)

4D. PENITENTIAL RITE (SCRUTINY) (459–463)

PENITENTIAL RITE (Second Sunday of Lent)

Introductory Rite
Greeting and Introduction (464)
Prayer (465)

Liturgy of the Word
Reading (466)
Homily (467)
Invitation to Silent Prayer (468)
Intercessions for the Candidates (469)
Prayer over the Candidates (470)
[Dismissal of the Assembly] (471)

Signing of the Catechumens and of the Candidates with the Cross (514)
1. [Signing of the Forehead] (515)
2. [Signing of the Other Senses of the Catechumens] (516)
3. Signing of the Forehead (518)
4. [Signing of the Other Senses of the Candidates] (519)
5. Concluding Prayer (520)
Invitation to the Celebration of the Word of God (521)

Liturgy of the Word
Instruction (522)
Readings (523)
Homily (524–525)
Intercessions for the Catechumens and Candidates (526)
Prayer over the Catechumens and Candidates (527)
Dismissal of the Catechumens (528)

Liturgy of the Eucharist (529)

RITE 2. PARISH CELEBRATION FOR SENDING CATECHUMENS FOR ELECTION AND CANDIDATES FOR RECOGNITION BY THE BISHOP (OPTIONAL) (530–535)

Liturgy of the Word
Homily (536)
Presentation of the Catechumens (537)
Affirmation by the Godparents [and the Assembly] (538–539)
Presentation of the Candidates (540)
Affirmation by the Sponsors [and the Assembly] (541–542)
Intercessions for the Catechumens and Candidates (543)
Prayer over the Catechumens and Candidates (544)
Dismissal of the Catechumens (545)

Liturgy of the Eucharist (546)

RITE 3. CELEBRATION OF THE RITE OF ELECTION OF CATECHUMENS AND OF THE CALL TO CONTINUING CONVERSION OF CANDIDATES WHO ARE PREPARING FOR CONFIRMATION AND/OR EUCHARIST OR RECEPTION INTO THE FULL COMMUNION OF THE CATHOLIC CHURCH (547–549)

Liturgy of the Word
Homily (550)

Celebration of Election
Presentation of the Catechumens (551)
Affirmation by the Godparents [and the Assembly] (552)
Invitation and Enrollment of Names (553)
Act of Admission or Election (554)

Celebration of the Call to Continuing Conversion
Presentation of the Candidates (555)
Affirmation by the Sponsors [and the Assembly] (556)

Act of Recognition (557)
Intercessions for the Elect and the Candidates (558)
Prayer over the Elect and the Candidates (559)
Dismissal of the Elect (560)

Liturgy of the Eucharist (561)

**RITE 4. CELEBRATION AT THE EASTER VIGIL OF
THE SACRAMENTS OF INITIATION AND OF THE
RITE OF RECEPTION INTO THE FULL COMMUNION
OF THE CATHOLIC CHURCH (562–565)**

Service of Light

Liturgy of the Word

Celebration of Baptism (567)
Presentation of the Candidates for Baptism (568)
Invitation to Prayer (569)
Litany of the Saints (570) (See no. 221, above.)
Blessing of the Water (571)
Profession of Faith (572)
1. Renunciation of Sin (573) (See no. 224, above.)
2. Profession of Faith (574) (See no. 225, above.)
Baptism (575) (See no. 226, above.)
Explanatory Rites (576) (See no. 227, above.)
1. [Anointing after Baptism] (577) (See no. 228, above)
2. [Clothing with a Baptismal Garment] (578) (See no. 229, above.)
3. Presentation of a Lighted Candle (579)

Renewal of Baptismal Promises
Invitation (580)
Renewal of Baptismal Promises
1. Renunciation of Sin (581)
2. Profession of Faith (582)
Sprinkling with Baptismal Water (583)

NATIONAL CONFERENCE OF CATHOLIC BISHOPS UNITED STATES OF AMERICA

DECREE

In accord with the norms established by decree of the Sacred Congregation of Rites in *Cum, nostra aetate* (27 January 1966), this edition of the *Rite of Christian Initiation of Adults* is declared to be the vernacular typical edition of *Ordo initiationis christianae adultorum* in the dioceses of the United States of America, and is published by authority of the National Conference of Catholic Bishops.

The *Rite of Christian Initiation of Adults* was canonically approved by the National Conference of Catholic Bishops in plenary assembly on 11 November 1986 and was subsequently confirmed by the Apostolic See by decree of the Congregation for Divine Worship on 19 February 1987 (Prot. N. 1192/86).

On 1 July 1988 the *Rite of Christian Initiation of Adults* may be published and used in the liturgy. From 1 September 1988 the use of the *Rite of Christian Initiation of Adults* is mandatory in the dioceses of the United States of America. From that day forward no other English version may be used.

Given at the General Secretariat of the National Conference of Catholic Bishops, Washington, DC, on 18 March 1988, the memorial of Saint Cyril of Jerusalem, bishop and doctor of the Church.

+ John L. May
  Archbishop of Saint Louis
  President
  National Conference of Catholic Bishops

Daniel F. Hoye
General Secretary

FOREWORD

This edition of the *Rite of Christian Initiation of Adults* contains the approved English translation of the 1974 emended second printing of the *Ordo initiationis christianae adultorum* prepared by the International Commission on English in the Liturgy (ICEL) and a number of other rites and liturgical texts approved for use in the dioceses of the United States of America. An English translation of the *Praenotanda de initiatione christiana,* which was also included in the second Latin printing, is also included in this edition and is entitled *"Christian Initiation,* General Introduction." This document has its own self-contained enumeration of paragraphs, to which there are several cross-references in the *Rite of Christian Initiation of Adults.* The ICEL edition incorporates the emendations of the text necessitated by the Code of Canon Law of 1983 and issued by the Congregation for Divine Worship on 12 September 1983.

This final edition of the *Rite of Christian Initiation of Adults* replaces the interim or provisional translation issued by ICEL in 1974. In the United States, the provisional translation had been approved "ad interim" by the Executive Committee of the National Conference of Catholic Bishops and was confirmed by the Apostolic See on 23 September 1974 (Prot. N. 1993/74) and, in the same year, was published by authority of the Bishops' Committee on the Liturgy for use in the dioceses of the United States of America.

The main body of the text of the present edition begins with the Introduction proper to the *Rite of Christian Initiation of Adults.* In the interest of pastoral utility and convenience, the English edition somewhat rearranges the contents of the *praenotanda* of the Latin *editio typica.* The Introduction moves directly from the section entitled "Structure of the Initiation of Adults," which presents a general outline of the steps and periods of the process of Christian initiation, to the section entitled "Ministries and Offices." The paragraphs in the Latin typical edition (nos. 9–40) devoted to a detailed description of each of the steps and periods of the entire catechumenate have been integrated with the correlative paragraphs of the particular introductions to each of those steps and periods, so that all the relevant material is concentrated in its place of application. In the section entitled "Structure of the Initiation of Adults," cross-references are given to these particular introductions. This editorial rearrangement omits nothing from the Latin original, but it does entail a departure from the paragraph enumeration of the Latin edition. For each paragraph of the English edition bearing the number proper to this edition, the right-hand margin carries the reference number or numbers indicating the corresponding paragraph or paragraphs of the Latin edition. A reference number in the right-hand margin that is preceded by a letter indicates a text from a source other than the *Ordo initiationis christianae adultorum;* numbers that are preceded by the letters "RM" refer to *The Roman Missal;* numbers that are preceded by the letters "PC" refer to *Pastoral Care of the Sick: Rites of Anointing and Viaticum;* numbers preceded by "R" refer to the appendix of the *Ordo initiationis,* "Rite of Reception of Baptized Christians into the Full Communion of the Catholic Church"; and numbers preceded by "P" refer to the *Rite of Penance.* Rites and texts prepared specifically for use in the dioceses of the United States of America are designated "USA" in the margin.

After the introduction to the *Rite of Christian Initiation of Adults,* the new English edition of this ritual presents the contents in two parts:

Part I, entitled "Christian Initiation of Adults," consists of the steps and periods that make up the full and paradigmatic form of Christian initiation, in accord with the restoration of the integral catechumenate decreed by the Second Vatican Council.

Part II, entitled "Rites for Particular Circumstances," consists of material for: the adaptation of the rite to unbaptized children of catechetical age; exceptional circumstances in which the process of Christian initiation is not followed in its complete form; situations in which those already baptized are either to be catechized and complete their Christian initiation or are to become part of the full communion of the Catholic Church.

In accord with the provisions laid down by the *Constitution on the Liturgy* (art. 63, b) and by the Introduction of the *Rite of Christian Initiation of Adults* (nos. 32–33; see also *Christian Initiation,* "General Introduction," nos. 30–33), the National Conference of Catholic Bishops approved a number of adaptations to the *Rite of Christian Initiation of Adults* over which it has discretionary power. Accordingly, the present US edition includes several editorial modifications of the ICEL edition (e.g., all references to the anointing with the oil of catechumens have been removed from *Step Three: Celebration of the Sacraments of Initiation*, since the National Conference of Catholic Bishops determined that in the dioceses of the United States this anointing is to be reserved for use in the period of the catechumenate and in the period of purification and enlightenment, and not be included in the preparation rites on Holy Saturday or in the celebration of initiation at the Easter Vigil or at another time.)

The present edition also contains a number of other rites approved specifically for use in the dioceses of the United States of America. A few of these rites have been incorporated into the ICEL edition as follows.

Part I, "First Step: Acceptance into the Order of Catechumens": inclusion of an optional "Presentation of a Cross"; and "Rite Belonging to the Period of the Catechumenate": inclusion of an optional parish rite, "Sending of the Catechumens for Election," for use when the rite of election is to be celebrated by the bishop at a regional or diocesan celebration.

Part II, "Christian Initiation of Children Who Have Reached Catechetical Age": inclusion of an optional "Rite of Election"; and "Preparation of Uncatechized Adults for Confirmation and Eucharist": inclusion of four (4) optional rites for baptized but previously uncatechized adults— "Welcoming the Candidates," "Sending the Candidates for Recognition by the Bishop," "Calling the Candidates to Continuing Conversion," "Penitential Rite" (Scrutiny).

Appendix I: "Additional (Combined) Rites" contains the "Celebration at the Easter Vigil of the Sacraments of Initiation and of the Rite of Reception into the Full Communion of the Catholic Church." This rite was prepared by ICEL at the request of the conferences of bishops for use in those situations when pastoral circumstances warrant the integration of the rite of reception with the sacraments of initiation in the same celebration of the Easter Vigil. In addition to this order, Appendix I contains three other "combined" rites which may be used in celebrations when both catechumens preparing for Christian initiation and baptized but previously uncatechized candidates preparing either for the sacraments of confirmation and/or eucharist or for reception into the full communion of the Catholic Church are present. All new liturgical rites and texts for this present edition are designated "USA" in the margin to indicate a variance from the ICEL edition.

Careful attention to the convenience of the minister has guided the format and presentation of each of the rites. An outline preceding each rite gives the minister a concise overview of the structure. The various options and alternatives provided within the rites are indicated simply and distinctly; introductory material, rubrics, and liturgical texts for each rite are typographically set off from each other. The full texts of the readings and psalms required for the liturgy of the word in celebrations are not printed out, since it is presumed that, in keeping with liturgical norms, they will be proclaimed from a Lectionary or Bible. Accordingly, either references to the *Lectionary for Mass* are given for the readings and psalms belonging to each celebration or a list of citations of suitable readings is given at the place of their occurrence in the particular rite.

This new edition of the *Rite of Christian Initiation of Adults* was approved for use in the dioceses of the United States of America by the National Conference of Catholic Bishops on 11 November 1986 and confirmed by the Apostolic See on 19 February 1988 (Prot. N. 1192/86).

Baptism is "the door to life and to the kingdom of God" (General Introduction, no. 3). May all those who have already been claimed for Christ draw others to the Lord and, through the rites and prayers of this ritual, forge greater bonds of unity in the Church.

+ Joseph P. Delaney
  Bishop of Fort Worth
  Chairman, Bishops' Committee on the Liturgy
  National Conference of Catholic Bishops

13 March 1988
Fourth Sunday of Lent

CONGREGATION FOR DIVINE WORSHIP

Prot. no. 15/72

DECREE

The Second Vatican Council prescribed the revision of the rite of baptism of adults and decreed that the catechumenate for adults, divided into several steps, should be restored. By this means the time of the catechumenate, which is intended as a period of well-suited instruction, would be sanctified by liturgical rites to be celebrated at successive intervals of time. The Council likewise decreed that both the solemn and simple rites of adult baptism should be revised, with proper attention to the restored catechumenate.

In observance of these decrees, the Congregation for Divine Worship prepared a new rite for the Christian initiation of adults, which Pope Paul VI has approved. The Congregation now publishes it and declares the present edition to be the *editio typica*, to replace the rite of baptism of adults now in the Roman Ritual. It likewise decrees that this new rite may be used in Latin at once and in the vernacular from the day appointed by the conference of bishops, after it has prepared a translation and had it confirmed by the Apostolic See.

All things to the contrary notwithstanding.

From the office of the Congregation for Divine Worship, 6 January 1972, Epiphany.

Arturo Cardinal Tabera
Prefect

A. Bugnini
Secretary

RITE OF CHRISTIAN INITIATION OF ADULTS

There is one Lord, one faith, one baptism, one God, the Father of all

INTRODUCTION

1. The rite of Christian initiation presented here is designed for adults who, after hearing the mystery of Christ proclaimed, consciously and freely seek the living God and enter the way of faith and conversion as the Holy Spirit opens their hearts. By God's help they will be strengthened spiritually during their preparation and at the proper time will receive the sacraments fruitfully.

2. This rite includes not simply the celebration of the sacraments of baptism, confirmation, and eucharist, but also all the rites belonging to the catechumenate. Endorsed by the ancient practice of the Church, a catechumenate that would be suited to contemporary missionary activity in all regions was so widely requested that the Second Vatican Council decreed its restoration, revision, and adaptation to local traditions.[1]

3. So that the rite of initiation will be more useful for the work of the Church and for individual, parochial, and missionary circumstances, the rite is first presented in Part I of this book in its complete and usual form (nos. 36–251). This is designed for the preparation of a group of candidates, but by simple adaptation parish priests (pastors) can devise a form suited to one person.

Part II provides rites for special circumstances: the Christian initiation of children (nos. 252–330), a simple form of the rite for adults to be carried out in exceptional circumstances (nos. 331–369), and a short form of the rite for those in danger of death (nos. 370–399). Part II also includes guidelines for preparing uncatechized adults for confirmation and eucharist (nos. 400–410) along with four (4) optional rites which may be used with such candidates, and the rite of

---

[1]See Vatican Council II, Constitution on the Liturgy *Sacrosanctum Concilium*, art. 64–66; Decree on the Church's Missionary Activity *Ad gentes*, no. 14; Decree on the Pastoral Office of Bishops *Christus Dominus*, no. 14.

reception of baptized Christians into the full communion of the Catholic Church (nos. 473–504).

Rites for catechumens and baptized but previously uncatechized adults celebrated in combination, along with a rite combining the reception of baptized Christians into the full communion of the Catholic Church with the celebration of Christian initiation at the Easter Vigil (nos. 562–594), are contained in Appendix I. The two additional appendices contain acclamations, hymns, and songs, and the National Statutes for the Catechumenate in the Dioceses of the United States of America.

STRUCTURE OF THE INITIATION OF ADULTS

4. The initiation of catechumens is a gradual process that takes place within the community of the faithful. By joining the catechumens in reflecting on the value of the paschal mystery and by renewing their own conversion, the faithful provide an example that will help the catechumens to obey the Holy Spirit more generously.

5. The rite of initiation is suited to a spiritual journey of adults that varies according to the many forms of God's grace, the free cooperation of the individuals, the action of the Church, and the circumstances of time and place.

6. This journey includes not only the periods for making inquiry and for maturing (see no. 7), but also the steps marking the catechumens' progress, as they pass, so to speak, through another doorway or ascend to the next level.

   1. The first step: reaching the point of initial conversion and wishing to become Christians, they are accepted as catechumens by the Church.
   2. The second step: having progressed in faith and nearly completed the catechumenate, they are accepted into a more intense preparation for the sacraments of initiation.
   3. The third step: having completed their spiritual preparation, they receive the sacraments of Christian initiation.

These three steps are to be regarded as the major, more intense moments of initiation and are marked by three liturgical rites: the first by the rite of acceptance into the order of catechumens (nos. 41–74); the second by the rite of election or enrollment of names (nos. 118–137); and the third by the celebration of the sacraments of Christian initiation (nos. 206–243).

7. The steps lead to periods of inquiry and growth; alterna- 7 tively the periods may also be seen as preparing for the ensuing step.

1. The first period consists of inquiry on the part of the candidates and of evangelization and the precatechumenate on the part of the Church. It ends with the rite of acceptance into the order of catechumens.

2. The second period, which begins with the rite of acceptance into the order of catechumens and may last for several years, includes catechesis and the rites connected with catechesis. It comes to an end on the day of election.

3. The third and much shorter period, which follows the rite of election, ordinarily coincides with the Lenten preparation for the Easter celebration and the sacraments of initiation. It is a time of purification and enlightenment and includes the celebration of the rites belonging to this period.

4. The final period extends through the whole Easter season and is devoted to the postbaptismal catechesis or mystagogy. It is a time for deepening the Christian experience, for spiritual growth, and for entering more fully into the life and unity of the community.

Thus there are four continuous periods: the precatechumenate, the period for hearing the first preaching of the Gospel (nos. 36–40); the period of the catechumenate, set aside for a thorough catechesis and for the rites belonging to this period (nos. 75–117); the period of purification and enlightenment (Lenten preparation), designed for a more intense spiritual preparation, which is assisted by the celebration of the scrutinies and presentations (nos. 138–205); and the period of postbaptismal catechesis or mystagogy, marked by the new experience of sacraments and community (nos. 244–251).

8. The whole initiation must bear a markedly paschal char- 8 acter, since the initiation of Christians is the first sacramental sharing in Christ's dying and rising and since, in addition, the period of purification and enlightenment ordi-

narily coincides with Lent[2] and the period of postbaptismal catechesis or mystagogy with the Easter season. All the resources of Lent should be brought to bear as a more intense preparation of the elect and the Easter Vigil should be regarded as the proper time for the sacraments of initiation. Because of pastoral needs, however, the sacraments of initiation may be celebrated at other times (see nos. 26–30).

MINISTRIES AND OFFICES

9. In light of what is said in *Christian Initiation*, General Introduction (no. 7), the people of God, as represented by the local Church, should understand and show by their concern that the initiation of adults is the responsibility of all the baptized.[3] Therefore the community must always be fully prepared in the pursuit of its apostolic vocation to give help to those who are searching for Christ. In the various circumstances of daily life, even as in the apostolate, all the followers of Christ have the obligation of spreading the faith according to their abilities.[4] Hence, the entire community must help the candidates and the catechumens throughout the process of initiation: during the period of the precatechumenate, the period of the catechumenate, the period of purification and enlightenment, and the period of postbaptismal catechesis or mystagogy. In particular:

    1. During the period of evangelization and precatechumenate, the faithful should remember that for the Church and its members the supreme purpose of the apostolate is that Christ's message is made known to the world by word and deed and that his grace is communicated.[5] They should therefore show themselves ready to give the candidates evidence of the spirit of the Christian community and to welcome them into their homes, into personal conversation, and into community gatherings.

    2. At the celebrations belonging to the period of the catechumenate, the faithful should seek to be present when-

41

[2]See Vatican Council II, Constitution on the Liturgy *Sacrosanctum Concilium,* art. 109.
[3]See Vatican Council II, Decree on the Church's Missionary Activity *Ad gentes,* no. 14.
[4]See Vatican Council II, Dogmatic Constitution on the Church *Lumen gentium,* no. 17.
[5]See Vatican Council II, Decree on the Apostolate of the Laity *Apostolicam actuositatem,* no. 6.

ever possible and should take an active part in the responses, prayers, singing, and acclamations.

3. On the day of election, because it is a day of growth for the community, the faithful, when called upon, should be sure to give honest and carefully considered testimony about the catechumens.

4. During Lent, the period of purification and enlightenment, the faithful should take care to participate in the rites of the scrutinies and presentations and give the elect the example of their own renewal in the spirit of penance, faith, and charity. At the Easter Vigil, they should attach great importance to renewing their own baptismal promises.

5. During the period immediately after baptism, the faithful should take part in the Masses for neophytes, that is, the Sunday Masses of the Easter season (see no. 25), welcome the neophytes with open arms in charity, and help them to feel more at home in the community of the baptized.

10. A sponsor accompanies any candidate seeking admission as a catechumen. Sponsors are persons who have known and assisted the candidates and stand as witnesses to the candidates' moral character, faith, and intention. It may happen that it is not the sponsor for the rite of acceptance and the period of the catechumenate but another person who serves as godparent for the periods of purification and enlightenment and of mystagogy. 42

11. Their godparents (for each a godmother or godfather, or both) accompany the candidates on the day of election, at the celebration of the sacraments of initiation, and during the period of mystagogy.[6] Godparents are persons chosen by the candidates on the basis of example, good qualities, and friendship, delegated by the local Christian community, and approved by the priest. It is the responsibility of godparents to show the candidates how to practice the Gospel in personal and social life, to sustain the candidates in moments of hesitancy and anxiety, to bear witness, and to guide the candidates' progress in the baptismal life. Chosen before the candidates' election, godparents fulfill this office publicly from the day of the rite of election, when they give testimony to the community about the candidates. They 43

[6]See *Christian Initiation*, General Introduction, nos. 8 and 10,1.

continue to be important during the time after reception of the sacraments when the neophytes need to be assisted so that they remain true to their baptismal promises.

12. The bishop,[7] in person or through his delegate, sets up, regulates, and promotes the program of pastoral formation for catechumens and admits the candidates to their election and to the sacraments. It is hoped that, presiding if possible at the Lenten liturgy, he will himself celebrate the rite of election and, at the Easter Vigil, the sacraments of initiation, at least for the initiation of those who are fourteen years old or older. Finally, when pastoral care requires, the bishop should depute catechists, truly worthy and properly prepared, to celebrate the minor exorcisms (nos. 90–94) and the blessings of the catechumens (nos. 95–97).

44

13. Priests, in addition to their usual ministry for any celebration of baptism, confirmation, and the eucharist,[8] have the responsibility of attending to the pastoral and personal care of the catechumens,[9] especially those who seem hesitant and discouraged. With the help of deacons and catechists, they are to provide instruction for the catechumens; they are also to approve the choice of godparents and willingly listen to and help them; they are to be diligent in the correct celebration and adaptation of the rites throughout the entire course of Christian initiation (see no. 35).

45

14. The priest who baptizes an adult or a child of catechetical age should, when the bishop is absent, also confer confirmation,[10] unless this sacrament is to be given at another time (see no. 24). When there are a large number of candidates to be confirmed, the minister of confirmation may associate priests with himself to administer the sacrament. It is preferable that the priests who are so invited:

46

1. either have a particular function or office in the diocese, being, namely, either vicars general, episcopal vicars, or district or regional vicars;

2. or be the pastors of the places where confirmation is conferred, pastors of the places where the candidates be-

7See ibid., no. 12.
8See ibid., nos. 13–15.
9See Vatican Council II, Decree on the Ministry and Life of Priests *Presbyterorum Ordinis*, no. 6.
10See *Rite of Confirmation*, Introduction, no. 7,b.

long, or priests who have had a special part in the catechetical preparation of the candidates.[11]

15. Deacons should be ready to assist in the ministry to catechumens. Conferences of bishops that have decided in favor of the permanent diaconate should ensure that the number and distribution of permanent deacons are adequate for the carrying out of the steps, periods, and formation programs of the catechumenate wherever pastoral needs require.[12]   47

16. Catechists, who have an important office for the progress of the catechumens and for the growth of the community, should, whenever possible, have an active part in the rites. When deputed by the bishop (see no. 12), they may perform the minor exorcisms and blessings contained in the ritual.[13] When they are teaching, catechists should see that their instruction is filled with the spirit of the Gospel, adapted to the liturgical signs and the cycle of the Church's year, suited to the needs of the catechumens, and as far as possible enriched by local traditions.   48

TIME AND PLACE OF INITIATION

17. As a general rule, pastors should make use of the rite of initiation in such a way that the sacraments themselves are celebrated at the Easter Vigil and the rite of election takes place on the First Sunday of Lent. The rest of the rites are spaced on the basis of the structure and arrangement of the catechumenate as described previously (nos. 6–8). For pastoral needs of a more serious nature, however, it is lawful to arrange the schedule for the entire rite of initiation differently, as will be detailed later (nos. 26–30).   49

PROPER OR USUAL TIMES

18. The following should be noted about the time of celebrating the rite of acceptance into the order of catechumens (nos. 41–74).   50

[11]See ibid., no. 8.
[12]See Vatican Council II, Dogmatic Constitution on the Church *Lumen gentium*, no. 26; Decree on the Church's Missionary Activity *Ad gentes*, no. 16.
[13]See Vatican Council II, Constitution on the Liturgy *Sacrosanctum Concilium*, art. 79.

1. It should not be too early, but should be delayed until the candidates, according to their own dispositions and situation, have had sufficient time to conceive an initial faith and to show the first signs of conversion (see no. 42).

2. In places where the number of candidates is smaller than usual, the rite of acceptance should be delayed until a group is formed that is sufficiently large for catechesis and the liturgical rites.

3. Two dates in the year, or three if necessary, are to be fixed as the usual times for carrying out this rite.

19. The rite of election or enrollment of names (nos. 118–137) should as a rule be celebrated on the First Sunday of Lent. As circumstances suggest or require, it may be anticipated somewhat or even celebrated on a weekday.   51

20. The scrutinies (nos. 150–156, 164–177) should take place on the Third, Fourth, and Fifth Sundays of Lent, or, if necessary, on the other Sundays of Lent, or even on convenient weekdays. Three scrutinies should be celebrated. The bishop may dispense from one of them for serious reasons or, in extraordinary circumstances, even from two (see nos. 34.3; 331). When, for lack of time, the election is held early, the first scrutiny is also to be held early; but in this case care is to be taken not to prolong the period of purification and enlightenment beyond eight weeks.   52

21. By ancient usage, the presentations, since they take place after the scrutinies, are part of the same period of purification and enlightenment. They are celebrated during the week. The presentation of the Creed to the catechumens (nos. 157–163) takes place during the week after the first scrutiny; the presentation of the Lord's Prayer (nos. 178–184) during the week after the third scrutiny. For pastoral reasons, however, to enrich the liturgy in the period of the catechumenate, each presentation may be transferred and celebrated during the period of the catechumenate as a kind of "rite of passage" (see nos. 79, 104–105).   53

22. On Holy Saturday, when the elect refrain from work and spend their time in recollection, the various preparation rites may be celebrated: the recitation or "return" of the Creed by the elect, the ephphetha rite, and the choosing of a Christian name (nos. 185–205).   54

23. The celebration of the sacraments of Christian initiation 55
(nos. 206–243) should take place at the Easter Vigil itself
(see nos. 8, 17). But if there are a great many catechumens,
the sacraments are given to the majority that night and reception of the sacraments by the rest may be transferred to
days within the Easter octave, whether at the principal
church or at a mission station. In this case either the Mass
of the day or one of the ritual Masses "Christian Initiation:
Baptism" may be used and the readings are chosen from
those of the Easter Vigil.

24. In certain cases when there is serious reason, confirma- 56
tion may be postponed until near the end of the period of
postbaptismal catechesis, for example, Pentecost Sunday
(see no. 249).

25. On all the Sundays of the Easter season after Easter 57
Sunday, the so-called Masses for neophytes are to be sched-
uled. The entire community and the newly baptized with
their godparents should be encouraged to participate (see
nos. 247–248).

OUTSIDE THE USUAL TIMES

26. The entire rite of Christian initiation is normally ar- 58
ranged so that the sacraments will be celebrated during the
Easter Vigil. Because of unusual circumstances and pastoral
needs, however, the rite of election and the rites belonging
to the period of purification and enlightenment may be
held outside Lent and the sacraments of initiation may be
celebrated at a time other than the Easter Vigil or Easter
Sunday.

Even when the usual time has otherwise been observed, it
is permissible, but only for serious pastoral needs (for example, if there are a great many people to be baptized), to
choose a day other than the Easter Vigil or Easter Sunday,
but preferably one during the Easter season, to celebrate
the sacraments of initiation; the program of initiation during Lent, however, must be maintained.

When the time is changed in either way, even though the
rite of Christian initiation occurs at a different point in the
liturgical year, the structure of the entire rite, with its properly spaced intervals, remains the same. But the following
adjustments are made.

27. As far as possible, the sacraments of initiation are to be 59 celebrated on a Sunday, using, as occasion suggests, the Sunday Mass or one of the ritual Masses "Christian Initiation: Baptism" (see nos. 23, 208).

28. The rite of acceptance into the order of catechumens is 60 to take place when the time is right (see no. 18).

29. The rite of election is to be celebrated about six weeks 61 before the sacraments of initiation, so that there is sufficient time for the scrutinies and the presentations. Care should be taken not to schedule the celebration of the rite of election on a solemnity of the liturgical year.

30. The scrutinies should not be celebrated on solemnities, 62 but on Sundays or even on weekdays, with the usual intervals.

PLACE OF CELEBRATION

31. The rites should be celebrated in the places appropriate 63 to them as indicated in the ritual. Consideration should be given to special needs that arise in secondary stations of mission territories.

ADAPTATIONS BY THE CONFERENCES OF BISHOPS IN THE USE OF THE ROMAN RITUAL

32. In addition to the adaptations envisioned in *Christian* 64 *Initiation*, General Introduction (nos. 30–33), the rite of Christian initiation of adults allows for other adaptations that will be decided by the conference of bishops.

33. Each conference of bishops has discretionary power to 65 make the following decisions:

1. to establish for the precatechumenate, where it seems advisable, some way of receiving inquirers who are interested in the catechumenate (see no. 39);

2. to insert into the rite of acceptance into the order of catechumens a first exorcism and a renunciation of false worship, in regions where paganism is widespread (see nos. 69–72) [The National Conference of Catholic Bishops has approved leaving to the discretion of the diocesan bishop this inclusion of a first exorcism and a renunciation of

false worship in the rite of acceptance into the order of catechumens];

3. to decide that in the same rite the tracing of the sign of the cross upon the forehead (nos. 54–55) be replaced by making that sign in front of the forehead, in regions where the act of touching may not seem proper [The National Conference of Catholic Bishops has established as the norm in the dioceses of the United States the tracing of the cross on the forehead. It leaves to the discretion of the diocesan bishop the substitution of making the sign of the cross in front of the forehead for those persons in whose culture the act of touching may not seem proper];

4. to decide that in the same rite candidates receive a new name in regions where it is the practice of non-Christian religions to give a new name to initiates immediately (no. 73) [The National Conference of Catholic Bishops establishes as the norm in the dioceses of the United States that there is to be no giving of a new name. It also approves leaving to the discretion of the diocesan bishop the giving of a new name to persons from those cultures in which it is the practice of non-Christian religions to give a new name];

5. to allow within the same rite, according to local customs, additional rites that symbolize reception into the community (no. 74) [The National Conference of Catholic Bishops has approved the inclusion of an optional presentation of a cross (no. 74) while leaving to the discretion of the diocesan bishop the inclusion of additional rites that symbolize reception into the community];

6. to establish during the period of the catechumenate, in addition to the usual rites (nos. 81–97), "rites of passage": for example, early celebration of the presentations (nos. 157–163, 178–184), the ephphetha rite, the catechumens' recitation of the Creed, or even an anointing of the catechumens (nos. 98–103) [The National Conference of Catholic Bishops approves the use of the anointing with the oil of catechumens during the period of the catechumenate as a kind of "rite of passage" (cf. no. 33.7). In addition it approves, when appropriate in the circumstances, the early celebration of the presentations (nos. 157–163, 178–184), the ephphetha rite (nos. 197–199), and the catechumens' recitation of the Creed (nos. 193–196)];

7. to decide on the omission of the anointing with the oil of catechumens or its transferral to the preparation rites

for Holy Saturday or its use during the period of the catechumenate as a kind of "rite of passage" (nos. 98–103) [The National Conference of Catholic Bishops approves the omission of the anointing with the oil of catechumens both in the celebration of baptism and in the optional preparation rites for Holy Saturday. Thus, anointing with the oil of catechumens is reserved for use in the period of the catechumenate and in the period of purification and enlightenment and is not to be included in the preparation rites on Holy Saturday or in the celebration of initiation at the Easter Vigil or at another time];

8. to make more specific and detailed the formularies of renunciation for the rite of acceptance into the order of catechumens (nos. 70–72) and for the celebration of baptism (no. 224) [The National Conference of Catholic Bishops has established as the norm in the dioceses of the United States that the formularies of renunciation should not be adapted. But for those cases where certain catechumens may be from cultures in which false worship is widespread it has approved leaving to the discretion of the diocesan bishop this matter of making more specific and detailed the formularies of renunciation in the rite of acceptance into the order of catechumens and in the celebration of baptism].

ADAPTATIONS BY THE BISHOP

34. It pertains to the bishop for his own diocese: 66

1. to set up the formation program of the catechumenate and to lay down norms according to local needs (see no. 12);

2. to decide whether and when, as circumstances warrant, the entire rite of Christian initiation may be celebrated outside the usual times (see no. 26);

3. to dispense, on the basis of some serious obstacle, from one scrutiny or, in extraordinary circumstances, even from two (see no. 331);

4. to permit the simple rite to be used in whole or in part (see no. 331);

5. to depute catechists, truly worthy and properly prepared, to give the exorcisms and blessings (see nos. 12, 16);

6. to preside at the rite of election and to ratify, personally or through a delegate, the admission of the elect (see no. 12);

7. in keeping with the provisions of law,[14] to stipulate the requisite age for sponsors (see *Christian Initiation*, General Introduction, no. 10.2).

ADAPTATIONS BY THE MINISTER

35. Celebrants should make full and intelligent use of the freedom given to them either in *Christian Initiation*, General Introduction (no. 34) or in the rubrics of the rite itself. In many places the manner of acting or praying is intentionally left undetermined or two alternatives are offered, so that ministers, according to their prudent pastoral judgment, may accommodate the rite to the circumstances of the candidates and others who are present. In all the rites the greatest freedom is left in the invitations and instructions, and the intercessions may always be shortened, changed, or even expanded with new intentions, in order to fit the circumstances or special situation of the candidates (for example, a sad or joyful event occurring in a family) or of the others present (for example, sorrow or joy common to the parish or civic community).

67

The minister will also adapt the texts by changing the gender and number as required.

[14]See *Codex Iuris Canonici*, can. 874, §1, 2°.

PART I

CHRISTIAN INITIATION OF ADULTS
Our Savior Jesus Christ has done away with death and brought us life through his Gospel

OUTLINE FOR CHRISTIAN INITIATION OF ADULTS

PERIOD OF EVANGELIZATION AND PRECATECHUMENATE

This is a time, of no fixed duration or structure, for inquiry and introduction to Gospel values, an opportunity for the beginnings of faith.

FIRST STEP: ACCEPTANCE INTO THE ORDER OF CATECHUMENS

This is the liturgical rite, usually celebrated on some annual date or dates, marking the beginning of the catechumenate proper, as the candidates express and the Church accepts their intention to respond to God's call to follow the way of Christ.

PERIOD OF THE CATECHUMENATE

This is the time, in duration corresponding to the progress of the individual, for the nurturing and growth of the catechumens' faith and conversion to God; celebrations of the word and prayers of exorcism and blessing are meant to assist the process.

SECOND STEP: ELECTION OR ENROLLMENT OF NAMES

This is the liturgical rite, usually celebrated on the First Sunday of Lent, by which the Church formally ratifies the catechumens' readiness for the sacraments of initiation and the catechumens, now the elect, express the will to receive these sacraments.

PERIOD OF PURIFICATION AND ENLIGHTENMENT

This is the time immediately preceding the elects' initiation, usually the Lenten season preceding the celebration of this initiation at the Easter Vigil; it is a time of reflection, intensely centered on conversion, marked by celebration of the scrutinies and presentations and of the preparation rites on Holy Saturday.

THIRD STEP: CELEBRATION OF THE SACRAMENTS OF INITIATION

This is the liturgical rite, usually integrated into the Easter Vigil, by which the elect are initiated through baptism, confirmation, and the eucharist.

PERIOD OF POSTBAPTISMAL CATECHESIS OR MYSTAGOGY

This is the time, usually the Easter season, following the celebration of initiation, during which the newly initiated experience being fully a part of the Christian community by means of pertinent catechesis and particularly by participation with all the faithful in the Sunday eucharistic celebration.

PERIOD OF EVANGELIZATION AND PRECATECHUMENATE

I, the light, have come into the world, so that whoever believes in me need not remain in the dark any more

36. Although the rite of initiation begins with admission to the catechumenate, the preceding period or precatechumenate is of great importance and as a rule should not be omitted. It is a time of evangelization: faithfully and constantly the living God is proclaimed and Jesus Christ whom he has sent for the salvation of all. Thus those who are not yet Christians, their hearts opened by the Holy Spirit, may believe and be freely converted to the Lord and commit themselves sincerely to him. For he who is the way, the truth, and the life fulfills all their spiritual expectations, indeed infinitely surpasses them.[1]   9

37. From evangelization, completed with the help of God, come the faith and initial conversion that cause a person to feel called away from sin and drawn into the mystery of God's love. The whole period of the precatechumenate is set aside for this evangelization, so that the genuine will to follow Christ and seek baptism may mature.   10

38. During this period, priests and deacons, catechists and other laypersons are to give the candidates a suitable explanation of the Gospel (see no. 42). The candidates are to receive help and attention so that with a purified and clearer intention they may cooperate with God's grace. Opportunities should be provided for them to meet families and other groups of Christians.   11

39. It belongs to the conference of bishops to provide for the evangelization proper to this period. The conference may also provide, if circumstances suggest and in keeping with local custom, a preliminary manner of receiving those interested in the precatechumenate, that is, those inquirers who, even though they do not fully believe, show some leaning toward the Christian faith (and who may be called "sympathizers").   12

[1]See Vatican Council II, Decree on the Church's Missionary Activity *Ad gentes*, no. 13.

1. Such a reception, if it takes place, will be carried out without any ritual celebration; it is the expression not yet of faith, but of a right intention.

2. The reception will be adapted to local conditions and to the pastoral situation. Some candidates may need to see evidence of the spirit of Christians that they are striving to understand and experience. For others, however, whose catechumenate will be delayed for one reason or another, some initial act of the candidates or the community that expresses their reception may be appropriate.

3. The reception will be held at a meeting or gathering of the local community, on an occasion that will permit friendly conversation. An inquirer or "sympathizer" is introduced by a friend and then welcomed and received by the priest or some other representative member of the community.

40. During the precatechumenate period, parish priests (pastors) should help those taking part in it with prayers suited to them, for example, by celebrating for their spiritual well-being the prayers of exorcism and the blessings given in the ritual (nos. 94, 97).

13
111
120

FIRST STEP: ACCEPTANCE INTO THE ORDER OF CATECHUMENS

Lord, let your mercy be on us, as we place our trust in you

41. The rite that is called the rite of acceptance into the order of catechumens is of the utmost importance. Assembling publicly for the first time, the candidates who have completed the period of the precatechumenate declare their intention to the Church and the Church in turn, carrying out its apostolic mission, accepts them as persons who intend to become its members. God showers his grace on the candidates, since the celebration manifests their desire publicly and marks their reception and first consecration by the Church.

14
15
68

42. The prerequisite for making this first step is that the beginnings of the spiritual life and the fundamentals of Christian teaching have taken root in the candidates.[1] Thus there must be evidence of the first faith that was conceived during the period of evangelization and precatechumenate and of an initial conversion and intention to change their lives and to enter into a relationship with God in Christ. Consequently, there must also be evidence of the first stirrings of repentance, a start to the practice of calling upon God in prayer, a sense of the Church, and some experience of the company and spirit of Christians through contact with a priest or with members of the community. The candidates should also be instructed about the celebration of the liturgical rite of acceptance.

15
68

43. Before the rite is celebrated, therefore, sufficient and necessary time, as required in each case, should be setaside to evaluate and, if necessary, to purify the candidates' motives and dispositions. With the help of the sponsors (see no. 10), catechists and deacons, pastors have the responsibility for judging the outward indications of such dispositions.[2] Because of the effect of baptism once validly received (see *Christian Initiation*, General Introduction, no. 4), it is the duty of pastors to see to it that no baptized person

16
69

[1]See Vatican Council II, Decree on the Church's Missionary Activity *Ad gentes*, no. 14.
[2]See ibid., no. 13.

seeks for any reason whatever to be baptized a second time.

44. The rite will take place on specified days during the year (see no. 18) that are suited to local conditions. The rite consists in the reception of the candidates, the celebration of the word of God, and the dismissal of the candidates; celebration of the eucharist may follow.

By decision of the conference of bishops, the following may be incorporated into this rite: a first exorcism and renunciation of false worship (nos. 70–72), the giving of a new name (no. 73), and additional rites signifying reception into the community (no. 74). [See no. 33 for the decisions made by the National Conference of Catholic Bishops regarding these matters.]

45. It is desirable that the entire Christian community or some part of it, consisting of friends and acquaintances, catechists and priests, take an active part in the celebration. The presiding celebrant is a priest or a deacon. The sponsors should also attend in order to present to the Church the candidates they have brought.

46. After the celebration of the rite of acceptance, the names of catechumens are to be duly inscribed in the register of the catechumens, along with the names of the sponsors and the minister and the date and place of the celebration.

47. From this time on the Church embraces the catechumens as its own with a mother's love and concern. Joined to the Church, the catechumens are now part of the household of Christ,[3] since the Church nourishes them with the word of God and sustains them by means of liturgical celebrations. The catechumens should be eager, then, to take part in celebrations of the word of God and to receive blessings and other sacramentals. When two catechumens marry or when a catechumen marries an unbaptized person, the appropriate rite is to be used.[4] One who dies during the catechumenate receives a Christian burial.

[3]See Vatican Council II, Dogmatic Constitution on the Church *Lumen gentium*, no. 14; Decree on the Church's Missionary Activity *Ad gentes*, no. 14.
[4] See *Rite of Marriage*, nos. 55–66.

RITE OF ACCEPTANCE INTO THE ORDER OF CATECHUMENS

RECEIVING THE CANDIDATES

48. The candidates, their sponsors, and a group of the   73
faithful gather outside the church (or inside at the entrance
or elsewhere) or at some other site suitable for this rite. As
the priest or deacon, wearing an alb or surplice, a stole,
and, if desired, a cope of festive color, goes to meet them,
the assembly of the faithful may sing a psalm or an appropriate song.

GREETING

49. The celebrant greets the candidates in a friendly man-   74
ner. He speaks to them, their sponsors, and all present,
pointing out the joy and happiness of the Church. He may
also recall for the sponsors and friends the particular experience and religious response by which the candidates, following their own spiritual path, have come to this first
step.

Then he invites the sponsors and candidates to come forward. As they are taking their places before the celebrant,
an appropriate song may be sung, for example, Psalm 63:1–
8.

OPENING DIALOGUE

50. Unless the candidates are already known to all present,   75
the celebrant asks for or calls out their given names. The
candidates answer one by one, even if, because of a large
number, the question is asked only once. One of the following or something similar may be used.

A   The celebrant asks:
What is your name?

Candidate:
N.

B   The celebrant calls out the name of each candidate.

The candidate answers:
Present.

The celebrant continues with the following questions for the individual candidates or, when there are a large number, for the candidates to answer as a group. The celebrant may use other words than those provided in asking the candidates about their intentions and may let them answer in their own words: for example, to the first question, "What do you ask of the Church of God?" or "What do you desire?" or "For what reason have you come?", he may receive such answers as "The grace of Christ" or "Entrance into the Church" or "Eternal life" or other suitable responses. The celebrant then phrases his next question according to the answer received.

Celebrant:
What do you ask of God's Church?

Candidate:
Faith.

Celebrant:
What does faith offer you?

Candidate:
Eternal life.

> 51. By decision of the diocesan bishop, the candidates' first USA
> acceptance of the Gospel (no. 52) may be replaced by the
> rite of exorcism and renunciation of false worship (nos. 70–
> 72) (see no. 33.2).

CANDIDATES' FIRST ACCEPTANCE OF THE GOSPEL

52. The celebrant addresses the candidates, adapting one 76
of the following formularies or similar words to the answers
received in the opening dialogue.

A
God gives light to everyone who comes into this 76
world; though unseen, he reveals himself through the
works of his hand, so that all people may learn to
give thanks to their Creator.

You have followed God's light and the way of the
Gospel now lies open before you. Set your feet
firmly on that path and acknowledge the living God,
who truly speaks to everyone. Walk in the light of

Christ and learn to trust in his wisdom. Commit your lives daily to his care, so that you may come to believe in him with all your heart.

This is the way of faith along which Christ will lead you in love toward eternal life. Are you prepared to begin this journey today under the guidance of Christ?

Candidates:
I am.

B

God is our Creator and in him all living things have their existence. He enlightens our minds, so that we may come to know and worship him. He has sent his faithful witness, Jesus Christ, to announce to us what he has seen and heard, the mysteries of heaven and earth. 370:1

Since you acknowledge with joy that Christ has come, now is the time to hear his word, so that you may possess eternal life by beginning, in our company, to know God and to love your neighbor. Are you ready, with the help of God, to live this life?

Candidates:
I am.

C

This is eternal life: to know the one true God and Jesus Christ, whom he has sent. Christ has been raised from the dead and appointed by God as the Lord of life and ruler of all things, seen and unseen. 370:2

If, then, you wish to become his disciples and members of his Church, you must be guided to the fullness of the truth that he has revealed to us. You must learn to make the mind of Christ Jesus your own. You must strive to pattern your life on the teachings of the Gospel and so to love the Lord your God and your neighbor. For this was Christ's command and he was its perfect example.

Is each of you ready to accept these teachings of the Gospel?

Candidates:
I am.

AFFIRMATION BY THE SPONSORS AND THE ASSEMBLY

53. Then the celebrant turns to the sponsors and the assembly and asks them in these or similar words. 77 81

Sponsors, you now present these candidates to us; are you, and all who are gathered here with us, ready to help these candidates find and follow Christ?

All:
We are.

With hands joined, the celebrant says:
Father of mercy, 82
we thank you for these your servants.
You have sought and summoned them in many ways and they have turned to seek you.

You have called them today and they have answered in our presence: we praise you, Lord, and we bless you.

All sing or say:
We praise you, Lord, and we bless you.

SIGNING OF THE CANDIDATES WITH THE CROSS

54. Next the cross is traced on the forehead of the candidates (or, at the discretion of the diocesan bishop, in front of the forehead for candidates in whose culture the act of touching may not seem proper—see no. 33.3); at the discretion of the celebrant the signing of one, several, or all of the senses may follow. The celebrant alone says the formularies accompanying each signing. 83 85

SIGNING OF THE FOREHEAD

55. One of the following options is used, depending on the number of candidates.

A

If there are only a few candidates, the celebrant invites them and their sponsors in these or similar words.   83

Come forward now with your sponsors to receive the sign of your new way of life as catechumens.

With their sponsors, the candidates come one by one to the celebrant; with his thumb he traces a cross on the forehead; then, if there is to be no signing of the senses, the sponsor does the same. The celebrant says:
N., receive the cross on your forehead.
It is Christ himself who now strengthens you
with this sign of his love.
Learn to know him and follow him.

All sing or say the following or another suitable acclamation.   86
Glory and praise to you, Lord Jesus Christ!

B

If there are a great many candidates, the celebrant speaks to them in these or similar words.*   84

Dear candidates, your answers mean that you wish to share our life and hope in Christ. To admit you as catechumens I now mark you with the sign of Christ's cross and call upon your catechists and sponsors to do the same. The whole community welcomes you with love and stands ready to help you.

Then the celebrant makes the sign of the cross over all together, as a cross is traced by a sponsor or catechist on the forehead of each candidate. The celebrant says:
Receive the cross on your forehead.
It is Christ himself who now strengthens you
with this sign of his love.**
Learn to know him and follow him.

---

*In those exceptional cases when, at the discretion of the diocesan bishop, a renunciation of false worship (no. 72) has been included in the rite of acceptance: "Dear candidates, your answers mean that you have rejected false worship and wish to share our life and hope in Christ. . . ."
**In those exceptional cases when, at the discretion of the diocesan bishop, there has been a renunciation of false worship: "with this sign of his victory."   86

All sing or say the following or another suitable acclamation.
Glory and praise to you, Lord Jesus Christ!

SIGNING OF THE OTHER SENSES

56. The signing is carried out by the catechists or the sponsors. (If required by special circumstances, this may be done by assisting priests or deacons.) The signing of each sense may be followed by an acclamation in praise of Christ, for example, "Glory and praise to you, Lord Jesus Christ!" 85 86

While the ears are being signed, the celebrant says:
Receive the sign of the cross on your ears,
that you may hear the voice of the Lord.

While the eyes are being signed:
Receive the sign of the cross on your eyes,
that you may see the glory of God.

While the lips are being signed:
Receive the sign of the cross on your lips,
That you may respond to the word of God.

While the breast is being signed:
Receive the sign of the cross over your heart,
that Christ may dwell there by faith.

While the shoulders are being signed:
Receive the sign of the cross on your shoulders,
that you may bear the gentle yoke of Christ.

[While the hands are being signed: USA
Receive the sign of the cross on your hands,
that Christ may be known in the work which you do.

While the feet are being signed: USA
Receive the sign of the cross on your feet,
that you may walk in the way of Christ.]

Without touching them, the celebrant alone makes the sign of the cross over all the candidates at once (or, if they are few, over each individually), saying:
I sign you with the sign of eternal life
in the name of the Father, and of the Son, ✠
and of the Holy Spirit.

Catechumens:
Amen.

CONCLUDING PRAYER

57. The celebrant concludes the signing of the forehead   87
(and senses) with one of the following prayers.

Let us pray.

A
Lord,   87
we have signed these catechumens
with the sign of Christ's cross.

Protect them by its power,
so that, faithful to the grace which has begun in
   them,
they may keep your commandments
and come to the glory of rebirth in baptism.

We ask this through Christ our Lord.
R̹. Amen.

B
Almighty God,   87
by the cross and resurrection of your Son
you have given life to your people.

Your servants have received the sign of the cross:
make them living proof of its saving power
and help them to persevere in the footsteps of Christ.

We ask this through Christ our Lord.
R̹. Amen.

---

58. At the discretion of the diocesan bishop, the giving of   USA
a new name (no. 73) may take place at this time.

59. At the discretion of the diocesan bishop, the invitation   USA
to the celebration of the word of God may be preceded or
followed by additional rites signifying reception into the
community, for example, the presentation of a cross (no.
74) or some other symbolic act.

INVITATION TO THE CELEBRATION OF THE WORD OF GOD

60. The celebrant next invites the catechumens and their sponsors to enter the church (or the place where the liturgy of the word will be celebrated). He uses the following or similar words, accompanying them with some gesture of invitation.

**N. and N., come into the church,
to share with us at the table of God's word.**

During the entry an appropriate song is sung or the following antiphon with Psalm 34:2, 3, 6, 9, 10, 11, 16.
**Come, my children, and listen to me;
I will teach you the fear of the Lord.**

LITURGY OF THE WORD

INSTRUCTION

61. After the catechumens have reached their places, **the** celebrant speaks to them briefly, helping them to understand the dignity of God's word, which is proclaimed and heard in the church.

The Lectionary for Mass or the Bible is carried in procession and placed with honor on the lectern, where it may be incensed.

Celebration of the liturgy of the word follows.

READINGS

62. The readings may be chosen from any of the readings in the Lectionary for Mass that are suited to the new catechumens or the following may be used.

FIRST READING

Genesis 12:1–4a—*Leave your country, and come into the land I will show you.*

RESPONSORIAL PSALM

Psalm 33:4–5, 12–13, 18–19, 20 and 22
℟. **(v.12b) Happy the people the Lord has chosen to be his own.**

Or:

R⁄. (v.22) Lord, let your mercy be on us, as we place our trust in you.

VERSE BEFORE THE GOSPEL

John 1:41, 17b

We have found the Messiah: Jesus Christ, who brings us truth and grace.

GOSPEL

John 1:35–42—*This is the Lamb of God. We have found the Messiah.*

HOMILY

63. A homily follows that explains the readings.   92

PRESENTATION OF A BIBLE

64. A book containing the Gospels may be given to the   93
catechumens by the celebrant; a cross may also be given,
unless this has already been done as one of the additional
rites (see no. 74). The celebrant may use words suited to
the gift presented, for example, "Receive the Gospel of Jesus Christ, the Son of God," and the catechumens may respond in an appropriate way.

INTERCESSIONS FOR THE CATECHUMENS

65. Then the sponsors and the whole congregation join in   94
the following or a similar formulary of intercession for the
catechumens.

[If it is decided, in accord with no. 68, that after the dismissal of the catechumens the usual general intercessions of
the Mass are to be omitted and that the liturgy of the eucharist is to begin immediately, intentions for the Church and
the whole world are to be added to the following intentions
for the catechumens.]

Celebrant:

These catechumens, who are our brothers and sisters,
have already traveled a long road. We rejoice with
them in the gentle guidance of God who has brought
them to this day. Let us pray that they may press on-

wards, until they come to share fully in our way of life.

Assisting minister:
That God our Father may reveal his Christ to them more and more with every passing day, let us pray to the Lord:
℟. **Lord, hear our prayer.**

Assisting minister:
That they may undertake with generous hearts and souls whatever God may ask of them, let us pray to the Lord:
℟. **Lord, hear our prayer.**

Assisting minister:
That they may have our sincere and unfailing support every step of the way, let us pray to the Lord:
℟. **Lord, hear our prayer.**

Assisting minister:
That they may find in our community compelling signs of unity and generous love, let us pray to the Lord:
℟. **Lord, hear our prayer.**

Assisting minister:
That their hearts and ours may become more responsive to the needs of others, let us pray to the Lord:
℟. **Lord, hear our prayer.**

Assisting minister:
That in due time they may be found worthy to receive the baptism of new birth and renewal in the Holy Spirit, let us pray to the Lord:
℟. **Lord, hear our prayer.**

PRAYER OVER THE CATECHUMENS

66. After the intercessions, the celebrant, with hands out- 95
stretched over the catechumens, says one of the following prayers.
Let us pray.

A

[God of our forebears and] God of all creation,   95
we ask you to look favorably on your servants N.
   and N.;
make them fervent in spirit,
joyful in hope,
and always ready to serve your name.

Lead them, Lord, to the baptism of new birth,
so that, living a fruitful life in the company of your
   faithful,
they may receive the eternal reward that you promise.

We ask this in the name of Jesus the Lord.
℞. Amen.

B

Almighty God,   95
source of all creation,
you have made us in your image.
Welcome with love those who come before you today.

They have listened among us to the word of Christ;
by its power renew them
and by your grace refashion them,
so that in time they may assume the full likeness of
   Christ,
who lives and reigns for ever and ever.
℞. Amen.

DISMISSAL OF THE CATECHUMENS

67. If the eucharist is to be celebrated, the catechumens are 96
normally dismissed at this point by use of option A or B; if
the catechumens are to stay for the celebration of the eucharist, option C is used; if the eucharist is not to be celebrated, the entire assembly is dismissed by use of option D.

A

The celebrant recalls briefly the great joy with which the
catechumens have just been received and urges them to
live according to the word of God they have just heard. Af-

ter the dismissal formulary, the group of catechumens goes
out but does not disperse. With the help of some of the
faithful, the catechumens remain together to share their joy
and spiritual experiences. For the dismissal the following or
similar words are used.

**Catechumens, go in peace, and may the Lord remain
with you always.**

Catechumens:
Thanks be to God.

B
As an optional formulary for dismissing the catechumens, USA
the celebrant may use these or similar words.

**My dear friends, this community now sends you
forth to reflect more deeply upon the word of God
which you have shared with us today. Be assured of
our loving support and prayers for you. We look forward to the day when you will share fully in the
Lord's Table.**

C If for serious reasons the catechumens cannot leave (see 96
no. 75.3) and must remain with the baptized, they are to be
instructed that though they are present at the eucharist,
they cannot take part in it as the baptized do. They may be
reminded of this by the celebrant in these or similar words.

**Although you cannot yet participate fully in the
Lord's eucharist, stay with us as a sign of our hope
that all God's children will eat and drink with the
Lord and work with his Spirit to re-create the face of
the earth.**

D
The celebrant dismisses those present, using these or similar words.

**Go in peace, and may the Lord remain with you
always.**

All:
Thanks be to God.

An appropriate song may conclude the celebration.

LITURGY OF THE EUCHARIST

68. When the eucharist is to follow, intercessory prayer is   97
resumed with the usual general intercessions for the needs
of the Church and the whole world; then, if required, the
profession of faith is said. But for pastoral reasons these
general intercessions and the profession of faith may be
omitted. The liturgy of the eucharist then begins as usual
with the preparation of the gifts.

OPTIONAL RITES

69. By decision of the National Conference of Catholic Bish-   USA
ops the presentation of a cross (no. 74) may be included as
a symbol of reception into the community. At the discretion
of the diocesan bishop, one or more additional rites may be
incorporated into the "Rite of Acceptance into the Order of
Catechumens": a first exorcism and renunciation of false
worship, the giving of a new name, as well as additional
rites that symbolize acceptance into the community (cf. no.
33.2, 33.4, 33.5, 33.8).

EXORCISM AND RENUNCIATION OF FALSE WORSHIP

70. In regions where false worship is widespread, whether   78
in worshiping spiritual powers or in calling on the shades
of the dead or in using magical arts, the diocesan bishop
may permit the introduction of a first exorcism and a renunciation of false worship; this replaces the candidates' first acceptance of the Gospel (no. 52).

EXORCISM

71. After giving a brief introduction to the rite, the cele-   79
brant breathes lightly toward the face of each candidate
and, with a symbolic gesture, for example, holding up his
right hand, or without any gesture, says the formulary of
exorcism.

[If there are a great many candidates, the breathing is omitted and the formulary said only once; the breathing is also omitted in places where it would be unacceptable.]

Celebrant:

**By the breath of your mouth, O Lord,
drive away the spirits of evil.
Command them to depart,
for your kingdom has come among us.**

RENUNCIATION OF FALSE WORSHIP

72. If the diocesan bishop judges it suitable to have the candidate openly renounce false worship and spirits or magical arts, he should see to the preparation of a formulary for the questions and renunciation relevant to the local situation. As long as the language is not offensive to members of other religious groups, this may be expressed using one of the following formularies or similar words.   80

A Celebrant: 80

Dear candidates, you have set out toward your baptism. You have answered God's call and been helped by his grace; you have decided to serve and worship him alone and the one he has sent, Jesus Christ. Since you have made this choice, now is the time to renounce publicly those powers that are not of God and those forms of worship that do not rightly honor him. Are you, therefore, resolved to remain loyal to God and his Christ, and never to serve ungodly powers?

Candidates:

Yes, we are.

Celebrant:

Do you reject the worship of N. and N.?

Candidates:

Yes, we do.

He continues in the same way for each form of worship to be renounced.

B Celebrant: 371

Dear candidates, the true God has called you and led you here. You sincerely desire to worship and serve

him alone, and his Son Jesus Christ. Now, in the presence of this community, you must reject all rites and forms of worship that do not honor the true God. Are you determined never to abandon him and his Son, Jesus Christ, and never to return to the service of other masters?

Candidates:
We are.

Celebrant:
Christ Jesus, Lord of the living and the dead, has power over all spirits and demons. Are you determined never to abandon him and never again to serve N.*?

Candidates:
We are.

Celebrant:
Christ Jesus alone has the power to protect us. Are you determined never to abandon him and never again to seek [wear/use] N.**?

Candidates:
We are.

Celebrant:
Christ Jesus alone is truth. Are you determined never to abandon him and never to seek out soothsayers, magicians, or witch doctors?

Candidates:
We are.

The celebration then continues with the affirmation by the sponsors and the assembly (no. 53).

GIVING OF A NEW NAME

73. At the discretion of the diocesan bishop, the giving of a new name to persons from cultures in which it is the practice of non-Christian religions to give a new name may fol-

*Here mention is made of the images worshiped in false rites, such as fetishes.
**Here mention is made of the objects that are used superstitiously, such as amulets.

low the signing of the candidates with the cross (nos. 54–56).* This may be either a Christian name or one familiar in the culture, provided such a name is not incompatible with Christian beliefs. (In some cases it will suffice to explain the Christian understanding of the catechumens' given names.) If a new name is given, one of the following formularies may be used.

A Celebrant:
By what name do you wish to be called?

Catechumen:
N.

B Celebrant:
N., from now on you will [also] be called N.

The catechumen gives the following or another suitable reply.
Amen.

The celebration then continues with the optional presentation of the cross (no. 74) and/or with an additional rite determined by the diocesan bishop to symbolize acceptance into the community (cf. no. 33.5) or with the invitation to the celebration of the word of God (no. 60).

PRESENTATION OF A CROSS

74. The presentation of a cross on occasion may be incorpo- USA
rated into the rite either before or after the invitation to the celebration of the word of God (no. 60).

Celebrant:
You have been marked with the cross of Christ. Receive now the sign of his love.

Catechumens:
Amen.

*If so, this rite is not repeated on Holy Saturday; see no. 200.

PERIOD OF THE CATECHUMENATE

Leave your country, and come into the land I will show you

75. The catechumenate is an extended period during
which the candidates are given suitable pastoral formation
and guidance, aimed at training them in the Christian life.[1]
In this way, the dispositions manifested at their acceptance
into the catechumenate are brought to maturity. This is
achieved in four ways.

1. A suitable catechesis is provided by priests or deacons,
or by catechists and others of the faithful, planned to be gradual and complete in its coverage, accommodated to the liturgical year, and solidly supported by celebrations of the word.
This catechesis leads the catechumens not only to an appropriate acquaintance with dogmas and precepts but also to a pro-
found sense of the mystery of salvation in which they desire
to participate.

2. As they become familiar with the Christian way of
life and are helped by the example and support of sponsors, godparents, and the entire Christian community, the
catechumens learn to turn more readily to God in prayer, to
bear witness to the faith, in all things to keep their hopes
set on Christ, to follow supernatural inspiration in their
deeds, and to practice love of neighbor, even at the cost of
self-renunciation. Thus formed, "the newly converted set
out on a spiritual journey. Already sharing through faith in
the mystery of Christ's death and resurrection, they pass
from the old to a new nature made perfect in Christ. Since
this transition brings with it a progressive change of outlook and conduct, it should become manifest by means of
its social consequences and it should develop gradually during the period of the catechumenate. Since the Lord in
whom they believe is a sign of contradiction, the newly converted often experience divisions and separations, but they
also taste the joy that God gives without measure."[2]

3. The Church, like a mother, helps the catechumens
on their journey by means of suitable liturgical rites, which
purify the catechumens little by little and strengthen them
with God's blessing. Celebrations of the word of God are

19

[1]See Vatican Council II, Decree on the Church's Missionary Activity *Ad gentes*, no. 14.

[2]Ibid., no. 13.

arranged for their benefit, and at Mass they may also take part with the faithful in the liturgy of the word, thus better preparing themselves for their eventual participation in the liturgy of the eucharist. Ordinarily, however, when they are present in the assembly of the faithful they should be kindly dismissed before the liturgy of the eucharist begins (unless their dismissal would present practical or pastoral problems). For they must await their baptism, which will join them to God's priestly people and empower them to participate in Christ's new worship (see no. 67 for formularies of dismissal).

    4. Since the Church's life is apostolic, catechumens should also learn how to work actively with others to spread the Gospel and build up the Church by the witness of their lives and by professing their faith.[3]

76. The duration of the catechumenate will depend on the grace of God and on various circumstances, such as the program of instruction for the catechumenate, the number of catechists, deacons, and priests, the cooperation of the individual catechumens, the means necessary for them to come to the site of the catechumenate and spend time there, the help of the local community. Nothing, therefore, can be settled a priori.   20 98

The time spent in the catechumenate should be long enough—several years if necessary—for the conversion and faith of the catechumens to become strong. By their formation in the entire Christian life and a sufficiently prolonged probation the catechumens are properly initiated into the mysteries of salvation and the practice of an evangelical way of life. By means of sacred rites celebrated at successive times they are led into the life of faith, worship, and charity belonging to the people of God.

77. It is the responsibility of the bishop to fix the duration and to direct the program of the catechumenate. The conference of bishops, after considering the conditions of its people and region,[4] may also wish to provide specific guidelines. At the discretion of the bishop, on the basis of the spiritual preparation of the candidate, the period of the   20 98

[3]See Vatican Council II, Decree on the Church's Missionary Activity *Ad gentes*, no. 14.
[4]See Vatican Council II, Constitution on the Liturgy *Sacrosanctum Concilium*, art. 64.

catechumenate may in particular cases be shortened (see nos. 331–335); in altogether extraordinary cases the catechumenate may be completed all at once (see nos. 332, 336–369).

78. The instruction that the catechumens receive during this period should be of a kind that while presenting Catholic teaching in its entirety also enlightens faith, directs the heart toward God, fosters participation in the liturgy, inspires apostolic activity, and nurtures a life completely in accord with the spirit of Christ.　99

79. Among the rites belonging to the period of the catechumenate, then, celebrations of the word of God (nos. 81–89) are foremost. The minor exorcisms (nos. 90–94) and the blessings of the catechumens (nos. 95–97) are ordinarily celebrated in conjunction with a celebration of the word. In addition, other rites may be celebrated to mark the passage of the catechumens from one level of catechesis to another: for example, an anointing of the catechumens may be celebrated (nos. 98–103) and the presentations of the Creed and the Lord's Prayer may be anticipated (see nos. 104–105).　103

80. During the period of the catechumenate, the catechumens should give thought to choosing their godparents who will present them to the Church on the day of the election (see no. 11; also *Christian Initiation*, General Introduction, nos. 8–10).　104 105

Provision should also be made for the entire community involved in the formation of the catechumens—priests, deacons, catechists, sponsors, godparents, friends and neighbors—to participate in some of the celebrations belonging to the catechumenate, including any of the optional "rites of passage" (nos. 98–105).

RITES BELONGING TO THE PERIOD OF THE CATECHUMENATE

CELEBRATIONS OF THE WORD OF GOD

81. During the period of the catechumenate there should be celebrations of the word of God that accord with the liturgical season and that contribute to the instruction of the catechumens and the needs of the community. These celebrations of the word are: first, celebrations held specially for the catechumens; second, participation in the liturgy of the word at the Sunday Mass; third, celebrations held in connection with catechetical instruction.

100

82. The special celebrations of the word of God arranged for the benefit of the catechumens have as their main purpose:

106

    1. to implant in their hearts the teachings they are receiving: for example, the morality characteristic of the New Testament, the forgiving of injuries and insults, a sense of sin and repentance, the duties Christians must carry out in the world;

    2. to give them instruction and experience in the different aspects and ways of prayer;

    3. to explain to them the signs, celebrations, and seasons of the liturgy;

    4. to prepare them gradually to enter the worship assembly of the entire community.

83. From the very beginning of the period of the catechumenate the catechumens should be taught to keep holy the Lord's Day.

107

    1. Care should be taken that some of the special celebrations of the word just mentioned (no. 82) are held on Sunday, so that the catechumens will become accustomed to taking an active and practiced part in these celebrations.

    2. Gradually the catechumens should be admitted to the first part of the celebration of the Sunday Mass. After the liturgy of the word they should, if possible, be dismissed, but an intention for them is included in the general intercessions (see no. 67 for formularies of dismissal).

84. Celebrations of the word may also be held in connec-   106
tion with catechetical or instructional meetings of the catechumens, so that these will occur in a context of prayer.

MODEL FOR A CELEBRATION OF THE WORD OF GOD

85. For the celebrations of the word of God that are held
specially for the benefit of the catechumens (see no. 82), the
following structure (nos. 86–89) may be used as a model.

86. *Song:* An appropriate song may be sung to open the
celebration.

87. *Readings and Responsorial Psalms:* One or more readings
from Scripture, chosen for their relevance to the formation
of the catechumens, are proclaimed by a baptized member
of the community. A sung responsorial psalm should ordinarily follow each reading.

88. *Homily:* A brief homily that explains and applies the
readings should be given.

89. *Concluding Rites:* The celebration of the word may con-   USA
clude with a minor exorcism (no. 94) or with a blessing of
the catechumens (no. 97). When the minor exorcism is
used, it may be followed by one of the blessings (no. 97)
or, on occasion, by the rite of anointing (nos. 102–103).*

MINOR EXORCISMS

90. The first or minor exorcisms have been composed in   101
the form of petitions directly addressed to God. They draw
the attention of the catechumens to the real nature of Christian life, the struggle between flesh and spirit, the importance of self-denial for reaching the blessedness of God's
kingdom, and the unending need for God's help.

*Celebrations of the word that are held in connection with instructional ses-
sions may include, along with an appropriate reading, a minor exorcism
(no. 94) or a blessing of the catechumens (no. 97). When the minor exorcism is used, it may be followed by one of the blessings (no. 97) or, on
occasion, by the rite of anointing (nos. 102–103).
The meetings of the catechumens after the liturgy of the word of the Sunday Mass may also include a minor exorcism (no. 94) or a blessing (no.
97). Likewise, when the minor exorcism is used, it may be followed by
one of the blessings (no. 97) or, on occasion, by the rite of anointing (nos.
102–103)

91. The presiding celebrant for the minor exorcisms is a   109
priest, a deacon, or a qualified catechist appointed by the
bishop for this ministry (see no. 16).

92. The minor exorcisms take place within a celebration of   110
the word of God held in a church, a chapel, or in a center
for the catechumenate. A minor exorcism may also be held
at the beginning or end of a meeting for catechesis. When
there is some special need, one of these prayers of exorcism
may be said privately for individual catechumens.

93. The formularies for the minor exorcisms may be used   112
on several occasions, as different situations may suggest.

PRAYERS OF EXORCISM

94. As the catechumens bow or kneel, the celebrant, with   109
hands outstretched over them, says one of the following
prayers.

Let us pray.

A
God of power,   113
who promised us the Holy Spirit through Jesus your
    Son,
we pray to you for these catechumens,
who present themselves before you.

Protect them from the spirit of evil
and guard them against error and sin,
so that they may become the temple of your Holy
    Spirit.

Confirm what we profess in faith,
so that our words may not be empty,
but full of the grace and power
by which your Son has freed the world.

We ask this through Christ our Lord.
R̸. Amen.

B
Lord our God,   114
you make known the true life;

you cut away corruption and strengthen faith,
you build up hope and foster love.

In the name of your beloved Son,
our Lord Jesus Christ,
and in the power of the Holy Spirit,
we ask you to remove from these your servants
all unbelief and hesitation in faith,
[the worship of false gods and magic,
witchcraft and dealings with the dead],
the love of money and lawless passions,
enmity and quarreling,
and every manner of evil.

And because you have called them
to be holy and sinless in your sight,
create in them a spirit of faith and reverence,
of patience and hope,
of temperance and purity,
and of charity and peace.

We ask this through Christ our Lord.
℞. Amen.

C
God of power,
you created us in your image and likeness
and formed us in holiness and justice.

Even when we sinned against you,
you did not abandon us,
but in your wisdom chose to save us
by the incarnation of your Son.

Save these your servants:
free them from evil and the tyranny of the enemy.
Keep far from them the spirit of wickedness, false-
    hood, and greed.

Receive them into your kingdom
and open their hearts to understand your Gospel,
so that, as children of the light,
they may become members of your Church,

bear witness to your truth,
and put into practice your commands of love.

We ask this through Christ our Lord.
℟. Amen.

D
Lord Jesus Christ, 116
when you climbed the mountain to preach,
you turned your disciples from the paths of sin
and revealed to them the beatitudes of your kingdom.

Help these your servants, who hear the word of the
Gospel,
and protect them from the spirit of greed, of lust,
and of pride.
May they find the blessings of your kingdom
in poverty and in hunger,
in mercy and in purity of heart.
May they work for peace and joyfully endure persecution
and so come to share your kingdom
and experience the mercy you promised.
May they finally see God in the joy of heaven
where you live and reign for ever and ever.
℟. Amen.

E
O God, 117
Creator and Savior of all,
in your love you have formed these your servants;
in your mercy you have called them and received
them.

Probe their hearts today
and watch over them as they look forward to the coming of your Son.

Keep them in your providence
and complete in them the plan of your love.
Through their loyalty to Christ
may they be counted among his disciples on earth

and be acknowledged by him in heaven.

We ask this through Christ our Lord.
R̶̷. Amen.

F
Lord and God,   118
you know the secrets of our hearts
and reward us for the good we do.

Look kindly on the efforts and the progress of your
    servants.
Strengthen them on their way,
increase their faith,
and accept their repentance.
Open to them your goodness and justice
and lead them to share in your sacraments on earth,
until they finally enjoy your presence in heaven.

We ask this through Christ our Lord.
R̶̷. Amen.

G
Lord Jesus Christ,   373:1
loving Redeemer of all,
your name alone has the power to save,
that name before which every knee should bend
in the heavens, on the earth, and under the earth.

We pray for these your servants,
who worship you as the true God.

Look upon them and enlighten their hearts,
free them from the snares and malice of Satan,
heal their weakness and blot out their sins.

Give them discernment to know what pleases you
and the courage to live by your Gospel,
that they may become the dwelling place of your
    Spirit,
for you live and reign for ever and ever.
R̶̷. Amen.

H

Lord Jesus Christ,

373:2

sent by the Father and anointed by the Spirit,
when you read in the synagogue at Nazareth
you fulfilled the words of the prophet Isaiah
that proclaimed liberty to captives
and announced a season of forgiveness.

We pray for these your servants
who have opened their ears and hearts to your word.
Grant that they may grasp your moment of grace.

Do not let their minds be troubled
or their lives tied to earthly desires.
Do not let them remain
estranged from the hope of your promises
or enslaved by a spirit of unbelief.
Rather, let them believe in you,
whom the Father has established as universal Lord
and to whom he has subjected all things.
Let them submit themselves to the Spirit of grace,
so that, with hope in their calling,
they may join the priestly people
and share in the abundant joy of the new Jerusalem,
where you live and reign for ever and ever.
℟. Amen.

I

Lord Jesus Christ,

373:3

after calming the storms and freeing the possessed,
you gave us a sign of your mercy
by calling Matthew, the tax collector, to follow you.
You chose him to record for all time
your command to teach all nations.

We pray for these your servants
who confess that they are sinners.

Hold in check the power of the evil one,
and show them your mercy;
heal in them the wounds of sin
and fill their hearts with your peace.

May they delight in their discovery of the Gospel
and generously follow your call,
for you live and reign for ever and ever.
℟. Amen.

J
God of infinite wisdom,   373:4
you chose the apostle Paul
to proclaim your Son to every nation.

We pray that these your servants,
who look forward to baptism,
may follow in the footsteps of Paul
and trust not in flesh and blood,
but in the call of your grace.

Probe their hearts and purify them,
so that, freed from all deception,
they may never look back
but strive always toward what is to come.
May they count everything as loss
compared with the unsurpassed worth of knowing
   your Son,
and so gain him as their eternal reward,
for he is Lord for ever and ever.
℟. Amen.

K
Lord,   373:5
Creator and Redeemer of your holy people,
your great love has drawn these catechumens to seek
   and find you.
Look upon them today,
purify their hearts,
and bring to fulfillment in them the plan of your
   grace,
so that, faithfully following Christ,
they may come to drink the waters of salvation.

We ask this through Christ our Lord.
℟. Amen.

BLESSINGS OF THE CATECHUMENS

95. The blessings of the catechumens are a sign of God's   102
love and of the Church's tender care. They are bestowed on
the catechumens so that, even though they do not as yet
have the grace of the sacraments, they may still receive
from the Church courage, joy, and peace as they proceed
along the difficult journey they have begun.

96. The blessings may be given by a priest, a deacon, or a   119
qualified catechist appointed by the bishop (see no. 16).
The blessings are usually given at the end of a celebration
of the word; they may also be given at the end of a meeting
for catechesis. When there is some special need, the blessings may be given privately to individual catechumens.

PRAYERS OF BLESSING

97. The celebrant, with hands outstretched over the cate-   119
chumens, says one of the following prayers. After the
prayer of blessing, if this can be done conveniently, the
catechumens come before the celebrant, who lays hands on
them individually. Then the catechumens leave.

Let us pray.

A
Lord,   121
form these catechumens by the mysteries of the faith,
that they may be brought to rebirth in baptism
and be counted among the members of your Church.

We ask this through Christ our Lord.
R̸. Amen.

B
Father,   122
through your holy prophets
you proclaimed to all who draw near you,
"Wash and be cleansed,"
and through Christ you have granted us rebirth in
    the Spirit.

Bless these your servants
as they earnestly prepare for baptism.

Fulfill your promise:
sanctify them in preparation for your gifts,
that they may come to be reborn as your children
and enter the community of your Church.

We ask this through Christ our Lord.
R̰. Amen.

C
God of power,
look upon these your servants
as they deepen their understanding of the Gospel.

Grant that they may come to know and love you
and always heed your will
with receptive minds and generous hearts.

Teach them through this time of preparation
and enfold them within your Church,
so that they may share your holy mysteries
both on earth and in heaven.

We ask this through Christ our Lord.
R̰. Amen.

D
God our Father,
you have sent your only Son, Jesus Christ,
to free the world from falsehood.

Give to your catechumens fullness of understanding,
unwavering faith,
and a firm grasp of your truth.

Let them grow ever stronger,
that they may receive in due time the new birth of
  baptism
that gives pardon of sins,
and join with us in praising your name.

We ask this through Christ our Lord.
R̰. Amen.

E
Almighty and eternal God,   374:1
you dwell on high yet look on the lowly;
to bring us your gift of salvation
you sent Jesus your Son,
our Lord and God.

Look kindly on these catechumens,
who bow before you in worship;
prepare them for their rebirth in baptism,
the forgiveness of their sins,
and the garment of incorruptible life.

Enfold them in your holy, catholic, and apostolic
   Church,
that they may join with us
in giving glory to your name.

We ask this through Christ our Lord.
R̶̸. Amen.

F
Lord of all,   374:2
through your only begotten Son
you cast down Satan
and broke the chains that held us captive.

We thank you for these catechumens
whom you have called.

Strengthen them in faith,
that they may know you, the one true God,
and Jesus Christ, whom you have sent.

Keep them clean of heart and make them grow in
   virtue,
that they may be worthy to receive baptism
and enter into the holy mysteries.

We ask this through Christ our Lord.
R̶̸. Amen.

G

Lord God,   374:3
you desire that all be saved
and come to the knowledge of truth.

Enliven with faith those who are preparing for
baptism;
bring them into the fold of your Church,
there to receive the gift of eternal life.

We ask this through Christ our Lord.
℟. Amen.

H

God of power and Father of our Savior Jesus Christ,   374:4
look kindly upon these your servants.

Drive from their minds all taint of false worship
and stamp your law and commands on their hearts.

Lead them to full knowledge of the truth
and prepare them to be the temple of the Holy Spirit
through their rebirth in baptism.

Grant this through Christ our Lord.
℟. Amen.

I

Lord,   374:5
look with love on your servants,
who commit themselves to your name
and bow before you in worship.

Help them to accomplish what is good;
arouse their hearts,
that they may always remember your works and your
commands
and eagerly embrace all that is yours.

Grant this through Christ our Lord.
℟. Amen.

ANOINTING OF THE CATECHUMENS

98. During the period of the catechumenate, a rite of anointing the catechumens, through use of the oil of catechumens, may be celebrated wherever this seems beneficial or desirable. The presiding celebrant for such a first anointing of the catechumens is a priest or a deacon. 103
127

99. Care is to be taken that the catechumens understand the significance of the anointing with oil. The anointing with oil symbolizes their need for God's help and strength so that, undeterred by the bonds of the past and overcoming the opposition of the devil, they will forthrightly take the step of professing their faith and will hold fast to it unfalteringly throughout their lives. 212

100. The anointing ordinarily takes place after the homily in a celebration of the word of God (see no. 89), and is conferred on each of the catechumens; this rite of anointing may be celebrated several times during the course of the catechumenate. Further, for particular reasons, a priest or a deacon may confer the anointing privately on individual catechumens. 128

101. The oil used for this rite is to be the oil blessed by the bishop at the chrism Mass, but for pastoral reasons a priest celebrant may bless oil for the rite immediately before the anointing.[1] 129

PRAYER OF EXORCISM OR BLESSING OF OIL

102. When anointing with oil already blessed by the bishop, the celebrant first says the prayer of exorcism given as option A (or one of the other prayers of exorcism in no. 94); a priest celebrant who for pastoral reasons chooses to bless oil for the rite uses the blessing given as option B. 130

A
Prayer of Exorcism

Let us pray.

Lord Jesus Christ,
sent by the Father and anointed by the Spirit, 373:2

---

[1]See *Rite of the Blessing of Oils, Rite of Consecrating the Chrism*, Introduction, no. 7.

when you read in the synagogue at Nazareth,
you fulfilled the words of the prophet Isaiah
that proclaimed liberty to captives
and announced a season of forgiveness.

We pray for these your servants
who have opened their ears and hearts to your word.
Grant that they may grasp your moment of grace.

Do not let their minds be troubled
or their lives tied to earthly desires.
Do not let them remain
estranged from the hope of your promises
or enslaved by a spirit of unbelief.
Rather, let them believe in you,
whom the Father has established as universal Lord
and to whom he has subjected all things.

Let them submit themselves to the Spirit of grace,
so that, with hope in their calling,
they may join the priestly people
and share in the abundant joy of the new Jerusalem,
where you live and reign for ever and ever.
℟. Amen.

B
Blessing of Oil

Let us pray.

O God,
source of strength and defender of your people,
you have chosen to make this oil,
created by your hand,
an effective sign of your power.

Bless ✣ this oil
and strengthen the catechumens who will be
   anointed with it.
Grant them your wisdom to understand the Gospel
   more deeply
and your strength to accept the challenges of Christian life.

**Enable them to rejoice in baptism
and to partake of a new life in the Church
as true children of your family.**

**We ask this through Christ our Lord.
R̸. Amen.**

ANOINTING

103. Facing the catechumens, the celebrant says: 132

**We anoint you with the oil of salvation
in the name of Christ our Savior.
May he strengthen you with his power,
who lives and reigns for ever and ever.**

Catechumens:
Amen.

The celebrant anoints each catechumen with the oil of catechumens on the breast or on both hands or, if this seems
desirable, even on other parts of the body.

[If there are a great many catechumens, additional priests
or deacons may assist in the anointing.]

The anointing may be followed by a blessing of the catechumens (no. 97).

PRESENTATIONS [OPTIONAL]

104. The presentations normally take place during Lent,   125
the period of purification and enlightenment, after the first
and third scrutinies. But for pastoral advantage and because
the period of purification and enlightenment is rather short,
the presentations may be held during the period of the
catechumenate, rather than at the regular times. But the presentations are not to take place until a point during the
catechumenate when the catechumens are judged ready for
these celebrations.

105. Both the presentation of the Creed and the presenta-   126
tion of the Lord's Prayer may be anticipated; each may be
concluded with the ephphetha rite.[1] When the presenta-

[1]But if the rite of recitation of the Creed (nos. 193–196) is also anticipated
as one of the "rites of passage" (see no. 33.6), the ephphetha rite is used
only to begin this rite of recitation and not with the presentations

tions are anticipated, care is to be taken to substitute the term "catechumens" for the term "elect" in all formularies.

PRESENTATIONS

Presentation of the Creed: see nos. 157–162.

Presentation of the Lord's Prayer: see nos. 178–183.

Ephphetha Rite: see nos. 197–199.

SENDING OF THE CATECHUMENS FOR ELECTION [OPTIONAL]   USA

106. At the conclusion of the period of the catechumenate, a rite of sending the catechumens to their election by the bishop may be celebrated in parishes wherever this seems beneficial or desirable. When election will take place in the parish, this rite is not used.

107. As the focal point of the Church's concern for the catechumens, admission to election belongs to the bishop who is usually its presiding celebrant. It is within the parish community, however, that the preliminary judgment is made concerning the catechumens' state of formation and progress.

This rite offers that local community the opportunity to express its approval of the catechumens and to send them forth to the celebration of election assured of the parish's care and support.

108. The rite is celebrated in the parish church at a suitable time prior to the rite of election.

109. The rite takes place after the homily in a celebration of the word of God (see no. 89) or at Mass.

110. When the Rite of Sending Catechumens for Election is combined with the rite of sending for recognition by the bishop the (already baptized) adult candidates for the sacraments of confirmation and eucharist (*or:* for reception into the full communion of the Catholic Church), the alternate rite found on page 301 (Appendix I, Rite 2.) is used.

PRESENTATION OF THE CATECHUMENS

111. After the homily, the priest in charge of the catechumens' initiation, or a deacon, a catechist, or a representative of the community, presents the catechumens, using the following or similar words.

Reverend Father, these catechumens, whom I now present to you, are beginning their final period of preparation and purification leading to their initiation. They have found strength in God's grace and support in our community's prayers and example.

Now they ask that they be recognized for the progress they have made in their spiritual formation and that they receive the assurance of our blessings and prayers as they go forth to the rite of election celebrated this afternoon (*or:* next Sunday [*or* specify the day]) by Bishop N.

The celebrant replies:
Those who are to be sent to the celebration of election in Christ, come forward, together with those who will be your godparents.

One by one, the catechumens are called by name. Each catechumen, accompanied by a godparent (or godparents), comes forward and stands before the celebrant.

AFFIRMATION BY THE GODPARENTS [AND THE ASSEMBLY]

112. Then the celebrant addresses the assembly in these or similar words:

My dear friends, these catechumens who have been preparing for the sacraments of initiation hope that they will be found ready to participate in the rite of election and be chosen in Christ for the Easter sacraments. It is the responsibility of this community to inquire about their readiness before they are presented to the bishop.

He addresses the godparents:
I turn to you, godparents, for your testimony about these candidates. Have these catechumens taken their

**formation in the Gospel and in the Catholic way of
life seriously?**

Godparents:
They have.

Celebrant:
**Have they given evidence of their conversion by the
example of their lives?**

Godparents:
They have.

Celebrant:
**Do you judge them to be ready to be presented to the
bishop for the rite of election?**

Godparents:
We do.

[When appropriate in the circumstances, the celebrant may
also ask the entire assembly to express its approval of the
candidates.]

The celebrant concludes the affirmation by the following:
**My dear catechumens, this community gladly recom-
mends you to the bishop, who, in the name of
Christ, will call you to the Easter sacraments. May
God bring to completion the good work he has be-
gun in you.**

113. If the signing of the Book of the Elect is to take place
in the presence of the bishop, it is omitted here. However,
if the signed Book of the Elect is to be presented to the bishop in the rite of election, the catechumens may now come
forward to sign it or they should sign it after the celebration
or at another time prior to the rite of Election.

INTERCESSIONS FOR THE CATECHUMENS

114. Then the community prays for the catechumens by
use of the following or a similar formulary. The celebrant
may adapt the introduction and the intentions to fit various
circumstances.

[If it is decided, in accord with no. 117, that after the dismissal of the catechumens the usual general intercessions of
the Mass are to be omitted and that the liturgy of the eucha-

rist is to begin immediately, intentions for the Church and the whole world are to be added to the following intentions for the catechumens.]

Celebrant:

My brothers and sisters, we look forward to celebrating at Easter the life-giving mysteries of our Lord's suffering, death and resurrection. As we journey together to the Easter sacraments, these catechumens will look to us for an example of Christian renewal. Let us pray to the Lord for them and for ourselves, that we may be renewed by one another's efforts and together come to share the joys of Easter.

Assisting minister:

That these catechumens may be freed from selfishness and learn to put others first, let us pray to the Lord:
R̟. Lord, hear our prayer.

Assisting minister:

That their godparents may be living examples of the Gospel, let us pray to the Lord:
R̟. Lord, hear our prayer.

Assisting minister:

That their teachers may always convey to them the beauty of God's word, let us pray to the Lord:
R̟. Lord, hear our prayer.

Assisting minister:

That these catechumens may share with others the joy they have found in their friendship with Jesus, let us pray to the Lord:
R̟. Lord, hear our prayer.

Assisting minister:

That our community, during this (*or:* the coming) Lenten season, may grow in charity and be constant in prayer, let us pray to the Lord:
R̟. Lord, hear our prayer.

PRAYER OVER THE CATECHUMENS

115. After the intercessions, the celebrant, with hands outstretched over the catechumens, says the following prayer.

**Father of love and power,
it is your will to establish everything in Christ
and to draw us into his all-embracing love.**

**Guide these catechumens in the days and weeks
ahead:
strengthen them in their vocation,
build them into the kingdom of your Son,
and seal them with the Spirit of your promise.**

**We ask this through Christ our Lord.
R̸. Amen.**

DISMISSAL

116. If the eucharist is to be celebrated, the catechumens
are normally dismissed at this point by use of option A or
B; if the catechumens are to stay for the celebration of the
eucharist, option C is used; if the eucharist is not to be celebrated, the entire assembly is dismissed by use of option D.

A The celebrant dismisses the catechumens in these or
similar words.

**My dear friends, you are about to set out on the road
that leads to the glory of Easter. Christ will be your
way, your truth, and your life. In his name we send
you forth from this community to celebrate with the
bishop the Lord's choice of you to be numbered
among his elect. Until we meet again for the scrutinies, walk always in his peace.**

Catechumens:
Amen.

B As an optional formulary for dismissing the catechumens, the celebrant may use these or similar words.

**My dear friends, this community now sends you
forth to reflect more deeply upon the word of God
which you have shared with us today. Be assured of
our loving support and prayers for you. We look forward to the day when you will share fully in the
Lord's Table.**

C If for serious reasons the catechumens cannot leave (see no. 75.3) and must remain with the rest of the liturgical assembly, they are to be instructed that though they are present at the eucharist, they cannot take part in it as the baptized do. They may be reminded of this by the celebrant in these or similar words.

Although you cannot yet participate fully in the Lord's eucharist, stay with us as a sign of our hope that all God's children will eat and drink with the Lord and work with his Spirit to re-create the face of the earth.

D The celebrant dismisses those present, using these or similar words.

Go in peace, and may the Lord remain with you always.

All:
Thanks be to God.

An appropriate song may conclude the celebration.

LITURGY OF THE EUCHARIST

117. When the eucharist is to follow, intercessory prayer is resumed with the usual general intercessions for the needs of the Church and the whole world; then, if required, the profession of faith is said. But for pastoral reasons these general intercessions and the profession of faith may be omitted. The liturgy of the eucharist then begins as usual with the preparation of the gifts.

SECOND STEP: ELECTION OR ENROLLMENT OF NAMES

Your ways, O Lord, are love and truth to those who keep your covenant

118. The second step in Christian initiation is the liturgical 134
rite called both election and the enrollment of names,
which closes the period of the catechumenate proper, that
is, the lengthy period of formation of the catechumens'
minds and hearts. The celebration of the rite of election,
which usually coincides with the opening of Lent, also
marks the beginning of the period of final, more intense
preparation for the sacraments of initiation, during which
the elect will be encouraged to follow Christ with greater
generosity.

119. At this second step, on the basis of the testimony of 22
godparents and catechists and of the catechumens' reaffir- 133
mation of their intention, the Church judges their state of
readiness and decides on their advancement toward the sacraments of initiation. Thus the Church makes its "election,"
that is, the choice and admission of those catechumens who
have the dispositions that make them fit to take part, at the
next major celebration, in the sacraments of initiation.

This step is called election because the acceptance made by
the Church is founded on the election by God, in whose
name the Church acts. The step is also called the enrollment of names because as a pledge of fidelity the candidates inscribe their names in the book that lists those who
have been chosen for initiation.

120. Before the rite of election is celebrated, the catechu- 23
mens are expected to have undergone a conversion in mind
and in action and to have developed a sufficient acquaintance with Christian teaching as well as a spirit of faith and
charity. With deliberate will and an enlightened faith they
must have the intention to receive the sacraments of the
Church, a resolve they will express publicly in the actual
celebration of the rite.

121. The election, marked with a rite of such solemnity, is 135
the focal point of the Church's concern for the catechu-

mens. Admission to election therefore belongs to the bishop, and the presiding celebrant for the rite of election is the bishop himself or a priest or a deacon who acts as the bishop's delegate (see no. 12).

Before the rite of election the bishop, priests, deacons, catechists, godparents, and the entire community, in accord with their respective responsibilities and in their own way, should, after considering the matter carefully, arrive at a judgment about the catechumens' state of formation and progress. After the election, they should surround the elect with prayer, so that the entire Church will accompany and lead them to encounter Christ.

122. Within the rite of election the bishop celebrant or his delegate declares in the presence of the community the Church's approval of the candidates. Therefore to exclude any semblance of mere formality from the rite, there should be a deliberation prior to its celebration to decide on the catechumens' suitableness. This deliberation is carried out by the priests, deacons, and catechists involved in the formation of the catechumens, and by the godparents and representatives of the local community. If circumstances suggest, the group of catechumens may also take part. The deliberation may take various forms, depending on local conditions and pastoral needs. During the celebration of election, the assembly is informed of the decision approving the catechumens. [23] [137]

123. Before the rite of election godparents are chosen by the catechumens; the choice should be made with the consent of the priest, and the persons chosen should, as far as possible, be approved for their role by the local community (see no. 11). In the rite of election the godparents exercise their ministry publicly for the first time. They are called by name at the beginning of the rite to come forward with the catechumens (no. 130); they give testimony on behalf of the catechumens before the community (no. 131); they may also write their names along with the catechumens in the book of the elect (no. 132). [136]

124. From the day of their election and admission, the catechumens are called "the elect." They are also described as *competentes* ("co-petitioners"), because they are joined together in asking for and aspiring to receive the three sacra- [24]

ments of Christ and the gift of the Holy Spirit. They are
also called *illuminandi* ("those who will be enlightened"), because baptism itself has been called *illuminatio* ("enlightenment") and it fills the newly baptized with the light of
faith. In our own times, other names may be applied to the
elect that, depending on regions and cultures, are better
suited to the people's understanding and the idiom of the
language.

125. The bishop celebrant or his delegate, however much 138
or little he was involved in the deliberation prior to the rite,
has the responsibility of showing in the homily or elsewhere during the celebration the religious and ecclesial significance of the election. The celebrant also declares before
all present the Church's decision and, if appropriate in the
circumstances, asks the community to express its approval
of the candidates. He also asks the catechumens to give a
personal expression of their intention and, in the name of
the Church, he carries out the act of admitting them as
elect. The celebrant should open to all the divine mystery
expressed in the call of the Church and in the liturgical celebration of this mystery. He should remind the faithful to
give good example to the elect and along with the elect to
prepare themselves for the Easter solemnities.

126. The sacraments of initiation are celebrated during the 139
Easter solemnities, and preparation for these sacraments is
part of the distinctive character of Lent. Accordingly, the
rite of election should normally take place on the First Sunday of Lent and the period of final preparation of the elect
should coincide with the Lenten season. The plan arranged
for the Lenten season will benefit the elect by reason of
both its liturgical structure and the participation of the community. For urgent pastoral reasons, especially in secondary mission stations, it is permitted to celebrate the rite of
election during the week preceding or following the First
Sunday of Lent.

When, because of unusual circumstances and pastoral
needs, the rite of election is celebrated outside Lent, it is to
be celebrated about six weeks before the sacraments of initiation, in order to allow sufficient time for the scrutinies
and presentations. The rite is not to be celebrated on a solemnity of the liturgical year (see no. 29).

127. The rite should take place in the cathedral/church, in a parish or, if necessary, in some other suitable and fitting place.

140
USA

128. The rite is celebrated within Mass, after the homily, and should be celebrated within the Mass of the First Sunday of Lent. If, for pastoral reasons, the rite is celebrated on a different day, the texts and the readings of the ritual Mass "Christian Initiation: Election or Enrollment of Names" may always be used. When the Mass of the day is celebrated and its readings are not suitable, the readings are those given for the First Sunday of Lent or others may be chosen from elsewhere in the Lectionary.

140
141

When celebrated outside Mass, the rite takes place after the readings and the homily and is concluded with the dismissal of both the elect and the faithful.

[An optional parish rite to send catechumens for election by the bishop precedes the rite of election and is found at no. 106.]

RITE OF ELECTION OR ENROLLMENT OF NAMES

LITURGY OF THE WORD

HOMILY

129. After the readings (see no. 128), the bishop, or the   142
celebrant who acts as delegate of the bishop, gives the homily. This should be suited to the actual situation and should address not just the catechumens but the entire community of the faithful, so that all will be encouraged to give good example and to accompany the elect along the path of the paschal mystery.

PRESENTATION OF THE CATECHUMENS

130. After the homily, the priest in charge of the catechu-   143
mens' initiation, or a deacon, a catechist, or a representative of the community, presents the candidates, using the following or similar words.

Reverend Father, Easter is drawing near, and so these catechumens, whom I now present to you, are completing their period of preparation. They have found strength in God's grace and support in our community's prayers and example.

Now they ask that after the celebration of the scrutinies, they be allowed to participate in the sacraments of baptism, confirmation, and the eucharist.

The celebrant replies:
Those who are to be chosen in Christ, come forward, together with your godparents.

One by one, the candidates and godparents are called by name. Each candidate, accompanied by a godparent (or godparents), comes forward and stands before the celebrant.

[If there are a great many candidates, all are presented in groups, for example, each group by its own catechist. But in this case, the catechists should be advised to have a special celebration beforehand in which they call each candidate forward by name.]

AFFIRMATION BY THE GODPARENTS [AND THE ASSEMBLY]

131. Then the celebrant addresses the assembly. If he has taken part in the earlier deliberation on the candidates' suitableness (see no. 122), he may use either option A or option B or similar words; if he has not taken part in the earlier deliberation, he uses option B or similar words.

144
145

A

My dear friends, these catechumens have asked to be initiated into the sacramental life of the Church this Easter. Those who know them have judged them to be sincere in their desire. During the period of their preparation they have listened to the word of Christ and endeavored to follow his commands; they have shared the company of their Christian brothers and sisters and joined with them in prayer.

145

And so I announce to all of you here that our community has decided to call them to the sacraments. Therefore, I ask their godparents to state their opinion once again, so that all of you may hear.

He addresses the godparents:
As God is your witness, do you consider these candidates worthy to be admitted to the sacraments of Christian initiation?

Godparents:
We do.

When appropriate in the circumstances, the celebrant may also ask the entire assembly to express its approval of the candidates in these or similar words:

Celebrant:
Now I ask you, the members of this community: Are you willing to affirm the testimony expressed about these catechumens and support them in faith, prayer and example as we prepare to celebrate the Easter sacraments?

USA

All:
We are.

B

God's holy Church wishes to know whether these   144
candidates are sufficiently prepared to be enrolled
among the elect for the coming celebration of Easter.
And so I speak first of all to you their godparents.

He addresses the godparents:
Have they faithfully listened to God's word pro-
claimed by the Church?

Godparents:
They have.

Celebrant:
Have they responded to that word and begun to walk
in God's presence?

Godparents:
They have.

Celebrant:
Have they shared the company of their Christian
brothers and sisters and joined with them in prayer?

Godparents:
They have.

When appropriate in the circumstances, the celebrant may
also ask the entire assembly to express its approval of the
candidates in these or similar words:

Celebrant:
And now I speak to you, my brothers and sisters in   USA
this assembly:
Are you ready to support the testimony expressed
about these catechumens and include them in your
prayer and affection as we move toward Easter?

All:
We are.

INVITATION AND ENROLLMENT OF NAMES

132. Then addressing the catechumens in the following or   146
similar words, the celebrant advises them of their accep-   USA
tance and asks them to declare their own intention.

And now, my dear catechumens, I address you. Your own godparents and teachers [and this entire community] have spoken in your favor. The Church in the name of Christ accepts their judgment and calls you to the Easter sacraments.

Since you have already heard the call of Christ, you must now express your response to that call clearly and in the presence of the whole Church.

Therefore, do you wish to enter fully into the life of the Church through the sacraments of baptism, confirmation, and the eucharist?

Catechumens:
We do.

Celebrant:
Then offer your names for enrollment.

The candidates give their names, either going with their godparents to the celebrant or while remaining in place, and the actual inscription of the names may be carried out in various ways. The candidates may inscribe their names themselves or they may call out their names, which are inscribed by the godparents or by the minister who presented the candidates (see no. 130). As the enrollment is taking place, an appropriate song, for example, Psalm 16 or Psalm 33 with a refrain such as, **"Happy the people the Lord has chosen to be his own"** may be sung.

[If there are a great many candidates, the enrollment may simply consist in the presentation of a list of the names to the celebrant, with such words as: **"These are the names of the candidates"** or, when the bishop is celebrant and candidates from several parishes have been presented to him: **"These are the names of the candidates from the parish of N."**] USA

ACT OF ADMISSION OR ELECTION

133. The celebrant briefly explains the significance of the enrollment that has just taken place. Then, turning to the candidates, he says the following or similar words. 147

N. and N., I now declare you to be members of the elect, to be initiated into the sacred mysteries at the next Easter Vigil.

Candidates:
Thanks be to God.

He continues:
God is always faithful to those he calls: now it is your duty, as it is ours, both to be faithful to him in return and to strive courageously to reach the fullness of truth, which your election opens up before you.

Then the celebrant turns to the godparents and instructs them in the following or similar words.
Godparents, you have spoken in favor of these cate-chumens: accept them now as chosen in the Lord and continue to sustain them through your loving care and example, until they come to share in the sacraments of God's life.

He invites them to place their hand on the shoulder of the candidate whom they are receiving into their care, or to make some other gesture to indicate the same intent.

INTERCESSIONS FOR THE ELECT

134. The community may use either of the following for-   148
mularies, options A or B, or a similar formulary to pray for
the elect. The celebrant may adapt the introduction and the
intentions to fit various circumstances.

[If it is decided, in accord with no. 137, that after the dismissal of the elect the usual general intercessions of the
Mass are to be omitted and that the liturgy of the eucharist
is to begin immediately, intentions for the Church and the
whole world are to be added to the following intentions for
the elect.]

Celebrant:
My brothers and sisters, in beginning this period of Lent, we look forward to celebrating at Easter the life-giving mysteries of our Lord's suffering, death, and resurrection. These elect, whom we bring with us to the Easter sacraments, will look to us for an ex-ample of Christian renewal. Let us pray to the Lord for them and for ourselves, that we may be renewed by one another's efforts and together come to share the joys of Easter.

A Assisting minister: 148

That together we may fruitfully employ this Lenten season to renew ourselves through self-denial and works of holiness, let us pray to the Lord:
℟. **Lord, hear our prayer.**

Assisting minister:

That our catechumens may always remember this day of their election and be grateful for the blessings they have received from heaven, let us pray to the Lord:
℟. **Lord, hear our prayer.**

Assisting minister:

That their teachers may always convey the beauty of God's word to those who search for it, let us pray to the Lord:
℟. **Lord, hear our prayer.**

Assisting minister.

That their godparents may be living examples of the Gospel, let us pray to the Lord:
℟. **Lord, hear our prayer.**

Assisting minister:

That their families, far from placing any obstacles in the way of these catechumens, may help them to follow the promptings of the Spirit, let us pray to the Lord:
℟. **Lord, hear our prayer.**

Assisting minister:

That our community, during this Lenten period, may grow in charity and be constant in prayer, let us pray to the Lord:
℟. **Lord, hear our prayer.**

Assisting minister:

That those who have not yet overcome their hesitation may trust in Christ and come to join our community as our brothers and sisters, let us pray to the Lord:
℟. **Lord, hear our prayer.**

B Assisting minister:
**That these elect may find joy in daily prayer, we
 pray:**
Rɤ. Lord, hear our prayer.

Assisting minister:
**That, by praying to you often, they may grow ever
closer to you, we pray:**
Rɤ. Lord, hear our prayer.

Assisting minister:
**That they may read your word and joyfully dwell on
it in their hearts, we pray:**
Rɤ. Lord, hear our prayer.

Assisting minister:
**That they may humbly acknowledge their faults and
work wholeheartedly to correct them, we pray:**
Rɤ. Lord, hear our prayer.

Assisting minister:
**That they may dedicate their daily work as a pleasing
offering to you, we pray:**
Rɤ. Lord, hear our prayer.

Assisting minister:
**That each day of Lent they may do something in
your honor, we pray:**
Rɤ. Lord, hear our prayer.

Assisting minister:
**That they may abstain with courage from everything
that defiles the heart, we pray:**
Rɤ. Lord, hear our prayer.

Assisting minister:
**That they may grow to love and seek virtue and holi-
ness of life, we pray:**
Rɤ. Lord, hear our prayer.

Assisting minister:
**That they may renounce self and put others first, we
pray:**
Rɤ. Lord, hear our prayer.

Assisting minister:
That you will protect and bless their families, we pray:
R̸. Lord, hear our prayer.

Assisting minister:
That they may share with others the joy they have found in their faith, we pray:
R̸. Lord, hear our prayer.

PRAYER OVER THE ELECT

135. After the intercessions, the celebrant, with hands out-   149
stretched over the elect, says one of the following prayers.

A
Lord God,   149
you created the human race
and are the author of its renewal.
Bless all your adopted children
and add these chosen ones
to the harvest of your new covenant.
As true children of the promise,
may they rejoice in eternal life,
won, not by the power of nature,
but through the mystery of your grace.

We ask this through Christ our Lord.
R̸. Amen.

B
Father of love and power,   149
it is your will to establish everything in Christ
and to draw us into his all-embracing love.
Guide the elect of your Church:
strengthen them in their vocation,
build them into the kingdom of your Son,
and seal them with the Spirit of your promise.

We ask this through Christ our Lord.
R̸. Amen.

DISMISSAL OF THE ELECT

136. If the eucharist is to be celebrated, the elect are nor-   150
mally dismissed at this point by use of option A or B; if the

elect are to stay for the celebration of the eucharist, option C is used; if the eucharist is not to be celebrated, the entire assembly is dismissed by use of option D.

A The celebrant dismisses the elect in these or similar words.

150

My dear elect, you have set out with us on the road that leads to the glory of Easter. Christ will be your way, your truth, and your life. Until we meet again for the scrutinies, walk always in his peace.

The elect:
Amen.

B As an optional formulary for dismissing the catechu-   USA
mens, the celebrant may use these or similar words.
My dear friends, this community now sends you forth to reflect more deeply upon the word of God which you have shared with us today. Be assured of our loving support and prayers for you. We look forward to the day when you will share fully in the Lord's Table.

C If for serious reasons the elect cannot leave (see no.   150
75.3) and must remain with the baptized, they are to be instructed that though they are present at the eucharist, they cannot take part in it as the baptized do. They may be reminded of this by the celebrant in these or similar words.

Although you cannot yet participate fully in the Lord's eucharist, stay with us as a sign of our hope that all God's children will eat and drink with the Lord and work with his Spirit to re-create the face of the earth.

D The celebrant dismisses those present, using these or similar words.
Go in peace, and may the Lord remain with you always.

All:
Thanks be to God.

An appropriate song may conclude the celebration.

LITURGY OF THE EUCHARIST

137. When the eucharist is to follow, intercessory prayer is resumed with the usual general intercessions for the needs of the Church and the whole world; then, if required, the profession of faith is said. But for pastoral reasons these general intercessions and the profession of faith may be omitted. The liturgy of the eucharist then begins as usual with the preparation of the gifts.

151

PERIOD OF PURIFICATION AND ENLIGHTENMENT

The water that I shall give will turn into a spring of eternal life

138. The period of purification and enlightenment, which the rite of election begins, customarily coincides with Lent. In the liturgy and liturgical catechesis of Lent the reminder of baptism already received or the preparation for its reception, as well as the theme of repentance, renew the entire community along with those being prepared to celebrate the paschal mystery, in which each of the elect will share through the sacraments of initiation.[1] For both the elect and the local community, therefore, the Lenten season is a time for spiritual recollection in preparation for the celebration of the paschal mystery.

21
152

139. This is a period of more intense spiritual preparation, consisting more in interior reflection than in catechetical instruction, and is intended to purify the minds and hearts of the elect as they search their own consciences and do penance. This period is intended as well to enlighten the minds and hearts of the elect with a deeper knowledge of Christ the Savior. The celebration of certain rites, particularly the scrutinies (see nos. 141–146) and the presentations (see nos. 147–149), brings about this process of purification and enlightenment and extends it over the course of the entire Lenten season.

22
153

140. Holy Saturday is the day of proximate preparation for the celebration of the sacraments of initiation and on that day the rites of preparation (see nos. 185–192) may be celebrated.

26

[1]See Vatican Council II, Decree on the Church's Missionary Activity *Ad gentes*, no. 14.

RITES BELONGING TO THE PERIOD OF PURIFICATION AND ENLIGHTENMENT

THE SCRUTINIES

141. The scrutinies, which are solemnly celebrated on Sundays and are reinforced by an exorcism, are rites for self-searching and repentance and have above all a spiritual purpose. The scrutinies are meant to uncover, then heal all that is weak, defective, or sinful in the hearts of the elect; to bring out, then strengthen all that is upright, strong, and good. For the scrutinies are celebrated in order to deliver the elect from the power of sin and Satan, to protect them against temptation, and to give them strength in Christ, who is the way, the truth, and the life. These rites, therefore, should complete the conversion of the elect and deepen their resolve to hold fast to Christ and to carry out their decision to love God above all. 25
154

142. Because they are asking for the three sacraments of initiation, the elect must have the intention of achieving an intimate knowledge of Christ and his Church, and they are expected particularly to progress in genuine self-knowledge through serious examination of their lives and true repentance. 155

143. In order to inspire in the elect a desire for purification and redemption by Christ, three scrutinies are celebrated. By this means, first of all, the elect are instructed gradually about the mystery of sin, from which the whole world and every person longs to be delivered and thus saved from its present and future consequences. Second, their spirit is filled with Christ the Redeemer, who is the living water (gospel of the Samaritan woman in the first scrutiny), the light of the world (gospel of the man born blind in the second scrutiny), the resurrection and the life (gospel of Lazarus in the third scrutiny). From the first to the final scrutiny the elect should progress in their perception of sin and their desire for salvation. 157

144. In the rite of exorcism (nos. 154, 168, 175), which is celebrated by a priest or a deacon, the elect, who have already learned from the Church as their mother the mystery of deliverance from sin by Christ, are freed from the effects of sin and from the influence of the devil. They receive new 156

strength in the midst of their spiritual journey and they open their hearts to receive the gifts of the Savior.

145. The priest or deacon who is the presiding celebrant should carry out the celebration in such a way that the faithful in the assembly will also derive benefit from the liturgy of the scrutinies and join in the intercessions for the elect. 158

146. The scrutinies should take place within the ritual Masses "Christian Initiation: The Scrutinies," which are celebrated on the Third, Fourth, and Fifth Sundays of Lent; the readings with their chants are those given for these Sundays in the Lectionary for Mass, Year A. When, for pastoral reasons, these ritual Masses cannot be celebrated on their proper Sundays, they are celebrated on other Sundays of Lent or even convenient days during the week. 159

When, because of unusual circumstances and pastoral needs, the period of purification and enlightenment takes place outside Lent, the scrutinies are celebrated on Sundays or even on weekdays, with the usual intervals between celebrations. They are not celebrated on solemnities of the liturgical year (see no. 30).

In every case the ritual Masses "Christian Initiation: The Scrutinies" are celebrated and in this sequence: for the first scrutiny the Mass with the gospel of the Samaritan woman; for the second, the Mass with the gospel of the man born blind; for the third, the Mass with the gospel of Lazarus.

PRESENTATIONS

147. The presentations take place after the celebration of the scrutinies, unless, for pastoral reasons, they have been anticipated during the period of the catechumenate (see nos. 79, 104-105). Thus, with the catechumenal formation of the elect completed, the Church lovingly entrusts to them the Creed and the Lord's Prayer, the ancient texts that have always been regarded as expressing the heart of the Church's faith and prayer. These texts are presented in order to enlighten the elect. The Creed, as it recalls the wonderful deeds of God for the salvation of the human race, suffuses the vision of the elect with the sure light of faith. The Lord's Prayer fills them with a deeper realization of the new spirit of adoption by which they will call God 25
181

their Father, especially in the midst of the eucharistic assembly.

148. The first presentation to the elect is the presentation of the Creed, during the week following the first scrutiny. The elect are to commit the Creed to memory and they will recite it publicly (nos. 193–196) prior to professing their faith in accordance with that Creed on the day of their baptism.

183
184

149. The second presentation to the elect is the presentation of the Lord's Prayer, during the week following the third scrutiny (but, if necessary, this presentation may be deferred for inclusion in the preparation rites of Holy Saturday; see no. 185). From antiquity the Lord's Prayer has been the prayer proper to those who in baptism have received the spirit of adoption. When the elect have been baptized and take part in their first celebration of the eucharist, they will join the rest of the faithful in saying the Lord's Prayer.

188
189

FIRST SCRUTINY
(Third Sunday of Lent)
LITURGY OF THE WORD

READINGS
150. The texts and the readings for Mass are always those 160
given for the first scrutiny in the Missal and the Lectionary
for Mass among the ritual Masses, "Christian Initiation: The
Scrutinies."

HOMILY
151. After the readings and guided by them, the celebrant 161
explains in the homily the meaning of the first scrutiny in
the light of the Lenten liturgy and of the spiritual journey
of the elect.

INVITATION TO SILENT PRAYER
152. After the homily, the elect with their godparents 162
come forward and stand before the celebrant.

The celebrant first addresses the assembly of the faithful, inviting them to pray in silence and to ask that the elect will
be given a spirit of repentance, a sense of sin, and the true
freedom of the children of God.

The celebrant then addresses the elect, inviting them also to
pray in silence and suggesting that as a sign of their inner
spirit of repentance they bow their heads or kneel; he concludes his remarks with the following or similar words.

**Elect of God, bow your heads [kneel down] and
pray.**

The elect bow their heads or kneel, and all pray for some
time in silence. After the period of silent prayer, the community and the elect stand for the intercessions.

INTERCESSIONS FOR THE ELECT
153. Either of the following formularies, options A or B, 163
may be used for the intercessions for the elect and both the
introduction and the intentions may be adapted to fit various circumstances. During the intercessions the godparents
stand with their right hand on the shoulder of the elect.

[If it is decided, in accordance with no. 156, that after the
dismissal of the elect the usual general intercessions of the

Mass are to be omitted and that the liturgy of the eucharist is to begin immediately, intentions for the Church and the whole world are to be added to the following intentions for the elect.]

Celebrant:
Let us pray for these elect whom the Church has confidently chosen. May they successfully complete their long preparation and at the paschal feast find Christ in his sacraments.

A Assisting minister:
That they may ponder the word of God in their hearts and savor its meaning more fully day by day, let us pray to the Lord:
R̸. Lord, hear our prayer.

163

Assisting minister:
That they may learn to know Christ, who came to save what was lost, let us pray to the Lord:
R̸. Lord, hear our prayer.

Assisting minister:
That they may humbly confess themselves to be sinners, let us pray to the Lord:
R̸. Lord, hear our prayer.

Assisting minister:
That they may sincerely reject everything in their lives that is displeasing and contrary to Christ, let us pray to the Lord:
R̸. Lord, hear our prayer.

Assisting minister:
That the Holy Spirit, who searches every heart, may help them to overcome their weakness through his power, let us pray to the Lord:
R̸. Lord, hear our prayer.

Assisting minister:
That the same Holy Spirit may teach them to know the things of God and how to please him, let us pray to the Lord:
R̸. Lord, hear our prayer.

Assisting minister:
**That their families also may put their hope in Christ
and find peace and holiness in him, let us pray to
the Lord:**
℟. **Lord, hear our prayer.**

Assisting minister:
**That we ourselves in preparation for the Easter feast
may seek a change of heart, give ourselves to prayer,
and persevere in our good works, let us pray to the
Lord:**
℟. **Lord, hear our prayer.**

Assisting minister:
**That throughout the whole world whatever is weak
may be strengthened, whatever is broken restored,
whatever is lost found, and what is found redeemed,
let us pray to the Lord:**
℟. **Lord, hear our prayer.**

B Assisting minister: 378
**That, like the woman of Samaria, our elect may re-
view their lives before Christ and acknowledge their
sins, let us pray to the Lord:**
℟. **Lord, hear our prayer.**

Assisting minister:
**That they may be freed from the spirit of mistrust
that deters people from following Christ, let us pray
to the Lord:**
℟. **Lord, hear our prayer.**

Assisting minister:
**That while awaiting the gift of God, they may long
with all their hearts for the living water that brings
eternal life, let us pray to the Lord:**
℟. **Lord, hear our prayer.**

Assisting minister:
**That by accepting the Son of God as their teacher,
they may become true worshipers of the Father in
spirit and in truth, let us pray to the Lord:**
℟. **Lord, hear our prayer.**

Assisting minister:
**That they may share with their friends and neighbors
the wonder of their own meeting with Christ, let us
pray to the Lord:**
℟. **Lord, hear our prayer.**

Assisting minister:
**That those whose lives are empty for want of the
word of God may come to the Gospel of Christ, let
us pray to the Lord:**
℟. **Lord, hear our prayer.**

Assisting minister:
**That all of us may learn from Christ to do the Fa-
ther's will in love, let us pray to the Lord:**
℟. **Lord, hear our prayer.**

EXORCISM

154. After the intercessions, the rite continues with one of   164
the following exorcisms.

A The celebrant faces the elect and, with hands joined,   164
says:
**God of power,
you sent your Son to be our Savior.
Grant that these catechumens,
who, like the woman of Samaria, thirst for living
   water,
may turn to the Lord as they hear his word
and acknowledge the sins and weaknesses that weigh
   them down.**

**Protect them from vain reliance on self
and defend them from the power of Satan.**

**Free them from the spirit of deceit,
so that, admitting the wrong they have done,
they may attain purity of heart
and advance on the way to salvation.**

We ask this through Christ our Lord.
℟. **Amen.**

Here, if this can be done conveniently, the celebrant lays
hands on each one of the elect.

Then, with hands outstretched over all the elect, he
continues:
Lord Jesus,
you are the fountain for which they thirst,
you are the Master whom they seek.
In your presence
they dare not claim to be without sin,
for you alone are the Holy One of God.

They open their hearts to you in faith,
they confess their faults
and lay bare their hidden wounds.
In your love free them from their infirmities,
heal their sickness,
quench their thirst, and give them peace.

In the power of your name,
which we call upon in faith,
stand by them now and heal them.
Rule over that spirit of evil,
conquered by your rising from the dead.

Show your elect the way of salvation in the Holy
   Spirit,
that they may come to worship the Father in truth,
for you live and reign for ever and ever.
R̸. Amen.

B   The celebrant faces the elect and, with hands joined,
says: 379
All-merciful Father,
through your Son you revealed your mercy
to the woman of Samaria;
and moved by that same care
you have offered salvation to all sinners.

Look favorably on these elect,
who desire to become your adopted children
through the power of your sacraments.

Free them from the slavery of sin,
and for Satan's crushing yoke
exchange the gentle yoke of Jesus.

Protect them in every danger,
that they may serve you faithfully in peace and joy
and render you thanks for ever.
℞. Amen.

Here, if this can be done conveniently, the celebrant lays hands on each one of the elect.

Then, with hands outstretched over all the elect, he continues:
Lord Jesus,
in your merciful wisdom
you touched the heart of the sinful woman
and taught her to worship the Father
in spirit and in truth.

Now, by your power,
free these elect from the cunning of Satan,
as they draw near to the fountain of living water.

Touch their hearts with the power of the Holy Spirit,
that they may come to know the Father
in true faith, which expresses itself in love,
for you live and reign for ever and ever.
℞. Amen.

An appropriate song may be sung, for example, Psalm 6, 26, 32, 38, 39, 40, 51, 116:1–9, 130, 139, or 142.

DISMISSAL OF THE ELECT

155. If the eucharist is to be celebrated, the elect are normally dismissed at this point by use of option **A** or **B**; if the elect are to stay for the celebration of the eucharist, option **C** is used; if the eucharist is not to be celebrated, the entire assembly is dismissed by use of option **D**.

A   The celebrant dismisses the elect in these or similar words.

165

Dear elect, go in peace, and join us again at the next
scrutiny. May the Lord remain with you always.

Elect:
Amen.

B As an optional formulary for dismissing the catechu- USA
mens, the celebrant may use these or similar words.
**My dear friends, this community now sends you
forth to reflect more deeply upon the word of God
which you have shared with us today. Be assured of
our loving support and prayers for you. We look forward to the day when you will share fully in the
Lord's Table.**

C If for serious reasons the elect cannot leave (see no.
75.3) and must remain with the baptized, they are to be instructed that though they are present at the eucharist, they
cannot take part in it as the baptized do. They may be reminded of this by the celebrant in these or similar words.

**Although you cannot yet participate fully in the
Lord's eucharist, stay with us as a sign of our hope
that all God's children will eat and drink with the
Lord and work with his Spirit to re-create the face of
the earth.**

D The celebrant dismisses those present, using these or
similar words.
**Go in peace, and may the Lord remain with you
always.**

All:
Thanks be to God.

An appropriate song may conclude the celebration.

LITURGY OF THE EUCHARIST

156. When the eucharist is to follow, intercessory prayer is 166
resumed with the usual general intercessions for the needs
of the Church and the whole world; then, if required, the
profession of faith is said. But for pastoral reasons these
general intercessions and the profession of faith may be
omitted. The liturgy of the eucharist then begins as usual
with the preparation of the gifts. In the eucharistic prayer
there is to be a remembrance of the elect and their godparents (see ritual Mass "Christian Initiation: The Scrutinies").

PRESENTATION OF THE CREED
(Third Week of Lent)

157. The presentation of the Creed, which takes place dur- 182
ing the week after the first scrutiny, should preferably be 184
celebrated in the presence of a community of the faithful,
within Mass after the homily.

LITURGY OF THE WORD

READINGS

158. In place of the readings assigned for the weekday 185
Mass, the following readings are used, as indicated in the
Lectionary for Mass, ritual Masses, "Christian Initiation: Pre-
sentation of the Creed."

FIRST READING

Deuteronomy 6:1–7—*Listen, Israel: You shall love the Lord
your God with all your heart.*

RESPONSORIAL PSALM

Psalm 19:8, 9, 10, 11
℟. (John 6:68c) **Lord, you have the words of everlasting life.**

SECOND READING

Romans 10:8–13—*The confession of faith of the elect.*

Or:
1 Corinthians 15:1–8a (longer) or 1–4 (shorter)—*The Gospel
will save you only if you keep believing what I preached to you.*

VERSE BEFORE THE GOSPEL

John 3:16
**God loved the world so much, he gave us his only Son,
that all who believe in him might have eternal life.**

GOSPEL

Matthew 16:13–18—*On this rock I will build my Church.*

Or:

John 12:44–50—*I, the light, have come into the world, so that whoever believes in me need not remain in the dark any more.*

HOMILY

159. After the readings and guided by them, the celebrant 185 explains in the homily the meaning and importance of the Creed in relation to the teaching that the elect have already received and to the profession of faith that they must make at their baptism and uphold throughout their lives.

PRESENTATION OF THE CREED

160. After the homily, a deacon or other assisting minister 186 says:

Let the elect now come forward to receive the Creed from the Church.

Before beginning the Apostles' Creed (option A) or the Nicene Creed (option B), the celebrant addresses the elect in these or similar words.

My dear friends, listen carefully to the words of that faith by which you will be justified. The words are few, but the mysteries they contain are great. Receive them with a sincere heart and be faithful to them.

A *Apostles' Creed*
The celebrant alone begins:
I believe in God, the Father almighty,

As the elect listen, he continues with the assembly of the faithful.
creator of heaven and earth.

I believe in Jesus Christ, his only Son, our Lord.
  He was conceived by the power of the Holy Spirit
    and born of the Virgin Mary.
  He suffered under Pontius Pilate,
    was crucified, died, and was buried.
  He descended to the dead.
  On the third day he rose again.
  He ascended into heaven,
    and is seated at the right hand of the Father.
  He will come again to judge the living and the
    dead.

I believe in the Holy Spirit,
  the holy catholic Church,
  the communion of saints,
  the forgiveness of sins,
  the resurrection of the body,
  and the life everlasting. Amen.

B *Nicene Creed*
The celebrant alone begins:

We believe in one God,

As the elect listen, he continues with the assembly of the faithful.

  the Father, the Almighty,
  maker of heaven and earth,
  of all that is seen and unseen.

We believe in one Lord, Jesus Christ,
  the only Son of God,
  eternally begotten of the Father,
  God from God, Light from Light,
  true God from true God,
  begotten, not made,
  one in Being with the Father.
  Through him all things were made.
  For us men and for our salvation
    he came down from heaven:
  by the power of the Holy Spirit
    he was born of the Virgin Mary,
      and became man.
  For our sake he was crucified under Pontius Pilate;
    he suffered death and was buried.
    On the third day he rose again
      in fulfillment of the Scriptures;
    he ascended into heaven
      and is seated at the right hand of the Father.
  He will come again in glory to judge the living
    and the dead,
    and his kingdom will have no end.
  We believe in the Holy Spirit, the Lord, the giver
    of life,
  who proceeds from the Father and the Son.

With the Father and the Son he is worshiped and
glorified.
He has spoken through the Prophets.
We believe in one holy catholic and apostolic
Church.
We acknowledge one baptism for the forgiveness
of sins.
We look for the resurrection of the dead,
and the life of the world to come. Amen.

PRAYER OVER THE ELECT

161. Using the following or similar words, the celebrant in-   187
vites the faithful to pray.

Let us pray for these elect, that God in his mercy
may make them responsive to his love, so that
through the waters of rebirth they may receive pardon for their sins and have life in Christ Jesus our
Lord.

All pray in silence.

Then the celebrant, with hands outstretched over the elect,
says:
Lord,
eternal source of light, justice, and truth,
take under your tender care
your servants N. and N.

Purify them and make them holy;
give them true knowledge, sure hope, and sound
understanding,
and make them worthy
to receive the grace of baptism.

We ask this through Christ our Lord.
℟. Amen.

DISMISSAL OF THE ELECT

162. If the eucharist is to be celebrated, the elect are normally dismissed at this point by use of option A or B; if the
elect are to stay for the celebration of the eucharist, option
C is used; if the eucharist is not to be celebrated, the entire
assembly is dismissed by use of option D.

A The celebrant dismisses the elect in these or similar words.
Dear elect, go in peace, and may the Lord remain with you always.

Elect:
Amen.

B As an optional formulary for dismissing the catechumens, the celebrant may use these or similar words.
My dear friends, this community now sends you forth to reflect more deeply upon the word of God which you have shared with us today. Be assured of our loving support and prayers for you. We look forward to the day when you will share fully in the Lord's Table.

C If for serious reasons the elect cannot leave (see no. 75.3) and must remain with the baptized, they are to be instructed that though they are present at the eucharist, they cannot take part in it as the baptized do. They may be reminded of this by the celebrant in these or similar words.

Although you cannot yet participate fully in the Lord's eucharist, stay with us as a sign of our hope that all God's children will eat and drink with the Lord and work with his Spirit to re-create the face of the earth.

D The celebrant dismisses those present, using these or similar words.
Go in peace, and may the Lord remain with you always.

All:
Thanks be to God.

An appropriate song may conclude the celebration.

SECOND SCRUTINY
(Fourth Sunday of Lent)

LITURGY OF THE WORD

READINGS

164. The texts and readings for Mass are always those 167
given for the second scrutiny in the Missal and the
Lectionary for Mass among the ritual Masses, "Christian Initiation: The Scrutinies."

HOMILY

165. After the readings and guided by them, the celebrant 168
explains in the homily the meaning of the second scrutiny
in the light of the Lenten liturgy and of the spiritual journey of the elect.

INVITATION TO SILENT PRAYER

166. See no. 152 169

INTERCESSIONS FOR THE ELECT

167. Either of the following formularies, options A or B, 170
may be used for the intercessions for the elect and both the
introduction and the intentions may be adapted to fit various circumstances. During the intercessions the godparents
stand with their right hand on the shoulder of the elect.

[If it is decided, in accord with no. 170, that after the dismissal of the elect the usual general intercessions of the
Mass are to be omitted and that the liturgy of the eucharist
is to begin immediately, intentions for the Church and the
whole world are to be added to the following intentions for
the elect.]

Celebrant:
**Let us pray for these elect whom God has called, that
they may remain faithful to him and boldly give witness to the words of eternal life.**

A   Assisting minister: 170
**That, trusting in the truth of Christ, they may find
freedom of mind and heart and preserve it always,
let us pray to the Lord:**

℟. **Lord, hear our prayer.**

Assisting minister:
**That, preferring the folly of the cross to the wisdom
of the world, they may glory in God alone, let us
pray to the Lord:**
℟. **Lord, hear our prayer.**

Assisting minister:
**That, freed by the power of the Spirit, they may put
all fear behind them and press forward with confidence, let us pray to the Lord:**
℟. **Lord, hear our prayer.**

Assisting minister:
**That, transformed in the Spirit, they may seek those
things that are holy and just, let us pray to the Lord:**
℟. **Lord, hear our prayer.**

Assisting minister:
**That all who suffer persecution for Christ's name
may find their strength in him, let us pray to the
Lord:**
℟. **Lord, hear our prayer.**

Assisting minister:
**That those families and nations prevented from embracing the faith may be granted freedom to believe
the Gospel, let us pray to the Lord:**
℟. **Lord, hear our prayer.**

Assisting minister:
**That we who are faced with the values of the world
may remain faithful to the spirit of the Gospel, let us
pray to the Lord:**
℟. **Lord, hear our prayer.**

Assisting minister:
**That the whole world, which the Father so loves,
may attain in the Church complete spiritual freedom,
let us pray to the Lord:**
℟. **Lord, hear our prayer.**

B Assisting minister: 382

That God may dispel darkness and be the light that shines in the hearts of our elect, let us pray to the Lord:

℟. **Lord, hear our prayer.**

Assisting minister:

That he may gently lead them to Christ, the light of the world, let us pray to the Lord:

℟. **Lord, hear our prayer.**

Assisting minister:

That our elect may open their hearts to God and acknowledge him as the source of light and the witness of truth, let us pray to the Lord:

℟. **Lord, hear our prayer.**

Assisting minister:

That he may heal them and preserve them from the unbelief of this world, let us pray to the Lord:

℟. **Lord, hear our prayer.**

Assisting minister:

That, saved by him who takes away the sin of the world, they may be freed from the contagion and forces of sin, let us pray to the Lord:

℟. **Lord, hear our prayer.**

Assisting minister:

That, enlightened by the Holy Spirit, they may never fail to profess the Good News of salvation and share it with others, let us pray to the Lord:

℟. **Lord, hear our prayer.**

Assisting minister:

That all of us, by the example of our lives, may become in Christ the light of the world, let us pray to the Lord:

℟. **Lord, hear our prayer.**

Assisting minister:

That every inhabitant of the earth may acknowledge the true God, the Creator of all things, who bestows

upon us the gift of Spirit and life, let us pray to the
Lord:
R̸. Lord, hear our prayer.

EXORCISM

168. After the intercessions, the rite continues with one of   171
the following exorcisms.

A   The celebrant faces the elect and, with hands joined,   171
says:
Father of mercy,
you led the man born blind
to the kingdom of light
through the gift of faith in your Son.

Free these elect
from the false values that surround and blind them.
Set them firmly in your truth,
children of the light for ever.

We ask this through Christ our Lord.
R̸. Amen.

Here, if this can be done conveniently, the celebrant lays
hands on each one of the elect.

Then, with hands outstretched over all the elect, he
continues:
Lord Jesus,
you are the true light that enlightens the world.
Through your Spirit of truth
free those who are enslaved by the father of lies.

Stir up the desire for good in these elect,
whom you have chosen for your sacraments.

Let them rejoice in your light, that they may see,
and, like the man born blind whose sight you
** restored,**
let them prove to be staunch and fearless witnesses
** to the faith,**
for you are Lord for ever and ever.
R̸. Amen.

B   The celebrant faces the elect and, with hands joined, says:

Lord God,
source of unfailing light,
by the death and resurrection of Christ
you have cast out the darkness of hatred and lies
and poured forth the light of truth and love
upon the human family.

Hear our prayers for these elect,
whom you have called to be your adopted children.

Enable them to pass from darkness to light
and, delivered from the prince of darkness,
to live always as children of the light.

We ask this through Christ our Lord.
R̂. Amen.

Here, if this can be done conveniently, the celebrant lays hands on each one of the elect.

Then, with hands outstretched over all the elect, he continues:

Lord Jesus,
at your own baptism
the heavens were opened
and you received the Holy Spirit
to empower you to proclaim the Good News to the
    poor
and restore sight to the blind.

Pour out the same Holy Spirit on these elect,
who long for your sacraments.
Guide them along the paths of right faith,
safe from error, doubt, and unbelief,
so that with eyes unsealed
they may come to see you face to face,
for you live and reign for ever and ever.
R̂. Amen.

An appropriate song may be sung, for example, Psalm 6, 26, 32, 38, 39, 40, 51, 116:1–9, 130, 139, or 142.

DISMISSAL OF THE ELECT

169. See no. 155. 172

LITURGY OF THE EUCHARIST

170. See no. 156. 173

THIRD SCRUTINY
(Fifth Sunday of Lent)

LITURGY OF THE WORD

READINGS

171. The texts and readings for Mass are always those   174
given for the third scrutiny in the Missal and the Lectionary
for Mass among the ritual Masses, "Christian Initiation: The
Scrutinies."

HOMILY

172. After the readings and guided by them, the celebrant   175
explains in the homily the meaning of the third scrutiny in
the light of the Lenten liturgy and of the spiritual journey
of the elect.

INVITATION TO SILENT PRAYER

173. See no. 152.   176

INTERCESSIONS FOR THE ELECT

174. Either of the following formularies, options A or B,   177
may be used for the intercessions for the elect and both the
introduction and the intentions may be adapted to fit various circumstances. During the intercessions the godparents
stand with their right hand on the shoulder of the elect.

[If it is decided, in accord with no. 177, that after the dismissal of the elect the usual general intercessions of the
Mass are to be omitted and that the liturgy of the eucharist
is to begin immediately, intentions for the Church and the
whole world are to be added to the following intentions for
the elect.]

Celebrant:
**Let us pray for these elect whom God has chosen.
May the grace of the sacraments conform them to
Christ in his passion and resurrection and enable
them to triumph over the bitter fate of death.**

A   Assisting minister: 177
**That faith may strengthen them against worldly de-
ceits of every kind, let us pray to the Lord:
℟. Lord, hear our prayer.**

Assisting minister:
That they may always thank God, who has chosen to rescue them from their ignorance of eternal life and to set them on the way of salvation, let us pray to the Lord:
R̥. **Lord, hear our prayer.**

Assisting minister:
That the example and prayers of catechumens who have shed their blood for Christ may encourage these elect in their hope of eternal life, let us pray to the Lord:
R̥. **Lord, hear our prayer.**

Assisting minister:
That they may all have a horror of sin, which distorts life, let us pray to the Lord:
R̥. **Lord, hear our prayer.**

Assisting minister:
That those who are saddened by the death of family or friends may find comfort in Christ, let us pray to the Lord:
R̥. **Lord, hear our prayer.**

Assisting minister:
That we too at Easter may again be confirmed in our hope of rising to life with Christ, let us pray to the Lord:
R̥. **Lord, hear our prayer.**

Assisting minister:
That the whole world, which God has created in love, may flower in faith and charity and so receive new life, let us pray to the Lord:
R̥. **Lord, hear our prayer.**

B Assisting minister: 386
That these elect may be given the faith to acknowledge Christ as the resurrection and the life, we pray to the Lord:
R̥. **Lord, hear our prayer.**

Assisting minister:
That they may be freed from sin and grow in the holiness that leads to eternal life, we pray to the Lord:
℞. Lord, hear our prayer.

Assisting minister:
That liberated by repentance from the shackles of sin they may become like Christ by baptism, dead to sin and alive for ever in God's sight, we pray to the Lord:
℞. Lord, hear our prayer.

Assisting minister:
That they may be filled with the hope of the life-giving Spirit and prepare themselves thoroughly for their birth to new life, we pray to the Lord:
℞. Lord, hear our prayer.

Assisting minister:
That the eucharistic food, which they are soon to receive, may make them one with Christ, the source of life and of resurrection, we pray to the Lord:
℞. Lord, hear our prayer.

Assisting minister:
That all of us may walk in newness of life and show to the world the power of the risen Christ, we pray to the Lord:
℞. Lord, hear our prayer.

Assisting minister:
That all the world may find Christ and acknowledge in him the promises of eternal life, we pray to the Lord:
℞. Lord, hear our prayer.

EXORCISM

175. After the intercessions, the rite continues with one of the following exorcisms.   178

A The celebrant faces the elect and, with hands joined, says: 178
Father of life and God not of the dead but of the living,

you sent your Son to proclaim life,
to snatch us from the realm of death,
and to lead us to the resurrection.

Free these elect
from the death-dealing power of the spirit of evil,
so that they may bear witness
to their new life in the risen Christ,
for he lives and reigns for ever and ever.
R̊. Amen.

Here, if this can be done conveniently, the celebrant lays
hands on each one of the elect.

Then, with hands outstretched over all the elect, he
continues:
Lord Jesus,
by raising Lazarus from the dead
you showed that you came that we might have life
and have it more abundantly.

Free from the grasp of death
those who await your life-giving sacraments
and deliver them from the spirit of corruption.

Through your Spirit, who gives life,
fill them with faith, hope, and charity,
that they may live with you always
in the glory of your resurrection,
for you are Lord for ever and ever.
R̊. Amen.

B The celebrant faces the elect and, with hands joined,
says: 387
Father,
source of all life,
in giving life to the living you seek out the image of
    your glory
and in raising the dead you reveal your unbounded
    power.

Rescue these elect from the tyranny of death,
for they long for new life through baptism.

Free them from the slavery of Satan,
the source of sin and death,
who seeks to corrupt the world you created
and saw to be good.

Place them under the reign of your beloved Son,
that they may share in the power of his resurrection
and give witness to your glory before all.

We ask this through Christ our Lord.
R̸. Amen.

Here, if this can be done conveniently, the celebrant lays hands on each one of the elect.

Then, with hands outstretched over all the elect, he continues:
Lord Jesus Christ,
you commanded Lazarus to step forth alive from his
   tomb
and by your own resurrection freed all people from
   death.

We pray for these your servants,
who eagerly approach the waters of new birth
and hunger for the banquet of life.

Do not let the power of death hold them back,
for, by their faith,
they will share in the triumph of your resurrection,
for you live and reign for ever and ever.
R̸. Amen.

An appropriate song may be sung, for example, Psalm 6, 26, 32, 38, 39, 40, 51, 116:1–9, 130, 139, or 142.

DISMISSAL OF THE ELECT

176. See no. 162.

LITURGY OF THE EUCHARIST

177. See no. 156.

PRESENTATION OF THE LORD'S PRAYER
(Fifth Week of Lent)

178. The presentation of the Lord's Prayer, which takes   182
place during the week after the third scrutiny, should pref-   189
erably be celebrated in the presence of a community of the
faithful, within Mass.

LITURGY OF THE WORD

READINGS

179. In place of the first reading assigned for the weekday   190
Mass, the following two readings are used, as indicated in
the Lectionary for Mass, ritual Masses, "Christian Initiation:
Presentation of the Lord's Prayer."

FIRST READING

Hosea 11:1b, 3–4, 8c–9—*I have led you with cords of love.*

RESPONSORIAL PSALM

Psalm 23:1–3a, 3b–4, 5, 6
℟. **(v.1) The Lord is my shepherd; there is nothing I
shall want.**

Or:
Psalm 103:1–2, 8 and 10, 11–12, 13 and 18
℟. **(v.3) As a father is kind to his children, so kind is
the Lord to those who fear him.**

SECOND READING

Romans 8:14–17, 26–27—*You have received the Spirit that
makes you God's children and in that Spirit we cry out, "Abba,
Father!"*

Or:
Galatians 4:4–7—*God has sent the Spirit of his Son into our
hearts: the Spirit that cries, "Abba, Father!"*

VERSE BEFORE THE GOSPEL

Romans 8:15
**You have received the Spirit which makes us God's
children, and in that Spirit we call God our Father.**

GOSPEL READING (PRESENTATION OF THE LORD'S PRAYER)

180. After the first and second reading, an assisting dea-   191
con or other minister says:

Let those who are to receive the Lord's Prayer now come forward.

The celebrant first addresses the following or similar words to the elect.
Listen to the gospel reading in which our Lord teaches his followers how to pray.

The gospel reading follows.
A reading from the holy gospel according to Matthew.

At that time Jesus said to his disciples: "Say this when you pray:

**'Our Father,
who art in heaven,
hallowed be thy name;
thy kingdom come;
thy will be done on earth
as it is in heaven.
Give us this day our daily bread
and forgive us our trespasses
as we forgive those
who trespass against us;
and lead us not into temptation,
but deliver us from evil.' "**

HOMILY

181. After the gospel presentation, the celebrant in the   191
homily explains the meaning and importance of the Lord's Prayer.

PRAYER OVER THE ELECT

182. After the homily, the celebrant, using the following   192
or similar words, invites the faithful to pray.

Let us pray for these elect, that God in his mercy may make them responsive to his love, so that through the waters of rebirth they may receive par-

don for their sins and have life in Christ Jesus our
Lord.

All pray in silence.

Then the celebrant, with hands outstretched over the elect,
says:
**Almighty and eternal God,
you continually enlarge the family of your Church.**

**Deepen the faith and understanding
of these elect, chosen for baptism.
Give them new birth in your living waters,
so that they may be numbered among your adopted
   children.**

**We ask this through Christ our Lord.
Ŗ. Amen.**

DISMISSAL OF THE ELECT
183. See no. 162.

LITURGY OF THE EUCHARIST

184. After the elect leave, the celebration of Mass continues in the usual way.

PREPARATION RITES ON HOLY SATURDAY

185. In proximate preparation for the celebration of the sacraments of initiation: 26
193

1. The elect are to be advised that on Holy Saturday they should refrain from their usual activities, spend their time in prayer and reflection, and, as far as they can, observe a fast.

2. When it is possible to bring the elect together on Holy Saturday for reflection and prayer, some or all of the following rites may be celebrated as an immediate preparation for the sacraments: the presentation of the Lord's Prayer, if it has been deferred (see nos. 149, 178–180), the "return" or recitation of the Creed (nos. 193–196), the ephphetha rite (nos. 197–199), the choosing of a baptismal name (nos. 200–202).

186. The choice and arrangement of these rites should be guided by what best suits the particular circumstances of the elect, but the following should be observed with regard to their celebration: 195
197

1. In cases where celebration of the presentation of the Creed was not possible, the recitation of the Creed is not celebrated.

2. When both the recitation of the Creed and the ephphetha rite are celebrated, the ephphetha rite immediately precedes the "Prayer before the Recitation" (no. 194).

MODEL FOR A CELEBRATION OF THE PREPARATION RITES

187. *Song:* When the elect have gathered, the celebration begins with a suitable song.

188. *Greeting:* After the singing, the celebrant greets the elect and any of the faithful who are present, using one of the greetings for Mass or other suitable words.

189. *Reading of the Word of God:* Where indicated in the particular rites, the reading of the word of God follows; the readings may be chosen from those suggested for each rite. If more than one reading is used, a suitable psalm or hymn may be sung between the readings.

190. *Homily:* Where indicated in the particular rites, a brief homily or an explanation of the text follows the reading of the word of God.

191. *Celebration of the Rites Chosen:* See nos. 193–202.

192. *Concluding Rites:* The celebration may be concluded with the prayer of blessing and dismissal given in nos. 204–205.

RECITATION OF THE CREED

193. The rite of recitation of the Creed prepares the elect   194
for the profession of faith they will make immediately before they are baptized (no. 225); the rite also instructs them
in their duty to proclaim the message of the Gospel.

READING AND HOMILY

194. One of the following readings may be used, or an-   196
other appropriate reading may be chosen:

Matthew 16:13–17—*You are Christ, the Son of the living God.*

   Or:

John 6:35, 63–71—*To whom shall we go? You have the words of
eternal life.*

A brief homily follows.

[If the ephphetha rite (nos. 197–199) is to be included as a
preparation rite, it is celebrated before the following
prayer.]

PRAYER BEFORE THE RECITATION

195. The celebrant, with hands outstretched, says the fol-   198
lowing prayer.

Let us pray.

**Lord,
we pray to you for these elect,
who have now accepted for themselves
the loving purpose and the mysteries
that you revealed in the life of your Son.**

**As they profess their belief with their lips,
may they have faith in their hearts
and accomplish your will in their lives.**

**We ask this through Christ our Lord.
R̸. Amen.**

RECITATION OF THE CREED

196. The elect then recite the Creed. Depending on the ver-   199
sion that was entrusted to them at the presentation, they

recite either the Apostles' Creed, option A, or the Nicene Creed, option B.

A Apostles' Creed

Elect:

I believe in God, the Father almighty,
    creator of heaven and earth.

I believe in Jesus Christ, his only Son, our Lord . . .

The rest of the Creed is recited as in no. 160A.

B Nicene Creed

Elect:

We believe in one God,
    the Father, the Almighty . . .

The rest of the Creed is recited as in no. 160B.

EPHPHETHA RITE

197. By the power of its symbolism the ephphetha rite, or rite of opening the ears and mouth, impresses on the elect their need of grace in order that they may hear the word of God and profess it for their salvation.   200

READING AND INSTRUCTION

198. The reading is as indicated for this rite in the Lectionary for Mass; the celebrant gives a brief explanation of the text.   201

Mark 7:31–37—*Ephphetha, that is, be opened.*

EPHPHETHA

199. The elect come before the celebrant. A suitable song may be sung as the celebrant touches the right and left ear and the closed lips of each of the elect with his thumb and says the following formulary.   202

[If there are a great many elect, additional priests or deacons may assist in carrying out the rite.]

Ephphetha: that is, be opened,
that you may profess the faith you hear,
to the praise and glory of God.

CHOOSING A BAPTISMAL NAME

200. The rite of choosing a baptismal name may be cele-   203
brated on Holy Saturday, unless it was included in the rite
of acceptance into the order of catechumens (see nos. 33.4,
73). The elect may choose a new name, which is either a
traditional Christian name or a name of regional usage that
is not incompatible with Christian beliefs. Where it seems
better suited to the circumstances and the elect are not too
numerous, the naming may consist simply in an explanation of the given name of each of the elect.

READING AND INSTRUCTION

201. There may be a reading—chosen, for example, from   204
the following list—and a brief explanation by the celebrant.

1. Genesis 17:1–7—*You will be called Abraham.*

2. Isaiah 62:1–5—*You will be called by a new name.*

3. Revelation 3:11–13—*I will write my new name upon him.*

4. Matthew 16:13–18—*You are Peter.*

5. John 1:40–42—*You will be called Peter.*

NAMING OF THE ELECT

202. If as baptismal names the elect have chosen new   205
names, option A is used; if they are to use their given
names, option B is used.

A
The celebrant asks each of the elect to state the new name
chosen; then he says the following or similar words.

N., from now on you will [also] be called N.

The elect responds by saying **"Amen"** or in some other suitable way.

B
The celebrant applies some Christian interpretation to the
given name of each of the elect.

CONCLUDING RITES

203. The celebration of the preparation rites may be concluded with a prayer of blessing over the elect and a dismissal.

PRAYER OF BLESSING

204. The celebrant invites those present to pray.
Let us pray.

Then, with hands outstretched over the elect, the celebrant says the following prayer.
Father,
through your holy prophets
you proclaimed to all who draw near you,
"Wash and be cleansed,"
and through Christ you have granted us rebirth in
the Spirit.

122

Bless these your servants
as they earnestly prepare for baptism.

Fulfill your promise:
sanctify them in preparation for your gifts,
that they may come to be reborn as your children
and enter the community of your Church.

We ask this through Christ our Lord.
R̸. Amen.

DISMISSAL

205. The celebrant may inform the elect of the time and place they are to meet for the Easter Vigil; the celebrant then dismisses them, using the following or another suitable formulary.

May the Lord be with you
until we gather again
to celebrate his paschal mystery.

Elect:
Amen.

THIRD STEP: CELEBRATION OF THE SACRAMENTS OF INITIATION

When we were baptized we joined Jesus in death so that we might walk in the newness of his life

206. The third step in the Christian initiation of adults is the celebration of the sacraments of baptism, confirmation, and eucharist. Through this final step the elect, receiving pardon for their sins, are admitted into the people of God. They are graced with adoption as children of God and are led by the Holy Spirit into the promised fullness of time begun in Christ[1] and, as they share in the eucharistic sacrifice and meal, even to a foretaste of the kingdom of God.

27

207. The usual time for the celebration of the sacraments of initiation is the Easter Vigil (see no. 23), at which preferably the bishop himself presides as celebrant, at least for the initiation of those who are fourteen years old or older (see no. 12). As indicated in the Roman Missal, "Easter Vigil" (no. 44), the conferral of the sacraments follows the blessing of the water.

208

208. When the celebration takes place outside the usual time (see nos. 26–27), care should be taken to ensure that it has a markedly paschal character (see *Christian Initiation, General Introduction*, no. 6). Thus the texts for one of the ritual Masses "Christian Initiation: Baptism" given in the Roman Missal are used, and the readings are chosen from those given in the Lectionary for Mass, "Celebration of the Sacraments of Initiation apart from the Easter Vigil."

209

CELEBRATION OF BAPTISM

209. The celebration of baptism has as its center and high point the baptismal washing and the invocation of the Holy Trinity. Beforehand there are rites that have an inherent relationship to the baptismal washing: first, the blessing of water, then the renunciation of sin by the elect, and their profession of faith. Following the baptismal washing, the effects received through this sacrament are given expression in the explanatory rites: the anointing with chrism (when confirmation does not immediately follow baptism), the

28
33

[1]See Vatican Council II, Dogmatic Constitution on the Church *Lumen gentium*, no. 48; also Ephesians 1:10.

clothing with a white garment, and the presentation of a lighted candle.

210. *Prayer over the Water:* The celebration of baptism begins with the blessing of water, even when the sacraments of initiation are received outside the Easter season. Should the sacraments be celebrated outside the Easter Vigil but during the Easter season (see no. 26), the water blessed at the Vigil is used, but a prayer of thanksgiving, having the same themes as the blessing, is included. The blessing declares the religious meaning of water as God's creation and the sacramental use of water in the unfolding of the paschal mystery, and the blessing is also a remembrance of God's wonderful works in the history of salvation.

29
210

The blessing thus introduces an invocation of the Trinity at the very outset of the celebration of baptism. For it calls to mind the mystery of God's love from the beginning of the world and the creation of the human race; by invoking the Holy Spirit and proclaiming Christ's death and resurrection, it impresses on the mind the newness of Christian baptism, by which we share in his own death and resurrection and receive the holiness of God himself.

211. *Renunciation of Sin and Profession of Faith:* In their renunciation of sin and profession of faith those to be baptized express their explicit faith in the paschal mystery that has already been recalled in the blessing of water and that will be connoted by the words of the sacrament soon to be spoken by the baptizing minister. Adults are not saved unless they come forward of their own accord and with the will to accept God's gift through their own belief. The faith of those to be baptized is not simply the faith of the Church, but the personal faith of each one of them and each one of them is expected to keep it a living faith.

30
211

Therefore the renunciation of sin and the profession of faith are an apt prelude to baptism, the sacrament of that faith by which the elect hold fast to God and receive new birth from him. Because of the renunciation of sin and the profession of faith, which form the one rite, the elect will not be baptized merely passively but will receive this great sacrament with the active resolve to renounce error and to hold fast to God. By their own personal act in the rite of renouncing sin and professing their faith, the elect, as was prefigured in the first covenant with the patriarchs, renounce sin and Satan in order to commit themselves for ever to the promise of the Savior and to the mystery of the Trinity. By professing their faith before the celebrant and the entire community, the elect express the intention, developed to maturity during the preceding periods of initiation, to enter into a new covenant with Christ. Thus these adults embrace the faith that through divine help the Church has handed down, and are baptized in that faith.

212. *Baptism:* Immediately after their profession of living faith in Christ's paschal mystery, the elect come forward and receive that mystery as expressed in the washing with water; thus once the elect have professed faith in the Father, Son, and Holy Spirit, invoked by the celebrant, the divine persons act so that those they have chosen receive divine adoption and become members of the people of God. 31

213. Therefore in the celebration of baptism the washing with water should take on its full importance as the sign of that mystical sharing in Christ's death and resurrection through which those who believe in his name die to sin and rise to eternal life. Either immersion or the pouring of water should be chosen for the rite, whichever will serve in individual cases and in the various traditions and circumstances to ensure the clear understanding that this washing is not a mere purification rite but the sacrament of being joined to Christ. 32

214. *Explanatory Rites:* The baptismal washing is followed by rites that give expression to the effects of the sacrament just received. The anointing with chrism is a sign of the royal priesthood of the baptized and that they are now numbered in the company of the people of God. The clothing with the baptismal garment signifies the new dignity they have received. The presentation of a lighted candle shows that they are called to walk as befits the children of the light. 33

CELEBRATION OF CONFIRMATION

215. In accord with the ancient practice followed in the Roman liturgy, adults are not to be baptized without receiving confirmation immediately afterward, unless some serious reason stands in the way. The conjunction of the two cele- 34

brations signifies the unity of the paschal mystery, the close link between the mission of the Son and the outpouring of the Holy Spirit, and the connection between the two sacraments through which the Son and the Holy Spirit come with the Father to those who are baptized.

216. Accordingly, confirmation is conferred after the explanatory rites of baptism, the anointing after baptism (no. 228) being omitted.

THE NEOPHYTES' FIRST SHARING IN THE CELEBRATION OF THE EUCHARIST

217. Finally in the celebration of the eucharist, as they take part for the first time and with full right, the newly baptized reach the culminating point in their Christian initiation. In this eucharist the neophytes, now raised to the ranks of the royal priesthood, have an active part both in the general intercessions and, to the extent possible, in bringing the gifts to the altar. With the entire community they share in the offering of the sacrifice and say the Lord's Prayer, giving expression to the spirit of adoption as God's children that they have received in baptism. When in communion they receive the body that was given for us and the blood that was shed, the neophytes are strengthened in the gifts they have already received and are given a foretaste of the eternal banquet.

CELEBRATION OF THE SACRAMENTS OF INITIATION
(Easter Vigil)

CELEBRATION OF BAPTISM

218. The celebration of baptism begins after the homily. It   213
takes place at the baptismal font, if this is in view of the
faithful; otherwise in the sanctuary, where a vessel of water
for the rite should be prepared beforehand.

PRESENTATION OF THE CANDIDATES

219. Accordingly, one of the following procedures, options   213
A, B, or C, is chosen for the presentation of the candidates.

A *When Baptism Is Celebrated Immediately at the Baptismal
Font*
The celebrant accompanied by the assisting ministers goes
directly to the font. An assisting deacon or other minister
calls the candidates forward and their godparents present
them. Then the candidates and the godparents take their
place around the font in such a way as not to block the
view of the congregation. The invitation to prayer (no. 220)
and the Litany of the Saints (no. 221) follow.

[If there are a great many candidates, they and their godparents simply take their place around the font during the singing of the Litany of the Saints.]

B *When Baptism Is Celebrated after a Procession to the Font*
There may be a full procession to the baptismal font. In this
case an assisting deacon or other minister calls the candidates forward and their godparents present them.

[If there are a great many candidates, they and their godparents simply take their place in the procession.]

The procession is formed in this order: a minister carries
the Easter candle at the head of the procession (unless, outside the Easter Vigil, it already rests at the baptismal font),
the candidates with their godparents come next, then the
celebrant with the assisting ministers. The Litany of the
Saints (no. 221) is sung during the procession. When the
procession has reached the font, the candidates and their

godparents take their place around the font in such a way
as not to block the view of the congregation. The invitation
to prayer (no. 220) precedes the blessing of the water.

C *When Baptism Is Celebrated in the Sanctuary*
An assisting deacon or other minister calls the candidates
forward and their godparents present them. The candidates
and their godparents take their place before the celebrant in
the sanctuary in such a way as not to block the view of the
congregation. The invitation to prayer (no. 220) and the Litany of the Saints (no. 221) follow.

[If there are a great many candidates, they and their godparents simply take their place in the sanctuary during the
singing of the Litany of the Saints.]

INVITATION TO PRAYER

220. The celebrant addresses the following or a similar invi-   213
tation for the assembly to join in prayer for the candidates.

**Dear friends, let us pray to almighty God for our
brothers and sisters, N. and N., who are asking for
baptism. He has called them and brought them to
this moment; may he grant them light and strength to
follow Christ with resolute hearts and to profess the
faith of the Church. May he give them the new life
of the Holy Spirit, whom we are about to call down
on this water.**

LITANY OF THE SAINTS

221. The singing of the Litany of the Saints is led by can-   214
tors and may include, at the proper place, names of other
saints (for example, the titular of the church, the patron
saints of the place or of those to be baptized) or petitions
suitable to the occasion.

Lord, have mercy	**Lord, have mercy**
Christ, have mercy	**Christ, have mercy**
Lord, have mercy	**Lord, have mercy**
Holy Mary, Mother of God	**pray for us**
Saint Michael	**pray for us**
Holy Angels of God	**pray for us**

Saint John the Baptist	pray for us
Saint Joseph	pray for us
Saint Peter and Saint Paul	pray for us
Saint Andrew	pray for us
Saint John	pray for us
Saint Mary Magdalene	pray for us
Saint Stephen	pray for us
Saint Ignatius	pray for us
Saint Lawrence	pray for us
Saint Perpetua and Saint Felicity	pray for us
Saint Agnes	pray for us
Saint Gregory	pray for us
Saint Augustine	pray for us
Saint Athanasius	pray for us
Saint Basil	pray for us
Saint Martin	pray for us
Saint Benedict	pray for us
Saint Francis and Saint Dominic	pray for us
Saint Francis Xavier	pray for us
Saint John Vianney	pray for us
Saint Catherine	pray for us
Saint Teresa	pray for us
All holy men and women	pray for us

Lord, be merciful	Lord, save your people
From all evil	Lord, save your people
From every sin	Lord, save your people
From everlasting death	Lord, save your people
By your coming as man	Lord, save your people
By your death and rising to a new life	Lord, save your people
By your gift of the Holy Spirit	Lord, save your people

Be merciful to us sinners	Lord, hear our prayer
Give new life to these chosen ones by the grace of baptism	Lord, hear our prayer
Jesus, Son of the living God	Lord, hear our prayer
Christ, hear us	Christ, hear us
Lord Jesus, hear our prayer	Lord Jesus, hear our prayer

PRAYER OVER THE WATER

222. After the Litany of the Saints, the celebrant blesses   215
the water, using the blessing formulary given in option A.   216

When baptism is celebrated outside the Easter Vigil (see no.
26), the celebrant may use any of the blessing formularies
given in options A, B, and C.

But when baptism is celebrated during the Easter season
(see no. 26) and water already blessed at the Easter Vigil is
available, the celebrant uses either option D or option E, so
that this part of the celebration will retain the themes of
thanksgiving and intercession.

A
Blessing of the Water: Facing the font (or vessel) containing
the water, the celebrant sings the following text:

**Father,
you give us grace through sacramental signs,
which tell us of the wonders of your unseen power.**

**In baptism we use your gift of water,
which you have made a rich symbol of the grace
you give us in this sacrament.**

**At the very dawn of creation
your Spirit breathed on the waters,
making them the wellspring of all holiness.**

**The waters of the great flood
you made a sign of the waters of baptism
that make an end of sin
and a new beginning of goodness.**

**Through the waters of the Red Sea
you led Israel out of slavery
to be an image of God's holy people,
set free from sin by baptism.**

**In the waters of the Jordan
your Son was baptized by John
and anointed with the Spirit.**

**Your Son willed that water and blood should flow
   from his side
as he hung upon the cross.**

After his resurrection he told his disciples:
"Go out and teach all nations,
baptizing them in the name of the Father, and of the
    Son, and of the Holy Spirit."

Father,
look now with love upon your Church
and unseal for it the fountain of baptism.

By the power of the Holy Spirit
give to this water the grace of your Son,
so that in the sacrament of baptism
all those whom you have created in your likeness
may be cleansed from sin
and rise to a new birth of innocence
by water and the Holy Spirit.

Here, if this can be done conveniently, the celebrant before
continuing lowers the Easter candle into the water once or
three times, then holds it there until the acclamation at the
end of the blessing.
We ask you, Father, with your Son
to send the Holy Spirit upon the waters of this font.
May all who are buried with Christ in the death of
    baptism
rise also with him to newness of life.

We ask this through Christ our Lord.

All:
Amen.

The people sing or say the following or some other suitable
acclamation.
Springs of water, bless the Lord.
Give him glory and praise for ever.

B *Blessing of Water:* Facing the font (or vessel) containing
the water, the celebrant says the following.

Praise to you, almighty God and Father,   389
for you have created water to cleanse and to give life.

All sing or say the following or some other suitable
acclamation.
Blessed be God.

Celebrant:
**Praise to you, Lord Jesus Christ, the Father's only
Son,
for you offered yourself on the cross,
that in the blood and water flowing from your side
and through your death and resurrection
the Church might be born.**

All:
Blessed be God.

Celebrant:
**Praise to you, God the Holy Spirit,
for you anointed Christ at his baptism in the waters
of the Jordan,
that we might all be baptized in you.**

All:
Blessed be God.

Celebrant:
**Come to us, Lord, Father of all,
and make holy this water which you have created,
so that all who are baptized in it may be washed
clean of sin
and be born again to live as your children.**

All sing or say the following or some other suitable
invocation.
Hear us, Lord.

Celebrant:
**Make this water holy, Lord,
so that all who are baptized into Christ's death and
resurrection by this water
may become more perfectly like your Son.**

All:
Hear us, Lord.

The celebrant touches the water with his right hand and
continues.

Lord,
make holy this water which you have created,
so that all those whom you have chosen
may be born again by the power of the Holy Spirit
and may take their place among your holy people.

All:
Hear us, Lord.

C *Blessing of Water:* Facing the font (or vessel) containing the water, the celebrant says the following.

Father, God of mercy,   389
through these waters of baptism
you have filled us with new life as your very own
children.

All sing or say the following or some other suitable acclamation.
Blessed be God.

Celebrant:
From all who are baptized in water and the Holy
Spirit,
you have formed one people,
united in your Son, Jesus Christ.

All:
Blessed be God.

Celebrant:
You have set us free and filled our hearts with the
Spirit of your love,
that we may live in your peace.

All:
Blessed be God.

Celebrant:
You call those who have been baptized
to announce the Good News of Jesus Christ to people
everywhere.

All:
Blessed be God.

The celebrant concludes with the following.
You have called your children, N. and N.,
to this cleansing water and new birth,
that by sharing the faith of your Church they may
have eternal life.
Bless ✠ this water in which they will be baptized.

We ask this in the name of Jesus the Lord.

All:
Amen.

D *Easter-Season Thanksgiving over Water Already Blessed:* Facing the font (or vessel) containing the blessed water, the celebrant says the following.

Praise to you, almighty God and Father, 389
for you have created water to cleanse and to give life.

All sing or say the following or some other suitable acclamation.
Blessed be God.

Celebrant:
Praise to you, Lord Jesus Christ, the Father's only
Son,
for you offered yourself on the cross,
that in the blood and water flowing from your side
and through your death and resurrection
the Church might be born.

All:
Blessed be God.

Celebrant:
Praise to you, God the Holy Spirit,
for you anointed Christ at his baptism in the waters
of the Jordan,
that we might all be baptized in you.

All:
Blessed be God.

The celebrant concludes with the following prayer.
**You have called your children, N. and N., to this
cleansing water,
that they may share in the faith of your Church and
have eternal life.
By the mystery of this consecrated water
lead them to a new and spiritual birth.**

We ask this through Christ our Lord.

All:
Amen.

E *Easter-Season Thanksgiving over Water Already Blessed:* Facing the font (or vessel) containing the blessed water, the celebrant says the following.

**Father, God of mercy,
through these waters of baptism
you have filled us with new life as your very own
children.**

389

All sing or say a suitable acclamation or the following.
Blessed be God.

Celebrant:
**From all who are baptized in water and the Holy
Spirit,
you have formed one people,
united in your Son, Jesus Christ.**

All:
Blessed be God.

Celebrant:
**You have set us free and filled our hearts with the
Spirit of your love,
that we may live in your peace.**

All:
Blessed be God.

Celebrant:
**You call those who have been baptized
to announce the Good News of Jesus Christ to people
everywhere.**

All:
Blessed be God.

The celebrant concludes with the following.
**You have called your children, N. and N., to this
    cleansing water,
that they may share in the faith of your Church and
    have eternal life.
By the mystery of this consecrated water
lead them to a new and spiritual birth.**

We ask this through Christ our Lord.

All:
Amen.

PROFESSION OF FAITH

223. After the blessing of the water (or prayer of thanksgiv-   217
ing), the celebrant continues with the profession of faith,
which includes the renunciation of sin and the profession
itself.

RENUNCIATION OF SIN

224. Using one of the following formularies, the celebrant   217
questions all the elect together; or, after being informed of   USA
each candidate's name by the godparents, he may use the
same formularies to question the candidates individually.

[At the discretion of the diocesan bishop, the formularies
for the renunciation of sin may be made more specific and
detailed as circumstances might require (see no. 33.8).]

A Celebrant:
**Do you reject sin so as to live in the freedom of
God's children?**

Candidates:
I do.

Celebrant:
**Do you reject the glamor of evil,
and refuse to be mastered by sin?**

Candidates:
I do.

Celebrant:
Do you reject Satan, father of sin and prince of darkness?

Candidates:
I do.

B Celebrant:
**Do you reject Satan,
and all his works,
and all his empty promises?**

Candidates:
I do.

C Celebrant:
Do you reject Satan?

Candidates:
I do.

Celebrant:
And all his works?

Candidates:
I do.

Celebrant:
And all his empty promises?

Candidates:
I do.

PROFESSION OF FAITH

225. Then the celebrant, informed again of each candidate's name by the godparents, questions the candidates individually. Each candidate is baptized immediately after his or her profession of faith.

[If there are a great many to be baptized, the profession of faith may be made simultaneously either by all together or group by group, then the baptism of each candidate follows.]

Celebrant:
N., do you believe in God, the Father almighty, creator of heaven and earth?

Candidate:
I do.

Celebrant:

**Do you believe in Jesus Christ, his only Son, our
Lord,
who was born of the Virgin Mary,
was crucified, died, and was buried,
rose from the dead,
and is now seated at the right hand of the Father?**

Candidate:
I do.

Celebrant:

**Do you believe in the Holy Spirit,
the holy catholic Church, the communion of saints,
the forgiveness of sins, the resurrection of the body,
and the life everlasting?**

Candidate:
I do.

BAPTISM

226. The celebrant baptizes each candidate either by immersion, option A, or by the pouring of water, option B. Each baptism may be followed by a short acclamation (Appendix II, no. 595), sung or said by the people.

[If there are a great number to be baptized, they may be divided into groups and baptized by assisting priests or deacons. In baptizing, either by immersion, option A, or by the pouring of water, option B, these ministers say the sacramental formulary for each candidate. During the baptisms, singing by the people is desirable or readings from Scripture or simply silent prayer.]

A

If baptism is by immersion, of the whole body or of the head only, decency and decorum should be preserved. Either or both godparents touch the candidate. The celebrant, immersing the candidate's whole body or head three times, baptizes the candidate in the name of the Trinity.

N., I baptize you in the name of the Father,

He immerses the candidate the first time.

and of the Son,

He immerses the candidate the second time.

and of the Holy Spirit.

He immerses the candidate the third time.

B

If baptism is by the pouring of water, either or both godpar- 221
ents place the right hand on the shoulder of the candidate,
and the celebrant, taking baptismal water and pouring it
three times on the candidate's bowed head, baptizes the
candidate in the name of the Trinity.

N., I baptize you in the name of the Father,

He pours water the first time.

and of the Son,

He pours water the second time.

and of the Holy Spirit.

He pours water the third time.

EXPLANATORY RITES

227. The celebration of baptism continues with the explana- 223
tory rites, after which the celebration of confirmation normally follows.

ANOINTING AFTER BAPTISM

228. If the confirmation of those baptized is separated 224
from their baptism, the celebrant anoints them with chrism
immediately after baptism.

[When a great number have been baptized, assisting priests
or deacons may help with the anointing.]

The celebrant first says the following over all the newly baptized before the anointing.

**The God of power and Father of our Lord Jesus
  Christ
has freed you from sin
and brought you to new life
through water and the Holy Spirit.**

**He now anoints you with the chrism of salvation,
so that, united with his people,**

**you may remain for ever a member of Christ
who is Priest, Prophet, and King.**

Newly baptized:
Amen.

In silence each of the newly baptized is anointed with
chrism on the crown of the head.

CLOTHING WITH A BAPTISMAL GARMENT

229. The garment used in this rite may be white or of a   225
color that conforms to local custom. If circumstances suggest, this rite may be omitted.

The celebrant says the following formulary, and at the
words "Receive this baptismal garment" the godparents
place the garment on the newly baptized.

**N. and N., you have become a new creation
and have clothed yourselves in Christ.
Receive this baptismal garment
and bring it unstained to the judgment seat of our
    Lord Jesus Christ,
so that you may have everlasting life.**

Newly baptized:
Amen.

PRESENTATION OF A LIGHTED CANDLE

230. The celebrant takes the Easter candle in his hands or   226
touches it, saying to the godparents:

**Godparents, please come forward to give to the
newly baptized the light of Christ.**

A godparent of each of the newly baptized goes to the celebrant, lights a candle from the Easter candle, then presents
it to the newly baptized.

Then the celebrant says to the newly baptized:
**You have been enlightened by Christ.
Walk always as children of the light
and keep the flame of faith alive in your hearts.
When the Lord comes, may you go out to meet him
with all the saints in the heavenly kingdom.**

Newly baptized:
Amen.

[If the celebration of confirmation is to be deferred, the renewal of baptismal promises, as in the Roman Missal, "Easter Vigil" (no. 46), now takes place; then the neophytes are led back to their places among the faithful.]

[Outside the Easter Vigil, if confirmation is to be deferred, the neophytes are led back to their places among the faithful after the presentation of a lighted candle.]

CELEBRATION OF CONFIRMATION

231. Between the celebration of baptism and confirmation, the congregation may sing a suitable song. 227

The place for the celebration of confirmation is either at the baptismal font or in the sanctuary, depending on the place where, according to local conditions, baptism has been celebrated.

232. If the bishop has conferred baptism, he should now also confer confirmation. If the bishop is not present, the priest who conferred baptism is authorized to confirm. 228

[When there are a great many persons to be confirmed, the minister of confirmation may associate priests with himself as ministers of the sacrament (see no. 14).]

INVITATION

233. The celebrant first speaks briefly to the newly baptized in these or similar words. 229

My dear newly baptized, born again in Christ by baptism, you have become members of Christ and of his priestly people. Now you are to share in the outpouring of the Holy Spirit among us, the Spirit sent by the Lord upon his apostles at Pentecost and given by them and their successors to the baptized.

The promised strength of the Holy Spirit, which you are to receive, will make you more like Christ and help you to be witnesses to his suffering, death, and resurrection. It will strengthen you to be active mem-

bers of the Church and to build up the Body of
Christ in faith and love.

[The priests who will be associated with the celebrant as
ministers of the sacrament now stand next to him.]

With hands joined, the celebrant next addresses the people:
**My dear friends, let us pray to God our Father, that
he will pour out the Holy Spirit on these newly baptized to strengthen them with his gifts and anoint
them to be more like Christ, the Son of God.**

All pray briefly in silence.

LAYING ON OF HANDS

234. The celebrant holds his hands outstretched over the   229
entire group of those to be confirmed and says the following prayer.

[In silence the priests associated as ministers of the sacrament also hold their hands outstretched over the
candidates.]

All-powerful God, Father of our Lord Jesus Christ,   230
by water and the Holy Spirit
you freed your sons and daughters from sin
and gave them new life.

Send your Holy Spirit upon them
to be their helper and guide.

Give them the spirit of wisdom and understanding,
the spirit of right judgment and courage,
the spirit of knowledge and reverence.
Fill them with the spirit of wonder and awe in your
**   presence.**

We ask this through Christ our Lord.
℟. Amen.

ANOINTING WITH CHRISM

235. A minister brings the chrism to the celebrant.   231

[When the celebrant is the bishop, priests who are associated as ministers of the sacrament receive the chrism from
him.]

Each candidate, with godparent or godparents, goes to the celebrant (or to an associated minister of the sacrament); or, if circumstances require, the celebrant (associated ministers) may go to the candidates.

Either or both godparents place the right hand on the shoulder of the candidate and either a godparent or the candidate gives the candidate's name to the minister of the sacrament. During the conferral of the sacrament a suitable song may be sung.

The minister of the sacrament dips his right thumb in the chrism and makes the sign of the cross on the forehead of the one to be confirmed as he says:

N., be sealed with the Gift of the Holy Spirit.

Newly confirmed:
Amen.

The minister of the sacrament adds:
Peace be with you.

Newly confirmed:
And also with you.

236. At the Easter Vigil the renewal of baptismal promises by the congregation [nos. 237–240 below or in the Roman Missal, "Easter Vigil" (no. 46)] follows the celebration of confirmation. Then the neophytes are led to their places among the faithful.

[Outside the Easter Vigil, the neophytes are led to their places among the faithful immediately after confirmation. The general intercessions then begin (see no. 241).]

RENEWAL OF BAPTISMAL PROMISES (AT THE EASTER VIGIL)

USA
RM

INVITATION

237. After the celebration of baptism, the celebrant addresses the community, in order to invite those present to the renewal of their baptismal promises; the candidates for reception into full communion join the rest of the commu-

nity in this renunciation of sin and profession of faith. All stand and hold lighted candles. The celebrant may use the following or similar words.

Dear friends, through the paschal mystery we have been buried with Christ in baptism, so that we may rise with him to newness of life. Now that we have completed our Lenten observance, let us renew the promises we made in baptism, when we rejected Satan and his works and promised to serve God faithfully in his holy catholic Church.

RENEWAL OF BAPTISMAL PROMISES

RENUNCIATION OF SIN

238. The celebrant continues with one of the following formularies of renunciation.

[If circumstances require, the conference of bishops may adapt formulary A in accord with local conditions.]

A Celebrant:
Do you reject sin so as to live in the freedom of God's children?

All:
I do.

Celebrant:
Do you reject the glamor of evil, and refuse to be mastered by sin?

All:
I do.

Celebrant:
Do you reject Satan, father of sin and prince of darkness?

All:
I do.

B Celebrant:
Do you reject Satan?

All:
I do.

Celebrant:
And all his works?

All:
I do.

Celebrant:
And all his empty promises?

All:
I do.

PROFESSION OF FAITH

239. Then the celebrant continues:

**Do you believe in God, the Father Almighty,
  creator of heaven and earth?**

All:
I do.

Celebrant:
**Do you believe in Jesus Christ, his only Son, our
  Lord,
    who was born of the Virgin Mary,
    was crucified, died, and was buried,
    rose from the dead,
    and is now seated at the right hand of the Father?**

All:
I do.

Celebrant:
**Do you believe in the Holy Spirit,
    the holy catholic Church, the communion of saints,
    the forgiveness of sins, the resurrection of the
    body,
    and the life everlasting?**

All:
I do.

SPRINKLING WITH BAPTISMAL WATER

240. The celebrant sprinkles all the people with the blessed baptismal water, while all sing the following song or any other that is baptismal in character.

I saw water flowing
from the right side of the temple, alleluia.
It brought God's life and his salvation,
and the people sang in joyful praise:
alleluia, alleluia. (*See* Ezekiel 47:1–2,9)

The celebrant then concludes with the following prayer.

God, the all-powerful Father of our Lord Jesus
  Christ,
has given us a new birth by water and the Holy
  Spirit
and forgiven all our sins.
May he also keep us faithful to our Lord Jesus Christ
for ever and ever.

All:
Amen.

LITURGY OF THE EUCHARIST

241. Since the profession of faith is not said, the general intercessions begin immediately and for the first time the neophytes take part in them. Some of the neophytes also take part in the procession to the altar with the gifts. 232

242. With Eucharistic Prayers I, II, or III the special interpolations given in the Roman Missal, the ritual Masses, "Christian Initiation: Baptism," are used. 233

[Eucharistic Prayer IV, with its special interpolation, indicated in the same ritual Masses, may also be used but outside the Easter Vigil.]

243. It is most desirable that the neophytes, together with their godparents, parents, spouses, and catechists, receive communion under both kinds. 234

Before saying "This is the Lamb of God," the celebrant may briefly remind the neophytes of the preeminence of the eucharist, which is the climax of their initiation and the center of the whole Christian life.

PERIOD OF POSTBAPTISMAL CATECHESIS OR MYSTAGOGY

You are a chosen race, a royal priesthood, a holy people; praise
God who called you out of darkness and into his marvelous light

244. The third step of Christian initiation, the celebration of the sacraments, is followed by the final period, the period of postbaptismal catechesis or mystagogy. This is a time for the community and the neophytes together to grow in deepening their grasp of the paschal mystery and in making it part of their lives through meditation on the Gospel, sharing in the eucharist, and doing the works of charity. To strengthen the neophytes as they begin to walk in newness of life, the community of the faithful, their godparents, and their pastors should give them thoughtful and friendly help. 37

245. The neophytes are, as the term "mystagogy" suggests, introduced into a fuller and more effective understanding of mysteries through the Gospel message they have learned and above all through their experience of the sacraments they have received. For they have truly been renewed in mind, tasted more deeply the sweetness of God's word, received the fellowship of the Holy Spirit, and grown to know the goodness of the Lord. Out of this experience, which belongs to Christians and increases as it is lived, they derive a new perception of the faith, of the Church, and of the world. 38

246. Just as their new participation in the sacraments enlightens the neophytes' understanding of the Scriptures, so too it increases their contact with the rest of the faithful and has an impact on the experience of the community. As a result, interaction between the neophytes and the faithful is made easier and more beneficial. The period of postbaptismal catechesis is of great significance for both the neophytes and the rest of the faithful. Through it the neophytes, with the help of their godparents, should experience a full and joyful welcome into the community and enter into closer ties with the other faithful. The faithful, in turn, should derive from it a renewal of inspiration and of outlook. 39 235

247. Since the distinctive spirit and power of the period of   40
postbaptismal catechesis or mystagogy derive from the new,
personal experience of the sacraments and of the community,
its main setting is the so-called Masses for neophytes, that is,
the Sunday Masses of the Easter season. Besides being occasions for the newly baptized to gather with the community
and share in the mysteries, these celebrations include particularly suitable readings from the Lectionary, especially the
readings for Year A. Even when Christian initiation has been
celebrated outside the usual times, the texts for these Sunday
Masses of the Easter season may be used.

248. All the neophytes and their godparents should make   236
an effort to take part in the Masses for the neophytes and
the entire local community should be invited to participate
with them. Special places in the congregation are to be reserved for the neophytes and their godparents. The homily
and, as circumstances suggest, the general intercessions
should take into account the presence and needs of the
neophytes.

249. To close the period of postbaptismal catechesis, some   237
sort of celebration should be held at the end of the Easter
season near Pentecost Sunday; festivities in keeping with local custom may accompany the occasion.

250. On the anniversary of their baptism the neophytes   238
should be brought together in order to give thanks to God,
to share with one another their spiritual experiences, and to
renew their commitment.

251. To show his pastoral concern for these new members   239
of the Church, the bishop, particularly if he was unable to
preside at the sacraments of initiation himself, should arrange, if possible, to meet the recently baptized at least
once in the year and to preside at a celebration of the eucharist with them. At this Mass they may receive holy communion under both kinds.

PART II

RITES FOR PARTICULAR CIRCUMSTANCES

God loved the world so much, he gave us his only Son, that all who believe in him might have eternal life

1. CHRISTIAN INITIATION OF CHILDREN WHO HAVE REACHED CATECHETICAL AGE

Do not keep the children from me.

252. This form of the rite of Christian initiation is intended for children, not baptized as infants, who have attained the use of reason and are of catechetical age. They seek Christian initiation either at the direction of their parents or guardians or, with parental permission, on their own initiative. Such children are capable of receiving and nurturing a personal faith and of recognizing an obligation in conscience. But they cannot yet be treated as adults because, at this stage of their lives, they are dependent on their parents or guardians and are still strongly influenced by their companions and their social surroundings. **306**

253. The Christian initiation of these children requires both a conversion that is personal and somewhat developed, in proportion to their age, and the assistance of the education they need. The process of initiation thus must be adapted both to their spiritual progress, that is, to the children's growth in faith, and to the catechetical instruction they receive. Accordingly, as with adults, their initiation is to be extended over several years, if need be, before they receive the sacraments. Also as with adults, their initiation is marked by several steps, the liturgical rites of acceptance into the order of catechumens (nos. 260–276) the optional rite of election (nos. 277–290), penitential rites or scrutinies (nos. 291–303), and the celebration of the sacraments of initiation (nos. 304–329); corresponding to the periods of adult initiation are the periods of the children's catechetical formation that lead up to and follow the steps of their initiation. **307 USA**

254. The children's progress in the formation they receive   308
depends on the help and example of their companions and
on the influence of their parents. Both these factors should
therefore be taken into account.

1. Since the children to be initiated often belong to a
group of children of the same age who are already baptized
and are preparing for confirmation and eucharist, their initiation progresses gradually and within the supportive setting of this group of companions.

2. It is to be hoped that the children will also receive as
much help and example as possible from the parents,
whose permission is required for the children to be initiated
and to live the Christian life. The period of initiation will
also provide a good opportunity for the family to have contact with priests and catechists.

255. For the celebrations proper to this form of Christian   309
initiation, it is advantageous, as circumstances allow, to
form a group of several children who are in this same situation, in order that by example they may help one another
in their progress as catechumens.

256. In regard to the time for the celebration of the steps   310
of initiation, it is preferable that, if possible, the final period   USA
of preparation, begun by the second step, the penitential
rites (or by the optional rite of election), coincide with Lent
and that the final step, celebration of the sacraments of initiation, take place at the Easter Vigil (see no. 8). Nevertheless before the children are admitted to the sacraments at
Easter, it should be established that they are ready for the
sacraments. Celebration at this time must also be consistent
with the program of catechetical instruction they are receiving, since the candidates should, if possible, come to the
sacraments of initiation at the time that their baptized companions are to receive confirmation or eucharist.

257. For children of this age, at the rites during the pro-   311
cess of initiation, it is generally preferable not to have the
whole parish community present, but simply represented.
Thus these rites should be celebrated with the active participation of a congregation that consists of a suitable number
of the faithful, the parents, family, members of the
catechetical group, and a few adult friends.

258. Each conference of bishops may adapt and add to the   312
form of the rite given here, in order that the rite will more
effectively satisfy local needs, conditions, and pastoral requirements. [The National Conference of Catholic Bishops
has done this by providing an optional "Rite of Election" before "Second Step: Penitential Rites (Scrutinies)."] The rites
for the presentation of the Creed (nos. 157–162) and the
Lord's Prayer (nos. 178–183), adapted to the age of the children, may be incorporated. When the form of the rite of initiation for children is translated, the instructions and
prayers should be adapted to their understanding. Further-
more, in addition to any liturgical text translated from the
Latin *editio typica*, the conference of bishops may also approve an original, alternative text that says the same thing
in a way more suited to children (see *Christian Initiation*,
General Introduction, no. 32).

259. In following this form of the rite of Christian initia-   313
tion the celebrant should make full and wise use of the options mentioned in *Christian Initiation*, General Introduction
(nos. 34–35), in the *Rite of Baptism for Children*, Introduction
(no. 31), and in the *Rite of Christian Initiation of Adults*, Introduction (no. 35).

FIRST STEP: ACCEPTANCE INTO THE ORDER OF CATECHUMENS

Happy the people the Lord has chosen to be his own

260. It is important that this rite be celebrated with an actively participating but small congregation, since the presence of a large group might make the children uncomfortable (see no. 257). When possible, the children's parents or guardians should be present. If they cannot come, they should indicate that they have given consent to their children and their place should be taken by "sponsors" (see no. 10), that is, suitable members of the Church who act on this occasion for the parents and present the children. The presiding celebrant is a priest or deacon.   314

261. The celebration takes place in the church or in a place that, according to the age and understanding of the children, can help them to experience a warm welcome. As circumstances suggest, the first part of the rite, "Receiving the Children," is carried out at the entrance of the place chosen for the celebration, and the second part of the rite, "Liturgy of the Word," takes place inside.   315 329

The celebration is not normally combined with celebration of the eucharist.

RITE OF ACCEPTANCE INTO THE ORDER OF CATECHUMENS

RECEIVING THE CHILDREN

262. The priest or deacon, wearing an alb or surplice with stole, comes to the place where the children are waiting with their parents or guardians or, alternatively, with their sponsors. 316

GREETING

263. The celebrant and the community present greet the children simply and in a friendly manner. The celebrant then speaks to the children and their parents or sponsors, pointing out the joy and happiness of the Church at their presence. Next he invites the children and their parents or sponsors to come forward and stand before him. 316 317

OPENING DIALOGUE

264. The celebrant then asks the children individually to express their intention. He may do so by means of such questions and answers as those given here or he may use other words that will allow the children to give such answers as: "I want to do the will of God"; "I want to follow the word of God"; "I want to be baptized"; "I want to be a friend of Jesus Christ"; "I want to join the Christian family." 318

[If there are a great many children, the celebrant may question a few of them and then ask the rest to express agreement with the responses given.]

Celebrant:
What do you want to become?

Children:
A Christian.

Celebrant:
Why do you want to become a Christian?

Children:
Because I believe in Christ.

Celebrant:
What do you gain by believing in Christ?

Children:
Eternal life.

The celebrant concludes this opening dialogue with a brief   319
catechesis, suited to the children's age and circumstances,
on the step they are taking. He may use these or similar
words and may ask the children, as a sign of their assent,
to repeat the final quotation from the words of Christ.

**Since you already believe in Christ and want us to
prepare you for baptism, we welcome you joyfully
into our Christian family, where you will come to
know Christ better day by day. Together with us you
will try to live as children of God, for our Lord has
taught us: "Love God with all your heart and love
one another as I have loved you."**

AFFIRMATION BY THE PARENTS (SPONSORS) AND
THE ASSEMBLY

265. In the following or a similar way, the celebrant asks   320
the children to seek the consent of the parents or sponsors
who are presenting them.

**N. and N., go and ask your parents (sponsors) to
come here and stand with you so that they may give
their assent.**

The children go to their parents or sponsors and bring
them before the celebrant, who continues:
**Dear parents (sponsors), your children have asked to
be prepared for baptism. Do you consent to their
request?**

Parents or sponsors:
We do.

Celebrant:
**Are you willing to do your part in their preparation
for baptism?**

Parents or sponsors:
We are.

Then the celebrant questions the assembly, using these or   321
similar words.

These boys and girls have set out on the road to baptism. They will need the support of our faith and love. Are you, their families and friends, ready to give that help?

All:
We are.

SIGNING OF THE CANDIDATES WITH THE CROSS

266. Next the cross is traced on the forehead of each child (or, at the discretion of the diocesan bishop, in front of the forehead—see nos. 33.3 and 54); at the discretion of the celebrant, and especially if the children are somewhat older, the signing of the other senses may follow. The celebrant alone says the formularies accompanying each signing.

322
USA

SIGNING OF THE FOREHEAD

267. The celebrant first says the following formulary.

322

N. and N., Christ has called you to be his friends. Always remember him and be faithful to him.

Therefore I mark your forehead with the sign of the cross. It is the sign of Christians; let it remind you always of Christ and how much he loves you.

Then the celebrant goes to the children and in silence traces the cross on the forehead of each one.

Then, if there is to be no signing of the other senses, he may, in the following words, invite the parents or sponsors and the catechists to trace the sign of the cross on their candidate's forehead.

And I also invite you, parents (sponsors) and catechists [N. and N.], since you also belong to Christ, to sign the children with the sign of the cross.

All sing or say the following or another suitable acclamation.
Glory and praise to you, Lord Jesus Christ!

SIGNING OF THE OTHER SENSES

268. The signing of the other senses may be carried out by the celebrant, who says the following formulary for each

323

child. The signing of the candidates may also be carried out by their parents or sponsors or by their catechists, as the celebrant says the formulary in the plural over all the children at once. After the signing of each sense the assembly may sing or recite an acclamation in praise of Christ, for example, **"Glory and praise to you, Lord Jesus Christ!"**

While the ears are being signed the celebrant says:
I [we] mark your ears with the sign of the cross: hear the words of Christ.

While the eyes are being signed:
I [we] mark your eyes with the sign of the cross: see the works of Christ.

While the lips are being signed:
I [we] mark your lips with the sign of the cross: speak as Christ would speak.

While the breast is being signed:
I [we] mark the sign of the cross over your heart: make your heart the home of Christ.

While the shoulders are being signed:
I [we] mark your shoulders with the sign of the cross: be strong with the strength of Christ.

[While the hands are being signed:
I (we) mark your hands with the sign of the cross, touch others with the gentleness of Christ.

While the feet are being signed:
I (we) mark your feet with the sign of the cross, walk in the way of Christ.]

While the sign of the cross is traced above the whole person:
**I [we] place you entirely under the sign of Christ's cross
in the name of the Father, and of the Son, ✠
and of the Holy Spirit:
live with Jesus now and for ever.**

Child:
Amen.

INVITATION TO THE CELEBRATION OF THE WORD OF GOD

269. After the signing, the celebrant in the following or 324
similar words invites the children and their parents or sponsors to enter the church or other place chosen for the celebration. Once the invitation has been spoken, the children
enter and take places either with their parents or sponsors
or with the baptized companions of their catechetical group
(see no. 254.1), so that it is clear that they now are a part of
the assembly. During the entrance, Psalm 95 or Psalm 122
is sung or another suitable song.

Celebrant:
**Now you can take your place in the Christian assem-
bly. Come with us to listen to the Lord as he speaks
and to join us in prayer.**

LITURGY OF THE WORD

INSTRUCTION

270. When the children have reached their places, the cele- 325
brant speaks to them briefly, helping them to understand
the dignity of God's word, which is proclaimed and heard
in the Christian assembly.

The Lectionary or the Bible is carried in procession and
placed with honor on the lectern, where it may be incensed.

Celebration of the liturgy of the word follows.

READINGS

271. Scripture readings are chosen that can be adapted to 326
the understanding of the children and to their progress in
the catechetical formation they and their companions have
received. Such readings may be chosen from those given in
the Lectionary for Mass, ritual Masses, "Christian Initiation
apart from the Easter Vigil" or from elsewhere in the
Lectionary; the following texts may also be used.

FIRST READING

Genesis 12:1–4a—*Leave your country, and come into the land I
will show you.*

RESPONSORIAL PSALM

Psalm 33:4–5, 12–13, 18–19, 20 and 22

℟. (v.12b) **Happy the people the Lord has chosen to be his own.**

Or:

℟. (v.22) **Lord, let your mercy be on us, as we place our trust in you.**

VERSE BEFORE THE GOSPEL

John 1:41, 17b

We have found the Messiah: Jesus Christ, who brings us truth and grace.

GOSPEL

John 1:35–42—*This is the Lamb of God. We have found the Messiah.*

HOMILY

272. The celebrant then gives a brief homily in explanation of the readings. 327

It is recommended that after the homily he invite the children to spend a period in silent prayer.

Then a suitable song is sung.

PRESENTATION OF A BIBLE

273. During or after the song, a book containing the Gospels may be presented to the children. They should be prepared for this presentation either beforehand in the homily or by a few words of explanation at this moment. 328

INTERCESSIONS FOR THE CHILDREN

274. The intercessions follow in these or similar words. 329

Celebrant:

Let us pray for these children, your sons and daughters, your companions and friends, as they draw nearer to God.

Assisting minister:
**That they may steadily increase their desire to live
with Jesus, let us pray to the Lord:
℟. Lord, hear our prayer.**

Assisting minister:
**That by belonging to the Church they may find true
happiness, let us pray to the Lord:
℟. Lord, hear our prayer.**

Assisting minister:
**That they may be given the strength to persevere in
their preparation for baptism, let us pray to the Lord:
℟. Lord, hear our prayer.**

Assisting minister:
**That they may be preserved from the temptation of
discouragement and fear, let us pray to the Lord:
℟. Lord, hear our prayer.**

Assisting minister:
**That they may rejoice in the happiness of receiving
the sacraments of baptism, confirmation, and the eucharist, let us pray to the Lord:
℟. Lord, hear our prayer.**

PRAYER OVER THE CHILDREN

275. After the intercessions, the celebrant, with hands out-   329
stretched over the children, says the following prayer.

**Lord,
you have filled these children
with the desire to become perfect Christians.
As they grow in wisdom and knowledge,
respond to their hopes
and answer our prayers.**

**We ask this through Christ our Lord.
℟. Amen.**

DISMISSAL

276. After the prayer the children and the community are
dismissed and a suitable song concludes the celebration.

But if for some reason the eucharist is to be celebrated (see no. 261), the children are dismissed beforehand.

Celebrant:

Go in peace, and may the Lord remain with you always.

All:

Thanks be to God.

RITE OF ELECTION OR ENROLLMENT OF NAMES (OPTIONAL)

To just such as these the Kingdom of God belongs

277. The (optional) liturgical rite called both election and the enrollment of names may be celebrated with children of catechetical age, especially those whose catechumenate has extended over a long period of time. This celebration, which usually coincides with the beginning of Lent, marks the beginning of the period of final preparation for the sacraments of initiation, during which the children will be encouraged to follow Christ with greater generosity.

278. In the rite of election, on the basis of the testimony of parents, godparents and catechists and of the children's reaffirmation of their intention, the Church judges their state of readiness and decides on their advancement toward the sacraments of initiation. Thus the Church makes its "election," that is, the choice and admission of those children who have the dispositions that make them fit to take part, at the next major celebration, in the sacraments of initiation.

279. The rite should take place in the cathedral church, in a parish church or, if necessary, in some other suitable and fitting place. If the election of children of catechetical age is to take place within a celebration in which older catechumens are also to receive the Church's election, the rite for adults (nos. 129–137) should be used, with appropriate adaptation of the texts to be made by the celebrant.

280. The rite is celebrated within Mass, after the homily, and should be celebrated within the Mass of the First Sunday of Lent. If, for pastoral reasons, the rite is celebrated on a different day, the texts and the readings of the ritual Mass "Christian Initiation: Election or Enrollment of Names" may always be used. When the Mass of the day is celebrated and its readings are not suitable, the readings are those given for the First Sunday of Lent or others may be chosen from elsewhere in the Lectionary.

When celebrated outside Mass, the rite takes place after the readings and the homily and is concluded with the dismissal of both the elect and the faithful.

LITURGY OF THE WORD

HOMILY

281. The bishop, or the celebrant who acts as delegate of the bishop, gives the homily. This should be brief and suitable to the understanding of the children. If the celebrant finds it difficult in the homily to adapt himself to the mentality of the children, one of the adults, for example, the children's catechist, may speak to the children after the gospel. The entire community should be encouraged to give good example to the children and to show their support and interest in them as they prepare to celebrate the Easter sacraments.

PRESENTATION OF THE CHILDREN

282. After the homily, the priest in charge of the childrens' initiation, or a deacon, a catechist, or a representative of the community, presents the children, using the following or similar words.

Reverend Father, these children, whom I now present to you, are completing their preparation for Christian initiation. God's love has strengthened them, and our community has supported them with prayer and good example.

As Easter approaches, they ask to be admitted to the sacraments of baptism, confirmation, and the eucharist.

The celebrant replies:
My dear children who are to be chosen in Christ, come forward now with your parents and godparents.

One by one, the children are called by name. Each candidate, accompanied by one or both parents and/or godparents, comes forward and stands before the celebrant.

[If there are a great many children, all are presented in groups, for example, each group by its own catechist. But in this case, the catechists should be advised to have a special celebration beforehand in which they call each child forward by name.]

AFFIRMATION BY THE (PARENTS,) GODPARENTS
[AND THE ASSEMBLY]

283. Then the celebrant addresses the assembly in these or
similar words.

Dear parents, godparents and members of this assembly: These children have asked to be initiated into the sacramental life of the Church this Easter. In the name of God's holy Church, I invite you to give your recommendation on their behalf.

He addresses the parents, godparents (and assembly):
Have these children shown themselves to be sincere in their desire for baptism, confirmation, and the eucharist?

Parents, godparents (and assembly):
They have.

Celebrant:
Have they listened well to the word of God?

Parents, godparents (and assembly):
They have.

Celebrant:
Have they tried to live as his faithful followers?

Parents, godparents (and assembly):
They have.

Celebrant:
Have they taken part in this community's life of prayer and service?

Parents, godparents (and assembly):
They have.

INVITATION AND ENROLLMENT OF NAMES

284. Then addressing the children in the following or similar words, the celebrant advises them of their acceptance and asks them to declare their own intention.

My dear children, your parents and godparents (and this entire community) have spoken in your favor.

The Church in the name of Christ accepts their word and calls you to the Easter sacraments.

Now you must let the whole Church know that you have heard Christ calling you and that you want to follow him.

Therefore, do you wish to enter fully into the life of the Church through the sacraments of baptism, confirmation, and the eucharist?

Children:
We do.

Celebrant:
Then offer your names for enrollment.

The children give their names, either going with their godparents to the celebrant or while remaining in place, and the actual inscription of the names may be carried out in various ways. The candidates may inscribe their names themselves or they may call out their names, which are inscribed by the godparents or by the minister who presented the candidates (see no. 282). As the enrollment is taking place, an appropriate song, for example, Psalm 16 or Psalm 33 with a refrain such as, "**Happy the people the Lord has chosen to be his own,**" may be sung.

[If there are a great many candidates, the enrollment may simply consist in the presentation of a list of the names to the celebrant, with such words as: "**These are the names of the candidates**" or, when the bishop is celebrant and candidates from several parishes have been presented to him: "**These are the names of the candidates from the parish of N.**"]

ACT OF ADMISSION OR ELECTION

285. The celebrant briefly explains the significance of the enrollment that has just taken place. Then, turning to the children, he says the following or similar words.

Celebrant:
My dear children, I am happy to declare you among the elect of God. You have been chosen to be initi-

ated at Easter through the sacraments of baptism, confirmation, and the eucharist.

Children:
Thanks be to God.

He continues:
**God is always faithful to those he calls. On your
part, you must strive to know, love, and serve the
Lord more and more with each passing day. Continue
to rely upon your godparents, parents, and catechists
for the help you will need to be faithful to the way
of Jesus.**

Then the celebrant addresses the parents, godparents, and
the entire assembly:
**Dear friends, you have spoken in favor of these
young catechumens. Accept them as chosen in the
Lord. Encourage them to live the way of the Gospel.
Offer them the support of your love and concern.
And, above all, be a good model to them of Christian
living so that by your example they may grow deeper
in the faith of the Church.**

He invites parents and godparents to place their hand on
the shoulder of the candidate whom they are receiving into
their care, or to make some other gesture to indicate the
same intent.

RECOGNITION OF THE GODPARENT(S)

286. The celebrant may speak briefly of the new relationship which will exist between the parents and godparents
of the elect. He may conclude by placing his outstretched
hands over the parents and godparents while praying in
these or similar words.

Celebrant:
**May Almighty God bring joy to your hearts as you
see the hope of eternal life shine on these elect.
Steadfastly bear witness to your faith by what you
say and do. May these children grow as faithful members of God's holy people. And may you be a constant support to each other, in Christ Jesus our Lord.**

Parent(s) and godparent(s):
Amen.

INTERCESSIONS FOR THE ELECT

287. The community may use the following or a similar formulary to pray for the elect. The celebrant may adapt the introduction and the intentions to fit various circumstances.

[If it is decided, in accord with no. 290, that after the dismissal of the elect the usual general intercessions of the Mass are to be omitted and that the liturgy of the eucharist is to begin immediately, intentions for the Church and the whole world are to be added to the following intentions for the elect.]

Celebrant:
My brothers and sisters, as we begin this Lenten season, we look forward to the initiation of these children at Easter into the mystery of Christ's suffering, death, and resurrection. Let us pray that this Lent will be for them, and for all of us, a time of genuine Christian renewal.

Assisting minister:
That together we may grow this Lent in our love for God and neighbor, let us pray to the Lord:
℟. Lord, hear our prayer.

Assisting minister:
That these catechumens may be freed from selfishness and learn to put others first, let us pray to the Lord:
℟. Lord, hear our prayer.

Assisting minister:
That their parents, godparents, and catechists may be living examples of the Gospel to inspire these children, let us pray to the Lord:
℟. Lord, hear our prayer.

Assisting minister:
That their teachers may always convey to them the beauty of God's word, let us pray to the Lord:
℟. Lord, hear our prayer.

Assisting minister:
**That these children may share with others the joy
they have found in their friendship with Jesus, let us
pray to the Lord:**
℟. **Lord, hear our prayer.**

Assisting minister:
**That together with the adults who have been elected,
these children may learn to love the Church and
proudly profess what they believe, let us pray to the
Lord:**
℟. **Lord, hear our prayer.**

Assisting minister:
**That our community, during this Lenten period, may
grow in charity and be constant in prayer, let us pray
to the Lord:**
℟. **Lord, hear our prayer.**

PRAYER OVER THE ELECT

288. After the intercessions, the celebrant, with hands outstretched over the elect, says one of the following prayers.

A
**Lord God,
you created us
and you give us life.
Bless these children
and add them to your family.
May they be joyful in the life you won for us
through Christ our Lord.**
℟. **Amen.**

B
**Father of love and power,
it is your will to establish everything in Christ
and to draw us into his all-embracing love.
Guide the elect of your Church:
strengthen them in their vocation,
build them into the kingdom of your Son,
and seal them with the Spirit of your promise.**

We ask this through Christ our Lord.
℟. **Amen.**

DISMISSAL OF THE ELECT

289. If the eucharist is to be celebrated, the elect are normally dismissed at this point by use of option A or B; if the elect are to stay for the celebration of the eucharist, option C is used; if the eucharist is not to be celebrated, the entire assembly is dismissed by use of option D.

A The celebrant dismisses the elect in these or similar words.

My dear children, elect of God, you have set out with us on the road that leads to the glory of Easter. Christ will be your way, your truth, and your life. Until we meet again, walk always in the Lord's peace.

The elect:
Amen.

B As an optional formulary for dismissing the elect, the celebrant may use these or similar words.

My dear children, go now. Think about God's word and know that we are with you and will pray for you. We look forward to the day when you will join us at the Lord's Table.

C If for serious reasons the elect cannot leave (see no. 75.3) and must remain with the baptized, they are to be instructed that though they are present at the eucharist, they cannot take part in it as the baptized do. They may be reminded of this by the celebrant in these or similar words.

Although you cannot join us at the Lord's Table, stay with us as a sign of our hope that all God's children will eat and drink with the Lord and work with his Spirit to make a new earth.

D The celebrant dismisses those present, using these or similar words.

Go in peace, and may the Lord remain with you always.

All:
Thanks be to God.

An appropriate song may conclude the celebration.

LITURGY OF THE EUCHARIST

290. When the eucharist is to follow, intercessory prayer is resumed with the usual general intercessions for the needs of the Church and the whole world; then, if required, the profession of faith is said. But for pastoral reasons these general intercessions and the profession of faith may be omitted. The liturgy of the eucharist then begins as usual with the preparation of the gifts.

SECOND STEP: PENITENTIAL RITES (SCRUTINIES)

Create in me a new heart and a new spirit

291. These penitential rites, which mark the second step in the children's Christian initiation, are major occasions in their catechumenate. They are held within a celebration of the word of God as a kind of scrutiny, similar to the scrutinies in the adult rite. Thus the guidelines given for the adult rite (nos. 141–146) may be followed and adapted, since the children's penitential rites have a similar purpose. 330

292. Because the penitential rites normally belong to the period of final preparation for baptism, the condition for their celebration is that the children are approaching the maturity of faith and understanding requisite for baptism. 331

293. Along with the children, their godparents and their baptized companions from the catechetical group participate in the celebration of these penitential rites. Therefore the rites are to be adapted in such a way that they also benefit the participants who are not catechumens. In particular, these penitential rites are a proper occasion for baptized children of the catechetical group to celebrate the sacrament of penance for the first time. When this is the case, care should be taken to include explanations, prayers, and ritual acts that relate to the celebration of the sacrament with these children. 332

294. The penitential rites are celebrated during Lent, if the catechumens are to be initiated at Easter; if not, at the most suitable time. At least one penitential rite is to be celebrated, and, if this can be arranged conveniently, a second should follow after an appropriate interval. The texts for a second celebration are to be composed on the model of the first given here, but the texts for the intercessions and prayer of exorcism given in the adult rite (nos. 153–154, 167–168, 174–175) are used, with the requisite modifications. 333

PENITENTIAL RITE (SCRUTINY)

LITURGY OF THE WORD

GREETING AND INTRODUCTION

295. The priest welcomes the assembly and in a few words   334
explains that the rite will have different meanings for the
different participants: the children who are catechumens,
the children who are already baptized, particularly those
who will celebrate the sacrament of penance for the first
time, the parents, godparents, catechists, priests, etc. All
these participants in their own different ways are going to
hear the comforting message of pardon for sin, for which
they will praise the Father's mercy.

A song may be sung that joyfully expresses faith in the
mercy of God our Father.

PRAYER

296. The celebrant then says one of the following prayers.   335

A
God of pardon and mercy,
you reveal yourself in your readiness to forgive
and manifest your glory by making us holy.

Grant that we who repent
may be cleansed from sin
and restored to your life of grace.

We ask this through Christ our Lord.
Ry. Amen.

B
Lord,
grant us your pardon and peace,
so that, cleansed of our sins,
we may serve you with untroubled hearts.

We ask this through Christ our Lord.
Ry. Amen.

READINGS

297. One or several readings may be chosen from those in   336
the following list; if there is more than one reading, one of
the responsorial psalms listed here from the ritual Masses,
"Christian Initiation apart from the Easter Vigil" (or any of
the others from the same Mass) or a song should be used
between the readings.

READINGS

1. Ezekiel 36:25–28—*A new heart and a new spirit.*

2. Isaiah 1:16–18—*The cleansing of sin.*

3. Mark 1:1–5, 14–15—*Repent and believe the Good News.*

4. Mark 2:1–12—*Healing of the paralytic.*

5. Luke 15:1–7—*Parable of the lost sheep.*

6. 1 John 1:8—2:2—*Jesus our Savior.*

Or the gospels used in the scrutinies of the adult rite:

7. John 4:1–14—*The Samaritan woman.*

8. John 9:1, 6–9, 13–17, 34–39—*The man born blind.*

9. John 11:3–7, 17, 20–27, 33b–45—*The raising of Lazarus.*

RESPONSORIAL PSALMS

1. Psalm 23:1–3a, 3b–4, 5–6
℞. (v.1) **The Lord is my shepherd; there is nothing I
shall want.**

2. Psalm 27:1, 4, 8b–9abc, 13–14
℞. (v.1a) **The Lord is my light and my salvation.**

3. Psalm 32:1–2, 5, 11
℞. (v.1a) **Happy are those whose sins are forgiven.**

4. Psalm 89:3–4, 16–17, 21–22, 25, 27
℞. (v.2a) **For ever I will sing the goodness of the
Lord.**

HOMILY

298. After the readings the celebrant explains the sacred texts in a short homily.

336
337

During the homily or immediately after it, the celebrant prepares all those in the assembly for conversion and repentance by speaking to them of appropriate themes, then pausing for periods of silent reflection.

If the assembly includes baptized children who will receive the sacrament of penance for the first time, the celebrant turns to them and invites them to show by some external sign their faith in Christ the Savior and their sorrow for their sins.

INTERCESSIONS

299. After a brief interval of silence to lead all present to sincere sorrow for sin, the celebrant introduces the following intercessions with an invitation addressed to the assembly.

338

For the celebrant's introduction and the intentions of the intercessions the texts in the adult rite (nos. 153, 167, 174) may also be used, with the requisite modifications.

Celebrant:
Let us pray for N. and N., who are preparing themselves for the sacraments of Christian initiation, [for N. and N., who will receive God's forgiveness in the sacrament of penance for the first time,] and for ourselves, who seek the mercy of Christ.

Assisting minister:
That we may open our hearts to the Lord Jesus with gratitude and faith, let us pray to the Lord:
℟. Lord, hear our prayer.

Assisting minister:
That we may honestly try to know our failures and recognize our sins, let us pray to the Lord:
℟. Lord, hear our prayer.

Assisting minister:
That, as children of God, we may openly admit our weaknesses and faults, let us pray to the Lord:
℟. Lord, hear our prayer.

Assisting minister:
That in the presence of Christ we may express sorrow for our sins, let us pray to the Lord:
℟. Lord, hear our prayer.

Assisting minister:
That we may be delivered from present evils and protected against those to come, let us pray to the Lord:
℟. Lord, hear our prayer.

Assisting minister:
That we may learn from our Father in heaven to triumph by his love over the powers of sin, let us pray to the Lord:
℟. Lord, hear our prayer.

EXORCISM

300. Then the celebrant, with hands outstretched over the   339
children, says one of the following.

Let us pray.

A
Father of mercies,   339
you sent your only Son
to rescue us from the slavery of sin
and to give us freedom as your children.

Look with love on these young people and fulfill
  their hopes;
they have already experienced temptation
and they acknowledge their faults.

Lead them from darkness into your unfailing light,
cleanse them from sin,
let them know the joy of your peace,
and guide them safely through life.

We ask this through Christ our Lord.
℟. Amen.

B
God of mercy and Father of all,   392
look upon N. and N., who will soon be baptized.

Children:
**We have heard the words of Jesus
and we love them.**

Celebrant:
**Even though they try to live as your children,
they sometimes find this difficult.**

Children:
**Father, we want always to do what pleases you,
but sometimes we find this hard.**

Celebrant:
**Loving Father,
free these young people
from whatever could make them bad
and help them always to walk in your light.**

Children:
**We want to walk with Jesus,
who gave his life for us.
Help us, Father, to follow him.**

Celebrant:
**If they stumble on the way
and do not please you,
help them up with the power of your hand,
that they may rise again
and continue on their journey to you
with Jesus Christ our Lord.**

Children:
Father, give us strength.

ANOINTING WITH THE OIL OF CATECHUMENS [OR LAYING ON OF HANDS]

301. The rite continues with the anointing with the oil of catechumens, option A. But for pastoral reasons, for example, if the children have been anointed already, a laying on of hands, option B, may be used.   340 USA

A *Anointing with the Oil of Catechumens:*

If, for pastoral reasons, the priest chooses to bless oil for the rite, he uses the following blessing.   USA

Let us pray.

O God, 131
source of strength and defender of your people,
you have chosen to make this oil,
created by your hand,
an effective sign of your power.

Bless ✠ this oil
and strengthen the catechumens who will be
  anointed with it.
Grant them your wisdom to understand the Gospel
  more deeply
and your strength to accept the challenges of Chris-
tian life.

Enable them to rejoice in baptism
and to partake of a new life in the Church
as true children of your family.

We ask this through Christ our Lord.
R̸. Amen.

The celebrant faces the children and says: 340
We anoint you with the oil of salvation 132
in the name of Christ our Savior.
May he strengthen you with his power,
who lives and reigns for ever and ever.

Children:
Amen.

Each child is anointed with the oil of catechumens on the breast or on both hands or even on other parts of the body, if this seems desirable.

[If there are a great many catechumens, additional priests or deacons may assist in the anointing.]

The anointing may be followed by a blessing of the catechumens (no. 97).

B *Laying on of Hands:* The celebrant faces the children and says:

**May Christ our Savior
strengthen you with his power,
for he is Lord for ever and ever.**

Children:
Amen.

Then, in silence, the celebrant lays his hands on the head
of each child.

DISMISSAL OF THE CHILDREN

302. The celebrant dismisses the children, option A, or   341
else sends them back to their places in the church, where
they remain, option B.

A   The celebrant dismisses the children, using these or
similar words.
**N. and N., here among us the Lord Jesus has opened
the arms of his mercy to you. Go now in peace.**

Children:
Thanks be to God.

B   The celebrant sends the children back to their places in
the church, using these or similar words.
**N. and N., here among us the Lord Jesus has opened
the arms of his mercy to you. Return to your places
now and continue with us in prayer.**

Children:
Thanks be to God.

LITURGY OF PENANCE

303. Next, the liturgy of the sacrament of penance begins   342
for baptized children who will celebrate this sacrament for
the first time. After the celebrant gives a brief instruction,
individual confession, first of the children, then of the others in the assembly, follows.

A suitable song or a prayer of thanksgiving follows the celebration of the sacrament; all then leave.

THIRD STEP: CELEBRATION OF THE SACRAMENTS OF INITIATION

Wake up and rise from death: Christ will shine upon you

304. In order to bring out the paschal character of baptism, celebration of the sacraments of initiation should preferably take place at the Easter Vigil or on a Sunday, the day that the Church devotes to the remembrance of Christ's resurrection (see *Rite of Baptism for Children*, Introduction, no. 9). But the provisions of no. 256 should also guide the choice of time for the celebration of the sacraments of initiation. 343

305. At this third step of their Christian initiation, the children will receive the sacrament of baptism, the bishop or priest who baptizes them will also confer confirmation, and the children will for the first time participate in the liturgy of the eucharist. 344

306. If the sacraments of initiation are celebrated at a time other than the Easter Vigil or Easter Sunday, the Mass of the day or one of the ritual Masses in the Roman Missal, "Christian Initiation: Baptism" is used. The readings are chosen from those given in the Lectionary for Mass, "Celebration of the Sacraments of Initiation apart from the Easter Vigil"; but the readings for the Sunday or feast on which the celebration takes place may be used instead. 345

307. All the children to be baptized are to be accompanied by their own godparent or godparents, chosen by themselves and approved by the priest (see no. 11; *Christian Initiation*, General Introduction, no. 10). 346

308. Baptized children of the catechetical group may be completing their Christian initiation in the sacraments of confirmation and the eucharist at this same celebration. When the bishop himself will not be the celebrant, he should grant the faculty to confirm such children to the priest who will be the celebrant.[1] For their confirmation, previously baptized children of the catechetical group are to have their own sponsors. If possible, these should be the persons who were godparents for their baptism, but other qualified persons may be chosen.[2]

[1]See *Rite of Confirmation*, Introduction, no. 7, b.
[2]See ibid., nos. 5 and 6.

CELEBRATION OF THE SACRAMENTS OF INITIATION

LITURGY OF THE WORD

309. When the children who are candidates for initiation, their parents or guardians, godparents, other children from the catechetical group, friends, and members of the parish have assembled, Mass begins.

347

The texts for the Mass and the readings in the liturgy of the word are those already indicated in no. 306. The homily follows the readings.

CELEBRATION OF BAPTISM

INVITATION TO PRAYER

310. After the homily, the celebrant and the children with their parents or guardians and godparents go to the baptismal font, if this is in view of the faithful; otherwise they gather in the sanctuary, where a vessel of water should be prepared beforehand. The celebrant speaks to the family, friends, and the entire assembly in these or similar words.

348

Dear friends, N. and N., with the approval of their parents, have asked to be baptized. Let us call upon the Father to number them among his adopted children in Christ.

PRAYER OVER THE WATER

311. Next, the celebrant blesses the water or says a prayer of thanksgiving over the water.

349
350

When baptism is celebrated at the Easter Vigil, the celebrant blesses the water, using option A; outside the Easter Vigil, in blessing the water he may use either option A or the other blessing formularies given in no. 222 as options B and C.

But when baptism is celebrated during the Easter season and water already blessed at the Easter Vigil is available, the celebrant uses option B, so that this part of the celebration will retain the themes of thanksgiving and intercession;

he may also use the second Easter-season thanksgiving formulary given in no. 222 as option E.

A

Blessing of the Water: Facing the font (or vessel) containing the water, the celebrant says the following prayer.   349

Father,
you give us grace through sacramental signs,
which tell us of the wonders of your unseen power.

In baptism we use your gift of water,
which you have made a rich symbol of the grace
you give us in this sacrament.

At the very dawn of creation
your Spirit breathed on the waters,
making them the wellspring of all holiness.

The waters of the great flood
you made a sign of the waters of baptism
that make an end of sin
and a new beginning of goodness.

Through the waters of the Red Sea
you led Israel out of slavery
to be an image of God's holy people,
set free from sin by baptism.

In the waters of the Jordan
your Son was baptized by John
and anointed with the Spirit.

Your Son willed that water and blood should flow
    from his side
as he hung upon the cross.

After his resurrection he told his disciples:
"Go out and teach all nations,
baptizing them in the name of the Father, and of the
    Son, and of the Holy Spirit."

Father,
look now with love upon your Church
and unseal for it the fountain of baptism.

By the power of the Holy Spirit
give to this water the grace of your Son,
so that in the sacrament of baptism
all those whom you have created in your likeness
may be cleansed from sin
and rise to a new birth of innocence
by water and the Holy Spirit.

The celebrant before continuing touches the water with his right hand.

[But at the Easter Vigil, if this can be done conveniently, the celebrant before continuing lowers the Easter candle into the water once or three times, then holds it there until the acclamation at the end of the blessing.]

We ask you, Father, with your Son
to send the Holy Spirit upon the waters of this font.
May all who are buried with Christ in the death of
baptism
rise also with him to newness of life.

We ask this through Christ our Lord.

All:
Amen.

The people sing the following or some other suitable acclamation.

Springs of water, bless the Lord.
Give him glory and praise for ever.

B
Easter-Season Thanksgiving over Water Already Blessed: Facing   389
the font (or vessel) containing the blessed water, the celebrant says the prayer as in no. 222 D.

COMMUNITY'S PROFESSION OF FAITH

312. Before the rite of the children's profession of faith,   351
the celebrant may, if this is in keeping with the circumstances, invite the parents or guardians, godparents, and all present to profess their faith.

N. and N. have completed a long preparation and are ready for baptism. They will receive new life from God who is love: they will become Christians.

From now on, we will need to help them even more. This is especially true of you, their parents, who have given them permission to be baptized and who have the primary responsibility for their upbringing. But all of us who have in any way prepared them to meet Christ today must always be ready to assist them.

And so, before these children make their profession of faith in our presence, let us in their presence publicly and with a deep sense of responsibility renew our own profession of faith, which is the faith of the Church.

Then together with the celebrant all recite the profession of faith, using either the Apostles' Creed, option A, or the Nicene Creed, option B.

A Apostles' Creed
All join the celebrant and say:

I believe in God, the Father almighty,
   creator of heaven and earth.

I believe in Jesus Christ, his only Son, our Lord.
   He was conceived by the power of the Holy Spirit
      and born of the Virgin Mary.
   He suffered under Pontius Pilate,
      was crucified, died, and was buried.
   He descended to the dead.
   On the third day he rose again.
   He ascended into heaven,
      and is seated at the right hand of the Father.
   He will come again to judge the living and the
      dead.

I believe in the Holy Spirit,
   the holy catholic Church,
   the communion of saints,
   the forgiveness of sins,
   the resurrection of the body,
   and the life everlasting. Amen.

B Nicene Creed
All join the celebrant and say:

We believe in one God,
   the Father, the Almighty,
   maker of heaven and earth,
   of all that is seen and unseen.

We believe in one Lord, Jesus Christ,
   the only Son of God,
   eternally begotten of the Father,
   God from God, Light from Light,
   true God from true God,
   begotten, not made,
   one in Being with the Father.
   Through him all things were made.
For us men and for our salvation
   he came down from heaven:
by the power of the Holy Spirit
   he was born of the Virgin Mary,
      and became man.
For our sake he was crucified under Pontius Pilate;
   he suffered death and was buried.
   On the third day he rose again
      in fulfillment of the Scriptures;
   he ascended into heaven
      and is seated at the right hand of the Father.
He will come again in glory to judge the living
   and the dead,
   and his kingdom will have no end.

We believe in the Holy Spirit, the Lord, the giver of
   life,
   who proceeds from the Father and the Son.
   With the Father and the Son he is worshiped and
      glorified.
   He has spoken through the Prophets.
   We believe in one holy catholic and apostolic
      Church.
   We acknowledge one baptism for the forgiveness
      of sins.
   We look for the resurrection of the dead,
      and the life of the world to come. Amen.

CHILDREN'S PROFESSION OF FAITH

313. The celebration of baptism continues with the rite of 352
the children's renunciation of sin and profession of faith.

The celebrant first addresses them briefly in these or similar
words.
**Children [N. and N.], you have spent a long time in
preparation and you have now asked to be baptized.
Your parents have agreed to your request; your teachers, companions, and friends have helped you; and
all who have come here today promise you the example of their faith and their loving support.**

**Before you are baptized, reject Satan and profess
your faith here in the presence of God's Church.**

RENUNCIATION OF SIN

314. The celebrant, using one of the following formularies, 353
questions all the children together.

A Celebrant:
**Do you reject sin so as to live in the freedom of
God's children?**

Children:
I do.

Celebrant:
**Do you reject the glamor of evil,
and refuse to be mastered by sin?**

Children:
I do.

Celebrant:
**Do you reject Satan, father of sin and prince of dark-
ness?**

Children:
I do.

B Celebrant:
**Do you reject Satan,
and all his works,
and all his empty promises?**

Children:
I do.

ANOINTING WITH THE OIL OF CATECHUMENS

315. If it has not been celebrated at another time during
the catechumenate of the children, particularly within the
penitential rite (no. 301), the anointing with the oil of catechumens now takes place between the renunciation of sin
and the profession of faith. Ordinarily, this rite is to be
omitted, as decreed by the National Conference of Catholic
Bishops (see no. 33.7).

354
USA

The celebrant, facing the children, says:
**We anoint you with the oil of salvation
in the name of Christ our Savior.
May he strengthen you with his power,
who lives and reigns for ever and ever.**

354

Children:
Amen.

Each of the children is anointed with the oil of catechumens
on both hands, on the breast, or on other parts of the
body, if this seems desirable.

[If there are a great number of children, additional priests
or deacons may assist with the anointings.]

PROFESSION OF FAITH

316. The celebrant, informed by the godparents of the
name of each child, asks the child individually to make the
profession of faith, then immediately baptizes the child.

355

Celebrant:
**N., do you believe in God, the Father almighty,
creator of heaven and earth?**

Child:
I do.

Celebrant:
**Do you believe in Jesus Christ, his only Son, our
Lord,
who was born of the Virgin Mary,**

was crucified, died, and was buried,
rose from the dead,
and is now seated at the right hand of the Father?

Child:
I do.

Celebrant:
Do you believe in the Holy Spirit,
the holy catholic Church, the communion of saints,
the forgiveness of sins, the resurrection of the
body,
and the life everlasting?

Child:
I do.

If there are a great many children to be baptized, the profes-   USA
sion of faith may be made simultaneously either by all together or group by group. The baptism of each candidate
follows.

BAPTISM

317. The celebrant baptizes each child either by immer-   356
sion, option A, or by the pouring of water, option B. Each
baptism may be followed by a short acclamation (Appendix
II, no. 595), sung or said by the people.

[If there are a great number of children to be baptized, they
may be divided into groups and baptized by assisting
priests or deacons. In baptizing, either by immersion, option A, or by the pouring of water, option B, these ministers say the sacramental formulary for each child. During
the baptisms, singing by the people is desirable or readings
from Scripture or simply silent prayer.]

A
If baptism is by immersion, of the whole body or of the   220
head only, decency and decorum should be preserved. Either or both godparents touch the child. The celebrant, immersing the child's whole body or head three times, baptizes the child in the name of the Trinity.

N., I baptize you in the name of the Father,

He immerses the child the first time.

and of the Son,

He immerses the child the second time.

and of the Holy Spirit.

He immerses the child the third time.

B

If baptism is by the pouring of water, either or both godpar-   356
ents place the right hand on the shoulder of the child, and
the celebrant, taking baptismal water and pouring it three
times on the child's bowed head, baptizes the child in the
name of the Trinity.

N., I baptize you in the name of the Father,

He pours water the first time.

and of the Son,

He pours water the second time.

and of the Holy Spirit.

He pours water the third time.

EXPLANATORY RITES

318. See no. 227.   357

ANOINTING AFTER BAPTISM

319. If the confirmation of those baptized is separated   358
from baptism, the celebrant anoints them with chrism immediately after baptism.

[When a great number have been baptized, assisting priests
or deacons may help with the anointing.]

The celebrant first says the following over all the newly baptized before the anointing.

**The God of power and Father of our Lord Jesus
  Christ
has freed you from sin
and brought you to new life
through water and the Holy Spirit.**

**He now anoints you with the chrism of salvation,
so that, united with his people,
you may remain for ever a member of Christ
who is Priest, Prophet, and King.**

Children:
Amen.

In silence each of the newly baptized is anointed with
chrism on the crown of the head.

CLOTHING WITH A BAPTISMAL GARMENT

320. The garment used in this rite may be white or of a
color that conforms to local custom. If circumstances suggest, this rite may be omitted.

359

The celebrant says the following formulary and at the
words "Receive this baptismal garment" the godparents
place the garment on the newly baptized children.

**N. and N., you have become a new creation
and have clothed yourselves in Christ.
Receive this baptismal garment
and bring it unstained to the judgment seat of our
Lord Jesus Christ,
so that you may have everlasting life.**

Children:
Amen.

PRESENTATION OF A LIGHTED CANDLE

321. The celebrant takes the Easter candle in his hands or
touches it, saying to the godparents:

360

**Godparents, please come forward to give to the
newly baptized the light of Christ.**

A godparent of each of the newly baptized goes to the celebrant, lights a candle from the Easter candle, then presents
it to the newly baptized child.

Then the celebrant says to the children:

**You have been enlightened by Christ.
Walk always as children of the light
and keep the flame of faith alive in your hearts.
When the Lord comes, may you go out to meet him
with all the saints in the heavenly kingdom.**

Children:
Amen.

CELEBRATION OF CONFIRMATION

322. Between the celebration of baptism and confirmation, the assembly may sing a suitable song. 361 362

The place for the celebration of confirmation is either at the baptismal font or in the sanctuary, depending on where, according to local conditions, baptism has been celebrated.

If previously baptized children of the catechetical group are to be confirmed, they with their sponsors join the newly baptized children to receive the sacrament.

323. If the bishop has conferred baptism, he should now also confer confirmation. If the bishop is not present, the priest who conferred baptism is authorized to confirm (see no. 308). 362

[When there are a great many children to be confirmed, the minister of confirmation may associate priests with himself as ministers of the sacrament (see no. 14).]

INVITATION

324. The celebrant first speaks briefly to the children in these or similar words. 363

My dear children, by your baptism you have been born again in Christ and you have become members of Christ and of his priestly people. Now you are to share in the outpouring of the Holy Spirit among us, the Spirit sent by the Lord upon his apostles at Pentecost and given by them and their successors to the baptized.

The promised strength of the Holy Spirit, which you are to receive, will make you more like Christ and help you to be witnesses to his suffering, death, and resurrection. It will strengthen you to be active members of the Church and to build up the Body of Christ in faith and love.

[The priests who will be associated with the celebrant as ministers of the sacrament now stand next to him.]

With hands joined, the celebrant next addresses the people:

My dear friends, let us pray to God our Father, that he will pour out the Holy Spirit on these children to strengthen them with his gifts and anoint them to be more like Christ, the Son of God.

All pray briefly in silence.

LAYING ON OF HANDS

325. See no. 234.

364

ANOINTING WITH CHRISM

326. A minister brings the chrism to the celebrant.

365

[When the celebrant is the bishop, priests who are associated as ministers of the sacrament receive the chrism from him.]

Each child to be confirmed, with godparent or godparents, sponsor or sponsors, goes to the celebrant (or to an associated minister of the sacrament); or, if circumstances require, the celebrant (associated ministers) may go to the children.

Either or both godparents or sponsors place the right hand on the shoulder of the child and a godparent or sponsor of each child gives the child's name or the child gives his or her name to the minister of the sacrament. During the conferral of the sacrament an appropriate song may be sung.

The minister of the sacrament dips his right thumb in the chrism and makes the sign of the cross on the forehead of the one to be confirmed as he says:

N., be sealed with the Gift of the Holy Spirit.

Child:
Amen.

The minister of the sacrament adds:
Peace be with you.

Child:
And also with you.

LITURGY OF THE EUCHARIST.

327. Since the profession of faith is not said, the general   366
intercessions begin immediately and for the first time the
newly baptized children take part in them. Some of the children also take part in the procession to the altar with the
gifts.

328. With Eucharistic Prayers I, II or III the special interpo-   367
lations given in the Roman Missal, the ritual Masses, "Christian Initiation: Baptism," are used.

Eucharistic Prayer IV, with its special interpolation indicated in the same ritual Masses, may also be used but outside the Easter Vigil.

329. It is most desirable that the newly baptized children,   368
together with their godparents, parents, and catechists, receive communion under both kinds.

Before saying "This is the Lamb of God," the celebrant may
briefly remind the newly baptized children of the preeminence of the eucharist, which is the climax of their initiation
and the center of the whole Christian life.

The celebrant should also pay special attention to any previously baptized children of the catechetical group who at
this celebration are to receive communion for the first time.
These children, together with their parents, godparents,
sponsors for confirmation, and catechists, may also receive
communion under both kinds.

PERIOD OF POSTBAPTISMAL CATECHESIS OR MYSTAGOGY

The Father chose us to be his adopted children through Jesus Christ

330. A period of postbaptismal catechesis or mystagogy should be provided to assist the young neophytes and their companions who have completed their Christian initiation. This period can be arranged by an adaptation of the guidelines given for adults (nos. 244–251).

369

2. CHRISTIAN INITIATION OF ADULTS IN EXCEPTIONAL CIRCUMSTANCES

He gave power to become children of God to all who believe in his name

331. Exceptional circumstances may arise in which the lo-   240
cal bishop, in individual cases, can allow the use of a form
of Christian initiation that is simpler than the usual, complete rite (see no. 34.4).

The bishop may permit this simpler form to consist in the
abbreviated form of the rite (nos. 340–369) that is carried
out in one celebration. Or he may permit an expansion of
this abbreviated rite, so that there are celebrations not only
of the sacraments of initiation but also of one or more of
the rites belonging to the period of the catechumenate and
to the period of purification and enlightenment (see nos.
332–335).

The extraordinary circumstances in question are either
events that prevent the candidate from completing all the
steps of the catechumenate or a depth of Christian conversion and a degree of religious maturity that lead the local
bishop to decide that the candidate may receive baptism
without delay.

EXPANDED FORM

332. Extraordinary circumstances, for example, sickness,   274
old age, change of residence, long absence for travel, may
sometimes either prevent a candidate from celebrating the
rite of acceptance that leads to the period of the
catechumenate or, having begun the catechumenate, from
completing it by participation in all the rites belonging to
the period. Yet merely to use the abbreviated form of the
rite given in nos. 340–369 could mean a spiritual loss for
the candidate, who would be deprived of the benefits of a
longer preparation for the sacraments of initiation. It is
therefore important that, with the bishop's permission, an
expanded form of initiation be developed by the incorporation of elements from the complete rite for the Christian initiation of adults.

333. Through such an expansion of the abbreviated rite a   275
new candidate can reach the same level as those who are

already advanced in the catechumenate, since some of the earlier elements from the full rite can be added, for example, the rite of acceptance into the order of catechumens (nos. 48–74) or the minor exorcisms (no. 94) and blessings (no. 97) from the period of the catechumenate. The expansion also makes it possible for a candidate who had begun the catechumenate with others, but was forced to interrupt it, to complete the catechumenate alone by celebrating, in addition to the sacraments of initiation (see nos. 206–217), elements from the full rite, for example, the rite of election (see nos. 118–128) and rites belonging to the period of purification and enlightenment (see nos. 141–149).

334. Pastors can arrange this expanded form of initiation   276
by taking the abbreviated form as a basis, then choosing wisely from the full rite to make adaptations in any of the following ways:

1. supplementing the abbreviated form: for example, adding rites belonging to the period of the catechumenate (nos. 81–102) or adding the presentations (nos. 157–162, 178–182);

2. making the rite of "Receiving the Candidate" or the "Liturgy of the Word" in the abbreviated rite separate or expanded celebrations. As to "Receiving the Candidate" (nos. 340–345), this can be expanded by replacing no. 342 and using elements from the rite of acceptance into the order of catechumens (nos. 48–74); or, depending on the candidate's state of preparation, by celebrating the rite of election (nos. 129–137) in place of nos. 343–344. As to the "Liturgy of the Word," after the readings, the intercessions, penitential rite, and prayer of exorcism, nos. 349–351, can be adapted by use of the elements in the scrutinies (nos. 152–154, 166– 168, 173–175);

3. replacing elements of the complete rite with elements of the abbreviated form; or combining the rite of acceptance into the order of catechumens (nos. 48–74) and the rite of election (nos. 129–137) at the time of receiving a properly disposed candidate (which is comparable to the time of receiving interested inquirers in the period of the precatechumenate; see no. 39.3).

335. When this expanded form of initiation is arranged,   277
care should be taken to ensure that:

1. the candidate has received a full catechesis;

2. the rite is celebrated with the active participation of an assembly;

3. after receiving the sacraments the neophyte has the benefit of a period of postbaptismal catechesis, if at all possible.

ABBREVIATED FORM

336. Before the abbreviated form of the rite is celebrated the candidate must have gone through an adequate period of instruction and preparation before baptism, in order to purify his or her motives for requesting baptism and to grow stronger in conversion and faith. The candidate should also have chosen godparents or a godparent (see no. 11) and become acquainted with the local Christian community (see nos. 39, 75.2). 241

337. This rite includes elements that express the presentation and welcoming of the candidate and that also express the candidate's clear and firm resolve to request Christian initiation, as well as the Church's approval of the candidate. A suitable liturgy of the word is also celebrated, then the sacraments of initiation. 242

338. Normally the rite is celebrated within Mass. The choice of readings should be in keeping with the character of the celebration; they may be either those of the day or those in the Lectionary for Mass, ritual Mass, "Christian Initiation apart from the Easter Vigil." The other Mass texts are those of one of the ritual Masses "Christian Initiation: Baptism" or of another Mass. After receiving baptism and confirmation, the candidate takes part for the first time in the celebration of the eucharist. 243

339. If at all possible, the celebration should take place on a Sunday (see no. 27), with the local community taking an active part. 244

CHRISTIAN INITIATION OF ADULTS IN EXCEPTIONAL CIRCUMSTANCES
(Abbreviated Form)

RECEIVING THE CANDIDATE

340. Before the celebration begins, the candidate with his   245
or her godparents and friends waits outside the church or
inside, at the entrance or some other convenient place. The
celebrant, wearing the vestments for Mass, goes to meet
them, as the faithful sing a psalm or another suitable song.

GREETING

341. The celebrant greets the candidate in a friendly man-   246
ner. He speaks to the candidate, godparents, and friends,
pointing out the joy and happiness of the Church. He recalls for the godparents and friends the particular experience and religious response that have led the candidate, following his or her own spiritual path, to the present celebration.

The celebrant then invites the godparents and the candidate
to come forward. As they are taking their place before him,
an appropriate song may be sung, for example, Psalm
63:1–8.

OPENING DIALOGUE

342. Facing the candidate, the celebrant asks the questions   247
that follow. In asking about the candidate's intention he
may use words other than those provided and may let the
candidate answer in his or her own words: for example, to
the first question, "What do you ask of the Church of
God?" or "What do you desire?" or "For what reason have
you come?", he may receive such answers as "The grace of
Christ" or "Entrance into the Church" or "Eternal life" or
other suitable responses. The celebrant will phrase his next
question according to the answer received.

Celebrant:
What do you ask of God's Church?

Candidate:
Faith.

Celebrant:
What does faith offer you?

Candidate:
Eternal life.

CANDIDATE'S DECLARATION

343. The celebrant addresses the candidate, adapting as re-   248
quired the following or similar words to the answers received in the opening dialogue.

**This is eternal life: to know the one true God and
Jesus Christ, whom he has sent. Christ has been
raised from the dead and appointed by God as the
Lord of life and ruler of all things, seen and unseen.**

**You would not ask for this life or seek baptism to-
day, unless you had already come to know Christ
and wanted to become his disciple. And I ask you,
have you listened to Christ's word and resolved to
keep his commandments? Have you shared our way
of life and joined with us in prayer? Have you done
all these things with the intention of becoming a
Christian?**

Candidate:
I have.

AFFIRMATION BY THE GODPARENTS

344. Then the celebrant turns to the godparents and asks: 249

**You are the candidate's godparents. As God is your
witness, do you consider him/her worthy to be admitted today to the sacraments of Christian initiation?**

Godparents:
I do.

Celebrant:
**You have spoken in N.'s favor. Are you prepared to
help him/her to serve Christ by your words and example?**

Godparents:
I am.

The celebrant, with hands joined, says: 250

Let us pray.

Father of mercy,
we thank you for your servant, N.
You have sought and summoned him/her in many
ways
and he/she has turned to seek you.

You have called him/her today
and he/she has answered in the presence of the
Church.

Look favorably upon him/her
and let your loving purpose be fulfilled within him/
her.

We ask this through Christ our Lord.
R̸. Amen.

INVITATION TO THE CELEBRATION OF THE WORD
OF GOD

345. Using the following or similar words, accompanied by   251
an appropriate gesture, the celebrant invites the candidate
and the godparents to enter the church.

Celebrant:
N., come into the church, to share with us at the ta-
ble of God's word.

During the entrance a suitable song is sung or the following
antiphon, with Psalm 34:2, 3, 6, 9, 10.

Come, my children, and listen to me;
I will teach you the fear of the Lord.

LITURGY OF THE WORD

346. When the candidate and the godparents have taken   252
their place in the church and the celebrant has reached the
sanctuary, the liturgy of the word begins; the usual introductory rites of the Mass are omitted.

READINGS

347. The readings are those already indicated in no. 338.   253

HOMILY

348. The homily follows the gospel reading.   253

INTERCESSIONS FOR THE CANDIDATE

349. After the homily, the candidate and the godparents   254
come before the celebrant. The entire assembly joins in offering the following or similar intercessions.

Celebrant:
**Let us pray for our brother/sister who asks for
Christ's sacraments, and let us pray for ourselves, sin-
ners that we are, that we may all draw nearer to
Christ in faith and repentance and walk untiringly in
newness of life.**

Assisting minister:
**That the Lord may kindle in all of us a spirit of true
repentance, let us pray to the Lord:
R̸. Lord, hear our prayer.**

Assisting minister:
**That we, who have died to sin and been saved by
Christ through baptism, may be living proof of his
grace, let us pray to the Lord:
R̸. Lord, hear our prayer.**

Assisting minister:
**That with trust in God's love and sorrow for sin our
brother/sister may prepare to meet Christ his/her Savior, let us pray to the Lord:
R̸. Lord, hear our prayer.**

Assisting minister:

That by following Christ, who takes away the sin of the world, our brother/sister may be healed of the infection of sin and freed from its power, let us pray to the Lord:

℟. **Lord, hear our prayer.**

Assisting minister:

That by the power of the Holy Spirit, he/she may be cleansed from sin and guided along the paths of holiness, let us pray to the Lord:

℟. **Lord, hear our prayer.**

Assisting minister:

That through burial with Christ in baptism he/she may die to sin and live always for God, let us pray to the Lord:

℟. **Lord, hear our prayer.**

Assisting minister:

That on the day of judgment he/she may come before the Father bearing fruits of holiness and love, let us pray to the Lord:

℟. **Lord, hear our prayer.**

Assisting minister:

That the entire world, for which the Father gave his beloved Son, may believe in his love and turn to him, let us pray to the Lord:

℟. **Lord, hear our prayer.**

PENITENTIAL RITE

350. The penitential rite may be omitted, as circumstances suggest. When it is celebrated, after the intercessions the candidate bows his or her head or kneels and joins the assembly in reciting the general confession of sins.

254

I confess to almighty God,
and to you, my brothers and sisters,
that I have sinned through my own fault

All strike their breast

in my thoughts and in my words,
in what I have done,

and in what I have failed to do;
and I ask blessed Mary, ever-virgin,
all the angels and saints,
and you, my brothers and sisters,
to pray for me to the Lord our God.

The absolution "May almighty God" is not said.

PRAYER OF EXORCISM

351. The celebrant concludes the intercessions (and peni-   255
tential rite) with the following prayer.

Father of mercies,
you sent your only Son
to rescue us from the slavery of sin
and to give us freedom as your children.

We pray for your servant N.;
he/she has faced the temptations of this world
and been tested by the cunning of Satan;
now he/she acknowledges his/her sinfulness
and professes his/her faith.

By the passion and resurrection of your Son
deliver him/her from the powers of darkness
and strengthen him/her through the grace of Christ,
that he/she may journey through life, shielded by
    your unfailing care.

We ask this through Christ our Lord.
℟. Amen.

ANOINTING WITH THE OIL OF CATECHUMENS OR
LAYING ON OF HANDS

352. If it has not been celebrated at another time, the   256
anointing with the oil of catechumens, option A, now takes   USA
place. Ordinarily, this rite is to be omitted, as decreed by
the National Conference of Catholic Bishops (see no. 33.7).
It is always permissible for the celebrant to substitute a laying on of hands, option B.

A   *Anointing with the Oil of Catechumens:* The celebrant
faces the candidate and says:

We anoint you with the oil of salvation
in the name of Christ our Savior.

**May he strengthen you with his power,
who lives and reigns for ever and ever.**

Candidate:
Amen.

The candidate is anointed with the oil of catechumens on
the breast or on both hands or even on other parts of the
body, if this seems desirable.

B *Laying on of Hands:* The celebrant faces the candidate
and says:

**May Christ our Savior
strengthen you with his power,
for he is Lord for ever and ever.**

Candidate:
Amen.

Then, in silence, the celebrant lays hands on the candidate.

CELEBRATION OF BAPTISM

INVITATION TO PRAYER

353. The candidate with the godparent or the godparents   257
goes to the baptismal font with the celebrant, then the celebrant addresses the following or a similar invitation for the
assembly to join in prayer for the candidate.

**Dear friends, let us pray to almighty God for our
brother/sister N., who is asking for baptism. He has
called N. and brought him/her to this moment; may
he grant N. light and strength to follow Christ with a
resolute heart and to profess the faith of the Church.
May he give N. the new life of the Holy Spirit,
whom we are about to call down on this water.**

PRAYER OVER THE WATER

354. Next, the celebrant blesses the water, using option A;   258
he may also use one of the other blessing formularies given
in no. 222 as option B and C.

But when baptism is celebrated during the Easter season
and water already blessed at the Easter Vigil is available,

the celebrant uses option B, so that this part of the celebration will retain the themes of thanksgiving and intercession; he may also use the second Easter-season thanksgiving formulary given in no. 222 as option E.

A *Blessing of the Water:* Facing the font (or vessel) containing the water, the celebrant says the following prayer.

**Father,
you give us grace through sacramental signs,
which tell us of the wonders of your unseen power.**

**In baptism we use your gift of water,
which you have made a rich symbol of the grace
you give us in this sacrament.**

**At the very dawn of creation
your Spirit breathed on the waters,
making them the wellspring of all holiness.**

**The waters of the great flood
you made a sign of the waters of baptism
that make an end of sin
and a new beginning of goodness.**

**Through the waters of the Red Sea
you led Israel out of slavery
to be an image of God's holy people,
set free from sin by baptism.**

**In the waters of the Jordan
your Son was baptized by John
and anointed with the Spirit.**

**Your Son willed that water and blood should flow
   from his side
as he hung upon the cross.**

**After his resurrection he told his disciples:
"Go out and teach all nations,
baptizing them in the name of the Father, and of the
   Son, and of the Holy Spirit."**

**Father,
look now with love upon your Church
and unseal for it the fountain of baptism.**

By the power of the Holy Spirit
give to this water the grace of your Son,
so that in the sacrament of baptism
all those whom you have created in your likeness
may be cleansed from sin
and rise to a new birth of innocence
by water and the Holy Spirit.

Before continuing, the celebrant pauses and touches the water with his right hand.

We ask you, Father, with your Son
to send the Holy Spirit upon the waters of this font.
May all who are buried with Christ in the death of
**   baptism**
rise also with him to newness of life.

We ask this through Christ our Lord.

All:
Amen.

B *Easter-Season Thanksgiving over Blessed Water:* See no. 222
D.
389

PROFESSION OF FAITH

355. See no. 223.
259

RENUNCIATION OF SIN

356. Using one of the following formularies, the celebrant questions the candidate.
259
USA

[At the discretion of the diocesan bishop, the formularies for the renunciation of sin may be made more specific and detailed as circumstances might require (see no. 33.8).]

A Celebrant:
Do you reject sin so as to live in the freedom of
**   God's children?**

Candidate:
I do.

Celebrant:
Do you reject the glamor of evil,
and refuse to be mastered by sin?

Candidate:
I do.

Celebrant:
Do you reject Satan, father of sin and prince of
darkness?

Candidate:
I do.

B   Celebrant:
Do you reject Satan,
and all his works,
and all his empty promises?

Candidate:
I do.

C   Celebrant:
Do you reject Satan?

Candidate:
I do.

Celebrant:
And all his works?

Candidate:
I do.

Celebrant:
And all his empty promises?

Candidate:
I do.

PROFESSION OF FAITH

357. Then the celebrant asks the candidate: 260

N., do you believe in God, the Father almighty, cre-
ator of heaven and earth?

Candidate:
I do.

Celebrant:

Do you believe in Jesus Christ, his only Son, our Lord,
who was born of the Virgin Mary,
was crucified, died, and was buried,
rose from the dead,
and is now seated at the right hand of the Father?

Candidate:

I do.

Celebrant:

Do you believe in the Holy Spirit,
the holy catholic Church, the communion of saints,
the forgiveness of sins, the resurrection of the body,
and the life everlasting?

Candidate:

I do.

BAPTISM

358. Immediately after the profession of faith the celebrant baptizes the candidate either by immersion, option A, or by the pouring of water, option B. After the baptism it is appropriate for the people to sing a short acclamation (Appendix II, no. 595). 260

A See no. 226 A. 261
B See no. 226 B. 262

EXPLANATORY RITES

359. The celebration of baptism proceeds immediately with the explanatory rites, after which the celebration of confirmation follows.

CLOTHING WITH A BAPTISMAL GARMENT

360. See no. 229. 264

PRESENTATION OF A LIGHTED CANDLE

361. The celebrant takes the Easter candle in his hands or touches it, saying to the godparent(s): 265

Please come forward to give to the newly baptized the light of Christ.

A godparent goes to the celebrant and lights a candle from the Easter candle, then presents it to the newly baptized.

Then the celebrant says to the newly baptized:

**You have been enlightened by Christ.
Walk always as a child of the light
and keep the flame of faith alive in your heart.
When the Lord comes, may you go out to meet him
with all the saints in the heavenly kingdom.**

Newly baptized:
Amen.

CELEBRATION OF CONFIRMATION

362. Between the celebration of baptism and confirmation, the assembly may sing an appropriate song. 266

363. If the bishop is not present, the celebrant who conferred baptism confers confirmation. 267

INVITATION

364. The celebrant first speaks briefly to the person newly baptized in these or similar words. 268

N., born again in Christ by baptism, you have become a member of Christ and of his priestly people. Now you are to share in the outpouring of the Holy Spirit among us, the Spirit sent by the Lord upon his apostles at Pentecost and given by them and their successors to the baptized.

The promised strength of the Holy Spirit, which you are to receive, will make you more like Christ and help you to be a witness to his suffering, death, and resurrection. It will strengthen you to be an active member of the Church and to build up the Body of Christ in faith and love.

With hands joined, the celebrant next addresses the people:

My dear friends, let us pray to God our Father, that he will pour out the Holy Spirit on our newly bap-

tized brother/sister to strengthen him/her with his gifts and anoint him/her to be more like Christ, the Son of God.

All pray briefly in silence.

LAYING ON OF HANDS

365. The celebrant then lays hands on the person to be confirmed and says the following prayer.

269

All-powerful God, Father of our Lord Jesus Christ, by water and the Holy Spirit you freed your son/daughter from sin and gave him/her new life.

Send your Holy Spirit upon him/her to be his/her helper and guide.

Give him/her the spirit of wisdom and understanding, the spirit of right judgment and courage, the spirit of knowledge and reverence. Fill him/her with the spirit of wonder and awe in your presence.

We ask this through Christ our Lord.
R̸. Amen.

ANOINTING WITH CHRISM

366. A minister brings the chrism to the celebrant.

270

The candidate, with the godparents, goes to the celebrant. Either or both godparents place the right hand on the shoulder of the candidate and either a godparent or the candidate gives the candidate's name to the celebrant. During the conferral of the sacrament an appropriate song may be sung.

The celebrant dips his right thumb in the chrism and makes the sign of the cross on the forehead of the one to be confirmed as he says:

N., be sealed with the Gift of the Holy Spirit.

Newly confirmed:
Amen.

The celebrant adds:
Peace be with you.

Newly confirmed:
And also with you.

LITURGY OF THE EUCHARIST

367. Since the profession of faith is not said, the general
intercessions begin immediately and for the first time the
neophyte takes part in them. He or she also helps to carry
the gifts when they are brought to the altar.

368. The eucharistic prayer is to include the special interpolations given for Eucharistic Prayers I, II, III, and IV in the
Roman Missal, ritual Masses, "Christian Initiation: Baptism."

369. It is most desirable that the neophyte, together with
his or her godparents, parents, spouse, and catechists, receive communion under both kinds.

Before saying "This is the Lamb of God" the celebrant may
briefly remind the neophyte of the preeminence of the eucharist, which is the climax of Christian initiation and the
center of the whole Christian life.

3. CHRISTIAN INITIATION OF A PERSON IN DANGER OF DEATH

By becoming coheirs with Christ, we share in his sufferings; we will also share in his glory

370. Persons, whether catechumens or not, who are in danger of death but are not at the point of death and so are able to hear and answer the questions involved may be baptized with this short rite.   278

371. Persons who have already been accepted as catechumens must make a promise that upon recovery they will complete the usual catechesis. Persons who are not catechumens must give serious indication of their conversion to Christ and renunciation of pagan worship and must not be seen to be attached to anything that conflicts with the moral life (for example, "simultaneous polygamy"). They must also promise that upon recovery they will go through the complete program of initiation as it applies to them.   279

372. This shorter rite is designed particularly for use by catechists and laypersons; a priest or a deacon may use it in a case of emergency. But normally a priest or a deacon is to use the abbreviated form of Christian initiation given in nos. 340–369, making any changes required by circumstances of place and time.   280

The minister of baptism who is a priest should, when the chrism is at hand and there is time, confer confirmation after the baptism; in this case there is no postbaptismal anointing.

The minister of baptism who is a priest, a deacon, or a catechist or layperson having permission to distribute communion should, if this is possible, give the eucharist to the newly baptized person. In this case before the beginning of the celebration of the rite the blessed sacrament is placed reverently on a table covered with a white cloth.

373. In the case of a person who is at the point of death, that is, whose death is imminent, and time is short, the minister, omitting everything else, pours natural water (even if not blessed) on the head of the sick person, while   281

saying the usual sacramental form (see *Christian Initiation, General Introduction*, no. 23).

374. If persons who were baptized when in danger of death or at the point of death recover their health, they are to be given a suitable formation, be welcomed at the church in due time, and there receive the other sacraments of initiation. In such cases the guidelines given in nos. 400–410 for baptized but uncatechized adults are followed, with the necessary changes. The same guidelines should be applied when sick persons recover after receiving not only baptism but also confirmation and eucharist as viaticum.

282
294

CHRISTIAN INITIATION OF A PERSON IN DANGER OF DEATH

375. The minister greets the family and then speaks with   283
the sick person about his or her request for baptism and, if
the sick person is not a catechumen, about his or her reasons for conversion. After deciding to baptize him or her,
the minister should, if necessary, instruct the person
briefly.

376. Then the minister invites the family, the person desig-   284
nated as godparent, and the friends and neighbors present
to gather around the sick person and selects one or two of
those present as witnesses. Water, even if it is not blessed,
is prepared.

INTRODUCTORY RITES

OPENING DIALOGUE

377. The minister addresses the sick person in these or   285
similar words.

**Dear brother/sister, you have asked to be baptized be-
cause you wish to have eternal life. This is eternal
life: to know the one, true God and Jesus Christ,
whom he has sent. This is the faith of Christians. Do
you acknowledge this?**

Candidate:
I do.

Minister:
**As well as professing your faith in Jesus Christ, you
must also be willing to follow his commands, as
Christians do. Are you willing to accept this?**

Candidate:
I am.

Minister.
Are you prepared to live as Christians do?

Candidate:
I am.

Minister:
**Promise, therefore, that once you have recovered
your strength, you will try to know Christ better and
follow a course of Christian formation. Do you so
promise?**

Candidate:
I do.

AFFIRMATION BY THE GODPARENT AND WITNESSES

378. Turning to the godparent and to the witnesses, the   286
minister asks them the following questions in these or similar words.

**You have heard N.'s promise. As his/her godparent
do you promise to remind him/her of it and to help
him/her to learn the teaching of Christ, to take part
in the life of our community, and to bear witness as
a true Christian?**

Godparent:
I do.

Minister
**And will the rest of you, who have witnessed this
promise, assist him/her in fulfilling it?**

Witnesses:
We will.

Then the minister turns to the sick person and says:

**Therefore you will now be baptized into eternal life,
in accordance with the command of our Lord Jesus
Christ.**

LITURGY OF THE WORD

GOSPEL READING

379. According to time and circumstances, the minister   287
reads some words from a gospel and explains them. One of
the following may be used

1. John 3:1–6—*Unless you are born again, you will not see the kingdom of heaven.*

2. John 6:44–47—*Whoever believes has eternal life.*

3. Matthew 22:35–40—*This is the greatest and the first commandment.*

4. Matthew 28:18–20—*Go and teach all people my Gospel, baptizing them in the name of the Father, and of the Son, and of the Holy Spirit.*

5. Mark 1:9–11—*Jesus was baptized by John in the Jordan.*

INTERCESSIONS FOR THE CANDIDATE

380. The minister may adapt or shorten the intercessions according to the condition of the sick person. The intercessions may be omitted if the sick person appears to be tiring. The minister begins:

Let us pray to the God of mercy for our sick brother/ sister who has asked for the gift of baptism; let us pray for his/her godparent and for all his/her family and friends.

Assisting minister:

Father, increase his/her faith in Christ, your Son and our Savior; in faith we make our prayer:
R̸. Lord, hear us.

Assisting minister:

Grant his/her desire to have eternal life and enter the kingdom of heaven; in faith we make our prayer:
R̸. Lord, hear us.

Assisting minister:

Fulfill his/her hope of knowing you, the Creator of the world and the Father of all; in faith we make our prayer:
R̸. Lord, hear us.

Assisting minister:

Through baptism forgive his/her sins and make him/ her holy; in faith we make our prayer:
R̸. Lord, hear us.

288

Assisting minister:
**Grant him/her the salvation that Christ won by his
death and resurrection; in faith we make our prayer:**
R̸. Lord, hear us.

Assisting minister:
**In your love adopt him/her into your family; in faith
we make our prayer:**
R̸. Lord, hear us.

[Assisting minister:
**Restore him/her to health so that he/she may have the
time to know and imitate Christ more perfectly; in
faith we make our prayer:**
R̸. Lord, hear us.]

Assisting minister:
**Keep united in faith and love all who have been bap-
tized into the one Body of Christ; in faith we make
our prayer:**
R̸. Lord, hear us.

PRAYER OVER THE CANDIDATE
381. The minister concludes the intercessions with the fol-   289
lowing prayer.

Father,
**look kindly upon the faith and longing of your ser-
     vant N.;**
through this water
**by which you have chosen to give us birth from
     above,**
join him/her to Christ's death and resurrection.

Forgive all his/her sins,
adopt him/her as your own,
and count him/her among your holy people.

[Grant also that he/she may be restored to health,
to render you thanks in your Church
and grow in faithfulness to the teaching of Christ.]

We ask this through Christ our Lord.
R̸. Amen.

CELEBRATION OF BAPTISM

RENUNCIATION OF SIN

382. The minister first asks the sick person to renounce   290
sin. The minister may use the following formulary or the
longer formulary given in no. 356 and may make pertinent
adaptations (see no. 72).

Minister:
**Do you reject Satan,
and all his works,
and all his empty promises?**

Candidate:
I do.

PROFESSION OF FAITH

383. A profession of faith is then made. One of the follow-   290
ing formularies may be used.

A Minister:
**N., do you believe in God, the Father almighty, cre-
ator of heaven and earth?**

Candidate:
I do.

Minister:
**Do you believe in Jesus Christ, his only Son, our
Lord,
who was born of the Virgin Mary,
was crucified, died, and was buried,
rose from the dead,
and is now seated at the right hand of the Father?**

Candidate:
I do.

Minister:
**Do you believe in the Holy Spirit,
the holy catholic Church, the communion of saints,
the forgiveness of sins, the resurrection of the
body,
and the life everlasting?**

Candidate:
I do.

B Candidate:
I believe in God, the Father almighty,
creator of heaven and earth.

I believe in Jesus Christ, his only Son, our Lord.
He was conceived by the power of the Holy Spirit
and born of the Virgin Mary.
He suffered under Pontius Pilate,
was crucified, died, and was buried.
He descended to the dead.
On the third day he rose again.
He ascended into heaven,
and is seated at the right hand of the Father.
He will come again to judge the living and the
dead.

I believe in the Holy Spirit,
the holy catholic Church,
the communion of saints,
the forgiveness of sins,
the resurrection of the body,
and the life everlasting. Amen.

BAPTISM

384. The minister, using the name the sick person desires   291
to have, baptizes him or her, saying:

N., I baptize you in the name of the Father,

The minister pours water the first time.

and of the Son,

The minister pours water the second time.

and of the Holy Spirit.

The minister pours water the third time.

ANOINTING AFTER BAPTISM

385. If the minister of baptism is a deacon, he says the fol-   292
lowing prayer, then in silence anoints the newly baptized
with chrism on the crown of the head.

The God of power and Father of our Lord Jesus
  Christ
has freed you from sin
and brought you to new life
through water and the Holy Spirit.

He now anoints you with the chrism of salvation,
so that, united with his people,
you may remain for ever a member of Christ
who is Priest, Prophet, and King.

Newly baptized:
Amen.

386. If the minister is not a priest, the rite continues with
the celebration of viaticum (no. 393).

387. If neither confirmation nor viaticum will be celebrated, one of the alternative concluding rites (no. 399) follows baptism.

CELEBRATION OF CONFIRMATION

388. If the minister of baptism is a priest, he should also   293
confer confirmation.

If there is not sufficient time because of the condition of the
sick person, the "Invitation" (no. 389) may be omitted; it is
enough for the priest to anoint with chrism, while saying
the words "**N. be sealed, . . .**"; if possible, he first lays
hands on the sick person with the prayer "**All-powerful
God.**"

INVITATION

389. The priest first speaks briefly to the newly baptized in   293
the following or similar words.

**N., born again in Christ by baptism, you have be-
come a member of Christ and of his priestly people.
Now you are to share in the outpouring of the Holy
Spirit among us, the Spirit sent by the Lord upon his**

apostles at Pentecost and given by them and their successors to the baptized.

All pray in silence for a short time.

LAYING ON OF HANDS

390. The priest lays hands on the newly baptized and says   293
the following prayer.

All-powerful God, Father of our Lord Jesus Christ,
by water and the Holy Spirit
you freed your son/daughter from sin
and gave him/her new life.

Send your Holy Spirit upon him/her
to be his/her helper and guide.

Give him/her the spirit of wisdom and understand-
ing,
the spirit of right judgment and courage,
the spirit of knowledge and reverence.
Fill him/her with the spirit of wonder and awe in
your presence.

We ask this through Christ our Lord.
R̸. Amen.

ANOINTING WITH CHRISM

391. The priest dips his right thumb in the chrism and   293
makes the sign of the cross on the forehead of the one to
be confirmed as he says:

N., be sealed with the Gift of the Holy Spirit.

Newly confirmed:
Amen.

The priest adds:
Peace be with you.

Newly confirmed:
And also with you.

392. If viaticum will not be celebrated, one of the alternative concluding rites (no. 399) follows confirmation.

CELEBRATION OF VIATICUM

393. Communion as viaticum is given immediately after 294
confirmation or, if confirmation is not celebrated, immediately after the celebration of baptism.

INVITATION TO PRAYER

394. The minister addresses the sick person: if viaticum follows the celebration of confirmation, the minister uses option A or similar words; if confirmation is not celebrated
and viaticum follows baptism, the minister uses option B or similar words.

A

N., God our Father has freed you from your sins, has 294
given you a new birth and made you his son/
daughter in Christ. Before you partake of the body of
the Lord and in the spirit of that adoption which you
have received today, join us now in praying as our
Lord himself taught us.

Then the sick person and all present join the minister in the
Lord's Prayer.
Our Father . . .

B

N., God our Father has freed you from your sins, has 294
given you a new birth and made you his son/
daughter in Christ. Soon, God willing, you will receive the fullness of the Holy Spirit through confirmation. Before you partake of the body of the Lord
and in the spirit of that adoption which you have received today, join us now in praying as our Lord himself taught us.

Then the sick person and all present join the minister in the
Lord's Prayer.
Our Father . . .

COMMUNION AS VIATICUM

395. The minister shows the eucharistic bread to those 294
present, using one of the following formularies.

A
Jesus Christ is the food for our journey;
he calls us to the heavenly table.

B
This is the Lamb of God
who takes away the sins of the world.
Happy are those who are called to his supper.

The sick person and all who are to receive communion say:
Lord, I am not worthy to receive you,
but only say the word and I shall be healed.

The minister goes to the sick person and, showing the
blessed sacrament, says:
The body of Christ.

The sick person answers:
Amen.

Then the minister says:
The blood of Christ.

The sick person answers:
Amen.

Immediately, or after giving communion to the sick person,   PC293
the minister adds the form for viaticum.
May the Lord Jesus Christ protect you and lead you
to eternal life.

The sick person answers:
Amen.

Others present who wish to receive communion then do so
in the usual way.

A short period of silent prayer may follow.

PRAYER AFTER COMMUNION
396. The minister says a concluding prayer.   294

Let us pray.

Pause for silent prayer, if this has not preceded.

**Father,
almighty and eternal God,
our brother/sister has received the eucharist
with faith in you and in your healing power.
May the body and blood of Christ
bring him/her eternal healing in mind and body.**

**We ask this in the name of Jesus the Lord.
R̶̷. Amen.**

CONCLUDING RITES

BLESSING

397. The minister blesses the sick person and the others   PC295
present, using one of the following blessings.

A   A minister who is a priest or deacon says:
**May the Lord be with you to protect you.
R̶̷. Amen.**

**May the Lord guide you and give you strength.
R̶̷. Amen.**

**May the Lord watch over you, keep you in his care,
and bless you with his peace.
R̶̷. Amen.**

**May almighty God bless you,
the Father, and the Son, ✠ and the Holy Spirit.
R̶̷. Amen.**

B   A lay minister invokes God's blessing and signs himself or herself with the sign of the cross, saying:
**May the Lord bless us,
protect us from all evil,
and bring us to everlasting life.
R̶̷. Amen.**

SIGN OF PEACE

398. The minister and the others present may then give   PC296
the sick person the sign of peace.

ALTERNATIVE CONCLUDING RITES

399. When the celebration is concluded after confirmation   292
and viaticum is not given, the rite is concluded by use of
option A. When the celebration concludes immediately after
baptism and neither confirmation nor viaticum is celebrated, the rite is concluded by use of option B.

A   The minister addresses the sick person in the following words.
**N., God our Father has freed you from your sins, has
given you a new birth and made you his son/
daughter in Christ. Soon, God willing, you will approach the altar of God to share the food of life at
the table of his sacrifice. In the spirit of that adoption which you have received today, join us now in
praying as our Lord himself taught us.**

Then the sick person and all present join the minister in
saying:
Our Father . . .

The blessing (no. 397) and sign of peace (no. 398) may then
be given.

B   The minister addresses the sick person in the following
words.
**N., God our Father has freed you from your sins, has
given you a new birth and made you his son/
daughter in Christ. Soon, God willing, you will receive the fullness of the Holy Spirit through confirmation and will approach the altar of God to share
the food of life at the table of his sacrifice. In his
spirit of that adoption which you have received today, join us now in praying as our Lord himself
taught us.**

Then the sick person and all present join the minister in
saying:
Our Father . . .

The blessing (no. 397) and sign of peace (no. 398) may then
be given.

4. PREPARATION OF UNCATECHIZED ADULTS FOR CONFIRMATION AND EUCHARIST

If then you have been raised with Christ, seek the things that are above, where Christ is seated at the right hand of God

400. The following pastoral guidelines concern adults who were baptized as infants either as Roman Catholics or as members of another Christian community but did not receive further catechetical formation nor, consequently, the sacraments of confirmation and eucharist. These suggestions may also be applied to similar cases, especially that of an adult who recovers after being baptized in danger of death or at the point of death (see no. 374).   **295 USA**

Even though uncatechized adults have not yet heard the message of the mystery of Christ, their status differs from that of catechumens, since by baptism they have already become members of the Church and children of God. Hence their conversion is based on the baptism they have already received, the effects of which they must develop.

401. As in the case of catechumens, the preparation of these adults requires a considerable time (see no. 76), during which the faith infused in baptism must grow in them and take deep root through the pastoral formation they receive. A program of training, catechesis suited to their needs, contact with the community of the faithful, and participation in certain liturgical rites are needed in order to strengthen them in the Christian life.   **296**

402. For the most part the plan of catechesis corresponds to the one laid down for catechumens (see no. 75,1). But in the process of catechesis the priest, deacon, or catechist should take into account that these adults have a special status because they are already baptized.   **297**

403. Just as it helps catechumens, the Christian community should also help these adults by its love and prayer (see nos. 4 and 75,2) and by testifying to their suitability when it is time for them to be admitted to the sacraments (see nos. 120, 121).   **298**

404. A sponsor presents these adults to the community   299
(see no. 10). During the period of their catechetical formation, they all choose godparents (a godfather, a godmother,
or both) approved by the priest. Their godparents work
with these adults as the representatives of the community
and have the same responsibilities as the godparents have
toward catechumens (see no. 11). The same persons who
were the godparents at the baptism of these adults may be
chosen as godparents at this time, provided they are truly
capable of carrying out the responsibilities of godparents.

405. The period of preparation is made holy by means of   300
liturgical celebrations. The first of these is a rite by which
the adults are welcomed into the community and acknowledge themselves to be part of it because they have already
been marked with the seal of baptism. [The Rite of Welcoming the Candidates, which follows in Part II, 4 A, is provided for this purpose.]

406. Once a rite of reception has been celebrated, these   301
adults take part in celebrations of the word of God, both
those of the entire Christian assembly and those celebrations arranged specially for the benefit of the catechumens
(see nos. 81–84).

407. As a sign of God's activity in this work of prepara-   302
tion, some of the rites belonging to the catechumenate, es-   USA
pecially suited to the condition and spiritual needs of these
baptized adults, can be used to advantage. Among these
are the presentation of the Creed (nos. 157–162) and of the
Lord's Prayer (nos. 178–182) or also a presentation of a
book of the Gospels (no. 64). [The additional rites in Part II,
4 B, 4 C, and 4 D, may also be used in accordance with the
individual needs and circumstances of the candidates.]

408. The period of catechesis for these adults should be   303
properly coordinated with the liturgical year. This is particularly true of its final phase, which should as a rule coincide
with Lent. During the Lenten season penitential services
should be arranged in such a way as to prepare these
adults for the celebration of the sacrament of penance.

409. The high point of their entire formation will normally   304
be the Easter Vigil. At that time they will make a profession
of the faith in which they were baptized, receive the sacra-

ment of confirmation, and take part in the eucharist. If, because neither the bishop nor another authorized minister is present, confirmation cannot be given at the Easter Vigil, it is to be celebrated as soon as possible and, if this can be arranged, during the Easter season.

410. These adults will complete their Christian formation and become fully integrated into the community by going through the period of postbaptismal catechesis or mystagogy with the newly baptized members of the Christian community.

305

OPTIONAL RITES FOR BAPTIZED BUT UNCATECHIZED ADULTS

4A. RITE OF WELCOMING THE CANDIDATES

Teach us your ways, O Lord

411. This optional rite welcomes baptized but previously uncatechized adults who are seeking to complete their Christian initiation through the sacraments of confirmation and eucharist or to be received into the full communion of the Catholic Church.

412. The prayers and ritual gestures acknowledge that such candidates are already part of the community because they have been marked by baptism. Now the Church surrounds them with special care and support as they prepare to be sealed with the gift of the Spirit in confirmation and take their place at the banquet table of Christ's sacrifice.

413. Once formally welcomed into the life of the community, these adults, besides regularly attending Sunday Eucharist, take part in celebrations of the word of God in the full Christian assembly and in celebrations arranged especially for the benefit of the candidates.

414. The rite will take place on specified days throughout the year (see no. 18) that are suited to local conditions.

415. When the rite of welcoming candidates for the sacraments of confirmation and eucharist is to be combined with the rite of acceptance into the order of catechumens, the alternate rite found on page 287 (Appendix I, Rite 1) is used.

RITE OF WELCOMING THE CANDIDATES

416. When this rite is celebrated within Mass, the entrance song or antiphon is sung as usual. Because they are already numbered among the baptized, the candidates are seated in a prominent place among the faithful.

GREETING

417. The celebrant greets the candidates in a friendly manner. He speaks to them, their sponsors, and all present,

pointing out the joy and happiness of the Church in welcoming them. He reminds the assembly that these candidates have already been baptized. If it seems opportune, he may also indicate briefly the particular path which has led the candidates to seek the completion of their Christian initiation.

Then he invites the sponsors and candidates to come forward. As they are taking their places before the celebrant, an appropriate song may be sung, for example, Psalm 63:1-8.

OPENING DIALOGUE

418. Unless the candidates are already known to all present, the celebrant asks for or calls out their given names. The candidates answer one by one, even if, because of a large number, the question is asked only once. One of the following formularies or similar words may be used.

A   The celebrant asks:
What is your name?

Candidate:
N.

B   The celebrant calls out the name of each candidate.

The candidate answers:
Present.

The celebrant continues with the following question for the individual candidates or, when there are a large number, for the candidates to answer as a group. The celebrant may use other words than those provided in asking the candidates about their intentions and may let them answer in their own words.

Celebrant:
What do you ask of God's Church?

Candidate:
To be accepted as a candidate for catechetical instruction leading to confirmation and eucharist (*or:* reception into the full communion of the Catholic Church).

CANDIDATES' DECLARATION OF INTENT

419. The celebrant addresses the candidates, adapting one of the following formularies or similar words to the answers received in the opening dialogue.

**A Blessed be the God and Father of our Lord Jesus Christ, who, in his great mercy has given us a new birth unto a living hope, a hope which draws its life from Christ's resurrection from the dead. By baptism into Christ Jesus, this hope of glory became your own. Christ opened for you the way of the Gospel that leads to eternal life. Now, under the guidance of the Holy Spirit, you desire to continue that journey of faith.
Are you prepared to reflect more deeply on the mystery of your baptism, to listen with us to the apostles' instruction, and to join with us in a life of prayer and service?**

Candidates:
I am.

B Celebrant:
Please declare before this community the reasons why you desire to enter more fully in the life of the Church.

The candidates respond with a brief personal witness.

AFFIRMATION BY THE SPONSORS AND THE ASSEMBLY

420. Then the celebrant turns to the sponsors and the assembly and asks them in these or similar words.

Sponsors, you now present these candidates to us. Are you, and all who are gathered with us, ready to help these candidates complete their Christian initiation (*or:* prepare for reception into the full communion of the Catholic Church)?

All:
We are.

With hands joined, the celebrant says:

**Father of mercy,
we thank you for these your servants.
You have already consecrated them in baptism
and now you call them
to the fullness of the Church's sacramental life:
we praise you, Lord, and we bless you.**

All sing or say:
We praise you, Lord, and we bless you.

SIGNING OF THE CANDIDATES WITH THE CROSS

421. Next the cross is traced on the forehead of the candidates; at the discretion of the celebrant the signing of one, several, or all of the senses may follow. The celebrant alone says the formularies accompanying each signing.

SIGNING OF THE FOREHEAD

422. The celebrant speaks to the candidates in these or similar words.

Dear candidates, you have expressed your desire to share fully in the life of the Catholic Church. I now mark you with the sign of Christ's cross and call upon your catechists and sponsors to do the same.

Then the celebrant makes the sign of the cross over all together, as a cross is traced by a sponsor or catechist on the forehead of each candidate. The celebrant says:

**Receive the cross on your forehead
as a reminder of your baptism into
Christ's saving death and resurrection.**

All sing or say the following or another suitable acclamation.
Glory and praise to you, Lord Jesus Christ!

SIGNING OF THE OTHER SENSES

423. The signing is carried out by the catechists or the sponsors. (If required by special circumstances, this may be done by assisting priests or deacons.) The signing of each sense may be followed by an acclamation in praise of

Christ, for example, "Glory and praise to you, Lord Jesus Christ!"

While the ears are being signed, the celebrant says:
Receive the sign of the cross on your ears,
that you may hear the voice of the Lord.

While the eyes are being signed:
Receive the sign of the cross on your eyes,
that you may see the glory of God.

While the lips are being signed:
Receive the sign of the cross on your lips,
that you may respond to the word of God.

While the breast is being signed:
Receive the sign of the cross over your heart,
that Christ may dwell there by faith.

While the shoulders are being signed:
Receive the sign of the cross on your shoulders,
that you may bear the gentle yoke of Christ.

[While the hands are being signed:
Receive the sign of the cross on your hands,
that Christ may be known in the work which you do.

While the feet are being signed:
Receive the sign of the cross on your feet,
that you may walk in the way of Christ.]

Without touching them the celebrant alone makes the sign of the cross over all the candidates at once (or, if they are few, over each individually), saying:

I sign you with the sign of eternal life
in the name of the Father, and of the Son, ✚
and of the Holy Spirit.

Candidates:
Amen.

CONCLUDING PRAYER

424. The celebrant concludes the signing of the forehead (and senses) with the opening prayer for the Mass of the day or with the following prayer.

Let us pray.

Almighty God,
by the cross and resurrection of your Son
you have given life to your people.

In baptism these your servants accepted the sign of
**   the cross:**
make them living proof of its saving power
and help them to persevere in the footsteps of Christ.

We ask this through Christ our Lord.
R̵. Amen.

LITURGY OF THE WORD

INSTRUCTION
425. The celebrant next speaks briefly to the candidates
and their sponsors, helping them to understand the dignity
of God's word proclaimed and heard in the church.

READINGS
426. The readings are those assigned for the day. According to the norms of the Lectionary, other appropriate readings may be substituted.

HOMILY
427. A homily follows that explains the readings.

PRESENTATION OF A BIBLE
428. A book containing the Gospels may be given to the
candidates by the celebrant. The celebrant may use words
suited to the gift presented, for example, **"Receive the Gos-**
pel of Jesus Christ, the Son of God." The candidates may
respond in an appropriate way.

PROFESSION OF FAITH
429. On Sundays and solemnities the profession of faith is
recited.

GENERAL INTERCESSIONS
430. Then the sponsors and the whole congregation join in
the general intercessions. One or more of the following in-

tentions for the candidates are added to the intentions for
the Church and the whole world.

Assisting minister:
**That God our Father may reveal his Christ to these
candidates more and more with every passing day,
let us pray to the Lord:**
℟. **Lord, hear our prayer.**

Assisting minister:
**That these candidates may come to a deeper apprecia-
tion of the gift of their baptism, which joined them
to Christ, let us pray to the Lord:**
℟. **Lord, hear our prayer.**

Assisting minister:
**That they may find in our community compelling
signs of unity and generous love, let us pray to the
Lord:**
℟. **Lord, hear our prayer.**

Assisting minister:
**That their hearts and ours may become more respon-
sive to the needs of others, let us pray to the Lord:**
℟. **Lord, hear our prayer.**

Assisting minister:
**That in due time these candidates may be (embraced
by the Father's merciful forgiveness,) sealed with the
gift of the Holy Spirit and know the joy of being one
with us at the table of Christ's sacrifice, let us pray to
the Lord:**
℟. **Lord, hear our prayer.**

PRAYER OVER THE CANDIDATES

431. After the intercessions, the celebrant, with hands outstretched over the candidates, says the following prayer.

**Almighty and eternal God,
whose love gathers us together as one,
receive the prayers of your people.**

**Look kindly on these your servants,
already consecrated to you in baptism,
and draw them into the fullness of faith.**

**Keep your family one in the bonds of love
through Christ our Lord.**

R̸. Amen.

DISMISSAL OF THE ASSEMBLY

432. If the eucharist is not to be celebrated, the entire assembly is dismissed by use of the following formulary or similar words.

Celebrant:
Go in peace, and may the Lord remain with you always.

All:
Thanks be to God.

An appropriate song may conclude the celebration.

LITURGY OF THE EUCHARIST

433. The liturgy of the eucharist begins as usual with the preparation of the gifts.

4B. RITE OF SENDING THE CANDIDATES FOR RECOGNITION BY THE BISHOP AND FOR THE CALL TO CONTINUING CONVERSION

USA

My sheep hear my voice and follow me

434. This optional rite is provided for parishes whose candidates seeking to complete their Christian initiation or to be received into the full communion of the Catholic Church will be recognized by the bishop in a subsequent celebration (for example, at the cathedral with the bishop).

435. Because he is the sign of unity within the particular Church, it is fitting for the bishop to recognize these candidates. It is the responsibility of the parish community, however, to prepare the candidates for their fuller life in the Church. Through the experience of worship, daily life and service in the parish community the candidates deepen their appreciation of the Church's tradition and universal character.

This rite offers that local community the opportunity to express its joy in the candidates' decision and to send them forth to the celebration of recognition assured of the parish's care and support.

436. The rite is celebrated in the parish church at a suitable time prior to the rite of recognition and call to continuing conversion.

437. When the rite of sending candidates for recognition is to be combined with the rite of sending catechumens for election, the alternate rite found on page 301 (Appendix I, Rite 2) is used.

RITE OF SENDING THE CANDIDATES FOR RECOGNITION BY THE BISHOP AND FOR THE CALL TO CONTINUING CONVERSION

LITURGY OF THE WORD

HOMILY

438. After the readings the celebrant gives the homily. This should be suited to the actual situation and should address not just the candidates but the entire community of the faithful, so that all will be encouraged to give good example and to accompany the candidates along the path leading to their complete initiation.

PRESENTATION OF THE CANDIDATES

439. After the homily, the priest in charge of the candidates' formation, or a deacon, a catechist, or a representative of the community, presents the candidates, using the following or similar words.

Reverend Father, these candidates, whom I now present to you, are beginning their final period of preparation for the sacraments of confirmation and eucharist (*or:* preparation to be received into the full communion of the Catholic Church). They have found strength in God's grace and support in our community's prayers and example.

Now they ask that they be recognized for the progress they have made in their spiritual formation and that they receive the assurance of our blessings and prayers as they go forth for recognition by Bishop N. this afternoon (*or:* next Sunday [*or:* specify the day]).

The celebrant replies:
Those who are to be recognized, come forward, together with your sponsors.

One by one, the candidates are called by name. Each candidate, accompanied by a sponsor, comes forward and stands before the celebrant.

AFFIRMATION BY THE SPONSORS [AND THE
ASSEMBLY]

440. Then the celebrant addresses the assembly in these or
similar words.

**My dear friends, these candidates, already one with
us by reason of their baptism in Christ, have asked
to complete their initiation (*or:* to be received into
the full communion of the Catholic Church). Those
who know them have judged them to be sincere in
their desire. During the period of their catechetical
formation they have listened to the word of Christ
and endeavored to follow his commands more perfectly; they have shared the company of their Christian brothers and sisters in this community and
joined with them in prayer.**

**And so I announce to all of you here that our commu-
nity ratifies their desire to complete their initiation
(*or:* to be received into full communion). Therefore, I
ask their sponsors to state their opinion once again,
so that all of you may hear.**

He addresses the sponsors:
**As God is your witness, do you consider these candi-
dates ready to receive the sacraments of confirmation
and eucharist?**

Sponsors:
We do.

[When appropriate in the circumstances, the celebrant may
also ask the entire assembly to express its approval of the
candidates.]

441. The celebrant concludes the affirmation by the following:

**And now, my dear friends, I address you. Your own
sponsors (and this entire community) have spoken in
your favor. The Church, in the name of Christ, accepts their testimony and sends you to Bishop N.,
who will exhort you to live in deeper conformity to
the life of Christ.**

GENERAL INTERCESSIONS

442. Then the sponsors and the whole congregation join in the general intercessions. One or more of the following intentions for the candidates are added to the intentions for the Church and the whole world.

Assisting minister:

That these candidates may be freed from selfishness and learn to put others first, let us pray to the Lord:
R̊. Lord, hear our prayer.

Assisting minister:

That their godparents and sponsors may be living examples of the Gospel, let us pray to the Lord:
R̊. Lord, hear our prayer.

Assisting minister:

That their teachers may always convey to them the beauty of God's word, let us pray to the Lord:
R̊. Lord, hear our prayer.

Assisting minister:

That these candidates may share with others the joy they have found in their friendship with Jesus, let us pray to the Lord:
R̊. Lord, hear our prayer.

Assisting minister:

That our community, during the coming Lenten season, may grow in charity and be constant in prayer, let us pray to the Lord:
R̊. Lord, hear our prayer.

PRAYER OVER THE CANDIDATES

443. After the intercessions, the celebrant, with hands outstretched over the candidates, says the following prayer.

Father of love and power,
it is your will to establish everything in Christ
and to draw us into his all-embracing love.

Guide these candidates in the days and weeks ahead:
strengthen them in their vocation,
build them into the kingdom of your Son,
and seal them with the Spirit of your promise.

We ask this through Christ our Lord.

R̶. Amen.

DISMISSAL OF THE ASSEMBLY

444. If the eucharist is not to be celebrated, the entire assembly is dismissed by use of the following formulary or similar words.

Celebrant:
Go in peace, and may the Lord remain with you always.

All:
Thanks be to God.

An appropriate song may conclude the celebration.

LITURGY OF THE EUCHARIST

445. When the eucharist is to follow, intercessory prayer is resumed with the usual general intercessions for the needs of the Church and the whole world; then, if required, the profession of faith is said. But for pastoral reasons these general intercessions and the profession of faith may be omitted. The liturgy of the eucharist then begins as usual with the preparation of the gifts.

4C. RITE OF CALLING THE CANDIDATES   USA
TO CONTINUING CONVERSION

As members of one body, you have been called to his peace

446. This rite may be celebrated with baptized but previously uncatechized adults who wish to complete their Christian initiation through the sacraments of confirmation and eucharist or who wish to be received into the full communion of the Catholic Church.

447. The rite is intended for celebrations in communities where there are no catechumens.

448. The rite is celebrated at the beginning of Lent. The presiding celebrant is the pastor of the parish.

449. If the calling of candidates to continuing conversion is to be combined with the rite of election of catechumens (either in a parish celebration or at one in which the bishop is celebrant) the alternate rite given on page 309 (Appendix I, Rite 3) is used.

RITE OF CALLING THE CANDIDATES TO CONTINUING CONVERSION

LITURGY OF THE WORD

HOMILY

450. After the readings, the celebrant gives the homily. This should be suited to the actual situation and should address not just the candidates but the entire community of the faithful, so that all will be encouraged to give good example and to accompany the candidates in their final preparation leading to the celebration of confirmation and eucharist.

PRESENTATION OF THE CANDIDATES FOR CONFIRMATION AND EUCHARIST

451. After the homily, the priest in charge of the candidates' formation, or a deacon, a catechist, or a representative of the community, presents the candidates, using the following or similar words.

Reverend Father, (since Easter is drawing near,) I am pleased to present to you the candidates who seek to complete their Christian initiation (*or:* who are preparing to be received into the full communion of the Catholic Church). They have found strength in God's grace and support in our community's prayers and example.

Now they ask that after this Lenten season, they be admitted to confirmation and the eucharist (*or:* to full eucharistic sharing).

The celebrant replies:
Those who desire to participate fully in the sacramental life of the Church, come forward, together with your sponsors.

One by one, the candidates are called by name. Each candidate, accompanied by a sponsor, comes forward and stands before the celebrant.

AFFIRMATION BY THE SPONSORS [AND THE ASSEMBLY]

452. Then the celebrant addresses the assembly. If he has taken part in the earlier deliberation on the candidates' suitableness (see no. 122), he may use either option A or option B or similar words; if he has not taken part in the earlier deliberation, he uses option B or similar words.

A

My dear friends, these candidates, our brothers and sisters, have asked to be able to participate fully in the sacramental life of the Catholic Church. Those who know them have judged them to be sincere in their desire. During the period of their preparation they have reflected on the mystery of their baptism and have come to appreciate more deeply the presence of Christ in their lives. They have shared the company of their brothers and sisters, joined with them in prayer, and endeavored to follow Christ's commands more perfectly.

And so I am pleased to recognize their desire to participate fully in the sacramental life of the Church. I ask their sponsors now to state their opinion once again, so that all of you may hear.

He addresses the sponsors:
Do you consider these candidates ready to receive the sacraments of confirmation and the eucharist (or: to be received into the full communion of the Catholic Church)?

Sponsors:
We do.

453. When appropriate in the circumstances, the celebrant may also ask the entire assembly to express its approval of the candidates in these or similar words:

Celebrant:
Now I ask you, the members of this community: Are you willing to affirm the testimony expressed about these candidates and support them in faith,

prayer, and example as they prepare to participate more fully in the Church's sacraments?

All:
We are.

B
The Christian life and the demands that flow from the sacraments cannot be taken lightly. Therefore, before granting these candidates their request to share fully in the Church's sacraments, it is important that the Church hear the testimony of their sponsors about their readiness.

He addresses the sponsors:
Have they faithfully listened to the apostles' instruction proclaimed by the Church?

Sponsors:
They have.

Celebrant:
Have they come to a deeper appreciation of their baptism, in which they were joined to Christ and his Church?

Sponsors:
They have.

Celebrant:
Have they reflected sufficiently on the tradition of the Church, which is their heritage, and joined their brothers and sisters in prayer?

Sponsors:
They have.

Celebrant:
Have they advanced in a life of love and service of others?

Sponsors:
They have.

When appropriate in the circumstances, the celebrant may also ask the entire assembly to express its approval of the candidates in these or similar words:

Celebrant:
And now I speak to you, my brothers and sisters in this assembly:
Are you ready to support the testimony expressed about these candidates and include them in your prayer and affection as we move toward Easter?

All:
We are.

ACT OF RECOGNITION

454. Then the celebrant says:

N. and N., the Church recognizes your desire (to be sealed with the gift of the Holy Spirit and) to have a place at Christ's eucharistic table. Join with us this Lent in a spirit of repentance. Hear the Lord's call to conversion and be faithful to your baptismal covenant.

Candidates:
Thanks be to God.

Then the celebrant turns to the sponsors and instructs them in the following or similar words.
Sponsors, continue to support these candidates with your guidance and concern. May they see in you a love for the Church and a sincere desire for doing good. Lead them this Lent to the joys of the Easter mysteries.

He invites them to place their hand on the shoulder of the candidate whom they are receiving into their care, or to make some other gesture to indicate the same intent.

GENERAL INTERCESSIONS

455. Then the sponsors and the whole congregation join in the general intercessions. One or more of the following intentions for the candidates are added to the intentions for the Church and the whole world.

Assisting minister:
That these candidates may come to a deeper appreciation of their baptism into Christ's death and resurrection, let us pray to the Lord:
R̸. Lord, hear our prayer.

Assisting minister:
That God bless those who have nurtured these candidates in faith, let us pray to the Lord:
R̸. Lord, hear our prayer.

Assisting minister:
That these candidates may embrace the discipline of Lent as a means of purification and approach the sacrament of reconciliation with trust in God's mercy, let us pray to the Lord:
R̸. Lord, hear our prayer.

Assisting minister:
That they may open their hearts to the promptings of God's Holy Spirit, let us pray to the Lord:
R̸. Lord, hear our prayer.

Assisting minister:
That they may approach the table of Christ's sacrifice with thanksgiving and praise, let us pray to the Lord:
R̸. Lord, hear our prayer.

Assisting minister:
That our community, during this Lenten period, may grow in charity and be constant in prayer, let us pray to the Lord:
R̸. Lord, hear our prayer.

PRAYER OVER THE CANDIDATES

456. After the intercessions, the celebrant, with hands outstretched over the candidates, says the following prayer.

Lord God,
whose love brings us to life
and whose mercy gives us new birth,
look favorably upon these candidates,
and conform their lives
to the pattern of Christ's suffering.

May he become their wealth and wisdom,
and may they know in their lives
the power flowing from his resurrection,
who is Lord for ever and ever.

℞. Amen.

DISMISSAL OF THE ASSEMBLY

457. If the eucharist is not to be celebrated, the entire assembly is dismissed by use of the following formulary or similar words.

Celebrant:
Go in peace, and may the Lord remain with you always.

All:
Thanks be to God.

An appropriate song may conclude the celebration.

LITURGY OF THE EUCHARIST

458. The liturgy of the eucharist begins as usual with the preparation of the gifts.

4D. PENITENTIAL RITE (SCRUTINY)

May you all be kept blameless, spirit, soul and body, for the coming of our Lord Jesus Christ

459. This penitential rite can serve to mark the Lenten purification of baptized but previously uncatechized adults who are preparing to receive the sacraments of confirmation and eucharist or to be received into the full communion of the Catholic Church. It is held within a celebration of the word of God as a kind of scrutiny, similar to the scrutinies for catechumens.

460. Because the penitential rite normally belongs to the period of final preparation for the sacraments, its celebration presumes that the candidates are approaching the maturity of faith and understanding requisite for fuller life in the community.

461. Along with the candidates, their sponsors and the larger liturgical assembly also participate in the celebration of the penitential rite. Therefore the rite is to be adapted in such a way that it benefits all the participants. This penitential rite may also help to prepare the candidates to celebrate the sacrament of penance.

462. This penitential rite may be celebrated on the Second Sunday of Lent or on a Lenten weekday, if the candidates are to receive the sacraments of confirmation and eucharist and/or be received into the full communion of the Catholic Church at Easter; if not, at the most suitable time.

463. This penitential rite is intended solely for celebrations with baptized adults preparing for confirmation and eucharist or reception into the full communion of the Catholic Church. Because the prayer of exorcism in the three scrutinies for catechumens who have received the Church's election properly belongs to the elect and uses numerous images referring to their approaching baptism, those scrutinies of the elect and this penitential rite for those preparing for confirmation and eucharist have been kept separate and distinct. Thus, no combined rite has been included in Appendix I.

PENITENTIAL RITE (SCRUTINY)
(SECOND SUNDAY OF LENT)

GREETING AND INTRODUCTION

464. The priest welcomes the assembly and in a few words explains that the rite will have different meanings for the different participants: the candidates who are already baptized, particularly those who are preparing to celebrate the sacrament of penance for the first time, the sponsors, catechists, priests, etc. All these participants in their own different ways are going to hear the comforting message of pardon for sin, for which they will praise the Father's mercy.

A song may be sung that joyfully expresses faith in the mercy of God the Father.

PRAYER

465. The celebrant then says the prayer for the Second Sunday of Lent or, on another day, the following prayer.

Lord of infinite compassion and steadfast love,
your sons and daughters stand before you
in humility and trust.
Look with compassion on us
as we acknowledge our sinfulness.
Stretch out your hand
to save us and raise us up.
Do not allow the power of darkness
to triumph over us,
but keep us free from sin
as members of Christ's body,
and sheep of your own flock.

We ask this through our Lord Jesus Christ, your Son,
who lives and reigns with you and the Holy Spirit,
one God, for ever and ever.

℟. Amen.

LITURGY OF THE WORD

READINGS

466. On the Second Sunday of Lent the readings for Mass are those assigned by the Lectionary for Mass. On other days, appropriate readings from the Lectionary are used.

HOMILY

467. After the readings the celebrant explains the sacred texts in the homily. He should prepare all those in the assembly for conversion and repentance and give the meaning of the penitential rite (scrutiny) in the light of the Lenten liturgy and of the spiritual journey of the candidates.

INVITATION TO SILENT PRAYER

468. After the homily, the candidates with their sponsors come forward and stand before the celebrant.

The celebrant first addresses the assembly of the faithful, inviting them to pray in silence and to ask that the candidates will be given a spirit of repentance, a deepened sense of sin, and the true freedom of the children of God.

The celebrant then addresses the candidates, inviting them also to pray in silence and suggesting that as a sign of their inner spirit of repentance they bow their heads or kneel; he concludes his remarks with the following or similar words.

Candidates, bow your heads [kneel down] and pray.

The candidates bow their heads or kneel, and all pray for some time in silence. After the period of silent prayer, the community and the candidates stand for the intercessions.

INTERCESSIONS FOR THE CANDIDATES

469. Then the sponsors and the whole congregation join in the intercessions for the candidates. If the eucharist is to be celebrated, intentions for the Church and for the whole world should be added to the following intentions for the candidates.

Celebrant:
My brothers and sisters, let us pray for these candidates (N. and N.). Christ has already ransomed them in baptism. Now they seek the forgiveness of their

sins and the healing of their weakness, so that they may be ready to be (sealed with the gift of the Father and) fed at the Lord's table. Let us also pray for ourselves, who seek the mercy of Christ.

Assisting minister:
That these candidates may come to a deeper appreciation of their baptism into Christ's death and resurrection, let us pray to the Lord:
℟. Lord, hear our prayer.

Assisting minister:
That these candidates may embrace the discipline of Lent as a means of purification and approach the sacrament of reconciliation with trust in God's mercy, let us pray to the Lord:
℟. Lord, hear our prayer.

Assisting minister:
That they may grow to love and seek virtue and holiness of life, let us pray to the Lord:
℟. Lord, hear our prayer.

Assisting minister:
That they may renounce self and put others first, let us pray to the Lord:
℟. Lord, hear our prayer.

Assisting minister:
That they may share with others the joy they have found in their faith, let us pray to the Lord:
℟. Lord, hear our prayer.

Assisting minister:
That they may accept the call to conversion with an open heart and not hesitate to make the personal changes it may require of them, let us pray to the Lord:
℟. Lord, hear our prayer.

Assisting minister:
That the Holy Spirit, who searches every heart, may help them to overcome their weakness through his power, let us pray to the Lord:
℟. Lord, hear our prayer.

Assisting minister:
**That their families also may put their hope in Christ
and find peace and holiness in him, let us pray to
the Lord:**
℟. **Lord, hear our prayer.**

Assisting minister:
**That we ourselves in preparation for the Easter feast
may seek a change of heart, give ourselves to prayer,
and persevere in our good works, let us pray to the
Lord:**
℟. **Lord, hear our prayer.**

PRAYER OVER THE CANDIDATES

470. After the intercessions, the rite continues with the
prayer over the candidates, option A (particularly when
celebrated on the Second Sunday of Lent) or option B.

A The celebrant faces the candidates and, with hands
joined, says:

**Lord God,
in the mystery of the transfiguration
your Son revealed his glory to the disciples
and prepared them for his death and resurrection.**

**Open the minds and hearts of these candidates
to the presence of Christ in their lives.
May they humbly acknowledge their sins and fail-
    ings
and be freed of whatever obstacles and falsehoods
    that
keep them from adhering wholeheartedly to your
    kingdom.**

We ask this through Christ our Lord.
℟. **Amen.**

Here, if this can be done conveniently, the celebrant lays
hands on each one of the candidates.
Then, with hands outstretched over all of them, he continues:

**Lord Jesus,
you are the only-begotten Son,**

whose kingdom these candidates acknowledge
and whose glory they seek.
Pour out upon them the power of your Spirit,
that they may be fearless witnesses to your Gospel
and one with us in the communion of love,
for you are Lord for ever and ever.

R̸. Amen.

B The celebrant faces the candidates and, with hands
joined, says:

Lord our God,
you created us in love
and redeemed us in mercy
through the blood of your Son.
Enlighten these men and women by your grace,
that, clearly seeing their sins and failings,
they may place all their trust in your mercy
and resist all that is deceitful and harmful.

We ask this through Christ our Lord.
R̸. Amen.

Here, if this can be done conveniently, the celebrant lays
hands on each one of the candidates.
Then, with hands outstretched over all of them, he continues:

Lord Jesus,
whose love reaches out in mercy
to embrace and heal the contrite of heart,
lead these candidates along the way of holiness,
and heal the wounds of their sins.
May they ever keep safe in all its fullness
the gift your love once gave them
and your mercy now restores,
for you are Lord for ever and ever.

R̸. Amen.

An appropriate song may be sung, for example, Psalm 6,
26, 32, 38, 39, 40, 51, 116:1–9, 130, 139, or 142.

DISMISSAL OF THE ASSEMBLY

471. If the eucharist is not to be celebrated, the entire assembly is dismissed by use of the following formulary or similar words.

Celebrant:
Go in peace, and may the Lord remain with you always.

All:
Thanks be to God.

An appropriate song may conclude the celebration.

LITURGY OF THE EUCHARIST

472. When the eucharist is to follow, the profession of faith, if required, is said. But for pastoral reasons it may be omitted. The liturgy of the eucharist then begins as usual with the preparation of the gifts.

5. RECEPTION OF BAPTIZED CHRISTIANS INTO THE FULL COMMUNION OF THE CATHOLIC CHURCH

All of you are one, united in Christ Jesus

473. This is the liturgical rite by which a person born and **R1** baptized in a separated ecclesial Community is received, according to the Latin rite,[1] into the full communion of the Catholic Church. The rite is so arranged that no greater burden than necessary (see Acts 15:28) is required for the establishment of communion and unity.[2]

474. In the case of Eastern Christians who enter into the **R2** fullness of Catholic communion, no liturgical rite is required, but simply a profession of Catholic faith, even if such persons are permitted, in virtue of recourse to the Apostolic See, to transfer to the Latin rite.[3]

475. In regard to the manner of celebrating the rite of **R3** reception:

1. The rite should appear clearly as a celebration of the Church and have as its high point eucharistic communion. For this reason the rite should normally take place within Mass.

2. Any appearance of triumphalism should be carefully avoided and the manner of celebrating this Mass should be decided beforehand and with a view to the particular circumstances. Both the ecumenical implications and the bond between the candidate and the parish community should be considered. Often it will be preferable to celebrate the Mass with only a few relatives and friends. If for a serious reason Mass cannot be celebrated, the reception should at least take place within a liturgy of the word, whenever this is possible. The person to be received into full communion should be consulted about the form of reception.

[1] See Vatican Council II, Constitution on the Liturgy *Sacrosanctum Concilium*, art. 69, b; Decree on Ecumenism *Unitatis redintegratio*, no. 3. Secretariat for Christian Unity, *Ecumenical Directory I*, no. 19: AAS 59 (1967), 581.
[2] See Vatican Council II, Decree on Ecumenism *Unitatis redintegratio*, no. 18.
[3] See Vatican Council II, Decree on the Eastern Catholic Churches *Orientalium Ecclesiarum*, nos. 25 and 4.

476. If the rite of reception is celebrated outside Mass, the R4
Mass in which for the first time the newly received will
take part with the Catholic community should be celebrated
as soon as possible, in order to make clear the connection
between the reception and eucharistic communion.

477. The baptized Christian is to receive both doctrinal R5
and spiritual preparation, adapted to individual pastoral requirements, for reception into the full communion of the
Catholic Church. The candidate should learn to deepen an
inner adherence to the Church, where he or she will find
the fullness of his or her baptism. During the period of
preparation the candidate may share in worship in conformity with the provisions of the *Ecumenical Directory*.

Anything that would equate candidates for reception with
those who are catechumens is to be absolutely avoided.

478. During the period of their doctrinal and spiritual USA
preparation individual candidates for reception into the full
communion of the Catholic Church may benefit from the
celebration of liturgical rites marking their progress in formation. Thus, for pastoral reasons and in light of the
catechesis in the faith which these baptized Christians have
received previously, one or several of the rites included in
Part II, 4—"Preparation of Uncatechized Adults for Confirmation and Eucharist"—may be celebrated as they are presented or in similar words. In all cases, however, discernment should be made regarding the length of catechetical
formation required for each individual candidate for reception into the full communion of the Catholic Church.

479. One who was born and baptized outside the visible R6
communion of the Catholic Church is not required to make
an abjuration of heresy, but simply a profession of faith.[4]

480. The sacrament of baptism cannot be repeated and R7
therefore it is not permitted to confer it again conditionally,
unless there is a reasonable doubt about the fact or validity
of the baptism already conferred. If serious investigation
raises such prudent doubt and it seems necessary to confer
baptism again conditionally, the minister should explain be-

[4]See Secretariat for Christian Unity, *Ecumenical Directory I*, nos. 19 and 20:
AAS 59 (1967), 581.

forehand the reasons why this is being done and a nonsolemn form of baptism is to be used.[5]

The local Ordinary is to decide in each case what rites are to be included or excluded in conferring conditional baptism.

481. It is the office of the bishop to receive baptized Christians into the full communion of the Catholic Church. But a priest to whom the bishop entrusts the celebration of the rite has the faculty of confirming the candidate within the rite of reception,[6] unless the person received has already been validly confirmed.

R8

482. If the profession of faith and reception take place within Mass, the candidate, according to his or her own conscience, should make a confession of sins beforehand, first informing the confessor that he or she is about to be received into full communion. Any confessor who is lawfully approved may hear the candidate's confession.

R9

483. At the reception, the candidate should be accompanied by a sponsor and may even have two sponsors. If someone has had the principal part in guiding or preparing the candidate, he or she should be the sponsor.

R10

484. In the eucharistic celebration within which reception into full communion takes place or, if the reception takes place outside Mass, in the Mass that follows at a later time, communion under both kinds is permitted for the person received, the sponsor, the parents and spouse who are Catholics, lay catechists who may have instructed the person, and, if the number involved and other circumstances make this feasible, for all Catholics present.

R11

485. The conferences of bishops may, in accord with the provisions of the Constitution on the Liturgy, art. 63, adapt the rite of reception to various circumstances. The local Ordinary, by expanding or shortening the rite, may arrange it to suit the particular circumstances of the persons and place involved.[7]

R12

[5]See ibid., nos. 14–15: AAS 59 (1967), 580.
[6]See *Rite of Confirmation*, Introduction, no. 7,b.
[7]See Secretariat for Christian Unity, *Ecumenical Directory I*, no. 19: AAS 59 (1967), 581.

486. The names of those received into the full communion   R13
of the Catholic Church should be recorded in a special
book, with the date and place of their baptism also noted.

RECEPTION WITHIN MASS

487. If the rite of reception into full communion takes   R14
place on a solemnity or on a Sunday, the Mass of the day
should be celebrated; on other days it is permissible to celebrate the Mass "For the Unity of Christians" from the
Masses for Various Needs.

LITURGY OF THE WORD

READINGS

488. The readings may be taken in whole or in part from   R14
those provided in the Lectionary for Mass for the day, for
the rite of reception into full communion, or for the Mass
"For the Unity of Christians."

HOMILY

489. In the homily following the readings, the celebrant   R14
should express gratitude to God for those being received
and allude to their own baptism as the basis for their reception, to the sacrament of confirmation already received or
about to be received, and to the eucharist, which for the
first time they will celebrate with the Catholic community.

CELEBRATION OF RECEPTION

INVITATION

490. At the end of the homily, the celebrant in the follow-   R14
ing or similar words invites the candidate to come forward
with his or her sponsor and to make the profession of faith
with the community. He may use these or similar words.

**N., of your own free will you have asked to be re-
ceived into the full communion of the Catholic
Church. You have made your decision after careful
thought under the guidance of the Holy Spirit. I now
invite you to come forward with your sponsor and in
the presence of this community to profess the Catholic faith. In this faith you will be one with us for the**

first time at the eucharistic table of the Lord Jesus,
the sign of the Church's unity.

PROFESSION OF FAITH

491. The one to be received then joins the community in
reciting the Nicene Creed, which is always said at this
Mass.   R15

The celebrant then asks the one to be received to add the
following profession of faith. The candidate says:

**I believe and profess all that the holy Catholic
Church believes, teaches, and proclaims to be revealed by God.**

ACT OF RECEPTION

492. The celebrant lays his right hand on the head of the
candidate for reception and says the following. (The gesture
is omitted when confirmation is to be conferred
immediately.)   R16

**N., the Lord receives you into the Catholic Church.
His loving kindness has led you here,
so that in the unity of the Holy Spirit
you may have full communion with us
in the faith that you have professed in the presence
   of his family.**

If confirmation is not celebrated, the celebrant's sign of welcome (no. 495) follows.

CELEBRATION OF CONFIRMATION

LAYING ON OF HANDS

493. If the person being received has not yet received the
sacrament of confirmation, the celebrant lays hands on the
candidate's head and begins the rite of confirmation with
the following prayer.   R17

**All-powerful God, Father of our Lord Jesus Christ,
by water and the Holy Spirit
you freed your son/daughter from sin
and gave him/her new life.**

**Send your Holy Spirit upon him/her
to be his/her helper and guide.**

**Give him/her the spirit of wisdom and understand-
ing,
the spirit of right judgment and courage,
the spirit of knowledge and reverence.
Fill him/her with the spirit of wonder and awe in
your presence.**

**We ask this through Christ our Lord.
R̶. Amen.**

ANOINTING WITH CHRISM

494. The sponsor places the right hand on the shoulder of   R17
the candidate.

The celebrant dips his right thumb in the chrism and makes
the sign of the cross on the forehead of the one to be confirmed as he says:

N., be sealed with the Gift of the Holy Spirit.

Newly confirmed:
Amen.

The celebrant adds:
Peace be with you.

Newly confirmed:
And also with you.

CELEBRANT'S SIGN OF WELCOME

495. The celebrant then takes the hands of the newly re-   R18
ceived person into his own as a sign of friendship and acceptance. With the permission of the Ordinary, another suitable gesture may be substituted, depending on local and
other circumstances.

GENERAL INTERCESSIONS

496. In the introduction to the general intercessions the   R19
celebrant should mention baptism, (confirmation,) and the
eucharist, and express gratitude to God. The one received
into full communion is mentioned at the beginning of the
intercessions. The celebrant may use these or similar
words.

Brothers and sisters: our brother/sister N. has already R30
been united to Christ through baptism [and confirma-
tion] and now, with thanksgiving to God, we have received him/her into the full communion of the Catholic Church [and confirmed him/her with the gifts of
the Holy Spirit]. Soon he/she will share with us at
the table of the Lord. As we rejoice at the reception
of a new member into the Catholic Church, let us
join with him/her in asking for the grace and mercy
of our Savior.

Assisting minister:
For N., whom we have welcomed today as one of us,
that he/she may have the help and guidance of the
Holy Spirit to persevere faithfully in the choice he/
she has made, we pray to the Lord:
℟. Lord, hear our prayer.

Assisting minister:
For all who believe in Christ and for the Communities to which they belong, that they may come to perfect unity, we pray to the Lord:
℟. Lord hear our prayer.

Assisting minister:
For the Church [Communion] in which N. was baptized and received his/her formation as a Christian,
that it may always grow in knowledge of Christ and
proclaim him more effectively, we pray to the Lord:
℟. Lord, hear our prayer.

Assisting minister:
For all in whom the spark of desire for God already
burns, that they may be led to the fullness of truth in
Christ, we pray to the Lord:
℟. Lord, hear our prayer.

Assisting minister:
For those who do not yet believe in Christ the Lord,
that they may enter the way of salvation by the light
of the Holy Spirit, we pray to the Lord:
℟. Lord, hear our prayer.

Assisting minister:

**For all people, that they may be freed from hunger
and war and live in peace and tranquility, we pray to
the Lord:
℟. Lord, hear our prayer.**

Assisting minister:

**For ourselves, that as we have received the gift of
faith, so too we may persevere in it to the end of our
lives, we pray to the Lord:
℟. Lord, hear our prayer.**

The celebrant then says:

**God our Father,
hear the prayers we offer
that we may continue our loving service to you.**

**Grant this through Christ our Lord.
℟. Amen.**

SIGN OF PEACE

497. After the general intercessions the sponsor and the en- R20
tire assembly, if not too numerous, may greet the newly received person in a friendly manner. In this case the sign of
peace before communion may be omitted. Finally, the one
who has been received returns to his or her place.

LITURGY OF THE EUCHARIST

498. Then the Mass continues. It is fitting that the person R21
received and all those mentioned in no. 484 receive communion under both kinds.

RECEPTION OUTSIDE MASS

499. If, for a serious reason, the rite of reception into full communion takes place outside Mass, a liturgy of the word is to be celebrated. R22

[If, in exceptional circumstances, not even a liturgy of the word is possible, just the celebration of the reception itself takes place as described in nos. 490–497. It begins with introductory words in which the celebrant quotes from Scripture, for example, a text in praise of the mercy of God that has guided the candidate, and speaks of the eucharistic communion that will follow on the earliest day possible.] R28

500. The celebrant, vested in alb, or at least surplice, with a stole of festive color, greets those present. R23

501. A suitable song may be sung, then there are one or more readings from Scripture, which the celebrant explains in the homily (see no. 489). R24

The readings may be chosen from those provided in the Lectionary for Mass for the day, for the ritual Mass "Christian Initiation apart from the Easter Vigil," or for the Mass "For the Unity of Christians"; but they are preferably chosen from those listed here, as indicated for the rite of reception into full communion.

NEW TESTAMENT READING

1. Romans 8:28–39——*He predestined us to become true images of his Son.*

2. 1 Corinthians 12:31–13:13—*Love never ends.*

3. Ephesians 1:3–14—*The Father chose us in Christ to be holy and spotless in love.*

4. Ephesians 4:1–7, 11–13—*There is one Lord, one faith, one baptism, one God, the Father of all.*

5. Philippians 4:4–8—*Fill your minds with everything that is holy.*

6. 1 Thessalonians 5:16–24—*May you all be kept blameless, spirit, soul, and body, for the coming of our Lord Jesus Christ.*

RESPONSORIAL PSALM

1. Psalm 27:1, 4, 8–9, 13–14
℟. **(v.1a) The Lord is my light and my salvation.**

2. Psalm 42:2–3; Psalm 43:3,4
℟. **(Psalm 42:3a) My soul is thirsting for the living God.**

3. Psalm 61:2–6, 9
℟. **(v.4a) Lord, you are my refuge.**

4. Psalm 63:2–6, 8–9
℟. **(v.3b) My soul is thirsting for you, O Lord my God.**

5. Psalm 65:2–6
℟. **(v.2a) It is right to praise you in Zion, O God.**

6. Psalm 121
℟. **(v.2a) Our help is from the Lord.**

GOSPEL

1. Matthew 5:2–12a—*Rejoice and be glad, for your reward will be great in heaven.*

2. Matthew 5:13–16—*Let your light shine before all people.*

3. Matthew 11:25–30—*You have hidden these things from the learned and the clever and revealed them to children.*

4. John 3:16–21—*Everyone who believes in him will have everlasting life.*

5. John 14:15–23, 26–27—*My Father will love them, and we will come to them.*

6. John 15:1–6—*I am the vine and you are the branches.*

502. The reception itself, as given in nos. 489–495, follows.　R25

503. Next there are intercessions, in the form given in no.　R26
496 or in a similar form.

504. The rite is concluded as follows:　R26

After the concluding prayer of the intercessions, the cele-　R31
brant introduces the Lord's Prayer, in the following or similar words.

**Brothers and sisters, let us join together and pray to
God as our Lord Jesus Christ taught us to pray:**

All:
Our Father . . .

If the person received was accustomed in his or her Community to the final doxology "**For the kingdom . . . ,**" it
should be added here to the Lord's Prayer.

The celebrant gives the blessing in the usual manner. Then　R26
the sponsor and the entire assembly, if not too numerous,　R27
may offer to the newly received person some sign of welcome into the community. All then depart in peace.

APPENDIX I

ADDITIONAL (COMBINED) RITES

My soul is thirsting for the living God

RITE 1: CELEBRATION OF THE RITE OF ACCEPTANCE INTO THE ORDER OF CATECHUMENS AND OF THE RITE OF WELCOMING BAPTIZED BUT PREVIOUSLY UNCATECHIZED ADULTS WHO ARE PREPARING FOR CONFIRMATION AND/OR EUCHARIST OR RECEPTION INTO THE FULL COMMUNION OF THE CATHOLIC CHURCH

USA

I am the good shepherd: I know my sheep and mine know me

505. This rite is for use in communities where catechumens are preparing for initiation and where baptized but previously uncatechized adults are beginning catechetical formation either prior to completing their Christian initiation in the sacraments of confirmation and eucharist or prior to being received into the full communion of the Catholic Church.

506. In the catechesis of the community and in the celebration of these rites, care must be taken to maintain the distinction between the catechumens and the baptized candidates.

CELEBRATION OF THE RITE OF ACCEPTANCE INTO THE ORDER OF CATECHUMENS AND OF THE RITE OF WELCOMING BAPTIZED BUT PREVIOUSLY UNCATECHIZED ADULTS WHO ARE PREPARING FOR CONFIRMATION AND/OR EUCHARIST OR RECEPTION INTO THE FULL COMMUNION OF THE CATHOLIC CHURCH

RECEIVING THE CANDIDATES

507. Those who are to be accepted into the order of catechumens, along with those who are candidates for the sacraments of confirmation and eucharist, their sponsors, and a group of the faithful gather outside the church (or inside at the entrance or elsewhere) or at some other site suitable for this rite. As the priest or deacon, wearing an alb or surplice, a stole, and, if desired, a cope of festive color, goes to meet them, the assembly of the faithful may sing a psalm or an appropriate song.

GREETING

508. The celebrant greets the candidates in a friendly manner. He speaks to them, their sponsors, and all present, pointing out the joy and happiness of the Church. He may also recall for the sponsors and friends the particular experience and religious response by which the candidates, following their own spiritual path, have come to this celebration. He uses these or similar words.

Dear friends, the Church joyfully welcomes today those who will be received into the order of catechumens. In the months to come they will prepare for their initiation into the Christian faith by baptism, confirmation, and eucharist.

We also greet those who, already one with us by baptism, now wish to complete their Christian initiation through confirmation and eucharist or to be received into the full communion of the Catholic Church.

For all of these, we give thanks and praise to the God who has led them by various paths to oneness

in faith. My dear candidates, you are welcomed in the name of Christ.

Then he invites the sponsors and candidates to come forward. As they are taking their places before the celebrant, an appropriate song may be sung, for example, Psalm 63:1–8.

OPENING DIALOGUE WITH CANDIDATES FOR THE CATECHUMENATE AND WITH CANDIDATES FOR POST-BAPTISMAL CATECHESIS

509. Unless the candidates are already known to all present, the celebrant asks for or calls out their given names. The names of the candidates for the catechumenate are given first, followed by the names of the candidates for post-baptismal catechesis. The candidates answer one by one, even if, because of a large number, the question is asked only once for each group. One of the following formularies or similar words may be used.

A The celebrant asks:
What is your name?

Candidate:
N.

B The celebrant calls out the name of each candidate.

The candidate answers:
Present.

The celebrant continues with the following questions for the individual candidates for the catechumenate. When there are a large number the candidates may answer as a group. The celebrant may use other words than those provided in asking the candidates about their intentions and may let them answer in their own words: for example, to the first question, **"What do you ask of the Church of God?"** or **"What do you desire?"** or **"For what reason have you come?"**, he may receive such answers as **"The grace of Christ"** or **"Entrance into the Church"** or **"Eternal life"** or other suitable responses. The celebrant then phrases his next question according to the answer received.

Celebrant:
What do you ask of God's Church?

Candidate:
Faith.

Celebrant:
What does faith offer you?

Candidate:
Eternal life.

The celebrant then addresses the following questions to the individual candidates for post-baptismal catechesis. Again when there are a large number the candidates may answer as a group. The celebrant may use other words than those provided in asking the candidates about their intentions and may let them answer in their own words. The celebrant then phrases his next question according to the answer received.

What do you ask of God's Church?

Candidate:
To be accepted as a candidate for catechetical instruction leading to confirmation and eucharist (*or:* leading to reception into the full communion of the Catholic Church).

Celebrant:
What does this period of formation offer you?

Candidate:
A fuller sharing in the life of the Church.

---

510. At the discretion of the diocesan bishop, the catechumens' first acceptance of the Gospel (which follows in no. 511) may be replaced by the rite of exorcism and renunciation of false worship (nos. 70–72) [see no. 33.2].

CATECHUMENS' FIRST ACCEPTANCE OF THE GOSPEL

511. The celebrant addresses the candidates for the catechumenate, adapting the following formulary to the answers received in the opening dialogue.

God is our Creator and in him all living things have their existence. He enlightens our minds, so that we may come to know and worship him. He has sent his

faithful witness, Jesus Christ, to announce to us what he has seen and heard, the mysteries of heaven and earth.

Since you acknowledge with joy that Christ has come, now is the time to hear his word, so that you may possess eternal life by beginning, in our company, to know God and to love your neighbor. Are you ready, with the help of God, to live this life?

Candidates:
I am.

CANDIDATES' DECLARATION OF INTENT

512. The celebrant then addresses the candidates for post-baptismal catechesis, adapting the following formulary to the answers received in the opening dialogue.

Those of you who seek to complete your Christian initiation (*or:* be received into the full communion of the Catholic Church,) are you prepared to listen to the apostles' instruction, gather with us for prayer, and join us in the love and service of others?

Candidates:
I am.

AFFIRMATION BY THE SPONSORS AND THE ASSEMBLY

513. Then the celebrant turns to the sponsors and the assembly and asks them in these or similar words.

Sponsors, you now present these candidates to us; are you, and all who are gathered with us, ready to help these candidates follow Christ?

All:
We are.

With hands joined, the celebrant says:

Father of mercy,
we thank you for these your servants.
You have sought and summoned them in many ways
and they have turned to seek you.

**You have called them today
and they have answered in our presence:
we praise you, Lord, and we bless you.**

All sing or say:
We praise you, Lord, and we bless you.

SIGNING OF THE CATECHUMENS AND OF THE CANDIDATES WITH THE CROSS

514. Next the cross is traced on the forehead of the cate-chumens (or, at the discretion of the diocesan bishop, in front of the forehead for those in whose culture the act of touching may not seem proper); at the discretion of the cele-brant the signing of one, several, or all of the senses may follow. The celebrant alone says the formularies accompany-ing each signing.

SIGNING OF THE FOREHEAD OF THE CATECHUMENS

515. The celebrant speaks to the catechumens and their sponsors in these or similar words.*

Celebrant:
Catechumens, come forward now with your sponsors to receive the sign of your new way of life as catechu-mens.

With their sponsors, the catechumens come one by one to the celebrant; with his thumb he traces a cross on the fore-head; then, if there is to be no signing of the senses, the sponsor does the same. The celebrant says:

**N., receive the cross on your forehead.
It is Christ himself who now strengthens you
with this sign of his love.**
Learn to know him and follow him.

All sing or say the following or another suitable acclamation.

Glory and praise to you, Lord Jesus Christ!

---

*In those exceptional cases when, at the discretion of the diocesan bishop, a renunciation of false worship (no. 72) has been included in the rite of acceptance: "Dear candidates, your answers mean that you have rejected false worship and wish to share our life and hope in Christ. . ."
**In those exceptional cases when, at the discretion of the diocesan bishop, there has been a renunciation of false worship: "with this sign of his vic-tory."

SIGNING OF THE OTHER SENSES OF THE CATECHUMENS

516. The signing is carried out by the catechists or the sponsors. (If required by special circumstances, this may be done by assisting priests or deacons.) The signing of each sense may be followed by an acclamation in praise of Christ, for example, **"Glory and praise to you, Lord Jesus Christ!"**

While the ears are being signed, the celebrant says:
**Receive the sign of the cross on your ears,
that you may hear the voice of the Lord.**

While the eyes are being signed:
**Receive the sign of the cross on your eyes,
that you may see the glory of God.**

While the lips are being signed:
**Receive the sign of the cross on your lips,
that you may respond to the word of God.**

While the breast is being signed:
**Receive the sign of the cross over your heart,
that Christ may dwell there by faith.**

While the shoulders are being signed:
**Receive the sign of the cross on your shoulders,
that you may bear the gentle yoke of Christ.**

[While the hands are being signed:
**Receive the sign of the cross on your hands,
that Christ may be known in the work which you do.**

While the feet are being signed:
**Receive the sign of the cross on your feet,
that you may walk in the way of Christ.]**

Without touching them the celebrant alone makes the sign of the cross over all the candidates at once (or, if they are few, over each individually), saying:

**I sign you with the sign of eternal life
in the name of the Father, and of the Son, ✠
and of the Holy Spirit.**

Catechumens:
Amen.

517. Next the cross is traced on the forehead of the candidates for confirmation and eucharist (or reception into the full communion of the Catholic Church); at the discretion of the celebrant the signing of one, several, or all of the senses may follow. The celebrant alone says the formularies accompanying each signing.

SIGNING OF THE FOREHEAD OF THE CANDIDATES

518. The celebrant speaks to the candidates for confirmation and the eucharist and their sponsors in these or similar words.

Celebrant:

Candidates for confirmation and the eucharist (*or:* reception into full communion), come forward now with your sponsors to receive the sign of your life in Christ.

With their sponsors, the candidates come one by one to the celebrant; with his thumb he traces a cross on the forehead; then, if there is to be no signing of the senses, the sponsor does the same. The celebrant says:

**N., receive the cross on your forehead
as a reminder of your baptism
into Christ's saving death and resurrection.**

All sing or say the following or another suitable acclamation.

Glory and praise to you, Lord Jesus Christ!

SIGNING OF THE OTHER SENSES OF THE CANDIDATES

519. The signing is carried out by the catechists or the sponsors. (If required by special circumstances, this may be done by assisting priests or deacons.) The signing of each sense may be followed by an acclamation in praise of Christ, for example, "**Glory and praise to you, Lord Jesus Christ!**"

While the ears are being signed, the celebrant says:
**Receive the sign of the cross on your ears,
that you may hear the voice of the Lord.**

While the eyes are being signed:
**Receive the sign of the cross on your eyes,
that you may see the glory of God.**

While the lips are being signed:
**Receive the sign of the cross on your lips,
that you may respond to the word of God.**

While the breast is being signed:
**Receive the sign of the cross over your heart,
that Christ may dwell there by faith.**

While the shoulders are being signed:
**Receive the sign of the cross on your shoulders,
that you may bear the gentle yoke of Christ.**

[While the hands are being signed:
**Receive the sign of the cross on your hands,
that Christ may be known in the work which you do.**

While the feet are being signed:
**Receive the sign of the cross on your feet,
that you may walk in the way of Christ.]**

Without touching them the celebrant alone makes the sign of the cross over all the candidates at once (or, if they are few, over each individually), saying:

**I sign you with the sign of eternal life
in the name of the Father, and of the Son, ✠
and of the Holy Spirit.**

Candidates:
Amen.

CONCLUDING PRAYER

520. The celebrant concludes the signing of the forehead (and senses) with the following prayer.

Let us pray.

**Almighty God,
by the cross and resurrection of your Son
you have given life to your people.**

**Your servants have received the sign of the cross:
make them living proof of its saving power
and help them to persevere in the footsteps of Christ.**

**We ask this through Christ our Lord.
R̸. Amen.**

INVITATION TO THE CELEBRATION OF THE WORD OF GOD

521. The celebrant next invites the catechumens and candidates and their sponsors to enter the church (or the place where the liturgy of the word will be celebrated). He uses the following or similar words, accompanying them with some gesture of invitation.

N. and N., come into the church, to share with us at the table of God's word.

The Lectionary for Mass or the Bible is carried in procession and placed with honor on the lectern, where it may be incensed.

During the entry an appropriate song is sung or the following antiphon, with Psalm 34:2, 3, 6, 9, 10, 11, 16.

**Come, my children, and listen to me;
I will teach you the fear of the Lord.**

LITURGY OF THE WORD

INSTRUCTION

522. After the catechumens and candidates have reached their places, the celebrant speaks to them briefly, helping them to understand the dignity of God's word, which is proclaimed and heard in the church.

Celebration of the liturgy of the word follows.

READINGS

523. The readings are those assigned for the day. According to the norms of the Lectionary, other appropriate readings, such as the following, may be used.

FIRST READING

Genesis 12:1–4a—*Leave your country, and come into the land I will show you.*

RESPONSORIAL PSALM

Psalm 33:4–5, 12–13, 18–19, 20 and 22
℟. (v. 12b) **Happy the people the Lord has chosen to be his own.**
Or:
℟. (v. 22) **Lord, let your mercy be on us, as we place our trust in you.**

VERSE BEFORE THE GOSPEL

John 1:41, 17b
We have found the Messiah: Jesus Christ, who brings us truth and grace.

GOSPEL

John 1:35–42—*This is the Lamb of God. We have found the Messiah.*

HOMILY

524. A homily follows that explains the readings.

PRESENTATION OF A BIBLE

525. A book containing the Gospels may be given to the catechumens and candidates by the celebrant; a cross may also be given, unless this has already been done as one of the additional rites (see no. 74). The celebrant may use words suited to the gift presented, for example, "**Receive the Gospel of Jesus Christ, the Son of God.**" The catechumens and candidates may respond in an appropriate way.

INTERCESSIONS FOR THE CATECHUMENS AND CANDIDATES

526. Then the sponsors and the whole congregation join in the following or a similar formulary of intercession for the catechumens and candidates.

[If it is decided, in accord with no. 529 that after the dismissal of the catechumens the usual general intercessions of the Mass are to be omitted and that the liturgy of the eucharist is to begin immediately, intentions for the Church and the whole world are to be added to the following intentions for the catechumens and candidates.]

Celebrant:
These catechumens and candidates, who are our brothers and sisters, have already traveled a long road. We rejoice with them in the gentle guidance of God who has brought them to this day. Let us pray that they may press onwards, until they come to share fully in our way of life.

Assisting minister:
That God our Father may reveal his Christ to them more and more with every passing day, let us pray to the Lord:
R̸. **Lord, hear our prayer.**

Assisting minister:
That they may undertake with generous hearts and souls whatever God may ask of them, let us pray to the Lord:
R̸. **Lord, hear our prayer.**

Assisting minister:
That they may have our sincere and unfailing support every step of the way, let us pray to the Lord:
R̸. **Lord, hear our prayer.**

Assisting minister:
That they may find in our community compelling signs of unity and generous love, let us pray to the Lord:
R̸. **Lord, hear our prayer.**

Assisting minister:
That their hearts and ours may become more responsive to the needs of others, let us pray to the Lord:
R̸. **Lord, hear our prayer.**

Assisting minister:
That in due time the catechumens may be found worthy to receive the baptism of new birth and renewal in the Holy Spirit and the candidates may be found

worthy to complete their initiation through the sacraments of confirmation and eucharist (*or* be received
into the full communion of the Catholic Church), let
us pray to the Lord:
℟. Lord, hear our prayer.

PRAYER OVER THE CATECHUMENS AND
CANDIDATES

527. After the intercessions, the celebrant, with hands outstretched over the catechumens and candidates, says the following prayer.

Almighty God,
source of all creation,
you have made us in your image.

Receive with love those who come before you.
Lead our catechumens to the baptism of new birth,
and our candidates to a deeper share
  in the paschal mystery,
so that, living a fruitful life
  in the company of your faithful,
they may receive the eternal reward that you
  promise.

We ask this in the name of Jesus the Lord.
℟. Amen.

DISMISSAL OF THE CATECHUMENS

528. If the eucharist is to be celebrated, the catechumens
are normally dismissed at this point by use of option **A** or
B; if the catechumens are to stay for the celebration of the
eucharist, option **C** is used; if the eucharist is not to be celebrated, the entire assembly is dismissed by use of option **D**.

A The celebrant dismisses the catechumens in these or
similar words.

Catechumens, go in peace, and may the Lord remain
with you always.

Catechumens:
Amen.

B   As an optional formulary for dismissing the catechumens, the celebrant may use these or similar words.

My dear friends, this community now sends you forth to reflect more deeply upon the word of God which you have shared with us today. Be assured of our loving support and prayers for you. We look forward to the day when you will share fully in the Lord's Table.

C   If for serious reasons the catechumens cannot leave (see no. 75.3) and must remain with the rest of the liturgical assembly, they, along with the candidates, are to be instructed that though they are present at the eucharist, they cannot take part in it as the Catholic faithful do. They may be reminded of this by the celebrant in these or similar words.

Although you cannot yet participate fully in the Lord's eucharist, stay with us as a sign of our hope that all God's children will eat and drink with the Lord and work with his Spirit to re-create the face of the earth.

D   The celebrant dismisses those present, using these or similar words.

Go in peace, and may the Lord remain with you always.

All:
Thanks be to God.

An appropriate song may conclude the celebration.

LITURGY OF THE EUCHARIST

529. When the eucharist is to follow, intercessory prayer is resumed with the usual general intercessions for the needs of the Church and the whole world; then, if required, the profession of faith is said. But for pastoral reasons these general intercessions and the profession of faith may be omitted. The liturgy of the eucharist then begins as usual with the preparation of the gifts.

RITE 2: PARISH CELEBRATION FOR SENDING CATECHUMENS FOR ELECTION AND CANDIDATES FOR RECOGNITION BY THE BISHOP [OPTIONAL]

The community was of one mind and one heart

530. This optional rite is provided for parishes whose catechumens will celebrate their election and whose adult candidates for confirmation and eucharist or reception into the full communion of the Catholic Church will celebrate their recognition in a subsequent celebration (e.g., at the cathedral with the bishop).

531. As the focal point of the Church's concern for the catechumens, admission to election belongs to the bishop who is usually its presiding celebrant. It is within the parish community, however, that the preliminary judgment is made concerning the catechumens' state of formation and progress.

This rite offers that local community the opportunity to express its approval of the catechumens and to send them forth to the celebration of election assured of the parish's care and support.

532. In addition, those who either are completing their initiation through the sacraments of confirmation and the eucharist or are preparing for reception into the full communion of the Catholic Church are also included in this rite, since they too will be presented to the bishop at the celebration of the rite of election for the catechumens.

533. The rite is celebrated in the parish church at a suitable time prior to the rite of election.

534. The rite takes place after the homily in a celebration of the word of God (see no. 89) or at Mass.

535. In the catechesis of the community and in the celebration of these rites, care must be taken to maintain the distinction between the catechumens and the baptized candidates.

PARISH CELEBRATION FOR SENDING CATECHUMENS FOR ELECTION AND CANDIDATES FOR RECOGNITION BY THE BISHOP [OPTIONAL]

LITURGY OF THE WORD

HOMILY

536. After the readings, the celebrant gives the homily. This should be suited to the actual situation and should address not just the catechumens and candidates but the entire community of the faithful, so that all will be encouraged to give good example and to accompany the candidates along the path of the paschal mystery.

PRESENTATION OF THE CATECHUMENS

537. After the homily, the priest in charge of the catechumens' initiation, or a deacon, a catechist, or a representative of the community, presents the catechumens using the following or similar words.

Reverend Father, these catechumens, N. and N., are beginning their final period of preparation and purification leading to their initiation. They have found strength in God's grace and support in our community's prayers and example.

Now they ask that they be recognized for the progress they have made in their spiritual formation and that they receive the assurance of our blessings and prayers as they go forth to the rite of election celebrated this afternoon (or *next Sunday* or [*specify the day*]) by Bishop N.

The celebrant replies:
Those who are to be sent to the celebration of election in Christ, come forward, together with those who will be your godparents.

One by one, the catechumens are called by name. Each catechumen, accompanied by a godparent (or godparents), comes forward and stands before the celebrant.

AFFIRMATION BY THE GODPARENTS [AND THE ASSEMBLY]

538. Then the celebrant addresses the assembly in these or similar words:

My dear friends, these catechumens who have been preparing for the sacraments of initiation hope that they will be found ready to participate in the rite of election and be chosen in Christ for the Easter sacraments. It is the responsibility of this community to inquire about their readiness before they are presented to the bishop.

He addresses the godparents:

I turn to you, godparents, for your testimony about these candidates. Have these catechumens taken their formation in the Gospel and in the Catholic way of life seriously?

Godparents:
They have.

Celebrant:
Have they given evidence of their conversion by the example of their lives?

Godparents:
They have.

Celebrant:
Do you judge them to be ready to be presented to the bishop for the rite of election?

Godparents:
We do.

[When appropriate in the circumstances, the celebrant may also ask the entire assembly to express its approval of the candidates.]

The celebrant concludes the affirmation by the following:

My dear catechumens, this community gladly recommends you to the bishop, who, in the name of Christ, will call you to the Easter sacraments. May

God bring to completion the good work he has begun in you.

539. If the signing of the Book of the Elect is to take place in the presence of the bishop, it is omitted here. However, if the signed Book of the Elect is to be presented to the bishop in the rite of election, the catechumens may now come forward to sign it or they should sign it after the celebration or at another time prior to the Rite of Election.

PRESENTATION OF THE CANDIDATES

540. The priest in charge of the candidates' formation, or a deacon, a catechist, or a representative of the community, presents the candidates, using the following or similar words.

Reverend Father, I now present to you the candidates who are beginning their final preparation for the sacraments of confirmation and eucharist (*and/or:* reception into the full communion of the Catholic Church). They have found strength in God's grace and support in our community's prayers and example.

Now they ask that they be recognized for the progress they have made in their spiritual formation and that they receive the assurance of our blessings and prayers as they go forth for recognition by Bishop N. this afternoon (or *next Sunday* or [*specify the day*]).

The celebrant replies:
Those who are to be recognized, come forward, together with your sponsors.

One by one, the candidates are called by name. Each candidate, accompanied by a sponsor, comes forward and stands before the celebrant.

AFFIRMATION BY THE SPONSORS [AND THE ASSEMBLY]

541. Then the celebrant addresses the assembly in these or similar words:

My dear friends, these candidates, already one with us by reason of their baptism in Christ, have asked to be able to participate fully in the sacramental life of the Catholic Church. Those who know them have judged them to be sincere in their desire. During the period of their catechetical formation they have listened to the word of Christ and endeavored to follow his commands more perfectly; they have shared the company of their Christian brothers and sisters in this community and joined with them in prayer.

And so I announce to all of you here that our community supports these candidates in their desire. Therefore, I ask their sponsors to state their opinion once again, so that all of you may hear.

He addresses the sponsors:
As God is your witness, do you consider these candidates ready to receive the sacraments of confirmation and eucharist (*or:* ready to be received into the full communion of the Catholic Church)?

Sponsors:
We do.

[When appropriate in the circumstances, the celebrant may also ask the entire assembly to express its approval of the candidates.]

542. The celebrant concludes the affirmation by the following:

And now, my dear friends, I address you. Your own sponsors (and this entire community) have spoken in your favor. The Church, in the name of Christ, accepts their testimony and sends you to Bishop N., who will exhort you to live in deeper conformity to the life of Christ.

INTERCESSIONS FOR THE CATECHUMENS AND CANDIDATES

543. Then the community prays for the catechumens and candidates by use of the following or a similar formulary.

The celebrant may adapt the introduction and the intentions to fit various circumstances.

[If it is decided, in accord with no. 546, that after the dismissal of the catechumens the usual general intercessions of the Mass are to be omitted and that the liturgy of the eucharist is to begin immediately, intentions for the Church and the whole world are to be added to the following intentions for the catechumens and candidates.]

Celebrant:
My brothers and sisters, we look forward to celebrating at Easter the life-giving mysteries of our Lord's suffering, death and resurrection. As we journey together to the Easter sacraments, these catechumens and candidates will look to us for an example of Christian renewal. Let us pray to the Lord for them and for ourselves, that we may be renewed by one another's efforts and together come to share the joys of Easter.

Assisting minister:
That these catechumens and candidates may be freed from selfishness and learn to put others first, let us pray to the Lord:
R̃. Lord, hear our prayer.

Assisting minister:
That their godparents and sponsors may be living examples of the Gospel, let us pray to the Lord:
R̃. Lord, hear our prayer.

Assisting minister:
That their teachers may always convey to them the beauty of God's word, let us pray to the Lord:
R̃. Lord, hear our prayer.

Assisting minister:
That these catechumens and candidates may share with others the joy they have found in their friendship with Jesus, let us pray to the Lord:
R̃. Lord, hear our prayer.

Assisting minister:
That our community, during the (coming) Lenten season, may grow in charity and be constant in prayer, let us pray to the Lord:
R̷. Lord, hear our prayer.

PRAYER OVER THE CATECHUMENS AND CANDIDATES

544. After the intercessions, the celebrant, with hands outstretched over the catechumens and candidates, says the following prayer.

Father of love and power,
it is your will to establish everything in Christ
and to draw us into his all-embracing love.

Guide these catechumens and candidates
in the days and weeks ahead:
strengthen them in their vocation,
build them into the kingdom of your Son,
and seal them with the Spirit of your promise.

We ask this through Christ our Lord.
R̷. Amen.

DISMISSAL OF THE CATECHUMENS

545. If the eucharist is to be celebrated, the catechumens are normally dismissed at this point by use of option **A** or **B**; if the catechumens are to stay for the celebration of the eucharist, option **C** is used; if the eucharist is not to be celebrated, the entire assembly is dismissed by use of option **D**.

A The celebrant dismisses the catechumens in these or similar words.

My dear friends, you are about to set out on the road that leads to the glory of Easter. Christ will be your way, your truth, and your life. In his name we send you forth from this community to celebrate with the bishop the Lord's choice of you to be numbered among his elect. Until we meet again for the scrutinies, walk always in his peace.

Catechumens:
Amen.

B As an optional formulary for dismissing the catechumens, the celebrant may use these or similar words.

My dear friends, this community now sends you forth to reflect more deeply upon the word of God which you have shared with us today. Be assured of our loving support and prayers for you. We look forward to the day when you will share fully in the Lord's Table.

C If for serious reasons the catechumens cannot leave (see no. 75.3) and must remain with the rest of the liturgical assembly, they, along with the candidates, are to be instructed that though they are present at the eucharist, they cannot take part in it as the Catholic faithful do. They may be reminded of this by the celebrant in these or similar words.

Although you cannot yet participate fully in the Lord's eucharist, stay with us as a sign of our hope that all God's children will eat and drink with the Lord and work with his Spirit to re-create the face of the earth.

D The celebrant dismisses those present, using these or similar words.

Go in peace, and may the Lord remain with you always.

All:
Thanks be to God.

An appropriate song may conclude the celebration.

LITURGY OF THE EUCHARIST

546. When the eucharist is to follow, intercessory prayer is resumed with the usual general intercessions for the needs of the Church and the whole world; then, if required, the profession of faith is said. But for pastoral reasons these general intercessions and the profession of faith may be omitted. The liturgy of the eucharist then begins as usual with the preparation of the gifts.

RITE 3: CELEBRATION OF THE RITE OF ELECTION OF CATECHUMENS AND OF THE CALL TO CONTINUING CONVERSION OF CANDIDATES WHO ARE PREPARING FOR CONFIRMATION AND/OR EUCHARIST OR RECEPTION INTO THE FULL COMMUNION OF THE CATHOLIC CHURCH

USA

The body is one and has many members

547. This rite is for use when the election of catechumens and the call to continuing conversion of candidates preparing either for confirmation and/or eucharist or reception into the full communion of the Catholic Church are celebrated together.

548. The rite should normally take place on the First Sunday of Lent, and the presiding celebrant is the bishop or his delegate.

549. In the catechesis of the community and in the celebration of these rites, care must be taken to maintain the distinction between the catechumens and the baptized candidates.

CELEBRATION OF THE RITE OF ELECTION OF CATECHUMENS AND OF THE CALL TO CONTINUING CONVERSION OF CANDIDATES WHO ARE PREPARING FOR CONFIRMATION AND/OR EUCHARIST OR RECEPTION INTO THE FULL COMMUNION OF THE CATHOLIC CHURCH

LITURGY OF THE WORD

HOMILY

550. After the readings (see no. 128), the bishop, or the celebrant who acts as delegate of the bishop, gives the homily. This should be suited to the actual situation and should address not just the catechumens and the candidates, but the entire community of the faithful, so that all will be encouraged to give good example and to accompany the catechumens and candidates during the time of their Lenten preparation for celebrating the Easter sacraments.

CELEBRATION OF ELECTION

PRESENTATION OF THE CATECHUMENS

551. After the homily, the priest in charge of the catechumens' initiation, or a deacon, a catechist, or a representative of the community, presents the catechumens, using the following or similar words.

Reverend Father, Easter is drawing near, and so these catechumens, whom I now present to you, are completing their period of preparation. They have found strength in God's grace and support in our community's prayers and example.

Now they ask that after the celebration of the scrutinies, they be allowed to participate in the sacraments of baptism, confirmation, and the eucharist.

The celebrant replies:
Those who are to be chosen in Christ, come forward, together with your godparents.

One by one, the catechumens are called by name. Each catechumen, accompanied by a godparent (or godparents), comes forward and stands before the celebrant.

[If there are a great many catechumens, all are presented in groups, for example, each group by its own catechist. But in this case, the catechists should be advised to have a special celebration beforehand in which they call each catechumen forward by name.]

AFFIRMATION BY THE GODPARENTS [AND THE ASSEMBLY]

552. Then the celebrant addresses the assembly. If he has taken part in the earlier deliberation on the catechumens' suitableness (see no. 122), he may use either option **A** or option **B** or similar words; if he has not taken part in the earlier deliberation, he uses option **B** or similar words.

A

My dear friends, these catechumens have asked to be initiated into the sacramental life of the Church this Easter. Those who know them have judged them to be sincere in their desire. During the period of their preparation they have listened to the word of Christ and endeavored to follow his commands; they have shared the company of their Christian brothers and sisters and joined with them in prayer.

And so I announce to all of you here that our community has decided to call them to the sacraments. Therefore, I ask their godparents to state their opinion once again, so that all of you may hear.

He addresses the godparents:
As God is your witness, do you consider these catechumens worthy to be admitted to the sacraments of Christian initiation?

Godparents:
We do.

When appropriate in the circumstances, the celebrant may also ask the entire assembly to express its approval of the catechumens in these or similar words:

Celebrant:
Now I ask you, the members of this community:

Are you willing to affirm the testimony expressed about these catechumens and support them in faith, prayer, and example as we prepare to celebrate the Easter sacraments?

All:
We are.

B
God's holy Church wishes to know whether these catechumens are sufficiently prepared to be enrolled among the elect for the coming celebration of Easter. And so I speak first of all to you their godparents.

He addresses the godparents:
Have they faithfully listened to God's word proclaimed by the Church?

Godparents:
They have.

Celebrant:
Have they responded to that word and begun to walk in God's presence?

Godparents:
They have.

Celebrant:
Have they shared the company of their Christian brothers and sisters and joined with them in prayer?

Godparents:
They have.

When appropriate in the circumstances, the celebrant may also ask the entire assembly to express its approval of the catechumens in these or similar words:

Celebrant:
And now I speak to you, my brothers and sisters in this assembly:
Are you ready to support the testimony expressed about these catechumens and include them in your prayer and affection as we move toward Easter?

All:
We are.

INVITATION AND ENROLLMENT OF NAMES

553. Then addressing the catechumens in the following or similar words, the celebrant advises them of their acceptance and asks them to declare their own intention.

And now, my dear catechumens, I address you. Your own godparents and teachers [and this entire community] have spoken in your favor. The Church in the name of Christ accepts their judgment and calls you to the Easter sacraments.

Since you have already heard the call of Christ, you must now express your response to that call clearly and in the presence of the whole Church.

Therefore, do you wish to enter fully into the life of the Church through the sacraments of baptism, confirmation, and the eucharist?

Catechumens:
We do.

Celebrant:
Then offer your names for enrollment.

The catechumens give their names, either going with their godparents to the celebrant or while remaining in place, and the actual inscription of the names may be carried out in various ways. The catechumens may inscribe their names themselves or they may call out their names, which are inscribed by the godparents or by the minister who presented the catechumens (see no. 117). As the enrollment is taking place, an appropriate song, for example, Psalm 16 or Psalm 33 with a refrain such as, "Happy the people the Lord has chosen to be his own" may be sung.

[If there are a great many candidates, the enrollment may simply consist in the presentation of a list of the names to the celebrant, with such words as: "These are the names of the candidates" or, when the bishop is celebrant and candidates from several parishes have been presented to him: "These are the names of the candidates from the parish of N."]

ACT OF ADMISSION OR ELECTION

554. The celebrant briefly explains the significance of the enrollment that has just taken place. Then, turning to the catechumens, he says the following or similar words.

N. and N., I now declare you to be members of the elect, to be initiated into the sacred mysteries at the next Easter Vigil.

Catechumens:
Thanks be to God.

He continues:
God is always faithful to those he calls: now it is your duty, as it is ours, both to be faithful to him in return and to strive courageously to reach the fullness of truth, which your election opens up before you.

Then the celebrant turns to the godparents and instructs them in the following or similar words.

Godparents, you have spoken in favor of these catechumens: accept them now as chosen in the Lord and continue to sustain them through your loving care and example, until them come to share in the sacraments of God's life.

He invites them to place their hand on the shoulder of the catechumen whom they are receiving into their care, or to make some other gesture to indicate the same intent.

CELEBRATION OF THE CALL TO CONTINUING CONVERSION

PRESENTATION OF THE CANDIDATES

555. The priest in charge of the candidates' formation, or a deacon, a catechist, or a representative of the community, presents the candidates, using the following or similar words.

Reverend Father, I now present to you the candidates who seek to complete their Christian initiation (or: who are preparing to be received into the full communion of the Catholic Church). They too have found strength in God's grace and support in our community's prayers and example.

Now they ask that after this Lenten season, they be admitted to confirmation and the eucharist (or: to full eucharistic sharing).

The celebrant replies:

Those who desire to participate fully in the sacramental life of the Church, come forward, together with your sponsors.

One by one, the candidates are called by name. Each candidate, accompanied by a sponsor, comes forward and stands before the celebrant.

[If there are a great many candidates, all are presented in groups, for example, each group by its own catechist. But in this case, the catechists should be advised to have a special celebration beforehand in which they call each candidate forward by name.]

AFFIRMATION BY THE SPONSORS [AND THE ASSEMBLY]

556. Then the celebrant addresses the assembly. If he has taken part in the earlier deliberation on the candidates' suitableness (see no. 122), he may use either option A or option B or similar words; if he has not taken part in the earlier deliberation, he uses option B or similar words.

A

My dear friends, these candidates, our brothers and sisters, have asked to be able to participate fully in the sacramental life of the Catholic Church. Those who know them have judged them to be sincere in their desire. During the period of their preparation they have reflected on the mystery of their baptism and have come to appreciate more deeply the presence of Christ in their lives. They have shared the company of their brothers and sisters, joined with them in prayer, and endeavored to follow Christ's commands more perfectly.

And so I am pleased to recognize their desire to participate fully in the sacramental life of the Church. I ask their sponsors now to state their opinion once again, so that all of you may hear.

He addresses the sponsors:

Do you consider these candidates ready to receive the sacraments of confirmation and the eucharist?

Sponsors:
We do.

When appropriate in the circumstances, the celebrant may
also ask the entire assembly to express its approval of the
candidates in these or similar words:

Celebrant:
**Now I ask you, the members of this community:
Are you willing to affirm the testimony expressed
about these candidates and support them in faith,
prayer and example as they prepare to participate
more fully in the Church's sacraments?**

All:
We are.

B
**The Christian life and the demands that flow from
the sacraments cannot be taken lightly. Therefore, before granting these candidates their request to share
fully in the Church's sacraments, it is important that
the Church hear the testimony of their sponsors
about their readiness.**

He addresses the sponsors:
**Have they faithfully listened to the apostles' instruc-
tion proclaimed by the Church?**

Sponsors:
They have.

Celebrant:
**Have they come to a deeper appreciation of their bap-
tism, in which they were joined to Christ and his
Church?**

Sponsors:
They have.

Celebrant:
**Have they reflected sufficiently on the tradition of
the Church, which is their heritage, and joined their
brothers and sisters in prayer?**

Sponsors:
They have.

Celebrant:
Have they advanced in a life of love and service of others?

Sponsors:
They have.

When appropriate in the circumstances, the celebrant may also ask the entire assembly to express its approval of the candidates in these or similar words:

Celebrant:
And now I speak to you, my brothers and sisters in this assembly:

Are you ready to support the testimony expressed about these candidates and include them in your prayer and affection as we move toward Easter?

All:
We are.

ACT OF RECOGNITION

557. The celebrant then says:

N. and N., the Church recognizes your desire (to be sealed with the gift of the Holy Spirit and) to have a place at Christ's eucharistic table. Join with us this Lent in a spirit of repentance. Hear the Lord's call to conversion and be faithful to your baptismal covenant.

Candidates:
Thanks be to God.

Then the celebrant turns to the sponsors and instructs them in the following or similar words.

Sponsors, continue to support these candidates with your guidance and concern. May they see in you a love for the Church and a sincere desire for doing good. Lead them this Lent to the joys of the Easter mysteries.

He invites them to place their hand on the shoulder of the candidate whom they are receiving into their care, or to make some other gesture to indicate the same intent.

INTERCESSIONS FOR THE ELECT AND THE
CANDIDATES

558. The community may use either of the following formularies, options **A** or **B,** or a similar formulary to pray for
the elect and the candidates. The celebrant may adapt the
introduction and the intentions to fit various circumstances.

[If it is decided, in accord with no. 561, that after the dismissal of the elect the usual general intercessions of the
Mass are to be omitted and that the liturgy of the eucharist
is to begin immediately, intentions for the Church and the
whole world are to be added to the following intentions for
the elect and candidates.]

Celebrant:
**My brothers and sisters, in beginning this period of
Lent, we look forward to celebrating at Easter the
life-giving mysteries of our Lord's suffering, death,
and resurrection. These elect and candidates, whom
we bring with us to the Easter sacraments, will look
to us for an example of Christian renewal. Let us
pray to the Lord for them and for ourselves, that we
may be renewed by one another's efforts and together come to share the joys of Easter.**

A Assisting minister:
**That together we may fruitfully employ this Lenten
season to renew ourselves through self-denial and
works of holiness, let us pray to the Lord:**
℟. **Lord, hear our prayer.**

Assisting minister:
**That our catechumens may always remember this day
of their election and be grateful for the blessings
they have received from heaven, let us pray to the
Lord:**
℟. **Lord, hear our prayer.**

Assisting minister:
**That our candidates preparing for confirmation and
eucharist (*or:* reception into the full communion of
the Catholic Church) may grow daily in fidelity to
their baptismal covenant, let us pray to the Lord:**
℟. **Lord, hear our prayer.**

Assisting minister:
That their teachers may always convey the beauty of
God's word to those who search for it, let us pray to
the Lord:
℟. Lord, hear our prayer.

Assisting minister:
That their godparents and sponsors may be living ex-
amples of the Gospel, let us pray to the Lord:
℟. Lord, hear our prayer.

Assisting minister:
That their families may help them to follow the
promptings of the Spirit, let us pray to the Lord:
℟. Lord, hear our prayer.

Assisting minister:
That our community, during this Lenten period, may
grow in charity and be constant in prayer, let us pray
to the Lord:
℟. Lord, hear our prayer.

Assisting minister:
That those who have not yet overcome their hesita-
tion may trust in Christ and come to join our commu-
nity as our brothers and sisters, let us pray to the
Lord:
℟. Lord, hear our prayer.

B Assisting minister:
That these elect and candidates may find joy in daily
prayer, we pray:
℟. Lord, hear our prayer.

Assisting minister:
That by praying to you often, they may grow ever
closer to you, we pray:
℟. Lord, hear our prayer.

Assisting minister:
That they may read your word and joyfully dwell on
it in their hearts, we pray:
℟. Lord, hear our prayer.

Assisting minister:
**That they may humbly acknowledge their faults and
work wholeheartedly to correct them, we pray:**
R̝. Lord, hear our prayer.

Assisting minister:
**That they may dedicate their daily work as a pleasing
offering to you, we pray:**
R̝. Lord, hear our prayer.

Assisting minister:
**That each day of Lent they may do something in
your honor, we pray:**
R̝. Lord, hear our prayer.

Assisting minister:
**That they may abstain with courage from everything
that defiles the heart, we pray:**
R̝. Lord, hear our prayer.

Assisting minister:
**That they may grow to love and seek virtue and holi-
ness of life, we pray:**
R̝. Lord, hear our prayer.

Assisting minister:
**That they may renounce self and put others first, we
pray:**
R̝. Lord, hear our prayer.

Assisting minister:
**That you will protect and bless their families, we
pray:**
R̝. Lord, hear our prayer.

Assisting minister:
**That they may share with others the joy they have
found in their faith, we pray:**
R̝. Lord, hear our prayer.

PRAYER OVER THE ELECT AND THE CANDIDATES

559. After the intercessions, the celebrant, with hands outstretched over the elect and the candidates, says one of the
following prayers.

A
Lord God,
you created the human race
and are the author of its renewal.

Bless all your adopted children
and add these chosen ones
to the harvest of your new covenant.
As true children of the promise,
may they rejoice in eternal life,
won, not by the power of nature,
but through the mystery of your grace.

We ask this through Christ our Lord.
R̝. Amen.

B
Father of love and power,
it is your will to establish everything in Christ
and to draw us into his all-embracing love.

Guide these chosen ones:
strengthen them in their vocation,
build them into the kingdom of your Son,
and seal them with the Spirit of your promise.

We ask this through Christ our Lord.
R̝. Amen.

DISMISSAL OF THE ELECT
560. If the eucharist is to be celebrated, the elect are normally dismissed at this point by use of option **A** or **B**; if the elect are to stay for the celebration of the eucharist, option **C** is used; if the eucharist is not to be celebrated, the entire assembly is dismissed by use of option **D**.

A The celebrant dismisses the elect in these or similar words.

My dear children, you have set out with us on the road that leads to the glory of Easter. Christ will be your way, your truth, and your life. Until we meet again for the scrutinies, walk always in his peace.

The elect:
Amen.

B As an optional formulary for dismissing the elect, the celebrant may use these or similar words.

My dear friends, this community now sends you forth to reflect more deeply upon the word of God which you have shared with us today. Be assured of our loving support and prayers for you. We look forward to the day when you will share fully in the Lord's Table.

C If for serious reasons the elect cannot leave (see no. 75.3) and must remain with the rest of the liturgical assembly, they, along with the candidates, are to be instructed that though they are present at the eucharist, they cannot take part in it as the Catholic faithful do. They may be reminded of this by the celebrant in these or similar words.

Although you cannot yet participate fully in the Lord's eucharist, stay with us as a sign of our hope that all God's children will eat and drink with the Lord and work with his Spirit to re-create the face of the earth.

D The celebrant dismisses those present, using these or similar words.

Go in peace, and may the Lord remain with you always.

All:
Thanks be to God.

An appropriate song may conclude the celebration.

LITURGY OF THE EUCHARIST

561. When this rite is celebrated with the bishop, the liturgy of the eucharist is usually omitted. However, when the eucharist is to follow, intercessory prayer is resumed with the usual general intercessions for the needs of the Church and the whole world; then, if required, the profession of faith is said. But for pastoral reasons these general intercessions and the profession of faith may be omitted. The liturgy of the eucharist then begins as usual with the preparation of the gifts.

RITE 4: CELEBRATION AT THE EASTER VIGIL OF THE SACRAMENTS OF INITIATION AND OF THE RITE OF RECEPTION INTO THE FULL COMMUNION OF THE CATHOLIC CHURCH

The Father chose us in Christ to be holy and spotless in love

562. Pastoral considerations may suggest that along with the celebration of the sacraments of Christian initiation the Easter Vigil should include the rite of reception of already baptized Christians into the full communion of the Catholic Church. But such a decision must be guided by the theological and pastoral directives proper to each rite. The model provided here simply arranges the ritual elements belonging to such a combined celebration. But the model can only be used properly in the light of nos. 206–217, regarding celebration of the sacraments of Christian initiation, and of nos. 473–486, regarding the rite of reception into the full communion of the Catholic Church.

563. Inclusion at the Easter Vigil of the rite of reception into full communion may also be opportune liturgically, especially when the candidates have undergone a lengthy period of spiritual formation coinciding with Lent. In the liturgical year the Easter Vigil, the preeminent commemoration of Christ's paschal mystery, is the preferred occasion for the celebration in which the elect will enter the paschal mystery through baptism, confirmation, and eucharist. Candidates for reception, who in baptism have already been justified by faith and incorporated into Christ,[1] are entering fully into a community that is constituted by its communion both in faith and in the sacramental sharing of the paschal mystery. The celebration of their reception at the Easter Vigil provides the candidates with a privileged opportunity to recall and reaffirm their own baptism, "the sacramental bond of unity [and] foundation of communion between all Christians."[2] At the Easter Vigil these candidates can make their profession of faith by joining the community in the re-

[1]See Secretariat for Christian Unity, *Ecumenical Directory I*, no. 11: AAS 59 (1967), 578–579. Vatican Council II, Decree on Ecumenism *Unitatis redintegratio*, no. 3.
[2]See *Ecumenical Directory I*, no. 11: AAS 59 (1967), 578. Vatican Council II, Decree on Ecumenism *Unitatis redintegratio*, no. 22.

newal of the baptismal promises, and, if they have not yet been confirmed, they can receive the sacrament of confirmation, which is intimately connected with baptism. Since of its nature baptism points to complete entrance into eucharistic communion,[3] the baptismal themes of the Easter Vigil can serve to emphasize why the high point of the candidates' reception is their sharing in the eucharist with the Catholic community for the first time (see no. 475.1).

564. The decision to combine the two celebrations at the Easter Vigil must be guided by the provision in the *Rite of Reception*, Introduction (no. 475.2). The decision should, then, be consistent in the actual situation with respect for ecumenical values and be guided by attentiveness both to local conditions and to personal and family preferences. The person to be received should always be consulted about the form of reception (see no. 475.2).

565. In its actual arrangement the celebration itself must reflect the status of candidates for reception into the full communion of the Catholic Church: such candidates have already been incorporated into Christ in baptism and anything that would equate them with catechumens is to be absolutely avoided (see no. 477).

[3]See Vatican Council II, Decree on Ecumenism *Unitatis redintegratio*, no. 22.

CELEBRATION AT THE EASTER VIGIL OF THE SACRAMENTS OF INITIATION AND OF THE RITE OF RECEPTION INTO THE FULL COMMUNION OF THE CATHOLIC CHURCH

566. Those who will be received into full communion at the Easter Vigil, along with their sponsors, should take places apart from the elect who will be called forward for the celebration of baptism.

The homily should include reference not only to the sacraments of initiation but also to reception into full communion (see no. 489).

CELEBRATION OF BAPTISM

567. The celebration of baptism begins after the homily. It takes place at the baptismal font, if this is in view of the faithful; otherwise in the sanctuary, where a vessel of water for the rite should be prepared beforehand.

PRESENTATION OF THE CANDIDATES FOR BAPTISM

568. Accordingly, one of the following procedures, options A, B, or C, is chosen for the presentation of the candidates for baptism.

A
When Baptism Is Celebrated Immediately at the Baptismal Font
The celebrant accompanied by the assisting ministers goes directly to the font. An assisting deacon or other minister calls the candidates for baptism forward and their godparents present them. Then the candidates and the godparents take their place around the font in such a way as not to block the view of the assembly. The invitation to prayer (no. 569) and the Litany of the Saints (no. 221) follow.

[If there are a great many candidates, they and their godparents simply take their place around the font during the singing of the Litany of the Saints.]

B
When Baptism Is Celebrated after a Procession to the Font
There may be a full procession to the baptismal font. In this case an assisting deacon or other minister calls the candi-

dates for baptism forward and their godparents present
them.

[If there are a great many candidates, they and their godparents simply take their place in the procession].

The procession is formed in this order: a minister carries
the Easter candle at the head of the procession (unless, outside the Easter Vigil, it already rests at the baptismal font),
the candidates with their godparents come next, then the
celebrant with the assisting ministers. The Litany of the
Saints (no. 221) is sung during the procession. When the
procession has reached the font, the candidates and their
godparents take their place around the font in such a way
as not to block the view of the assembly. The invitation to
prayer (no. 569) precedes the blessing of the water.

C
When Baptism Is Celebrated in the Sanctuary
An assisting deacon or other minister calls the candidates
for baptism forward and their godparents present them.
The candidates and their godparents take their place before
the celebrant in the sanctuary in such a way as not to block
the view of the assembly. The invitation to prayer (no. 569)
and the Litany of the Saints (no. 570, see no. 221) follow.

[If there are a great many candidates, they and their godparents simply take their place in the sanctuary during the
singing of the Litany of the Saints.]

INVITATION TO PRAYER

569. The celebrant addresses the following or a similar invitation for the assembly to join in prayer for the candidates
for baptism.

**Dear friends, let us pray to almighty God for our
brothers and sisters, N. and N., who are asking for
baptism. He has called them and brought them to
this moment; may he grant them light and strength to
follow Christ with resolute hearts and to profess the
faith of the Church. May he give them the new life
of the Holy Spirit, whom we are about to call down
on this water.**

LITANY OF THE SAINTS

570. See no. 221.

BLESSING OF THE WATER

571. After the Litany of the Saints, facing the font (or vessel) containing the water, the celebrant sings the following:

**Father,
you give us grace through sacramental signs,
which tell us of the wonders of your unseen power.**

**In baptism we use your gift of water,
which you have made a rich symbol of the grace
you give us in this sacrament.**

**At the very dawn of creation
your Spirit breathed on the waters,
making them the wellspring of all holiness.**

**The waters of the great flood
you made a sign of the waters of baptism
that make an end of sin
and a new beginning of goodness.**

**Through the waters of the Red Sea
you led Israel out of slavery
to be an image of God's holy people,
set free from sin by baptism.**

**In the waters of the Jordan
your Son was baptized by John
and anointed with the Spirit.**

**Your Son willed that water and blood should flow
   from his side
as he hung upon the cross.**

**After his resurrection he told his disciples:
"Go out and teach all nations,
baptizing them in the name of the Father, and of the
   Son, and of the Holy Spirit."**

**Father,
look now with love upon your Church
and unseal for it the fountain of baptism.**

By the power of the Holy Spirit
give to this water the grace of your Son,
so that in the sacrament of baptism
all those whom you have created in your likeness
may be cleansed from sin
and rise to a new birth of innocence
by water and the Holy Spirit.

Here, if this can be done conveniently, the celebrant before continuing lowers the Easter candle into the water once or three times, then holds it there until the acclamation at the end of the blessing.

We ask you, Father, with your Son
to send the Holy Spirit upon the waters of this font.
May all who are buried with Christ in the death of
     baptism
rise also with him to newness of life.

We ask this through Christ our Lord.

All:
Amen.

If the Easter candle has been held in the water, the celebrant then raises it and the people sing the following or another suitable acclamation.

Springs of water, bless the Lord.
Give him glory and praise for ever.

PROFESSION OF FAITH

572. After the blessing of the water, the celebrant continues with the profession of faith, which includes the renunciation of sin and the profession itself.

RENUNCIATION OF SIN

573. See no. 224.

PROFESSION OF FAITH

574. See no. 225.

BAPTISM

575. See no. 226.

EXPLANATORY RITES
576. See no. 227.

ANOINTING AFTER BAPTISM
577. See no. 228.

CLOTHING WITH A BAPTISMAL GARMENT
578. See no. 229.

PRESENTATION OF A LIGHTED CANDLE

579. The celebrant takes the Easter candle in his hands or touches it, saying:

Godparents, please come forward to give to the newly baptized the light of Christ.

A godparent of each of the newly baptized goes to the celebrant, lights a candle from the Easter candle, then presents it to the newly baptized.

Then the celebrant says to the newly baptized:
You have been enlightened by Christ.
Walk always as children of the light
and keep the flame of faith alive in your hearts.
When the Lord comes, may you go out to meet him
with all the saints in the heavenly kingdom.

Newly baptized:
Amen.

RENEWAL OF BAPTISMAL PROMISES

INVITATION

580. After the celebration of baptism, the celebrant addresses the community, in order to invite those present to the renewal of their baptismal promises; the candidates for reception into full communion join the rest of the community in this renunciation of sin and profession of faith. All stand and hold lighted candles. The celebrant may use the following or similar words.

Dear friends, through the paschal mystery we have been buried with Christ in baptism, so that we may rise with him to newness of life. Now that we have completed our Lenten observance, let us renew the promises we made in baptism, when we rejected Satan and his works and promised to serve God faithfully in his holy catholic Church.

RENEWAL OF BAPTISMAL PROMISES

RENUNCIATION OF SIN

581. The celebrant continues with one of the following formularies of renunciation.

[If circumstances require, the conference of bishops may adapt formulary A in accord with local conditions.]

A Celebrant:
Do you reject sin so as to live in the freedom of God's children?

All:
I do.

Celebrant:
Do you reject the glamor of evil, and refuse to be mastered by sin?

All:
I do.

Celebrant:
Do you reject Satan, father of sin and prince of darkness?

All:
I do.

B Celebrant:
Do you reject Satan?

All:
I do.

Celebrant:
And all his works?

All:
I do.

Celebrant:
And all his empty promises?

All:
I do.

PROFESSION OF FAITH

582. Then the celebrant continues:

**Do you believe in God, the Father almighty, creator
  of heaven and earth?**

All:
I do.

Celebrant:
**Do you believe in Jesus Christ, his only Son, our
  Lord,
  who was born of the Virgin Mary,
  was crucified, died, and was buried,
  rose from the dead,
  and is now seated at the right hand of the Father?**

All:
I do.

Celebrant:
**Do you believe in the Holy Spirit,
  the holy catholic Church, the communion of saints,
  the forgiveness of sins, the resurrection of the
  body,
  and the life everlasting?**

All:
I do.

SPRINKLING WITH BAPTISMAL WATER

583. The celebrant sprinkles all the people with the
blessed baptismal water, while all sing the following song
or any other that is baptismal in character.

I saw water flowing
from the right side of the temple, alleluia.
It brought God's life and his salvation,
and the people sang in joyful praise:
alleluia, alleluia. (See Ezekiel 47:1–2,9)

The celebrant then concludes with the following prayer.
God, the all-powerful Father of our Lord Jesus
Christ, has given us a new birth by water and the
Holy Spirit and forgiven all our sins.
May he also keep us faithful to our Lord Jesus Christ
for ever and ever.

All:
Amen.

CELEBRATION OF RECEPTION

INVITATION

584. If baptism has been celebrated at the font, the celebrant, the assisting ministers, and the newly baptized with their godparents proceed to the sanctuary. As they do so the assembly may sing a suitable song.

Then in the following or similar words the celebrant invites the candidates for reception, along with their sponsors, to come into the sanctuary and before the community to make a profession of faith.

N and N., of your own free will you have asked to
be received into the full communion of the Catholic
Church. You have made your decision after careful
thought under the guidance of the Holy Spirit. I now
invite you to come forward with your sponsors and
in the presence of this community to profess the
Catholic faith. In this faith you will be one with us
for the first time at the eucharistic table of the Lord
Jesus, the sign of the Church's unity.

PROFESSION BY THE CANDIDATES

585. When the candidates for reception and their sponsors have taken their places in the sanctuary, the celebrant asks the candidates to make the following profession of faith. The candidates say:

**I believe and profess all that the holy Catholic
Church believes, teaches, and proclaims to be revealed by God.**

ACT OF RECEPTION

586. Then the candidates with their sponsors go individually to the celebrant, who says to each candidate (laying his
right hand on the head of any candidate who is not to receive confirmation):

**N., the Lord receives you into the Catholic Church.
His loving kindness has led you here,
so that in the unity of the Holy Spirit
you may have full communion with us
in the faith that you have professed in the presence
  of his family.**

CELEBRATION OF CONFIRMATION

587. Before the celebration of confirmation begins, the assembly may sing a suitable song.

588. If the bishop has conferred baptism, he should now
also confer confirmation. If the bishop is not present, the
priest who conferred baptism and received the candidates
into full communion is authorized to confirm.

[When there are a great many persons to be confirmed, the
minister of confirmation may associate priests with himself
as ministers of the sacrament (see no. 14).]

INVITATION

589. The newly baptized with their godparents and, if
they have not received the sacrament of confirmation, the
newly received with their sponsors, stand before the celebrant. He first speaks briefly to the newly baptized and the
newly received in these or similar words.

**My dear candidates for confirmation, by your bap-
tism you have been born again in Christ and you
have become members of Christ and of his priestly
people. Now you are to share in the outpouring of
the Holy Spirit among us, the Spirit sent by the Lord**

upon his apostles at Pentecost and given by them
and their successors to the baptized.

The promised strength of the Holy Spirit, which you
are to receive, will make you more like Christ and
help you to be witnesses to his suffering, death, and
resurrection. It will strengthen you to be active members of the Church and to build up the Body of
Christ in faith and love.

[The priests who will be associated with the celebrant as
ministers of the sacrament now stand next to him.]

With hands joined, the celebrant next addresses the people:

My dear friends, let us pray to God our Father, that
he will pour out the Holy Spirit on these candidates
for confirmation to strengthen them with his gifts
and anoint them to be more like Christ, the Son of
God.

All pray briefly in silence.

LAYING ON OF HANDS

590. The celebrant holds his hands outstretched over the
entire group of those to be confirmed and says the following prayer.

[In silence the priests associated as ministers of the sacrament also hold their hands outstretched over the
candidates.]

All-powerful God, Father of our Lord Jesus Christ,
by water and the Holy Spirit
you freed your sons and daughters from sin
and gave them new life.

Send your Holy Spirit upon them
to be their helper and guide.

Give them the spirit of wisdom and understanding,
the spirit of right judgment and courage,
the spirit of knowledge and reverence.
Fill them with the spirit of wonder and awe in your
    presence.

We ask this through Christ our Lord.
R/. Amen.

ANOINTING WITH CHRISM

591. A minister brings the chrism to the celebrant.

[When the celebrant is the bishop, priests who are associated as ministers of the sacrament receive the chrism from him.]

Each candidate, with godparent or godparents or with sponsors, goes to the celebrant (or to an associated minister of the sacrament); or, if circumstances require, the celebrant (associated ministers) may go to the candidates.

Either or both godparents and sponsors place the right hand on the shoulder of the candidate; a godparent or a sponsor or the candidate gives the candidate's name to the minister of the sacrament. During the conferral of the sacrament an appropriate song may be sung.

The minister of the sacrament dips his right thumb in the chrism and makes the sign of the cross on the forehead of the one to be confirmed as he says:

N., be sealed with the Gift of the Holy Spirit.

Newly confirmed:
Amen.

The minister of the sacrament adds:
Peace be with you.

Newly confirmed:
And also with you.

After all have received the sacrament, the newly confirmed as well as the godparents and sponsors are led to their places in the assembly.

LITURGY OF THE EUCHARIST

592. Since the profession of faith is not said, the general intercessions begin immediately and for the first time the neophytes take part in them. Some of the neophytes also take part in the procession to the altar with the gifts.

593. With Eucharistic Prayers I, II, or III the special interpolations given in the Roman Missal, the ritual Mass, "Christian Initiation: Baptism" are used.

594. It is most desirable that the neophytes and newly received, together with their godparents, sponsors, parents, spouses, and catechists, receive communion under both kinds.

Before saying "This is the Lamb of God," the celebrant may briefly remind the neophytes of the preeminence of the eucharist, which is the climax of their initiation and the center of the whole Christian life. He may also mention that for those received into full communion this first full sharing with the Catholic community in eucharistic communion is the high point of their reception.

APPENDIX II

ACCLAMATIONS, HYMNS, AND SONGS

Praised be the Father of our Lord Jesus Christ, a God so merciful and kind

ACCLAMATIONS FROM SACRED SCRIPTURE

595. The following are acclamations from Sacred Scripture.   390

1.
Lord God, who is your equal?
Strong, majestic, and holy!
Worthy of praise, worker of wonders! (Exodus 15:11)

2.
God is light: in him there is no darkness. (1 John 1:5)

3.
God is love; those who live in love, live in God.
   (1 John 4:16)

4.
There is one God, one Father of all;
he is over all, and through all;
he lives in all of us. (Ephesians 4:6)

5.
Come to him and receive his light! (Psalm 34:6)

6.
Blessed be God who chose you in Christ. (See Ephesians 1:3–4)

7.
You are God's work of art, created in Christ Jesus.
   (Ephesians 2:10)

8.
You are now God's children, my dearest friends.
What you shall be in his glory has not yet been re-
vealed. (1 John 3:2)

9.
Think of how God loves you!
He calls you his own children,
and that is what you are. (1 John 3:1)

10.
Happy are those who have washed their robes clean,
washed in the blood of the Lamb! (Revelation 22:14)

11.
All of you are one,
united in Christ Jesus. (Galatians 3:28)

12.
Imitate God; walk in his love,
just as Christ loves us. (Ephesians 5:1–2)

HYMNS IN THE STYLE OF THE NEW TESTAMENT

596. The following are hymns in the style of the New Testament.

390

1.
Praised be the Father of our Lord Jesus Christ,
a God so merciful and kind!
He has given us a new birth, a living hope,
by raising Jesus his Son from death.
Salvation is our undying inheritance,
preserved for us in heaven,
salvation at the end of time. (1 Peter 1:3–5)

2.
How great the sign of God's love for us,
Jesus Christ our Lord:
promised before all time began,
revealed in these last days.
He lived and suffered and died for us,
but the Spirit raised him to life.
People everywhere have heard his message
and placed their faith in him.
What wonderful blessings he gives his people;
living in the Father's glory;
he fills all creation
and guides it to perfection. (See 1 Timothy 3:16)

SONGS FROM ANCIENT LITURGIES

597. The following are songs from ancient liturgies.

390

1.
We believe in you, Lord Jesus Christ.
Fill our hearts with your radiance
and make us the children of light!

2.
We come to you, Lord Jesus.
Fill us with your life.
Make us children of the Father
and one in you.

3.
Lord Jesus, from your wounded side
flowed streams of cleansing water;
the world was washed of all its sin,
all life made new again!

4.
The Father's voice calls us above the waters,
the glory of the Son shines on us,
the love of the Spirit fills us with life.

5.
Holy Church of God, stretch out your hand
and welcome your children,
newborn of water
and of the Spirit of God.

6.
Rejoice, you newly baptized,
chosen members of the Kingdom.
Buried with Christ in death,
you are reborn in him by faith.

7.
This is the fountain of life that floods the entire
    world,
the water that took its beginning
from the pierced side of Christ.
You who are born again of this water,
place your hope in the kingdom of heaven.

APPENDIX III

NATIONAL STATUTES FOR THE CATECHUMENATE

Imitate God; walk in his love, just as Christ loves us

NATIONAL STATUTES FOR THE CATECHUMENATE

Approved by the National Conference of Catholic Bishops on November 11, 1986

PRECATECHUMENATE

1. Any reception or service of welcome or prayer for inquirers at the beginning or during a precatechumenate (or in an earlier period of evangelization) must be entirely informal. Such meetings should take into account that the inquirers are not yet catechumens and that the rite of acceptance into the order of catechumens, intended for those who have been converted from unbelief and have initial faith, may not be anticipated.

CATECHUMENATE

2. The term "catechumen" should be strictly reserved for the unbaptized who have been admitted into the order of catechumens; the term "convert" should be reserved strictly for those converted from unbelief to Christian belief and never used of those baptized Christians who are received into the full communion of the Catholic Church.

3. This holds true even if elements of catechumenal formation are appropriate for those who are not catechumens, namely, (a) baptized Catholic Christians who have not received catechetical instruction and whose Christian initiation has not been completed by confirmation and eucharist and (b) baptized Christians who have been members of another Church or ecclesial community and seek to be received into the full communion of the Catholic Church.

4. If the catechumenal preparation takes place in a non-parochial setting such as a center, school, or other institution, the catechumens should be introduced into the Christian life of a parish or similar community from the very beginning of the catechumenate, so that after their initiation and mystagogy they will not find themselves isolated from the ordinary life of the Christian people.

5. In the celebration of the rite of acceptance into the order of catechumens, it is for the diocesan bishop to determine whether the additional rites listed in no. 74, *Rite of Christian Initiation of Adults,* are to be incorporated (see no. 33.5).

6. The period of catechumenate, beginning at acceptance into the order of catechumens and including both the catechumenate proper and the period of purification and enlightenment after election or enrollment of names, should extend for at least one year of formation, instruction, and probation. Ordinarily this period should go from at least the Easter season of one year until the next; preferably it should begin before Lent in one year and extend until Easter of the following year.

7. A thoroughly comprehensive catechesis on the truths of Catholic doctrine and moral life, aided by approved catechetical texts, is to be provided during the period of the catechumenate (see RCIA, no. 75).

CATECHUMENS

8. Catechumens should be encouraged to seek blessings and other suffrages from the Church, since they are of the household of Christ; they are entitled to Christian burial should they die before the completion of their initiation.

9. In this case, the funeral liturgy, including the funeral Mass, should be celebrated as usual, omitting only language referring directly to the sacraments which the catechumen has not received. In view of the sensibilities of the immediate family of the deceased catechumen, however, the funeral Mass may be omitted at the discretion of the pastor.

10. The marriages of catechumens, whether with other catechumens or with baptized Christians or even non-Christians, should be celebrated at a liturgy of the word

and never at the eucharistic liturgy. Chapter III of the *Rite of Marriage* is to be followed, but the nuptial blessing in Chapter I, no. 33, may be used, all references to eucharistic sharing being omitted.

MINISTER OF BAPTISM AND CONFIRMATION

11. The diocesan bishop is the proper minister of the sacraments of initiation for adults, including children of catechetical age, in accord with canon 852:1. If he is unable to celebrate the sacraments of initiation with all the candidates of the local church, he should at least celebrate the rite of election or enrollment of names, ordinarily at the beginning of Lent, for the catechumens of the diocese.

12. Priests who do not exercise a pastoral office but participate in a catechumenal program require a mandate from the diocesan bishop if they are to baptize adults; they then do not require any additional mandate or authorization in order to confirm, but have the faculty to confirm from the law, as do priests who baptize adults in the exercise of their pastoral office.

13. Since those who have the faculty to confirm are bound to exercise it in accord with canon 885:2, and may not be prohibited from using the faculty, a diocesan bishop who is desirous of confirming neophytes should reserve to himself the baptism of adults in accord with canon 863.

CELEBRATION OF THE SACRAMENTS OF INITIATION

14. In order to signify clearly the interrelation or coalescence of the three sacraments which are required for full Christian initiation (canon 842:2), adult candidates, including children of catechetical age, are to receive baptism, confirmation, and eucharist in a single eucharistic celebration, whether at the Easter Vigil or, if necessary, at some other time.

15. Candidates for initiation, as well as those who assist them and participate in the celebration of the Easter Vigil with them, are encouraged to keep and extend the paschal fast of Good Friday, as determined by canon 1251, throughout the day of Holy Saturday until the end of the Vigil itself, in accord with the Constitution on the Liturgy, *Sacrosanctum Concilium*, art. 110.

16. The rite of anointing with the oil of catechumens is to be omitted in the baptism of adults at the Easter Vigil.

17. Baptism by immersion is the fuller and more expressive sign of the sacrament and, therefore, is preferred. Although it is not yet a common practice in the United States, provision should be made for its more frequent use in the baptism of adults. At the least, the provision of the *Rite of Christian Initiation of Adults* for partial immersion, namely, immersion of the candidate's head, should be taken into account.

CHILDREN OF CATECHETICAL AGE

18. Since children who have reached the use of reason are considered, for purposes of Christian initiation, to be adults (canon 852:1), their formation should follow the general pattern of the ordinary catechumenate as far as possible, with the appropriate adaptations permitted by the ritual. They should receive the sacraments of baptism, confirmation, and eucharist at the Easter Vigil, together with the older catechumens.

19. Some elements of the ordinary catechetical instruction of baptized children before their reception of the sacraments of confirmation and eucharist may be appropriately shared with catechumens of catechetical age. Their condition and status as catechumens, however, should not be compromised or confused, nor should they receive the sacraments of initiation in any sequence other than that determined in the ritual of Christian initiation.

ABBREVIATED CATECHUMENATE

20. The abbreviated catechumenate, which the diocesan bishop may permit only in individual and exceptional cases, as described in nos. 307–308 of the *Rite of Christian Initiation of Adults*, should always be as limited as possible. It should extend over a substantial and appropriate period of time. The rites prior to sacramental initiation should not be unduly compressed, much less celebrated on a single occasion. The catechumenate of persons who move from one parish to another or from one diocese to another should not on that account alone be abbreviated.

21. Candidates who have received their formation in an abbreviated catechumenate should receive the sacraments of Christian initiation at the Easter Vigil, if possible, together with candidates who have participated in the more extended catechumenate. They should also participate in the period of mystagogy, to the extent possible.

MYSTAGOGY

22. After the completion of their Christian initiation in the sacraments of baptism, confirmation, and eucharist, the neophytes should begin the period of mystagogy by participating in the principal Sunday Eucharist of the community throughout the Easter season, which ends on Pentecost Sunday. They should do this as a body in company with their godparents and those who have assisted in their Christian formation.

23. Under the moderation of the diocesan bishop, the mystagogy should embrace a deepened understanding of the mysteries of baptism, confirmation, and the eucharist, and especially of the eucharist as the continuing celebration of faith and conversion.

24. After the immediate mystagogy or postbaptismal catechesis during the Easter season, the program for the neophytes should extend until the anniversary of Christian initiation, with at least monthly assemblies of the neophytes for their deeper Christian formation and incorporation into the full life of the Christian community.

UNCATECHIZED ADULT CATHOLICS

25. Although baptized adult Catholics who have never received catechetical instruction or been admitted to the sacraments of confirmation and eucharist are not catechumens, some elements of the usual catechumenal formation are appropriate to their preparation for the sacraments, in accord with the norms of the ritual, "Preparation of Uncatechized Adults for Confirmation and Eucharist."

26. Although it is not generally recommended, if the sacramental initiation of such candidates is completed with confirmation and eucharist on the same occasion as the celebration of the full Christian initiation of candidates for baptism, the condition and status of those already baptized should be carefully respected and distinguished.

27. The celebration of the sacrament of reconciliation with candidates for confirmation and eucharist is to be carried out at a time prior to and distinct from the celebration of confirmation and the eucharist. As part of the formation of such candidates, they should be encouraged in the frequent celebration of this sacrament.

28. Priests mentioned in canon 883:2 also have the faculty to confirm (a) in the case of the readmission to communion of a baptized Catholic who has been an apostate from the faith and also (b) in the case of a baptized Catholic who has without fault been instructed in a non-Catholic religion or adhered to a non-Catholic religion, but (c) not in the case of a baptized Catholic who without his or her fault never put the faith into practice.

29. In the instance mentioned in no. 28 c, in order to maintain the interrelationship and sequence of confirmation and eucharist as defined in canon 842:2, priests who lack the faculty to confirm should seek it from the diocesan bishop, who may, in accord with canon 884:1, grant the faculty if he judges it necessary.

RECEPTION INTO FULL CATHOLIC COMMUNION

30. Those who have already been baptized in another Church or ecclesial community should not be treated as catechumens or so designated. Their doctrinal and spiritual preparation for reception into full Catholic communion should be determined according to the individual case, that is, it should depend on the extent to which the baptized person has led a Christian life within a community of faith and been appropriately catechized to deepen his or her inner adherence to the Church.

31. Those who have been baptized but have received relatively little Christian upbringing may participate in the elements of catechumenal formation so far as necessary and appropriate, but should not take part in rites intended for the unbaptized catechumens. They may, however, participate in celebrations of the word together with catechumens. In addition they may be included with uncatechized adult

Catholics in such rites as may be appropriate among those included or mentioned in the ritual in Part II, 4, "Preparation of Uncatechized Adults for Confirmation and Eucharist." The rites of presentation of the Creed, the Lord's Prayer, and the book of the Gospels are not proper except for those who have received no Christian instruction and formation. Those baptized persons who have lived as Christians and need only instruction in the Catholic tradition and a degree of probation within the Catholic community should not be asked to undergo a full program parallel to the catechumenate.

32. The reception of candidates into the communion of the Catholic Church should ordinarily take place at the Sunday Eucharist of the parish community, in such a way that it is understood that they are indeed Christian believers who have already shared in the sacramental life of the Church and are now welcomed into the Catholic eucharistic community upon their profession of faith and confirmation, if they have not been confirmed, before receiving the eucharist.

33. It is preferable that reception into full communion not take place at the Easter Vigil lest there be any confusion of such baptized Christians with the candidates for baptism, possible misunderstanding of or even reflection upon the sacrament of baptism celebrated in another Church or ecclesial community, or any perceived triumphalism in the liturgical welcome into the Catholic eucharistic community.

34. Nevertheless if there are both catechumens to be baptized and baptized Christians to be received into full communion at the Vigil, for pastoral reasons and in view of the Vigil's being the principal annual celebration of the Church, the combined rite is to be followed: "Celebration at the Easter Vigil of the Sacraments of Initiation and of the Rite of Reception into the Full Communion of the Catholic Church." A clear distinction should be maintained during the celebration between candidates for sacramental initiation and candidates for reception into full communion, and ecumenical sensitivities should be carefully respected.

35. The "Rite of Reception into the Full Communion of the Catholic Church" respects the traditional sequence of confirmation before eucharist. When the bishop, whose office it

is to receive adult Christians into the full communion of the Catholic Church (*RCIA*, no. 481 [R8]) entrusts the celebration of the rite to a presbyter, the priest receives from the law itself (canon 883:2) the faculty to confirm the candidate for reception and is obliged to use it (canon 885:2); he may not be prohibited from exercising the faculty. The confirmation of such candidates for reception should not be deferred, nor should they be admitted to the eucharist until they are confirmed. A diocesan bishop who is desirous of confirming those received into full communion should reserve the rite of reception to himself.

36. The celebration of the sacrament of reconciliation with candidates for reception into full communion is to be carried out at a time prior to and distinct from the celebration of the rite of reception. As part of the formation of such candidates, they should be encouraged in the frequent celebration of this sacrament.

37. There may be a reasonable and prudent doubt concerning the baptism of such Christians which cannot be resolved after serious investigation into the fact and/or validity of baptism, namely, to ascertain whether the person was baptized with water and with the Trinitarian formula, and whether the minister and the recipient of the sacrament had the proper requisite intentions. If conditional baptism then seems necessary, this must be celebrated privately rather than at a public liturgical assembly of the community and with only those limited rites which the diocesan bishop determines. The reception into full communion should take place later at the Sunday Eucharist of the community.

DOCUMENTATION

The *Rite of Christian Initiation of Adults* incorporates the (slight) emendations of the introduction (*praenotanda*) occasioned by the promulgation of the Code of Canon Law in 1983. It does not, however, include the text of pertinent canons or the underlying conciliar decisions and statements on the catechumenate, although the latter are reflected in the introduction to the ritual. In order to have these texts available in one place, this documentary appendix has been compiled.

A. Conciliar Constitutions and Decrees (Unless otherwise noted all translations are from: *Documents on the Liturgy, 1963–1979: Conciliar, Papal, and Curial Texts* [Collegeville, MN: The Liturgical Press, 1982])

Constitution on the Liturgy *Sacrosanctum Concilium*, art. 64: "The catechumenate for adults, divided into several stages, is to be restored and put into use at the discretion of the local Ordinary. By this means the time of the catechumenate, which is intended as a period of well-suited instruction, may be sanctified by sacred rites to be celebrated at successive intervals of time."

Constitution on the Liturgy *Sacrosanctum Concilium*, art. 65: "With art. 37–40 of this Constitution as the norm, it is lawful in mission lands to allow, besides what is part of Christian tradition, those initiation elements in use among individual peoples, to the extent that such elements are compatible with the Christian rite of initiation."

Constitution on the Liturgy *Sacrosanctum Concilium*, art. 66: "Both of the rites for the baptism of adults are to be revised: not only the simpler rite, but also the more solemn one, with proper attention to the restored catechumenate. A special Mass 'On the Occasion of a Baptism' is to be incorporated into the Roman Missal."

Dogmatic Constitution on the Church *Lumen Gentium*, no. 14: "This holy Council first of all turns its attention to the Catholic faithful. Basing itself on scripture and tradition, it teaches that the Church, a pilgrim now on earth, is necessary for salvation: the one Christ is mediator and the way of salvation; he is present to us in his body which is the Church. He himself explicitly asserted the necessity of faith and baptism (cf. Mk. 16:16; Jn. 3:5), and thereby affirmed at the same time the necessity of the Church which men enter through baptism as through a door. Hence they could not be saved who, knowing that the Catholic Church was founded as necessary by God through Christ, would refuse either to enter it, or to remain in it.

"Fully incorporated into the Church are those who, possessing the Spirit of Christ, accept all the means of salvation given to the Church together with her entire organization, and who—by the bonds constituted by the profession of faith, the sacraments, ecclesiastical government, and communion—are joined in the visible structure of the Church of Christ, who rules her through the Supreme Pontiff and the bishops. Even though incorporated into the Church, one who does not however persevere in charity is not saved. He remains indeed in the bosom of the Church, but 'in body' not 'in heart.' All children of the Church should nevertheless remember that their exalted condition results, not from their own merits, but from the grace of Christ. If they fail to respond in thought, word and deed to that grace, not only shall they not be saved, but they shall be the more severely judged.

"Catechumens who, moved by the Holy Spirit, desire with an explicit intention to be incorporated into the Church, are by that very intention joined to her. With love and solicitude mother Church already embraces them as her own" (Flannery translation).

Decree on the Church's Missionary Activity *Ad gentes*, no. 13: "Whenever God opens a door for the word in order to declare the mystery of Christ (cf. Col. 4:3) then the living God, and he whom he has sent for the salvation of all, Jesus Christ (cf. 1 Th. 1:9–10; 1 Cor. 1:18–21; Gal. 1:31; Acts 14:15–17; 17:22–31), are confidently and perseveringly (cf. Acts 4:13, 29, 31; 9:27, 28; 13:40; 14:3; 19:8; 26:26; 28:31; 1 Th. 2:2; 2 Cor. 3:12; 7:4; Phil. 1:20; Eph. 3:12; 6:19–20) proclaimed (cf. 1 Cor. 9:15; Rom. 10:14) to all men (cf. Mk. 16:15). And this is in order that non-Christians, whose heart is being opened by the Holy Spirit (cf. Acts 16:4), might, while believing, freely turn to the Lord who, since he is the 'way, the truth and the life' (Jn. 14:6), will satisfy all their inner hopes, or rather infinitely surpass them.

"This conversion is, indeed, only initial; sufficient however to make a man realize that he has been snatched from sin, and is being led into the mystery of God's love, who invites him to establish a personal relationship with him in Christ. Under the movement of divine grace the new convert sets out on a spiritual journey by means of which, while already sharing through faith in the mystery of the death and resurrection, he passes from the old man to the new man who has been made perfect in Christ (cf. Col. 3:5–10; Eph. 4:20–24). This transition, which involves a progressive change of outlook and morals, should be manifested in its social implications and effected gradually during the period of catechumenate. Since the Lord in whom he believes is a sign of contradiction (cf. Lk. 2:34; Mt. 10:34–39) the convert often has to suffer misunderstanding and separation, but he also experiences those joys which are generously granted by God.

"The Church strictly forbids that anyone should be forced to accept the faith, or be induced or enticed by unworthy devices; as it likewise strongly defends the right that no one should be frightened away from the faith by unjust persecutions.

"In accordance with the very ancient practice of the Church, the motives for the conversion should be examined and, if necessary, purified" (Flannery translation).

Decree on the Church's Missionary Activity *Ad gentes*, no. 14: "Those who through the Church have accepted from the Father faith in Christ should be admitted to the catechumenate by means of liturgical ceremonies. The catechumenate means not simply a presentation of teachings and precepts, but a formation in the whole of Christian life and a sufficiently prolonged period of training; by these means the disciples will become bound to Christ as their master. Catechumens should therefore be properly initiated into the mystery of salvation and the practices of gospel living; by means of sacred rites celebrated at successive times, they should be led gradually into the life of faith, liturgy, and charity belonging to the people of God.

"Next, freed from the power of darkness, dying, buried, and risen again together with Christ through the sacraments of Christian initiation, they receive the Spirit of adoption of children, and with the whole people of God celebrate the memorial of the Lord's death and resurrection.

"There is a great need for a reform of the Lenten and Easter liturgy so that it will be a spiritual preparation of the catechumens for the celebration of the paschal mystery, the rites of which will include their being reborn to Christ through baptism.

"Christian initiation during the catechumenate is not the concern of catechists or priests alone, but of the whole community of believers and especially of godparents, so that from the outset the catechumens will have a sense of being part of the people of God. Moreover, because the Church's life is apostolic, catechumens should learn to take an active share in the evangelization and the building up of the Church through the witness of their life and the profession of their faith.

"Finally, the new code of canon law should set out clearly the juridic status of catechumens; they are already joined to the Church, already part of Christ's household, and are in many cases already living a life of faith, hope, and charity."

Decree on the Church's Missionary Activity *Ad gentes*, no. 15: "The Holy Spirit calls all to Christ through the seed of the word and the preaching of the Gospel and inspires in hearts the obedience of faith. When in the womb of the baptismal font the Spirit gives birth into a new life to those who believe in Christ, he gathers them all together into the one people of God, 'a chosen race, a royal priesthood, a holy nation, God's own people' (1 Pt. 2:9).

"As God's co-workers, therefore, missionaries are to create congregations of believers of a kind that, living in a way worthy of their calling, will carry out the divinely appointed offices of priest, prophet, and king. This is how the Christian community becomes a sign of God's presence in the world: by the eucharistic sacrifice it goes constantly with Christ to the Father; strengthened by God's word, it bears witness to Christ; it walks in charity and burns with the apostolic spirit. Right from the beginning the Christian community should be trained to be as far as possible self-sufficient in regard to its own needs."

Decree on the Pastoral Office of Bishops in the Church *Christus Dominus*, no. 14: "[Bishops] should . . . take steps toward restoring the instruction of adult catechumens or toward adapting it more effectively."

Decree on the Ministry and Life of Priests *Presbyterorum ordinis*, no. 5: "God, who alone is holy and the author of holiness, willed to take to himself as companions and helpers men who would humbly dedicate themselves to the work of making others holy. Through the ministry of the bishop God consecrates priests to be sharers by a special title in the priesthood of Christ. In exercising sacred functions they act therefore as the ministers of him who in the liturgy continually fulfills his priestly office on our behalf by the action of his Spirit. By baptism men and women are brought into the people of God and the Church; by the oil of the sick those who are ill find relief; by the celebration of Mass people sacramentally offer the sacrifice of Christ. But in administering all the sacraments, as St. Ignatius the Martyr already attested in the early days of the Church, priests, on various grounds, are linked hierarchically with their bishop and so, in a certain way, bring his presence to every gathering of the faithful.

"The other sacraments, like every ministry of the Church and every work of the apostolate, are linked with the holy eucharist and have it as their end. For the eucharist contains the Church's entire spiritual wealth, that is, Christ, himself. He is our Passover and living bread; through his flesh, made living and life-giving by the Holy Spirit, he is bringing life to people and thereby inviting them to offer themselves together with him, as well as their labors and all created things. The eucharist therefore stands as the source and apex of all evangelization: catechumens are led gradually toward a share in the eucharist and the faithful who already bear the seal of baptism and confirmation enter through the eucharist more fully into the Body of Christ."

Decree on the Ministry and Life of Priests *Presbyterorum ordinis*, no. 6: "The pastor's task is not limited to individual care of the faithful. It extends by right also to the formation of a genuine Christian community. But if a community spirit is to be properly cultivated it must embrace not only the local church but the universal Church. A local community ought not merely to promote the care of the faithful within itself, but should be imbued with the missionary spirit and smooth the path to Christ for all men. But it must regard as its special charge those under instruction and the newly converted who are gradually educated in knowing and living the Christian life" (Flannery translation).

B. Code of Canon Law (Translations are from: *Code of Canon Law: Latin—English Edition* [Washington, DC: The Canon Law Society of America, 1983])

206. *1.* Catechumens are in union with the Church in a special manner, that is, under the influence of the Holy Spirit, they ask to be incorporated into the Church by ex-

plicit choice and are therefore united with the Church by that choice just as by a life of faith, hope and charity which they lead; the Church already cherishes them as its own.
2. The Church has special care for catechumens; the Church invites them to lead the evangelical life and introduces them to the celebration of sacred rites, and grants them various prerogatives which are proper to Christians.

787. *1.* By the witness of their life and words missionaries are to establish a sincere dialogue with those who do not believe in Christ in order that through methods suited to their characteristics and culture avenues may be open to them by which they can be led to an understanding of the gospel message.
2. Missionaries are to see to it that they teach the truths of faith to those whom they judge to be ready to accept the gospel message so that these persons can be admitted to the reception of baptism when they freely request it.

788. *1.* After a period of pre-catechumenate has elapsed, persons who have manifested a willingness to embrace faith in Christ are to be admitted to the catechumenate in liturgical ceremonies and their names are to be registered in a book destined for this purpose.
2. Through instruction and an apprenticeship in the Christian life catechumens are suitably to be initiated into the mystery of salvation and introduced to the life of faith, liturgy, charity of the people of God and the apostolate.
3. It is the responsibility of the conference of bishops to issue statutes by which the catechumenate is regulated; these statutes are to determine what things are to be expected of catechumens and define what prerogatives are recognized as theirs.

789. Through a suitable instruction neophytes are to be formed to a more thorough understanding of the gospel truth and the baptismal duties to be fulfilled; they are to be imbued with a love of Christ and of His Church.

842. 2. The sacraments of baptism, confirmation, and the Most Holy Eucharist are so interrelated that they are required for full Christian initiation.

851. *1.* An adult who intends to receive baptism is to be admitted to the catechumenate and, to the extent possible, be led through the several stages to sacramental initiation, in accord with the order of initiation adapted by the conference of bishops and the special norms published by it.

852. *1.* What is prescribed in the canons on the baptism of an adult is applicable to all who are no longer infants but have attained the use of reason.

863. The baptism of adults, at least those who have completed fourteen years of age is to be referred to the bishop so that it may be conferred by him, if he judges it expedient.

865. *1.* To be baptized, it is required that an adult have manifested the will to receive baptism, be sufficiently instructed in the truths of faith and in Christian obligations and be tested in the Christian life by means of the catechumenate; the adult is also to be exhorted to have sorrow for personal sins.
2. An adult in danger of death may be baptized if, having some knowledge of the principal truths of faith, the person has in any way manifested an intention of receiving baptism and promises to observe the commandments of the Christian religion.

866. Unless a grave reason prevents it, an adult who is baptized is to be confirmed immediately after baptism and participate in the celebration of the Eucharist, also receiving Communion.

869. *1.* If there is a doubt whether one has been baptized or whether baptism was validly conferred and the doubt remains after serious investigation, baptism is to be conferred conditionally.
2. Those baptized in a non-Catholic ecclesial community are not to be baptized conditionally unless, after an examination of the matter and the form of words used in the conferral of baptism and after a consideration of the intention of an adult baptized person and of the minister of the baptism, a serious reason for doubting the validity of the baptism is present.
3. If the conferral or the validity of the baptism in the cases

mentioned in nos. 1 & 2 remains doubtful, baptism is not to be conferred until the doctrine of the sacrament of baptism is explained to the person, if an adult, and the reasons for the doubtful validity of the baptism have been explained to the adult recipient or, in the case of an infant, to the parents.

883. The following have the faculty of administering confirmation by the law itself:

1. within the limits of their territory, those who are equivalent in law to the diocesan bishop;

2. with regard to the person in question, the presbyter who by reason of office or mandate of the diocesan bishop baptizes one who is no longer an infant or one already baptized whom he admits into the full communion of the Catholic Church;

3. with regard to those in danger of death, the pastor or indeed any presbyter.

884. 1. The diocesan bishop is to administer confirmation personally or see that it is administered by another bishop, but if necessity requires he may give the faculty to administer this sacrament to one or more specified presbyters.
2. For a grave cause, a bishop and likewise a presbyter who has the faculty to confirm by virtue of law or special concession of competent authority may in individual cases associate presbyters with themselves so that they may administer the sacrament.

885. 2. A presbyter who has this faculty must use it for those in whose favor the faculty was granted.

1170. Blessings, to be imparted especially to Catholics, can also be given to catechumens and even to non-Catholics unless a church prohibition precludes this.

1183. 1. As regards funeral rites catechumens are to be considered members of the Christian faithful.

The Rite of Baptism for Children

RITE OF BAPTISM FOR CHILDREN

RITE OF BAPTISM FOR CHILDREN

Decree
Baptism of Children (1-31)

CHAPTER I
RITE OF BAPTISM FOR SEVERAL CHILDREN

Reception of the Children (32-43)

Liturgy of the Word
Scripture Readings and Homily (44-46)
Intercessions (Prayer of the Faithful) (47-48)
Prayer of Exorcism and Anointing before Baptism (49-52)

Celebration of the Sacrament (53)
Blessing and Invocation of God over Baptismal Water (54-55)
Renunciation of Sin and Profession of Faith (56-59)
Baptism (60-61)

Explanatory Rites
Anointing after Baptism (62)
Clothing with White Garment (63)
Lighted Candle (64)
Ephphetha or Prayer over Ears and Mouth (65-66)

Conclusion of the Rite (67)
Lord's Prayer (68-69)
Blessing and Dismissal (70-71)

CHAPTER II
RITE OF BAPTISM FOR ONE CHILD

Reception of the Child (72-80)

Liturgy of the Word
Scriptural Readings and Homily (81-83)
Intercessions (Prayer of the Faithful) (84-85)
Prayer of Exorcism and Anointing before Baptism (86-89)

Celebration of the Sacrament (90)
Blessing and Invocation of God over Baptismal Water (91-92)
Renunciation of Sin and Profession of Faith (93-96)
Baptism (97)

Explanatory Rites
Anointing after Baptism (98)
Clothing with the White Garment (99)
Lighted Candle (100)
Ephphetha or Prayer over Ears and Mouth (101)

Conclusion of the Rite (102)
Lord's Prayer (103-104)
Blessing and Dismissal (105-106)

CHAPTER III
RITE OF BAPTISM FOR A LARGE NUMBER OF
CHILDREN

Reception of the Children (107-111)

Liturgy of the Word
Scriptural Readings and Homily (112-113)
Intercessions (Prayer of the Faithful) (114)
Prayer of Exorcism (115-116)

Celebration of the Sacrament (117)
Blessing and Invocation of God over Baptismal Water (118-119)
Renunciation of Sin and Profession of Faith (120-123)
Baptism (124)

Explanatory Rites
Anointing after Baptism (125)
Clothing with White Garment (126)
Lighted Candle (127)

Conclusion of the Rite
Lord's Prayer (128-129)
Blessing and Dismissal (130-131)

CHAPTER IV
RITE OF BAPTISM FOR CHILDREN
ADMINISTERED BY A CATECHIST WHEN NO
PRIEST OR DEACON IS AVAILABLE

CHAPTER V
RITE OF BAPTISM FOR CHILDREN IN DANGER
OF DEATH WHEN NO PRIEST OR DEACON IS
AVAILABLE (157-164)

CHAPTER VI
RITE OF BRINGING A BAPTIZED CHILD TO
THE CHURCH

Explanatory Rites
Anointing after Baptism (178)
Clothing with White Garment (179)
Lighted Candle (180)

Conclusion of the Rite
Lord's Prayer (181-182)
Blessing and Dismissal (183-185)

CHAPTER VII
VARIOUS TEXTS FOR USE IN THE
CELEBRATION OF BAPTISM FOR CHILDREN

I. Scriptural Readings (186-215)
II. Other Forms of the Intercessions (Prayer of the Faithful)
(216-220)
III. Another Form of the Prayer of Exorcism (221)
IV. Blessing and Invocation of God over Baptismal Water
(222-224)
V. Acclamations and Hymns (225-245)
VI. Forms of the Final Blessing (246-249)

APPENDIX

Litany of the Saints

Special Invocations

SACRED CONGREGATION FOR DIVINE WORSHIP

Prot. n. R 23/969

DECREE

Vatican Council II decreed that the rite of baptism for children in the Roman Ritual was to be revised in order that: the rite might be better adapted to the actual condition of children; the role and responsibilities of parents and godparents might be more clearly expressed; suitable adaptations might be made for the baptism of a large number of people; suitable adaptations might likewise be made for a great number of recipients or for baptism administered by catechists in mission areas or by others in circumstances when the ordinary minister is unavailable; a rite would be composed to make it clear that children baptized according to the shorter rite have already been received into the Church (SC art. 67–69).

This revision has been carried out by the Consilium for the Implementation of the Constitution on the Sacred Liturgy. By his apostolic authority Pope Paul VI has approved and ordered the publication of this new rite of baptism for children to replace the rite given in the Roman Ritual.

Therefore this Sacred Congregation, acting on the express mandate of the Pope, promulgates this rite and sets 8 September 1969 as its effective date.

Anything to the contrary notwithstanding.

From the Congregation for Divine Worship, May 15, 1969, Feast of the Ascension.

Benno Cardinal Gut
Prefect

A. Bugnini
Secretary

INTRODUCTION

I. IMPORTANCE OF BAPTIZING CHILDREN

1. The term "children" or "infants" refers to those who have not yet reached the age of discernment and therefore cannot profess personal faith.

2. From the earliest times, the Church, to which the mission of preaching the Gospel and of baptizing was entrusted, has baptized not only adults but children as well. Our Lord said: "Unless a man is reborn in water and the Holy Spirit, he cannot enter the kingdom of God."[1] The Church has always understood these words to mean that children should not be deprived of baptism, because they are baptized in the faith of the Church, a faith proclaimed for them by their parents and godparents, who represent both the local Church and the whole society of saints and believers: "The whole Church is the mother of all and the mother of each."[2]

3. To fulfill the true meaning of the sacrament, children must later be formed in the faith in which they have been baptized. The foundation of this formation will be the sacrament itself that they have already received. Christian formation, which is their due, seeks to lead them gradually to learn God's plan in Christ, so that they may ultimately accept for themselves the faith in which they have been baptized.

II. MINISTRIES AND ROLES IN THE CELEBRATION OF BAPTISM

4. The people of God, that is, the Church, made present by the local community, has an important part to play in the baptism of both children and adults.

Before and after the celebration of the sacrament, the child has a right to the love and help of the community. During the rite, in addition to the ways of congregational participation mentioned in the General Introduction to Christian Initiation no. 7, the community exercises its duty when it expresses its assent together with the celebrant af-

[1]Jn 3:5.
[2]Augustine, *Ep.* 98, 5: PL 33, 362.

ter the profession of faith by the parents and godparents. In this way it is clear that the faith in which the children are baptized is not the private possession of the individual family, but the common treasure of the whole Church of Christ.

5. Because of the natural relationships, parents have a ministry and a responsibility in the baptism of infants more important than those of the godparents.

1. Before the celebration of the sacrament, it is of great importance that parents, moved by their own faith or with the help of friends or other members of the community, should prepare to take part in the rite with understanding. They should be provided with suitable means such as books, letters addressed to them, and catechisms designed for families. The pastor should make it his duty to visit them or see that they are visited; he should try to gather a group of families together and prepare them for the coming celebration by pastoral counsel and common prayer.

2. It is very important that the parents be present at the celebration in which their child is reborn in water and the Holy Spirit.

3. In the celebration of baptism, the father and mother have special parts to play. They listen to the words addressed to them by the celebrant, they join in prayer along with the congregation, and they exercise a genuine ministry when: a. they publicly ask that the child be baptized; b. they sign their child with the sign of the cross after the celebrant; c. they renounce Satan and recite the profession of faith; d. they (and especially the mother) carry the child to the font; e. they hold the lighted candle; f. they are blessed with the prayers formulated specifically for mothers and fathers.

4. A parent unable to make the profession of faith (for example, not being a Catholic) may keep silent. Such a parent, when making the request for the child's baptism is asked only to make arrangements or at least to give permission for the child's instruction in the faith of its baptism.

5. After baptism it is the responsibility of the parents, in their gratitude to God and in fidelity to the duty they have undertaken, to assist the child to know God, whose adopted child it has become, to prepare the child to receive

confirmation and participate in the holy eucharist. In this duty they are again to be helped by the parish priest (pastor) by suitable means.

6. Each child may have a godfather (*patrinus*) and a godmother (*matrina*), the word "godparents" is used in the rite to describe both.

7. In addition to what is said about the ordinary minister of baptism in the General Introduction to Christian Initiation nos. 11–15, the following should be noted:

1. It is the duty of the priest to prepare families for the baptism of their children and to help them in the task of Christian formation that they have undertaken. It is the duty of the bishop to coordinate such pastoral efforts in the diocese, with the help also of deacons and lay people.

2. It is also the duty of the priest to arrange that baptism is always celebrated with proper dignity and, as far as possible, adapted to the circumstances and wishes of the families concerned. All who perform the rite of baptism should do so with exactness and reverence; they must also try to be understanding and friendly to all.

III. TIME AND PLACE FOR BAPTISM OF CHILDREN

8. As for the time of baptism, the first consideration is the welfare of the child, that it may not be deprived of the benefit of the sacrament; then the health of the mother must be considered, so that, if at all possible, she too may be present. Then, as long as they do not interfere with the greater good of the child, there are pastoral considerations, such as allowing sufficient time to prepare the parents and to plan the actual celebration in order to bring out its true character effectively. Accordingly:

1. If the child is in danger of death, it is to be baptized without delay; this is permitted even when the parents are opposed and even when the infant is the child of non-Catholic parents. The baptism is conferred in the manner laid down in no. 21.

2. In other cases the parents, or at least one of them or whoever stands in the place of the parents, must consent to

the baptism of the infant. So that proper preparation may be made for the celebration of the sacrament, as soon as possible, if need be even before the child is born, the parents should be in touch with the pastor concerning the baptism.

3. An infant should be baptized within the first weeks after birth. In the complete absence of any well-founded hope that the infant will be brought up in the Catholic religion, the baptism is to be delayed, in conformity with the provisions of particular law (see no. 25), and the parents are to be informed of the reasons.

4. In the absence of the conditions laid down in nos. 2 and 3, it is for the pastor, keeping in mind whatever regulations have been laid down by the conference of bishops, to determine the time for the baptism of infants.

9. To bring out the paschal character of baptism, it is recommended that the sacrament be celebrated during the Easter Vigil or on Sunday, when the Church commemorates the Lord's resurrection. On Sunday, baptism may be celebrated even during Mass, so that the entire community may be present and the relationship between baptism and eucharist may be clearly seen; but this should not be done too often. Regulations for the celebration of baptism during the Easter Vigil or at Mass on Sunday will be set out later.

10. So that baptism may clearly appear as the sacrament of the Church's faith and of incorporation into the people of God, it should normally be celebrated in the parish church, which must have a baptismal font.

11. After consulting the local pastor, the local Ordinary may permit or direct that a baptismal font be placed in another church or oratory within the parish boundaries. In these places, too, the right to celebrate baptism belongs ordinarily to the pastor.

However, distance or other circumstances may make it seriously inconvenient for the candidate to go or be brought to the usual place for baptism. In such a case, the sacrament may and should be conferred in another, more accessible church or oratory, or even in some other suitable place. The provisions laid down here, nos. 8–9 and 15–22, on the time and the structure of the celebration are to be followed.

12. Outside a case of necessity, baptism is not to be celebrated in private homes, unless the local Ordinary has, for a serious reason, granted permission.

13. Unless the bishop decides otherwise (see no. 11), baptism should not be celebrated in hospitals, except in cases of emergency or some other compelling pastoral reason. But care should always be taken that the pastor is notified and that the parents are suitably prepared beforehand.

14. While the liturgy of the word is being celebrated, it is desirable that children should be taken to some other place. But provision must be made for the mothers or godmothers to attend the liturgy of the word; the children should therefore be entrusted to the care of other women.

IV. STRUCTURE OF THE RITE OF BAPTIZING CHILDREN

A. ORDER OF BAPTISM CELEBRATED BY THE ORDINARY MINISTER

15. Baptism, whether for one child, or for several, or even for a larger number, should be celebrated by the ordinary minister and with the full rite when there is no immediate danger of death.

16. The rite begins with the reception of the children. This is to indicate the desire of the parents and godparents, as well as the intention of the Church, concerning the celebration of the sacrament of baptism. These purposes are expressed in action when the parents and the celebrant trace the sign of the cross on the foreheads of the children.

17. Then the liturgy of the word is directed toward stirring up the faith of the parents, godparents, and congregation and toward praying in common for the fruits of baptism before the sacrament itself. This part of the celebration consists of the reading of one or more passages from holy Scripture; a homily, followed by a period of silence; the general intercessions, with its concluding prayer, drawn up in the style of an exorcism, to introduce either the anointing with the oil of catechumens or the laying on of hands.

18. In the celebration of the sacrament:

   1. The immediate preparation consists of:

   a. the solemn prayer of the celebrant, which, by invoking God and recalling his plan of salvation, blesses the water of baptism or makes reference to its earlier blessing;

   b. the renunciation of Satan on the part of parents and godparents and their profession of faith, to which is added the assent of the celebrant and the community; and the final interrogation of the parents and godparents.

   2. The sacrament itself consists of the washing in water by way of immersion or infusion, depending on local custom, and the invocation of the blessed Trinity.

   3. The completion of the sacrament consists, first, of the anointing with chrism, which signifies the royal priesthood of the baptized and enrollment into the company of the people of God; then of the ceremonies of the white garment, lighted candle, and *ephphetha* rite (the last of which is optional).

19. Before the altar to prefigure the future sharing in the eucharist, the celebrant introduces and all recite the Lord's Prayer, in which God's children pray to their Father in heaven. Finally, a prayer of blessing is said over the mothers, fathers, and all present, to ask the outpouring of God's grace upon them.

B. SHORTER RITE OF BAPTISM

20. In the shorter rite of baptism designed for the use of catechists,[3] the reception of the children, the celebration of the word of God, or the instruction by the minister, and the general intercessions are retained. Before the font, the minister offers a prayer invoking God and recalling the history of salvation as it relates to baptism. After the baptismal washing, an adapted formulary is recited in place of the anointing with chrism and the whole rite concludes in the customary way. The omissions, therefore, are the exorcism, the anointing with oil of catechumens and with chrism, and the *ephphetha* rite.

[3] See SC art. 68.

21. The shorter rite for baptizing a child in danger of death and in the absence of the ordinary minister has a twofold structure:

  1. At the moment of death or when there is urgency because of imminent danger of death, the minister,[4] omitting all other ceremonies, pours water (not necessarily blessed but real and natural water) on the head of the child and pronounces the customary formulary.[5]

  2. If, however, it is prudently judged that there is sufficient time, several of the faithful may be gathered together and, if one of them is able to lead the others in a short prayer, the following rite may be used: an explanation by the minister of the sacrament, a short set of general intercessions, the profession of faith by the parents or one godparent and the pouring of the water with the customary words. But if those present are uneducated, the minister of the sacrament should recite the profession of faith aloud and baptize according to the rite for use in danger of death.

22. In danger of death, the priest or deacon may also use this shorter form if necessary. If there is time and he has the sacred chrism, the pastor or other priest enjoying the same faculty should not fail to confer confirmation after baptism. In this case he omits the postbaptismal anointing with chrism.

V. ADAPTATIONS BY CONFERENCES OF BISHOPS OR BY BISHOPS

23. In addition to the adaptations provided for (see *Christian Initiation*, General Introduction, nos. 30–33), the baptismal rite for infants admits other variations, to be determined by the conferences of bishops.

24. As is indicated in the Roman Ritual, the following matters are left to the discretion of the conferences:

  1. As local customs may dictate, the questioning about the name of the child may be arranged in different ways: the name may have been given already or may be given during the rite of baptism.

  2. The anointing with oil of catechumens may be omitted (nos. 50, 87).

[4]See General Introduction to Christian Initiation no. 16.
[5]See ibid. no. 23.

3. The formulary of renunciation may be made more pointed and detailed (nos. 57, 94, 121).

4. If the number to be baptized is very great, the anointing with chrism may be omitted (no. 125).

5. The *ephphetha* rite may be retained (nos. 64, 101).

25. In many countries parents are sometimes not ready for the celebration of baptism or they ask for their children to be baptized even though the latter will not afterward receive a Christian education and will even lose the faith. Since to instruct such parents and to inquire about their faith in the course of the rite itself is not enough, conferences of bishops may issue pastoral directives, for the guidance of pastors, to determine a longer interval between birth and baptism.

26. It is for the bishop to decide for his diocese whether catechists may give the homily on their own or only by reading a written text.

VI. ADAPTATIONS BY THE MINISTER

27. During meetings to prepare the parents for the baptism of their children, it is important that the instruction should be supported by prayer and religious rites. For this the various elements provided in the rite of baptism for the celebration of the word of God will prove helpful.

28. When the baptism of children is celebrated as part of the Easter Vigil, the ritual should be arranged as follows:

1. At a convenient time and place before the Easter Vigil the rite of receiving the children is celebrated. The liturgy of the word may be omitted at the end, according to circumstances, and the prayer of exorcism is said, followed by the anointing with oil of catechumens.

2. The celebration of the sacrament (nos. 56–58, 60–63) takes place after the blessing of the water, as is indicated in the rite of the Easter Vigil.

3. The assent of the celebrant and community (no. 59) is omitted, as are the presentation of the lighted candle (no. 64) and the *ephphetha* rite (no. 65).

4. The conclusion of the rite (nos. 67–71) is omitted.

29. If baptism takes place during Sunday Mass, the Mass for that Sunday is used, or, on the Sundays of the Christmas season and of Ordinary Time, the Mass for the Baptism of Children, and the celebration takes place as follows:

1. The rite of receiving the children (nos. 33–43) takes place at the beginning of Mass and the greeting and penitential rite of the Mass are omitted.

2. In the liturgy of the word:

a. The readings are taken from the Mass of the Sunday. But in the Christmas season and in Ordinary Time they may also be taken from those given in the Lectionary for Mass (757–761) or in this baptismal rite (nos. 44, 186–215).

When a ritual Mass is prohibited, one of the readings may be taken from the texts provided for the celebration of baptism for children, with attention paid to the pastoral benefit of the faithful and the character of the liturgical day.

b. The homily is based on the sacred texts, but should take account of the baptism that is to take place.

c. The *Creed* is not said, since the profession of faith by the entire community before baptism takes its place.

d. The general intercessions are taken from those used in the rite of baptism (nos. 47–48). At the end, however, before the invocation of the saints, petitions are added for the universal Church and the needs of the world.

3. The celebration of baptism continues with the prayer of exorcism, anointing, and other ceremonies described in the rite (nos. 49–66).

4. After the celebration of baptism, the Mass continues in the usual way with the presentation of the gifts.

5. For the blessing at the end of Mass, the priest may use one of the formularies provided in the rite of baptism (nos. 70, 247–249).

30. If baptism is celebrated during Mass on weekdays, it is arranged in basically the same way as on Sunday, but the readings for the liturgy of the word may be taken from those that are provided in the rite of baptism (nos. 44, 186–194, 204–215).

31. In accordance with the General Introduction no. 34, the minister may make some adaptations in the rite as circumstances require, such as:

1. If the child's mother died in childbirth, this should be taken into account in the opening instruction (no. 36), general intercessions (nos. 47, 217–220), and final blessing (nos. 70, 247–248).

2. In the dialogue with the parents (nos. 37–38, 76–77), their answers should be taken into account: if they have not answered *Baptism*, but *Faith*, or *The grace of Christ*, or *Entrance into the Church*, or *Everlasting life*, then the minister does not begin by saying *Baptism*, but uses *Faith*, or *The grace of Christ*, and so forth.

3. The rite of bringing a child already baptized to the church (nos. 165–185), which has been drawn up for use only when the child has been baptized in danger of death, should be adapted to cover other contingencies, for example, when children have been baptized during a time of religious persecution or temporary disagreement between the parents.

(N.B. 1. The texts of the psalms and of the New Testament are taken from the Neo-Vulgate edition of the Bible. 2. Liturgical texts written in the masculine gender can be changed to the feminine; those written in the singular can be changed to the plural.)

CHAPTER I

RITE OF BAPTISM
FOR SEVERAL CHILDREN

RECEPTION OF THE CHILDREN

32. If possible, baptism should take place on Sunday, the day on which the Church celebrates the paschal mystery. It should be conferred in a communal celebration for all the recently born children, and in the presence of the faithful, or at least of relatives, friends, and neighbors, who are all to take an active part in the rite.

33. It is the role of the father and mother, accompanied by the godparents, to present the child to the Church for baptism.

34. If there are very many children, and if there are several priests or deacons present, these may help the celebrant in the parts referred to below.

35. The people may sing a psalm or hymn suitable for the occasion. Meanwhile the celebrating priest or deacon, vested in alb or surplice, with a stole (with or without a cope) of festive color, and accompanied by the ministers, goes to the entrance of the church or to that part of the church where the parents and godparents are waiting with those who are to be baptized.

36. The celebrant greets all present, and especially the parents and godparents, reminding them briefly of the joy with which the parents welcomed their children as gifts from God, the source of life, who now wishes to bestow his own life on these little ones.

37. First the celebrant questions the parents of each child.

Celebrant:
What name do you give your child? (or: have you given?)
Parents: **N.**

Celebrant:

What do you ask of God's Church for N.?

Parents: **Baptism.**

The celebrant may choose other words for this dialogue.
The first reply may be given by someone other than the parents
if local custom gives him/her the right to name the child.
In the second response the parents may use other words,
e.g., **faith** or **the grace of Christ** or **entrance into the Church**
or **eternal life.**

38. If there are many children to be baptized, the celebrant
asks the names from all the parents together, and each
family replies in turn. The second question may also be
asked of all together.

Celebrant:

**What name do you give each of these children? (or:
have you given?)**

Parents: **N., N.,** etc.

Celebrant:

What do you ask of God's Church for your children?

All: **Baptism.**

39. The celebrant speaks to the parents in these or similar
words:

**You have asked to have your children baptized. In
doing so you are accepting the responsibility of training them in the practice of the faith. It will be your
duty to bring them up to keep God's commandments
as Christ taught us, by loving God and our neighbor.
Do you clearly understand what you are undertaking?**

Parents: **We do.**

This response is given by each family individually. But if
there are many children to be baptized, the response may be
given by all together.

40. Then the celebrant turns to the godparents and addresses them in these or similar words:

**Are you ready to help these parents in their duty as
Christian mothers and fathers?**
All the godparents: **We are.**

41. The celebrant continues:
**N. and N. (or, My dear children), the Christian com-
munity welcomes you with great joy. In its name I
claim you for Christ our Savior by the sign of the
cross. I now trace the cross on your foreheads, and
invite your parents (and godparents) to do the same.**

He signs each child on the forehead, in silence. Then he
invites the parents and, if this seems appropriate, the godparents to do the same.

42. The celebrant invites the parents, godparents, and the
others to take part in the liturgy of the word. If circumstances permit, there is a procession to the place where this
will be celebrated, during which a song is sung, e.g., Psalm
85:7, 8, 9ab:

**Will you not give us life;
  and shall not your people rejoice in you?
Show us, O Lord, your kindness,
  and grant us your salvation.
I will hear what God proclaims;
  the Lord—for he proclaims peace to his people.**

43. The children to be baptized may be carried to a separate
place, where they remain until the end of the liturgy of the
word.

LITURGY OF THE WORD

READINGS AND HOMILY

44. One or even two of the following gospel passages are
read, during which all may sit if convenient.

John 3:1-6 The meeting with Nicodemus.
Matthew 28:18-20 The apostles are sent to preach the
gospel and to baptize.
Mark 1:9-11 The baptism of Jesus.

Mark 10:13-16 Let the little children come to me.

The passages listed in nos. 186-194 and 204-215 may be chosen, or other passages which better meet the wishes or needs of the parents. Between the readings, responsorial psalms or verses may be sung as given in nos. 195-203.

45. After the reading, the celebrant gives a short homily, explaining to those present the significance of what has been read. His purpose will be to lead them to a deeper understanding of the mystery of baptism and to encourage the parents and godparents to a ready acceptance of the responsibilities which arise from the sacrament.

46. After the homily, or in the course of or after the litany, it is desirable to have a period of silence while all pray at the invitation of the celebrant. If convenient, a suitable song follows, e.g., one chosen from nos. 225-245.

INTERCESSIONS (PRAYER OF THE FAITHFUL)

47. Then the intercessions (prayer of the faithful) are said:

Celebrant:

My brothers and sisters,* let us ask our Lord Jesus Christ to look lovingly on these children who are to be baptized, on their parents and godparents, and on all the baptized.

Assisting Minister:

By the mystery of your death and resurrection, bathe these children in light, give them the new life of baptism and welcome them into your holy Church.
All: **Lord, hear our prayer.**

Assisting Minister:

Through baptism and confirmation, make them your faithful followers and witnesses to your gospel.
All: **Lord, hear our prayer.**

---

*At the discretion of the priest, other words which seem more suitable under the circumstances, such as **friends** or **dearly beloved** or **brethren,** may be used. This also applies to parallel instances in the liturgy.

Assisting Minister:
Lead them by a holy life to the joys of God's kingdom.
All: **Lord, hear our prayer.**

Assisting Minister:
Make the lives of their parents and godparents examples of faith to inspire these children.
All: **Lord, hear our prayer.**

Assisting Minister:
Keep their families always in your love.
All: **Lord, hear our prayer.**

Assisting Minister:
Renew the grace of our baptism in each one of us.
All: **Lord, hear our prayer.**

Other forms may be chosen from nos. 217-220.

48. The celebrant next invites all to invoke the saints. At this point, if the children have been taken out, they are brought back.

Holy Mary, Mother of God,	**pray for us.**
Saint John the Baptist,	**pray for us.**
Saint Joseph,	**pray for us.**
Saint Peter and Saint Paul,	**pray for us.**

The names of other saints may be added, especially the patrons of the children to be baptized, and of the church or locality. The litany concludes:

All you saints of God,	**pray for us.**

PRAYER OF EXORCISM AND ANOINTING
BEFORE BAPTISM

49. After the invocations, the celebrant says:

A
Almighty and ever-living God,
you sent your only Son into the world
to cast out the power of Satan, spirit of evil,
to rescue man from the kingdom of darkness,

the United States, it may be omitted only when the minister of baptism judges the omission to be pastorally necessary or desirable.] In that case the celebrant says once only:

May you have strength in the power of Christ our Savior, who lives and reigns for ever and ever.
All: **Amen.**

And immediately he lays his hand on each child in silence.

52. If the baptistry is located outside the church or is not within view of the congregation, all go there in procession.

If the baptistry is located within view of the congregation, the celebrant, parents, and godparents go there with the children, while the others remain in their places.

If, however, the baptistry cannot accommodate the congregation, the baptism may be celebrated in a suitable place within the church, and the parents and godparents bring the child forward at the proper moment.

Meanwhile, if it can be done suitably, an appropriate song is sung, e.g., Psalm 23:

The Lord is my shepherd; I shall not want.
In verdant pastures he gives me repose;
Beside restful waters he leads me;
he refreshes my soul.
He guides me in right paths
for his name's sake.
Even though I walk in the dark valley
I fear no evil; for you are at my side
With your rod and your staff
that give me courage.
You spread the table before me
in the sight of my foes;
You anoint my head with oil;
my cup overflows.
Only goodness and kindness follow me
all the days of my life;
And I shall dwell in the house of the Lord
for years to come.

and bring him into the splendor of your kingdom of
  light.
We pray for these children:
set them free from original sin,
make them temples of your glory,
and send your Holy Spirit to dwell within them.
We ask this through Christ our Lord.
All: Amen.

Another form of the prayer of exorcism:

B
Almighty God,
you sent your only Son
to rescue us from the slavery of sin,
and to give us the freedom
only your sons and daughters enjoy.
We now pray for these children
who will have to face the world with its temptations,
and fight the devil in all his cunning.
Your Son died and rose again to save us.
By his victory over sin and death,
cleanse these children from the stain of original sin.
Strengthen them with the grace of Christ,
and watch over them at every step in life's journey.
We ask this through Christ our Lord.
All: **Amen.**

50. The celebrant continues:

We anoint you with the oil of salvation
in the name of Christ our Savior;
may he strengthen you with his power,
who lives and reigns for ever and ever.
All: **Amen.**

He anoints each child on the breast with the oil of catechumens. If the number of children is large, the anointing
may be done by several ministers.

51. If, for serious reasons, the conference of bishops so decides, the anointing before baptism may be omitted. [In

CELEBRATION OF THE SACRAMENT

53. When they come to the font, the celebrant briefly reminds the congregation of the wonderful work of God whose plan it is to sanctify man, body and soul, through water. He may use these or similar words:

A

My dear brothers and sisters, we now ask God to give these children new life in abundance through water and the Holy Spirit.

B

My dear brothers and sisters, God uses the sacrament of water to give his divine life to those who believe in him. Let us turn to him, and ask him to pour his gift of life from this font on the children he has chosen.

BLESSING AND INVOCATION OF GOD OVER BAPTISMAL WATER

54. Then, turning to the font, he says the following blessing (outside the Easter season):

A
Father,
you give us grace through sacramental signs,
which tell us of the wonders of your unseen power.

In baptism we use your gift of water,
which you have made a rich symbol of the grace
you give us in this sacrament.

At the very dawn of creation
your Spirit breathed on the waters,
making them the wellspring of all holiness.

The waters of the great flood
you made a sign of the waters of baptism
that make an end of sin
and a new beginning of goodness.

Through the waters of the Red Sea
you led Israel out of slavery

to be an image of God's holy people,
set free from sin by baptism.

In the waters of the Jordan
your Son was baptized by John
and anointed with the Spirit.

Your Son willed that water and blood should flow
   from his side
as he hung upon the cross.

After his resurrection he told his disciples:
"Go out and teach all nations,
baptizing them in the name of the Father, and of the
   Son, and of the Holy Spirit."

Father,
look now with love upon your Church
and unseal for it the fountain of baptism.

By the power of the Holy Spirit
give to this water the grace of your Son,
so that in the sacrament of baptism
all those whom you have created in your likeness
may be cleansed from sin
and rise to a new birth of innocence
by water and the Holy Spirit.

The celebrant touches the water with his right hand and
continues:

We ask you, Father, with your Son
to send the Holy Spirit upon the waters of this font.
May all who are buried with Christ in the death of
   baptism
rise also with him to newness of life.

We ask this through Christ our Lord.

All: **Amen.**

Other forms of the blessing, nos. 223-224, may be chosen.

55. During the Easter season, if there is baptismal water which was consecrated at the Easter Vigil, the blessing and invocation of God over the water are nevertheless included, so that this theme of thanksgiving and petition may find a place in the baptism. The forms of this blessing and invocation are those found in nos. 223-224, with the variation indicated at the end of each text.

RENUNCIATION OF SIN AND PROFESSION OF FAITH

56. The celebrant speaks to the parents and godparents in these words:

Dear parents and godparents: You have come here to present these children for baptism. By water and the Holy Spirit they are to receive the gift of new life from God, who is love.

On your part, you must make it your constant care to bring them up in the practice of the faith. See that the divine life which God gives them is kept safe from the poison of sin, to grow always stronger in their hearts.

If your faith makes you ready to accept this responsibility, renew now the vows of your own baptism. Reject sin; profess your faith in Christ Jesus. This is the faith of the Church. This is the faith in which these children are about to be baptized.

57. The celebrant questions the parents and godparents.

A
Celebrant:
Do your reject Satan?
Parents and godparents: **I do.**

Celebrant:
And all his works?
Parents and godparents: **I do.**

Celebrant:
And all his empty promises?
Parents and godparents: **I do.**

or **B**
Celebrant:
Do you reject sin so as to live in the freedom of God's children?
Parents and godparents: **I do.**

Celebrant:
Do you reject the glamor of evil, and refuse to be mastered by sin?
Parents and godparents: **I do.**

Celebrant:
Do you reject Satan, father of sin and prince of darkness?
Parents and godparents: **I do.**

According to circumstances, this second form may be expressed with greater precision by the conferences of bishops, especially in places where it is necessary for the parents and godparents to reject superstitious and magical practices used with children.

58. Next the celebrant asks for the threefold profession of faith from the parents and godparents:

Celebrant:
Do you believe in God, the Father almighty,
    creator of heaven and earth?
Parents and godparents: **I do.**

Celebrant:
Do you believe in Jesus Christ, his only Son, our Lord,
    who was born of the Virgin Mary,
    was crucified, died, and was buried,
    rose from the dead,
    and is now seated at the right hand of the Father?
Parents and godparents: **I do.**

Celebrant:
Do you believe in the Holy Spirit,
    the holy catholic Church, the communion of saints,

the forgiveness of sins, the resurrection of the body,
and the life everlasting?
Parents and godparents: **I do.**

59. The celebrant and the congregation give their assent to
the profession of faith:

Celebrant:
**This is our faith. This is the faith of the Church. We
are proud to profess it, in Christ Jesus our Lord.**
All: **Amen.**

If desired, some other formula may be used instead, or a
suitable song by which the community expresses its faith
with a single voice.

BAPTISM

60. The celebrant invites the first of the families to the
font. Using the name of the individual child, he questions
the parents and godparents.

Celebrant:
**Is it your will that N. should be baptized in the faith
of the Church, which we have all professed with
you?**
Parents and godparents: **It is.**

He baptizes the child, saying:

N., I baptize you in the name of the Father,

He immerses the child or pours water upon it.

and of the Son,

He immerses the child or pours water upon it a second
time.

and of the Holy Spirit.

He immerses the child or pours water upon it a third time.

He asks the same question and performs the same action
for each child.

After each baptism it is appropriate for the people to sing
a short acclamation. (See nos. 225-245).

If the baptism is performed by the pouring of water, it is preferable that the child be held by the mother (or father). Where, however, it is felt that the existing custom should be retained, the godmother (or godfather) may hold the child. If baptism is by immersion, the mother or father (godmother or godfather) lifts the child out of the font.

61. If the number of children to be baptized is large, and other priests or deacons are present, these may baptize some of the children in the way described above, and with the same form.

EXPLANATORY RITES

ANOINTING AFTER BAPTISM

62. Then the celebrant says:

The God of power and Father of our Lord Jesus Christ
has freed you from sin
and brought you to new life
through water and the Holy Spirit.

He now anoints you with the chrism of salvation,
so that, united with his people,
you may remain for ever a member of Christ
who is Priest, Prophet, and King.

All: **Amen.**

Next, the celebrant anoints each child on the crown of the head with chrism, in silence.
If the number of children is large and other priests or deacons are present, these may anoint some of the children with chrism.

CLOTHING WITH WHITE GARMENT

63. The celebrant says:

(N. and N.,) you have become a new creation, and have clothed yourselves in Christ.

See in this white garment the outward sign of your Christian dignity. With your family and friends to help you by word and example, bring that dignity unstained into the everlasting life of heaven.
All: **Amen.**

The white garments are put on the children. A different color is not permitted unless demanded by local custom. It is desirable that the families provide the garments.

LIGHTED CANDLE

64. The celebrant takes the Easter candle and says:

Receive the light of Christ.

Someone from each family (e.g., the father or godfather) lights the child's candle from the Easter candle.

The celebrant then says:

Parents and godparents, this light is entrusted to you to be kept burning brightly. These children of yours have been enlightened by Christ. They are to walk always as children of the light. May they keep the flame of faith alive in their hearts. When the Lord comes, may they go out to meet him with all the saints in the heavenly kingdom.

EPHPHETHA OR PRAYER OVER EARS AND MOUTH

65. If the conference of bishops decides to preserve the practice, the rite of *Ephphetha* follows. [In the United States it may be performed at the discretion of the minister.] The celebrant touches the ears and mouth of each child with his thumb, saying:

The Lord Jesus made the deaf hear and the dumb speak. May he soon touch your ears to receive his word, and your mouth to proclaim his faith, to the praise and glory of God the Father.
All: **Amen.**

66. If the number of children is large, the celebrant says the formula once, but does not touch the ears and mouth.

CONCLUSION OF THE RITE

67. Next there is a procession to the altar, unless the baptism was performed in the sanctuary. The lighted candles are carried for the children.
A baptismal song is appropriate at this time, e.g.:

**You have put on Christ,
in him you have been baptized.
Alleluia, alleluia.**

Other songs may be chosen from nos. 225-245.

LORD'S PRAYER

68. The celebrant stands in front of the altar and addresses the parents, godparents, and the whole assembly in these or similar words:

Dearly beloved, these children have been reborn in baptism. They are now called children of God, for so indeed they are. In confirmation they will receive the fullness of God's Spirit. In holy communion they will share the banquet of Christ's sacrifice, calling God

their Father in the midst of the Church. In their name, in the Spirit of our common sonship, let us pray together in the words our Lord has given us:

69. All present join the celebrant in singing or saying:

Our Father. . . .

BLESSING AND DISMISSAL

70. The celebrant first blesses the mothers, who hold the children in their arms, then the fathers, and lastly the entire assembly:

A
Celebrant:
God the Father, through his Son, the Virgin Mary's child, has brought joy to all Christian mothers, as they see the hope of eternal life shine on their children. May he bless the mothers of these children.

They now thank God for the gift of their children.
May they be one with them in thanking him for ever
in heaven, in Christ Jesus our Lord.
All: **Amen.**

Celebrant:
God is the giver of all life, human and divine. May he
bless the fathers of these children. With their wives
they will be the first teachers of their children in the
ways of faith. May they be also the best of teachers,
bearing witness to the faith by what they say and do,
in Christ Jesus our Lord.
All: **Amen.**

Celebrant:
By God's gift, through water and the Holy Spirit, we
are reborn to everlasting life. In his goodness, may he
continue to pour out his blessings upon all present,
who are his sons and daughters. May he make them
always, wherever they may be, faithful members of
his holy people. May he send his peace upon all who
are gathered here, in Christ Jesus our Lord.
All: **Amen.**

Celebrant:
May almighty God, the Father, and the Son, ✛ and
the Holy Spirit, bless you.
All: **Amen.**

Celebrant: **Go in peace.**
All: **Thanks be to God.**

Other forms of the final blessing, nos. 247, 248, and 249
may be chosen.

B
Celebrant:
May God the almighty Father, who filled the world
with joy by giving us his only Son, bless these
newly-baptized children. May they grow to be more
fully like Jesus Christ our Lord.
All: **Amen.**

Celebrant:
May almighty God, who gives life on earth and in heaven, bless the parents of these children. They thank him now for the gift he has given them. May they always show that gratitude in action by loving and caring for their children.
All: **Amen.**

Celebrant:
May almighty God, who has given us a new birth by water and the Holy Spirit, generously bless all of us who are his faithful children. May we always live as his people, and may he bless all here present with his peace.
All: **Amen.**

Celebrant:
May almighty God, the Father, and the Son, ✛ and the Holy Spirit, bless you.
All: **Amen.**

Celebrant:
Go in peace.
All: **Thanks be to God.**

C

Celebrant:
May God, the source of life and love, who fills the hearts of mothers with love for their children, bless the mothers of these newly-baptized children. As they thank God for a safe delivery, may they find joy in the love, growth, and holiness of their children.
All: **Amen.**

Celebrant:
May God, the Father and model of all fathers, help these fathers to give good example, so that their children will grow to be mature Christians in all the fullness of Jesus Christ.
All: **Amen.**

Celebrant:

May God, who loves all people, bless all the relatives and friends who are gathered here. In his mercy, may he guard them from evil and give them his abundant peace.
All: **Amen.**

Celebrant:

And may almighty God, the Father, and the Son, ✝ and the Holy Spirit, bless you.
All: **Amen.**

Celebrant:

Go in peace.
All: **Thanks be to God.**

D

Celebrant:

**My brothers and sisters, we entrust you all to the mercy and help of God the almighty Father, his only Son, and the Holy Spirit. May he watch over your life, and may we all walk by the light of faith, and attain the good things he has promised us.
And may almighty God, the Father, and the Son, ✝ and the Holy Spirit, bless you.**
All: **Amen.**

Celebrant:

Go in peace.
All: **Thanks be to God.**

71. After the blessing, all may sing a hymn which suitably expresses thanksgiving and Easter joy, or they may sing the song of the Blessed Virgin Mary, the Magnificat.

Where there is the practice of bringing the baptized child to the altar of the blessed Virgin, this custom is observed if appropriate.

CHAPTER II

RITE OF BAPTISM FOR ONE CHILD

RECEPTION OF THE CHILD

72. If possible, baptism should take place on Sunday, the day on which the Church celebrates the paschal mystery. It should be conferred in a communal celebration in the presence of the faithful, or at least of relatives, friends, and neighbors, who are all to take an active part in the rite.

73. It is the role of the father and mother, accompanied by the godparents, to present the child to the Church for baptism.

74. The people may sing a psalm or hymn suitable for the occasion. Meanwhile the celebrating priest or deacon, vested in alb or surplice, with a stole (with or without a cope) of festive color, and accompanied by the ministers, goes to the entrance of the church or to that part of the church where the parents and godparents are waiting with the child.

75. The celebrant greets all present, and especially the parents and godparents, reminding them briefly of the joy with which the parents welcomed this child as a gift from God, the source of life, who now wishes to bestow his own life on this little one.

76. First the celebrant questions the parents:

Celebrant:
What name do you give your child? (or: **have you given?**)
Parents: **N.**

Celebrant:
What do you ask of God's Church for N.?
Parents: **Baptism.**

The celebrant may choose other words for this dialogue.
The first reply may be given by someone other than the parents
if local custom gives him/her the right to name the child.

In the second response the parents may use other words, such as, **faith** or **the grace of Christ** or **entrance into the Church** or **eternal life.**

77. The celebrant speaks to the parents in these or similar words:

You have asked to have your child baptized. In doing so you are accepting the responsibility of training him (her) in the practice of the faith. It will be your duty to bring him (her) up to keep God's commandments as Christ taught us, by loving God and our neighbor. Do you clearly understand what you are undertaking?
Parents: **We do.**

78. Then the celebrant turns to the godparents and addresses them in these or similar words:

Are you ready to help the parents of this child in their duty as Christian parents?
Godparents: **We are.**

79. The celebrant continues:

N., the Christian community welcomes you with great joy. In its name I claim you for Christ our Savior by the sign of his cross. I now trace the cross on your forehead, and invite your parents (and godparents) to do the same.
He signs the child on the forehead, in silence. Then he invites the parents and (if it seems appropriate) the godparents to do the same.

80. The celebrant invites the parents, godparents, and the others to take part in the liturgy of the word. If circumstances permit, there is a procession to the place where this will be celebrated, during which a song is sung, e.g., Psalm 85:7, 8, 9ab:

Will you not give us life;
   and shall not your people rejoice in you?
Show us, O Lord, your kindness,
   and grant us your salvation.

I will hear what God proclaims;
   the Lord—for he proclaims peace to his people.

LITURGY OF THE WORD

READINGS AND HOMILY

81. One or even two of the following gospel passages are
read, during which all may sit if convenient.

John 3:1-6   The meeting with Nicodemus.
Matthew 28:18-20   The apostles are sent to preach the
   gospel and to baptize.
Mark 1:9-11   The baptism of Jesus.
Mark 10:13-16   Let the little children come to me.

The passages listed in nos. 186-194 and 204-215 may be
chosen, or other passages which better meet the wishes or
needs of the parents. Between the readings, responsorial
psalms or verses may be sung as given in nos. 195-203.

82. After the reading, the celebrant gives a short homily,
explaining to those present the significance of what has been
read. His purpose will be to lead them to a deeper understanding of the mystery of baptism and to encourage the
parents and godparents to a ready acceptance of the responsibilities which arise from the sacrament.

83. After the homily, or in the course of or after the litany,
it is desirable to have a period of silence while all pray at the
invitation of the celebrant. If convenient, a suitable song
follows, such as one chosen from nos. 225-245.

INTERCESSIONS (PRAYER OF THE FAITHFUL)

84. Then the intercessions (prayer of the faithful) are said:

Celebrant:
My dear brothers and sisters, let us ask our Lord Jesus
Christ to look lovingly on this child who is to be
baptized, on his (her) parents and godparents, and on
all the baptized.

Assisting Minister:

**By the mystery of your death and resurrection, bathe
this child in light, give him (her) the new life of
baptism and welcome him (her) into your holy
Church.**
All: **Lord, hear our prayer.**

Assisting Minister:

**Through baptism and confirmation, make him (her)
your faithful follower and a witness to your gospel.**
All: **Lord, hear our prayer.**

Assisting Minister:

**Lead him (her) by a holy life to the joys of God's
kingdom.**
All: **Lord, hear our prayer.**

Assisting Minister:

**Make the lives of his (her) parents and godparents
examples of faith to inspire this child.**
All: **Lord, hear our prayer.**

Assisting Minister:

Keep his (her) family always in your love.
All: **Lord, hear our prayer.**

Assisting Minister:

Renew the grace of our baptism in each one of us.
All: **Lord, hear our prayer.**

Other forms may be chosen from nos. 217-220.

85. The celebrant next invites all present to invoke the
saints.

Holy Mary, Mother of God,	**pray for us.**
Saint John the Baptist,	**pray for us.**
Saint Joseph,	**pray for us.**
Saint Peter and Saint Paul,	**pray for us.**

The names of other saints may be added, especially the
patrons of the child to be baptized, and of the church or
locality. The litany concludes:

All holy men and women,	**pray for us.**

PRAYER OF EXORCISM AND ANOINTING BEFORE BAPTISM

86. After the invocation, the celebrant says:

Almighty and ever-living God,
you sent your only Son into the world
to cast out the power of Satan, spirit of evil,
to rescue man from the kingdom of darkness,
and bring him into the splendor of your kingdom of
** light.**
We pray for this child:
set him (her) free from original sin,
make him (her) a temple of your glory,
and send your Holy Spirit to dwell with him (her).
We ask this through Christ our Lord.
All: **Amen.**

For another form of the prayer of exorcism, see no. 221.

87. The celebrant continues:

We anoint you with the oil of salvation
in the name of Christ our Savior;
may he strengthen you with his power,
who lives and reigns for ever and ever.
All: **Amen.**

He anoints the child on the breast with the oil of catechumens.

88. If, for serious reasons, the conference of bishops so decides, the anointing before baptism may be omitted. [In the United States, it may be omitted only when the minister of baptism judges the omission to be pastorally necessary or desirable.] In that case the celebrant says:

May you have strength in the power of Christ our
Savior, who lives and reigns for ever and ever.
All: **Amen.**

And immediately he lays his hand on the child in silence.

89. Then they go to the baptistry, or to the sanctuary when baptism is celebrated there on occasion.

CELEBRATION OF THE SACRAMENT

90. When they come to the font, the celebrant briefly reminds the congregation of the wonderful work of God whose plan it is to sanctify man, body and soul, through water. He may use these or similar words:

A
My dear brothers and sisters, we now ask God to give this child new life in abundance through water and the Holy Spirit.

or **B**
My dear brothers and sisters, God uses the sacrament of water to give his divine life to those who believe in him. Let us turn to him, and ask him to pour his gift of life from this font on this child he has chosen.

BLESSING AND INVOCATION OF GOD OVER BAPTISMAL WATER

91. Then, turning to the font, he says the following blessing (outside the Easter season):

Father,
you give us grace through sacramental signs,
which tell us of the wonders of your unseen power.

In baptism we use your gift of water,
which you have made a rich symbol of the grace
you give us in this sacrament.

At the very dawn of creation
your Spirit breathed on the waters,
making them the wellspring of all holiness.

The waters of the great flood
you made a sign of the waters of baptism
that make an end of sin
and a new beginning of goodness.

Through the waters of the Red Sea
you led Israel out of slavery
to be an image of God's holy people,
set free from sin by baptism.

In the waters of the Jordan
your Son was baptized by John
and anointed with the Spirit.
Your Son willed that water and blood should flow
    from his side
as he hung upon the cross.

After his resurrection he told his disciples:
"Go out and teach all nations,
baptizing them in the name of the Father,
    and of the Son, and of the Holy Spirit."

Father,
look now with love upon your Church
and unseal for it the fountain of baptism.

By the power of the Holy Spirit
give to this water the grace of your Son,
so that in the sacrament of baptism
all those whom you have created in your likeness
may be cleansed from sin
and rise to a new birth of innocence
by water and the Holy Spirit.

The celebrant touches the water with his right hand and
continues:

We ask you, Father, with your Son
to send the Holy Spirit upon the waters of this font.
May all who are buried with Christ in the death of
    baptism
rise also with him to newness of life.

We ask this through Christ our Lord.

All: **Amen.**

Other forms may be chosen from nos. 223-224.

92. During the Easter season, if there is baptismal water
which was consecrated at the Easter Vigil, the blessing and
invocation of God over the water are nevertheless included, so that this theme of thanksgiving and petition
may find a place in the baptism. The forms of this blessing
and invocation are those found in nos. 223-224 with the
variation indicated at the end of the text.

RENUNCIATION OF SIN AND PROFESSION OF FAITH

93. The celebrant speaks to the parents and godparents in these words:

Dear parents and godparents: You have come here to present this child for baptism. By water and the Holy Spirit he (she) is to receive the gift of new life from God, who is love.

On your part, you must make it your constant care to bring him (her) up in the practice of the faith. See that the divine life which God gives him (her) is kept safe from the poison of sin, to grow always stronger in his (her) heart.

If your faith makes you ready to accept this responsibility, renew now the vows of your own baptism. Reject sin; profess your faith in Christ Jesus. This is the faith of the Church. This is the faith in which this child is about to be baptized.

94. The celebrant questions the parents and godparents.

A
Celebrant:
Do you reject Satan?
Parents and godparents: **I do.**

Celebrant:
And all his works?
Parents and godparents: **I do.**

Celebrant:
And all his empty promises?
Parents and godparents: **I do.**

or **B**
Celebrant:
Do you reject sin so as to live in the freedom of God's children?
Parents and godparents: **I do.**

Celebrant:
Do you reject the glamor of evil, and refuse to be mastered by sin?

Parents and godparents: **I do.**

Celebrant:
**Do you reject Satan, father of sin and prince of
darkness?**
Parents and godparents: **I do.**

According to circumstances, this second form may be expressed with greater precision by the conferences of bishops, especially in places where it is necessary for the parents and godparents to reject superstitious and magical practices used with children.

95. Next the celebrant asks for the threefold profession of faith from the parents and godparents:

Celebrant:
**Do you believe in God, the Father almighty,
   creator of heaven and earth?**
Parents and godparents: **I do.**

Celebrant:
**Do you believe in Jesus Christ, his only Son, our Lord,
   who was born of the Virgin Mary,
   was crucified, died, and was buried,
   rose from the dead,
   and is now seated at the right hand of the Father?**
Parents and godparents: **I do.**

Celebrant:
**Do you believe in the Holy Spirit,
   the holy catholic Church, the communion of saints,
   the forgiveness of sins, the resurrection of the body,
   and the life everlasting?**
Parents and godparents: **I do.**

96. The celebrant and the congregation give their assent to this profession of faith:

Celebrant:
**This is our faith. This is the faith of the Church. We
are proud to profess it, in Christ Jesus our Lord.**
All: **Amen.**

If desired, some other formula may be used instead, or a suitable song by which the community expresses its faith with a single voice.

BAPTISM

97. The celebrant invites the family to the font and questions the parents and godparents:

Celebrant:
Is it your will that N. should be baptized in the faith of the Church, which we have all professed with you?
Parents and godparents: **It is.**

He baptizes the child, saying:

N., I baptize you in the name of the Father,

He immerses the child or pours water upon it.

and of the Son,

He immerses the child or pours water upon it a second time.

and of the Holy Spirit.

He immerses the child or pours water upon it a third time.

After the child is baptized, it is appropriate for the people to sing a short acclamation. (See nos. 225-245.)

If the baptism is performed by the pouring of water, it is preferable that the child be held by the mother (or father). Where, however, it is felt that the existing custom should be retained, the godmother (or godfather) may hold the child. If baptism is by immersion, the mother or father (godmother or godfather) lifts the child out of the font.

EXPLANATORY RITES

ANOINTING AFTER BAPTISM

98. Then the celebrant says:

The God of power and Father of our Lord Jesus
    Christ
has freed you from sin
and brought you to new life

through water and the Holy Spirit.

He now anoints you with the chrism of salvation,
so that, united with his people,
you may remain for ever a member of Christ
who is Priest, Prophet, and King.

All: **Amen.**

Then the celebrant anoints the child on the crown of the
head with the sacred chrism, in silence.

CLOTHING WITH WHITE GARMENT

99. The celebrant says:

N., you have become a new creation, and have
clothed yourself in Christ.

See in this white garment the outward sign of your
Christian dignity. With your family and friends to
help you by word and example, bring that dignity
unstained into the everlasting life of heaven.
All: **Amen.**

The white garment is put on the child. A different color is
not permitted unless demanded by local custom. It is desirable that the family provide the garment.

LIGHTED CANDLE

100. The celebrant takes the Easter candle and says:

Receive the light of Christ.

Someone from the family (such as the father or godfather)
lights the child's candle from the Easter candle.

The celebrant then says:

Parents and godparent (or godparents), this light is
entrusted to you to be kept burning brightly. This
child of yours has been enlightened by Christ. He
(she) is to walk always as a child of the light. May
he (she) keep the flame of faith alive in his (her)
heart. When the Lord comes, may he (she) go out to
meet him with all the saints in the heavenly king-
dom.

EPHPHETHA OR PRAYER OVER EARS AND MOUTH

101. If the conference of bishops decides to preserve the practice, the rite of *Ephphetha* follows. [In the United States it may be performed at the discretion of the minister.] The celebrant touches the ears and mouth of the child with his thumb, saying:

The Lord Jesus made the deaf hear and the dumb speak. May he soon touch your ears to receive his word, and your mouth to proclaim his faith, to the praise and glory of God the Father.
All: **Amen.**

[If baptism is celebrated during Sunday or weekday Mass, the Mass continues in the usual way with preparation of the altar and the gifts.]

CONCLUSION OF THE RITE

102. Next there is a procession to the altar, unless the baptism was performed in the sanctuary. The lighted candle is carried for the child.

A baptismal song is appropriate at this time, e.g.:

**You have put on Christ,
in him you have been baptized.
Alleluia, alleluia.**

Other songs may be chosen from nos. 225-245.

LORD'S PRAYER

103. The celebrant stands in front of the altar, and addresses the parents, godparents, and the whole assembly in these or similar words:

Dearly beloved, this child has been reborn in baptism. He (she) is now called the child of God, for so indeed he (she) is. In confirmation he (she) will receive the fullness of God's Spirit. In holy communion he (she) will share the banquet of Christ's sacrifice, calling God his (her) Father in the midst of the Church. In the name of this child, in the Spirit of our common sonship, let us pray together in the words our Lord has given us:

104. All present join the celebrant in singing or saying:

Our Father. . . .

BLESSING

105. The celebrant first blesses the mother, who holds the child in her arms, then the father, and lastly the entire assembly:

Celebrant:

God the Father, through his Son, the Virgin Mary's child, has brought joy to all Christian mothers, as they see the hope of eternal life shine on their children. May he bless the mother of this child. She now thanks God for the gift of her child. May she be one with him (her) in thanking him for ever in heaven, in Christ Jesus our Lord.
All: **Amen.**

Celebrant:

God is the giver of all life, human and divine. May he bless the father of this child. He and his wife will be the first teachers of their child in the ways of faith. May they be also the best of teachers, bearing witness to the faith by what they say and do, in Christ Jesus our Lord.
All: **Amen.**

Celebrant:

By God's gift, through water and the Holy Spirit, we are reborn to everlasting life. In his goodness, may he continue to pour out his blessings upon these sons and daughters of his. May he make them always, wherever they may be, faithful members of his holy people. May he send his peace upon all who are gathered here, in Christ Jesus our Lord.
All: **Amen.**

Celebrant:

May almighty God, the Father, and the Son, ✚ and the Holy Spirit, bless you.
All: **Amen.**

Celebrant: **Go in peace.**
All: **Thanks be to God.**

For other forms of the blessing, see nos. 247-249.

106. After the blessing, all may sing a hymn which suitably expresses thanksgiving and Easter joy, or they may sing the song of the Blessed Virgin Mary, the Magnificat.

Where there is a practice of bringing the baptized child to the altar of the Blessed Virgin Mary, this custom is observed if appropriate.

CHAPTER III

RITE OF BAPTISM FOR A LARGE NUMBER OF CHILDREN

RECEPTION OF THE CHILDREN

107. The people may sing a psalm or hymn suitable for the occasion. Meanwhile the celebrating priest or deacon, vested in alb or surplice, with a stole (with or without a cope) of festive color, and accompanied by the ministers, goes to the entrance of the church or to that part of the church where the parents and godparents are waiting with those who are to be baptized.

108. The celebrant greets all present, and especially the parents and godparents, reminding them briefly of the joy with which the parents welcomed their children as gifts from God, the source of life, who now wishes to bestow his own life on these little ones.

Then the celebrant questions the parents and godparents together:

A
Celebrant:
What name do you want to give your children?
Each family answers in turn, giving the names of the children.

Celebrant:
What do you ask of God's Church for these children?
All families together: **Baptism.**

But if there is a very large number to be baptized, he omits the first question and asks:

B
Celebrant:
Parents and godparents, what do you ask for these children?
All families together: **Baptism.**

109. The celebrant speaks to the parents in these or similar words:

You have asked to have your children baptized. In doing so you are accepting the responsibility of training them in the practice of the faith. It will be your duty to bring them up to keep God's commandments as Christ taught us, by loving God and our neighbor. Do you clearly understand what you are undertaking?
All parents together: **We do.**

110. Then the celebrant turns to the godparents and addresses them in these or similar words:

Are you ready to help these parents in their duty as Christian mothers and fathers?
All the godparents: **We are.**

111. The celebrant continues:

My dear children, the Christian community welcomes you with great joy. In its name I claim you for Christ our Savior by the sign of his cross.

He makes the sign of the cross over all the children together, and says:

Parents (or godparents), make the sign of Christ our Savior on the foreheads of your children.

Then the parents (or godparents) sign the children on their foreheads.

LITURGY OF THE WORD

READINGS AND HOMILY

112. The celebrant invites the parents, godparents and the others to take part in the liturgy of the word. Matthew 28:18-20 is read, telling how the apostles were sent to preach the gospel and to baptize.

Other passages may also be selected from nos. 44, 186-194, 204-215.

113. After the reading, the celebrant gives a short homily, explaining to those present the significance of what has been read. His purpose will be to lead them to a deeper understanding of the mystery of baptism and to encourage the parents and godparents to a ready acceptance of the responsibilities which arise from the sacrament.

INTERCESSIONS (PRAYER OF THE FAITHFUL)

114. Then the intercessions (prayer of the faithful) are said:

Celebrant:
My dear brothers and sisters, let us ask our Lord Jesus Christ to look lovingly on these children who are to be baptized, on their parents and godparents, and on all the baptized.

Assisting Minister:
By the mystery of your death and resurrection, bathe these children in light, give them the new life of baptism and welcome them into your holy Church.
All: **Lord, hear our prayer.**

Assisting Minister:
Through baptism and confirmation, make them your faithful followers and witnesses to your gospel.
All: **Lord, hear our prayer.**

Assisting Minister:
Lead them by a holy life to the joys of God's kingdom.
All: **Lord, hear our prayer.**

Assisting Minister:
Make the lives of their parents and godparents examples of faith to inspire these children.
All: **Lord, hear our prayer.**

Assisting Minister:
Keep their families always in your love.
All: **Lord, hear our prayer.**

Assisting Minister:
Renew the grace of our baptism in each one of us.
All: **Lord, hear our prayer.**

Other forms may be chosen from nos. 217-220. The invocation of the saints (see no. 48) may be omitted.

PRAYER OF EXORCISM

115. The prayer of the faithful is concluded with the prayer of exorcism:

Almighty and ever-living God,
you sent your only Son into the world
to cast out the power of Satan, spirit of evil,
to rescue man from the kingdom of darkness,
and bring him into the splendor of your kingdom of
     light.
We pray for these children:
set them free from original sin,
make them temples of your glory,
and send your Holy Spirit to dwell within them.
We ask this through Christ our Lord.
All: **Amen.**

For another form of the prayer of exorcism, see no. 221.

Because of the large number of children to be baptized, the celebrant does not anoint them with oil of catechumens. He imposes his hands over all the children at once and says:

May you have strength in the power of Christ our
Savior, who lives and reigns for ever and ever.
All: **Amen.**

116. Then they go to the place where baptism is celebrated.

CELEBRATION OF THE SACRAMENT

117. When they come to the font, the celebrant briefly reminds the congregation of the wonderful work of God whose plan it is to sanctify man, body and soul, through water. He may use these or similar words:

My dear brothers and sisters, God uses the sacrament
of water to give his divine life to those who believe
in him.

Let us turn to him in our faith, and ask him to pour
his gift of life from this font on the children he has
chosen.

BLESSING AND INVOCATION OF GOD OVER BAPTISMAL WATER

118. Facing the font (or vessel) containing the water, the
celebrant says the following.

Father, God of mercy,
through these waters of baptism
you have filled us with new life as your very own
 children.

All sing or say a suitable acclamation or the following.
Blessed be God.

Celebrant:
From all who are baptized in water and the Holy
 Spirit,
you have formed one people,
united in your Son, Jesus Christ.

All: **Blessed be God.**

Celebrant:
You have set us free and filled our hearts with the
 Spirit of your love,
that we may live in your peace.

All: **Blessed be God.**

Celebrant:
You call those who have been baptized
to announce the Good News of Jesus Christ to
 people everywhere.

All: **Blessed be God.**

The celebrant concludes with the following.
You have called your children, N. and N.,
to this cleansing water and new birth,

that by sharing the faith of your Church they may
have eternal life.
Bless ✛ this water in which they will be baptized.

We ask this in the name of Jesus the Lord.

All: **Amen.**

119. *Easter-Season Thanksgiving over Water Already Blessed:*
If the baptismal water has already been blessed,
the celebrant omits this last prayer and says:

You have called your children, N. and N., to this
cleansing water,
that they may share in the faith of your Church and
have eternal life.
By the mystery of this consecrated water
lead them to a new and spiritual birth.

We ask this through Christ our Lord.

All: **Amen.**

Other forms may be chosen from no. 223.

RENUNCIATION OF SIN AND PROFESSION OF FAITH

120. The celebrant speaks to the parents and godparents in
these words:

**Dear parents and godparents: You have come here to
present these children for baptism. By water and the
Holy Spirit they are to receive the gift of new life
from God, who is love.**

**On your part, you must make it your constant care to
bring them up in the practice of the faith. See that
the divine life which God gives them is kept safe
from the poison of sin, to grow always stronger in
their hearts.**

**If your faith makes you ready to accept this responsi-
bility, renew now the vows of your baptism. Reject
sin; profess your faith in Christ Jesus. This is the
faith of the Church. This is the faith in which these
children are about to be baptized.**

121. The celebrant questions the parents and godparents.

A
Celebrant:
Do you reject Satan?
Parents and godparents: **I do.**

Celebrant:
And all his works?
Parents and godparents: **I do.**

Celebrant:
And all his empty promises?
Parents and godparents: **I do.**

or **B**
Celebrant:
Do you reject sin so as to live in the freedom of God's children?
Parents and godparents: **I do.**

Celebrant:
Do you reject the glamor of evil, and refuse to be mastered by sin?
Parents and godparents: **I do.**

Celebrant:
Do you reject Satan, father of sin and prince of darkness?
Parents and godparents: **I do.**

According to circumstances, this second form may be expressed with greater precision by the conferences of bishops, especially in places where it is necessary for the parents and godparents to reject superstitious and magical practices used with children.

122. Next the celebrant asks for the threefold profession of faith from the parents and godparents:

Celebrant:
Do you believe in God, the Father almighty, creator of heaven and earth?
Parents and godparents: **I do.**

Celebrant:
Do you believe in Jesus Christ, his only Son, our Lord,

who was born of the Virgin Mary,
was crucified, died, and was buried,
rose from the dead,
and is now seated at the right hand of the Father?
Parents and godparents: **I do.**

Celebrant:
Do you believe in the Holy Spirit,
the holy catholic Church, the communion of saints,
the forgiveness of sins, the resurrection of the body,
and the life everlasting?
Parents and godparents: **I do.**

123. The celebrant and the congregation give their assent
to this profession of faith:

Celebrant:
This is our faith. This is the faith of the Church. We
are proud to profess it, in Christ Jesus our Lord.
All: **Amen.**

If desired, some other formula may be used instead, or a
suitable song by which the community expresses its faith
with a single voice.

BAPTISM

124. If there are several ministers because of the large
number to be baptized, each of them questions the parents
and godparents, using the name of the individual child:

Celebrant:
Is it your will that N. should be baptized in the faith
of the Church, which we have all professed with
you?
Parents and godparents: **It is.**

He baptizes the child, saying:

N., I baptize you in the name of the Father,

He immerses the child or pours water upon it.

and of the Son,

He immerses the child or pours water upon it a second
time.

and of the Holy Spirit.

He immerses the child or pours water upon it a third time.

He asks the same question and performs the same action for each child.

If the baptism is performed by the pouring of water, it is preferable that the child be held by the mother (or father). Where, however, it is felt that the existing custom should be retained, the godmother (or godfather) may hold the child.

If baptism is by immersion, the mother or father (godmother or godfather) lifts the child out of the font.

While the children are being baptized, the community can make acclamations or sing hymns (see nos. 225-245). Some passages from Scripture may also be read, or a sacred silence observed.

EXPLANATORY RITES

ANOINTING AFTER BAPTISM

125. Then the celebrant says the formula of anointing once for all the children:

**The God of power and Father of our Lord Jesus
    Christ
has freed you from sin
and brought you to new life
through water and the Holy Spirit.**

**He now anoints you with the chrism of salvation,
so that, united with his people,
you may remain for ever a member of Christ
who is Priest, Prophet, and King.**

Children: **Amen.**

Then the ministers anoint each child on the crown of the head with the sacred chrism, in silence.

But if the number of children is extremely large, the conferences of bishops may decide that the anointing with chrism may be omitted. [In the United States the anointing may not be omitted.] In this case, an adapted formula is used:

**The God of power and Father of our Lord Jesus
    Christ**

**has freed you from sin
and brought you to new life
through water and the Holy Spirit.**

**He has made you Christians now,
and has welcomed you into his holy people.
As Christ was anointed Priest, Prophet, and King,
so may you live always as members of his body,
sharing everlasting life.**

All: **Amen.**

CLOTHING WITH WHITE GARMENT

126. The celebrant says:

**My dear children, you have become a new creation,
and have clothed yourselves in Christ.**

**See in this white garment the outward sign of your
Christian dignity. With your family and friends to
help you by word and example, bring that dignity
unstained into the everlasting life of heaven.**
All: **Amen.**

The white garments are put on the children. A different
color is not permitted unless demanded by local custom. It
is desirable that the families provide the garments.

LIGHTED CANDLE

127. The celebrant takes the Easter candle and says:

**Receive the light of Christ. Parents and godparents,
this light is entrusted to you to be kept burning
brightly. These children of yours have been enlightened by Christ. They are to walk always as children
of the light. May they keep the flame of faith alive
in their hearts. When the Lord comes, may they go
out to meet him with all the saints in the heavenly
kingdom.**

Candles are distributed to the families. The head of one
family lights his candle from the Easter candle and passes
the flame on to the rest. Meanwhile the community sings a
baptismal song, such as:

You have put on Christ,
in him you have been baptized.
Alleluia, alleluia.

Other hymns may be chosen from nos. 225-245.

Meanwhile, unless the baptisms were performed in the sanctuary, there is a procession to the altar. The lighted candles are carried for the children.

CONCLUSION OF THE RITE

LORD'S PRAYER

128. The celebrant stands in front of the altar and addresses the parents, godparents, and the whole assembly in these or similar words:

Dearly beloved, these children have been reborn in baptism. They are now called children of God, for so indeed they are. In confirmation they will receive the fullness of God's Spirit. In holy communion they will share the banquet of Christ's sacrifice, calling God their Father in the midst of the Church. In their name, in the spirit of our common sonship, let us pray together in the words our Lord has given us:

129. All present join the celebrant in singing or saying:

Our Father. . . .

BLESSING AND DISMISSAL

130. The celebrant blesses the entire assembly, and dismisses them:

My brothers and sisters, we commend you to the mercy and grace of God our almighty Father, of his only Son, and of the Holy Spirit. May he protect your paths, so that walking in the light of faith, you may come to the good things he has promised us.

May almighty God, the Father, and the Son, ✝ and the Holy Spirit bless you.
All: Amen.

Celebrant: **Go in peace.**
All: **Thanks be to God.**

For other forms of the blessing, see nos. 70, 247-248.

131. After the blessing, all may sing a hymn which suitably
expresses thanksgiving and Easter joy, or they may sing the
song of the Blessed Virgin Mary, the Magnificat.

CHAPTER IV

RITE OF BAPTISM FOR CHILDREN ADMINISTERED BY A CATECHIST WHEN NO PRIEST OR DEACON IS AVAILABLE

RECEPTION OF THE CHILDREN

132. While the faithful sing a suitable psalm or hymn, the catechist and the ministers approach the door of the church or the part of the church where the parents, godparents, and the children to be baptized are waiting.

If there is a large group of persons to be baptized, the catechist may be assisted by others in the act of baptism, as noted below.

133. The catechist greets all present, and especially the parents and godparents, reminding them briefly of the joy with which the parents welcomed their children as gifts from God, the source of life, who now wishes to bestow his own life on these little ones.

Then he questions the parents and godparents together in these or similar words:

A
What name do you give your children? (or: **have you given?**)
Each family answers in turn, giving the names of the children.

Catechist:
What do you ask of God's Church for these children?
All families together: **Baptism.**

If there are many children to be baptized, the first question is omitted and the catechist asks:

B
Parents and godparents, what do you ask for these children?
All families together: **Baptism.**

134. Then the catechist speaks to the parents:

Parents, you have asked to have your children baptized. In doing so you are accepting the responsibility of training them in the practice of the faith. It will be your duty to bring them up to keep God's commandments as Christ taught us, by loving God and our neighbor. Do you clearly understand what you are undertaking?
All parents together: **We do.**

135. Then turning to the godparents, the catechist asks:

Godparents, are you ready to help these parents in their duty as Christian mothers and fathers?
All the godparents: **We are.**

136. The catechist continues:

My dear children, the Christian community welcomes you with great joy. In its name I claim for you Christ our Savior by the sign of his cross.

He makes the sign of the cross over all the children together, and says:

Parents (or godparents), make the sign of Christ our Savior on the foreheads of your children.

Then the parents (or godparents) sign the children on their foreheads.

LITURGY OF THE WORD

READING AND HOMILY OR SHORT TALK

137. The catechist invites the parents, godparents, and the others to take part in the liturgy of the word. Matthew

28:18-20 is read, telling how the apostles were sent to preach the gospel and to baptize.

Other passages may also be selected from nos. 186-194, 204-215. If songs and hymns are sung, see nos. 195-203. After the reading, the catechist can give a brief homily in the way determined by the bishop.

138. In the place of the Scripture reading and the homily, the catechist can, if necessary, give this talk:

In baptism, Christ will come to meet these children. He entrusted this sacrament to his Church when he sent forth his apostles with these words: "Go, make disciples of all nations, and baptize them in the name of the Father, and of the Son, and of the Holy Spirit."

As you know, these children will be given countless gifts in this great sacrament: they will be freed from sin; they will become members of the Church; they will become God's children. But since man is unable to accomplish such wonders, we must pray together with humility and faith for these blessings.

May God our Father see in the fellowship of our community the faith of his Church, and hear in our prayer the voice of Jesus his Son. As he promised us through Christ, may he bless these children by the power of his Holy Spirit.

INTERCESSIONS (PRAYER OF THE FAITHFUL)

139. Then the intercessions (prayer of the faithful) are said:

Catechist:
My dear brothers and sisters, let us ask our Lord Jesus Christ to look lovingly on these children who are to be baptized, on their parents and godparents, and on all the baptized.

Assisting Minister:
By the mystery of your death and resurrection, bathe these children in light, give them the new life of baptism and welcome them into your holy Church. All: Lord, hear our prayer.

Assisting Minister:

Through baptism and confirmation, make them your faithful followers and witnesses to your gospel.
All: **Lord, hear our prayer.**

Assisting Minister:

Lead them by a holy life to the joys of God's kingdom.
All: **Lord, hear our prayer.**

Assisting Minister:

Make the lives of their parents and godparents examples of faith to inspire these children.
All: **Lord, hear our prayer.**

Assisting Minister:

Keep their families always in your love.
All: **Lord, hear our prayer.**

Assisting Minister:

Renew the grace of our baptism in each one of us.
All: **Lord, hear our prayer.**

Other forms may be chosen from nos. 217-220.

Then the catechist invites all present to invoke the saints:

Holy Mary, Mother of God,	**pray for us.**
Saint John the Baptist,	**pray for us.**
Saint Joseph,	**pray for us.**
Saint Peter and Saint Paul,	**pray for us.**

The names of other saints may be added, especially the patrons of the children to be baptized, and of the church or locality. The litany concludes:

| **All holy men and women,** | **pray for us.** |

140. The prayer of exorcism and the anointing with oil of catechumens are omitted.

CELEBRATION OF THE SACRAMENT

BLESSING AND INVOCATION OF GOD OVER BAPTISMAL WATER

141. With the parents and godparents carrying the children who are to be baptized, the catechist comes to the font. He invites all to pray:

My dear brothers and sisters, let us ask God to give these children new life in abundance through water and the Holy Spirit.

142. If there is no blessed water available, the catechist stands before the font and says this invocation:

A
Catechist:
Father, God of mercy,
through these waters of baptism
you have filled us with new life as your very own
   children.

All sing or say a suitable acclamation or the following.
Blessed be God.

Catechist:
From all who are baptized in water and the Holy
   Spirit,
you have formed one people,
united in your Son, Jesus Christ.

All: **Blessed be God.**

Catechist:
You have set us free and filled our hearts with the
   Spirit of your love,
that we may live in your peace.

All: **Blessed be God.**

Catechist:
You call those who have been baptized
to announce the Good News of Jesus Christ to peo-
   ple everywhere.

All: **Blessed be God.**

The catechist concludes with the following.
**Come and bless this water
in which your servants are to be baptized.
You have called them to the washing of new life
in the Faith of your Church,
so that they may have eternal life.
We ask this through Christ our Lord.**

All: **Amen.**

143. If blessed water is available, he says the following
invocation:

**B
Father of our Lord Jesus Christ,
source of all life and love,
you are glorified throughout the world
by the simple joys and daily cares
of mothers and fathers.**

**In the beauty of a child's birth
and in the mystery of his rebirth to eternal life,
you give us a glimpse of all creation:
it is guided by your fatherly love,
unfolding in fruitfulness to perfection
in Jesus Christ your Son.**

**In your kindness
hear the prayers of the Church and of these parents.
Look upon these children with love,
and keep them from the power of sin.
Since they are a gift from you, Father,
welcome them into the kingdom of your Son.**

**You have created this water,
and made it clean, refreshing, and life-giving.
You have made it holy through the baptism of
  Christ,
that by the power of the Holy Spirit
it may give your people a new birth.**

**When these children are baptized into the mystery
of Christ's suffering, death, and resurrection,**

may they be worthy to become members of your Church,
your very own children.
Father, may they rejoice
with Jesus your Son and the Holy Spirit
for ever and ever.
All: **Amen.**

RENUNCIATION OF SIN AND PROFESSION OF FAITH

144. The catechist speaks to the parents and godparents in these words:

Dear parents and godparents: You have come here to present these children for baptism. By water and the Holy Spirit, they are to receive the gift of new life from God, who is love.

On your part, you must make it your constant care to bring them up in the practice of the faith. See that the divine life which God gives them is kept safe from the poison of sin, to grow always stronger in their hearts.

If your faith makes you ready to accept this responsibility, renew now the vows of your baptism. Reject sin; profess your faith in Christ Jesus. This is the faith of the Church. This is the faith in which these children are about to be baptized.

145. Then he asks them:

A
Catechist:
Do you reject Satan?
Parents and godparents: **I do.**

Catechist:
And all his works?
Parents and godparents: **I do.**

Catechist:
And all his empty promises?
Parents and godparents: **I do.**

or **B**
Catechist:
**Do you reject sin so as to live in the freedom of
God's children?**
Parents and godparents: **I do.**

Catechist:
**Do you reject the glamor of evil, and refuse to be
mastered by sin?**
Parents and godparents: **I do.**

Catechist:
**Do you reject Satan, father of sin and prince of
darkness?**
Parents and godparents: **I do.**

According to circumstances, this second form may be expressed with greater precision by the conference of bishops, especially in places where it is necessary for the parents and godparents to reject superstitious and magical practices used with children.

146. Then the catechist asks for the threefold profession of faith from the parents and godparents:

Catechist:
**Do you believe in God, the Father almighty,
    creator of heaven and earth?**
Parents and godparents: **I do.**

Catechist:
**Do you believe in Jesus Christ, his only Son, our Lord,
    who was born of the Virgin Mary,
    was crucified, died, and was buried,
    rose from the dead,
    and is now seated at the right hand of the Father?**
Parents and godparents: **I do.**

Catechist:
**Do you believe in the Holy Spirit,
    the holy catholic Church, the communion of saints,
    the forgiveness of sins, the resurrection of the body,
    and the life everlasting?**
Parents and godparents: **I do.**

147. The catechist and the congregation give their assent to this profession of faith:

Catechist:

This is our faith. This is the faith of the Church. We are proud to profess it, in Christ Jesus our Lord.
All: **Amen.**

If desired, some other formula may be used instead, or a suitable song by which the community expresses its faith with a single voice.

BAPTISM

148. The catechist invites the first of the families to approach the font. Using the name of the individual child, he asks the parents and godparents:

Is it your will that N. should be baptized in the faith of the Church, which we have all professed with you?
Parents and godparents: **It is.**

He baptizes the child, saying:

N., I baptize you in the name of the Father,

He immerses the child or pours water upon it.

and of the Son,

He immerses the child or pours water upon it a second time.

and of the Holy Spirit.

He immerses the child or pours water upon it a third time.

If baptism is performed by the pouring of water, it is preferable that the child be held by the mother or father. Where, however, it is felt that the existing custom should be retained, the godmother or godfather may hold the child. If baptism is by immersion, the parent or godparent lifts the child out of the font.

149. If the number of children to be baptized is large, and other catechists are present, these may baptize some of the children in the way described above, and with the same form (no. 148).

150. While the children are being baptized, the community can make acclamations or sing hymns (see nos. 225-245). Some passages from Scripture may also be read, or a sacred silence observed.

EXPLANATORY RITES

151. The anointing with chrism is omitted. The catechist says once for all the newly-baptized children:

**The God of power and Father of our Lord Jesus
  Christ
has freed you from sin
and brought you to new life
through water and the Holy Spirit.**

**He has made you Christians now,
and has welcomed you into his holy people.
As Christ was anointed Priest, Prophet, and King,
so may you live always as members of his body,
sharing everlasting life.**
All: **Amen.**

CLOTHING WITH WHITE GARMENT

152. The catechist says:

**My dear children, you have become a new creation,
and have clothed yourselves in Christ.**

**See in this white garment the outward sign of your
Christian dignity. With your family and friends to
help you by word and example, bring that dignity
unstained into the everlasting life of heaven.**
All: **Amen.**

The white garments are put on the children. A different color is not permitted unless demanded by local custom. It is desirable that the families provide the garments.

LIGHTED CANDLE

153. The catechist takes the Easter candle and says:

Receive the light of Christ. Parents and godparents, this light is entrusted to you to be kept burning brightly. These children of yours have been enlightened by Christ. They are to walk always as children of the light. May they keep the flame of faith alive in their hearts. When the Lord comes, may they go out to meet him with all the saints in the heavenly kingdom.

Candles are distributed to the families. The head of one family lights his candle from the Easter candle and passes the flame on to the rest. Meanwhile the community sings a baptismal song, such as:

**You have put on Christ,
in him you have been baptized.
Alleluia, alleluia.**

Other hymns may be chosen from nos. 225-245.

Meanwhile, unless the baptisms were performed in the sanctuary, there is a procession to the altar. The lighted candles are carried for the children.

CONCLUSION OF THE RITE

LORD'S PRAYER

154. The catechist stands in front of the altar and addresses the parents, godparents, and the whole assembly in these or similar words:

Dearly beloved, these children have been reborn in baptism. They are now called children of God, for so indeed they are. In confirmation they will receive the fullness of God's Spirit. In holy communion they will share the banquet of Christ's sacrifice, calling God their Father in the midst of the Church. In their name, in the spirit of common sonship, let us pray together in the words our Lord has given us:

155. All say together:

Our Father. . . .

BLESSING AND DISMISSAL

156. The catechist invokes the blessing of God and dismisses the assembly.

My brothers and sisters, we commend you to the mercy and grace of God our almighty Father, of his only Son, and of the Holy Spirit. May he protect your paths, so that walking in the light of faith, you may come to the good things he has promised us.

All: **Amen.**

Catechist:
Go in peace.
All: **Thanks be to God.**

After the blessing, all may sing a hymn which suitably expresses thanksgiving and Easter joy, or they may sing the canticle of the Blessed Virgin Mary, the Magnificat.

CHAPTER V

RITE OF BAPTISM FOR CHILDREN IN DANGER OF DEATH WHEN NO PRIEST OR DEACON IS AVAILABLE

157. Water, even though not blessed, is prepared for the rite. The parents, godparents, and if possible, some friends and neighbors of the family gather around the sick child. The minister, who is any suitable member of the Church, begins with this brief prayer of the faithful:

Let us ask almighty God to look with mercy on this child who is about to receive the grace of baptism, on his (her) parents and godparents, and on all baptized persons.
Through baptism, welcome this child into your Church.
R̸. Lord, hear our prayer.

Through baptism, make him (her) one of your adopted children.
R̸. Lord, hear our prayer.

Through baptism, he (she) is being buried in the likeness of Christ's death. May he (she) also share in the glory of his resurrection.
R̸. Lord, hear our prayer.

Renew the grace of our baptism in each one of us.
R̸. Lord, hear our prayer.

May all the followers of Christ, baptized into one body, always live united in faith and love.
R̸. Lord, hear our prayer.

158. The prayer of the faithful concludes with this prayer:

Father of our Lord Jesus Christ,
source of all life and love,
you know the anxiety of parents
and you lighten their burden
by your fatherly care for all children in danger.

You reveal the depth of your love
by offering them a new and eternal birth.

In your kindness, hear our prayers:
keep this child from the power of sin,
and welcome him (her) with love into the kingdom of
    your Son.

By water and by the power of the Holy Spirit,
may this child, whom we now call N.,
share in the mystery of Christ's death
so that he (she) may also share in the mystery of
    Christ's resurrection.

May he (she) become your adopted son (daughter),
and share in the inheritance of Christ.
Grant that he (she) may rejoice in the fellowship of
    your Church
with your only Son and the Holy Spirit
for ever and ever.
℟. Amen.

159. Then they make the profession of faith. The minister
says to all present:

A
Let us remember our own baptism, and profess our
faith in Jesus Christ. This is the faith of the Church,
the faith into which children are baptized.

Then the minister asks:

Do you believe in God, the Father almighty,
    creator of heaven and earth?
℟. I do.

Minister:
Do you believe in Jesus Christ, his only Son, our Lord,
    who was born of the Virgin Mary,
    was crucified, died, and was buried,
    rose from the dead,
    and is now seated at the right of the Father?
℟. I do.

Minister:
**Do you believe in the Holy Spirit,
the holy catholic Church, the communion of saints,
the forgiveness of sins, the resurrection of the body,
and the life everlasting?**
℟. **I do.**

The profession of faith may also be made, if desirable, by
reciting the Apostles' Creed:

B
**I believe in God, the Father almighty,
Creator of heaven and earth;
and in Jesus Christ, his only Son, our Lord,
who was conceived by the Holy Spirit,
born of the Virgin Mary,
suffered under Pontius Pilate,
was crucified, died, and was buried.
He descended into hell;
the third day he rose again from the dead;
he ascended into heaven,
sitteth at the right hand of God, the Father
almighty,
from thence he shall come to judge the living and
the dead.
I believe in the Holy Spirit,
the holy catholic Church,
the communion of saints,
the forgiveness of sins,
the resurrection of the body,
and the life everlasting. Amen.**

160. Then the minister baptizes the child, saying:

N., I baptize you in the name of the Father,

The minister pours water upon the child.

and of the Son,

The minister pours water upon the child a second time.

and of the Holy Spirit.

The minister pours water upon the child a third time.

161. Omitting all other ceremonies, the minister may give the white garment to the child. The minister says:

N., you have become a new creation, and have clothed yourself in Christ.

See in this white garment the outward sign of your Christian dignity. May you bring it unstained into the everlasting life of heaven.

162. The celebration concludes with the recitation of the Lord's Prayer:

Our Father . . .

163. If no one there is capable of directing the prayer, any member of the Church may baptize, after reciting the Apostles' Creed, by pouring water on the child while reciting the customary words (see no. 160, above). The creed may be omitted if necessary.

164. At the moment of death, it is sufficient for the minister to omit all other ceremonies and pour water on the child while saying the usual words (see no. 160, above). It is desirable that the minister, as far as possible, should use one or two witnesses.

CHAPTER VI

RITE OF BRINGING A BAPTIZED CHILD TO THE CHURCH

RECEPTION OF THE CHILD

165. The people may sing a psalm or song suitable for the occasion. Meanwhile the celebrating priest or deacon, vested in alb or surplice, with a stole (with or without a cope) of festive color, and accompanied by the ministers, goes to the entrance of the church where the parents and godparents are waiting with the child.

166. The celebrant greets all present, and especially the parents and godparents. He praises them for having had the child baptized without delay, and thanks God and congratulates the parents on the child's return to health.

167. First the celebrant questions the parents:

Celebrant:
What name have you given the child?
Parents: **N.**

Celebrant:
What do you ask of God's Church, now that your child has been baptized?
Parents: **We ask that the whole community will know that he (she) has been received into the Church.**

The first reply may be given by someone other than the parents if local custom gives him the right to name the child.

In the second response the parents may use other words, such as **that he (she) is a Christian** or **that he (she) has been baptized.**

168. Then the celebrant speaks to the parents in these or similar words:

Celebrant:
Do you realize that in bringing your child to the

Church, you are accepting the duty of raising him (her) in the faith, so that by observing the commandments he (she) will love God and neighbor as Christ taught us?
Parents: **We do.**

169. Then the celebrant turns to the godparents and addresses them in these or similar words:

Are you ready to help the mother and father of this child to carry out their duty as Christian parents?
Godparents: **We are.**

170. The celebrant continues:

N., the Christian community welcomes you with great joy, now that you have recovered your health. We now bear witness that you have been received as a member of the Church. In the name of the community I sign you with the cross of Christ, who gave you a new life in baptism and made you a member of his Church. I invite your parents (and godparents) to do the same.

He signs the child on the forehead, in silence. Then he invites the parents and (if it seems appropriate) the godparents to do the same.

171. The celebrant invites the parents, godparents, and all who are present to take part in the liturgy of the word. If circumstances permit, there is a procession to the place where this will be celebrated, during which a song is sung, such as Psalm 85:7, 8, 9ab:

Will you not give us life;
 and shall not your people rejoice in you?
Show us, O Lord, your kindness,
 and grant us your salvation.
I will hear what God proclaims:
 the Lord—for he proclaims peace to his people.

LITURGY OF THE WORD

READINGS AND HOMILY

172. One or even two of the following gospel passages are read, during which all may sit if convenient.

John 3:1-6 The meeting with Nicodemus..
Matthew 28:18-20 The apostles are sent to preach the gospel and to baptize.
Mark 1:9-11 The baptism of Jesus.
Mark 10:13-16 Let the little children come to me.

The passages listed in nos. 186-194 and 204-215 may also be chosen, or other passages which better meet the wishes or needs of the parents, such as the following:

1 Kings 17:17-24
2 Kings 4:8-37

Between the readings, responsorial psalms or verses may be sung, as given in nos. 195-203.

173. After the reading, the celebrant gives a brief homily, explaining to those present the significance of what has been read. His purpose will be to lead them to a deeper understanding of the mystery of baptism and to encourage parents and godparents to a ready acceptance of the responsibilities which arise from the sacrament.

174. After the homily, or in the course of or after the litany, it is desirable to have a period of silence while all pray at the invitation of the celebrant. A suitable hymn may follow, such as one chosen from nos. 225-245.

INTERCESSIONS (PRAYER OF THE FAITHFUL)

175. Then the intercessions (prayer of the faithful) are said:

Celebrant:
Let us ask our Lord Jesus Christ to look lovingly on this child, on his (her) parents and godparents, and on all the baptized.

Assisting Minister:
May this child always show gratitude to God for his (her) baptism and recovery.
All: **Lord, hear our prayer.**

Assisting Minister:
Help him (her) always to be a living member of your Church.
All: **Lord, hear our prayer.**

Assisting Minister:
Inspire him (her) to hear, follow, and witness to your gospel.
All: **Lord, hear our prayer.**

Assisting Minister:
May he (she) come with joy to the table of your sacrifice.
All: **Lord, hear our prayer.**

Assisting Minister:
Help him (her) to love God and neighbor as you have taught us.
All: **Lord, hear our prayer.**

Assisting Minister:
May he (she) grow in holiness and wisdom by listening to his (her) fellow Christians and following their example.
All: **Lord, hear our prayer.**

Assisting Minister:
Keep all your followers united in faith and love for ever.
All: **Lord, hear our prayer.**

176. The celebrant next invites all present to invoke the saints:

Holy Mary, Mother of God,	**pray for us.**
Saint John the Baptist,	**pray for us.**
Saint Joseph,	**pray for us.**
Saint Peter and Saint Paul,	**pray for us.**

The names of other saints may be added, especially the patrons of the child and of the church or locality. The litany concludes:

All holy men and women,   **pray for us.**

177. Then the celebrant says:

Father of our Lord Jesus Christ,
source of all life and love,
you are glorified by the loving care these parents
    have shown this child.
You rescue children from danger and save them in
    baptism.

Your Church thanks you and prays for your child N.
You have brought him (her) out of the kingdom of
    darkness
and into your marvelous light.
You have made him (her) your adopted child
and a temple of the Holy Spirit.

Help him (her) in all the dangers of this life
and strengthen him (her) in the constant effort to
    reach your kingdom,
through the power of Christ our Savior.
We ask this through Christ our Lord.
All: **Amen.**

EXPLANATORY RITES

ANOINTING AFTER BAPTISM

178. See no. 62.

CLOTHING WITH WHITE GARMENT

179. The celebrant says:

N., you have become a new creation, and have
clothed yourself in Christ.

See in this white garment the outward sign of your
Christian dignity. With your family and friends to
help you by word and example, bring that dignity

unstained into the everlasting life of heaven.
All: **Amen.**

LIGHTED CANDLE

180. The celebrant takes the Easter candle and says:

Receive the light of Christ.

Someone, such as the father or godfather, lights the child's candle from the Easter candle.

The celebrant then says:

Parents and godparents, this light is entrusted to you to be kept burning brightly. This child of yours has been enlightened by Christ. He (she) is to walk always as a child of the light. May he (she) keep the flame of faith alive in his (her) heart. When the Lord comes, may he (she) go out to meet him with all the saints in the heavenly kingdom.

A baptismal song is appropriate at this time, such as:

**You have put on Christ,
in him you have been baptized.
Alleluia, alleluia.**

Other songs may be chosen from nos. 225-245.

CONCLUSION OF THE RITE

LORD'S PRAYER

181. The celebrant stands in front of the altar and addresses the parents, godparents, and the whole assembly in these or similar words:

My dear brothers and sisters, this child has been reborn in baptism. He (she) is now called the child of God, for so indeed he (she) is. In confirmation he (she) will receive the fullness of God's Spirit. In holy communion he (she) will share the banquet of Christ's sacrifice, calling God his (her) Father in the midst of the Church. In the name of this child, in the spirit of our common sonship, let us pray together in the words our Lord has given us:

182. All present join the celebrant in singing or saying:

Our Father. . . .

BLESSING AND DISMISSAL

183. The celebrant first blesses the mother, who holds the child in her arms, then the father, and lastly the entire assembly:

Celebrant:
God the Father, through his Son, the Virgin Mary's child, has brought joy to all Christian mothers, as they see the hope of eternal life shine on their children. May he bless the mother of this child. She now thanks God for the gift of her child. May she be one with her son (daughter) in thanking God for ever in heaven, in Christ Jesus our Lord.
All: **Amen.**

Celebrant:
God is the giver of all life, human and divine. May he bless the father of this child. He and his wife will be the first teachers of their child in the ways of faith.

May they also be the best of teachers, bearing witness to the faith by what they say and do, in Christ Jesus our Lord.
All: **Amen.**

Celebrant:
By God's gift, through water and the Holy Spirit, we are reborn to everlasting life. In his goodness, may he continue to pour out his blessings on these sons and daughters of his. May he make them always, wherever they may be, faithful members of his holy people. May he send his peace upon all who are gathered here, in Christ Jesus our Lord.
All: **Amen.**

Celebrant:
May almighty God, the Father, and the Son, ✛ and the Holy Spirit, bless you.
All: **Amen.**

Celebrant:
Go in Peace.
All: **Thanks be to God.**

For other forms of the blessing, see nos. 247-249.

184. After the blessing, all may sing a hymn which suitably expresses thanksgiving and Easter joy, or they may sing the song of the Blessed Virgin Mary, the Magnificat.

Where there is the practice of bringing the baptized child to the altar of the blessed Virgin, this custom is observed if appropriate.

185. The above rite is followed even when the baptized child is brought to the church after other difficulties (such as persecution, disagreement between parents) which prevented the celebration of baptism in the church. In such cases, the celebrant should adapt the explanations, readings, intentions in the prayer of the faithful and other parts of the rite to the child's circumstances.

CHAPTER VII

VARIOUS TEXTS FOR USE IN THE CELEBRATION OF BAPTISM FOR CHILDREN

I. SCRIPTURAL READINGS

OLD TESTAMENT READINGS

186. **Exodus 17:3-7**   Water from the rock.

187. **Ezekiel 36:24-28**   Clean water, a new heart, a renewed spirit.

188. **Ezekiel 47:1-9, 12**   The water of salvation.

NEW TESTAMENT READINGS

189. **Romans 6:3-5**   Baptism: a sharing in Christ's death and resurrection.

190. **Romans 8:28-32**   We have become more perfectly like God's own Son.

191. **1 Corinthians 12:12-13**   Baptized in one Spirit to form one body.

192. **Galatians 3:26-28**   Now that you have been baptized you have put on Christ.

193. **Ephesians 4:1-6**   One Lord, one faith, one baptism.

194. **1 Peter 2:4-5, 9-10**   A chosen race, a royal priesthood.

RESPONSORIAL PSALMS

195. Psalm 23:1-3a, 3b-4, 5, 6
℞. (1) **The Lord is my shepherd; there is nothing I shall want.**

196. Psalm 27:1, 4, 8b-9abc, 13-14

℟. (1a) **The Lord is my light and my salvation.**

Or: Ephesians 5:14

Wake up and rise from death:
Christ will shine upon you!

197. Psalm 34:2-3, 6-7, 8-9, 14-15, 16-17, 18-19

℟. (6a) **Come to him and receive his light!**

Or: (9a) **Taste and see the goodness of the Lord.**

ALLELUIA VERSE AND VERSE BEFORE THE GOSPEL

198. John 3:16

God loved the world so much, he gave us his only
    Son,
that all who believe in him might have eternal life.

199. John 8:12

I am the light of the world, says the Lord;
the man who follows me will have the light of life.

200. John 14:5

I am the way, the truth, and the life, says the Lord;
no one comes to the Father, except through me.

201. Ephesians 4:5-6

One Lord, one faith, one baptism.
One God, the Father of all.

202. 2 Timothy 1:10b

Our Savior Jesus Christ has done away with death,
and brought us life through his gospel.

203. 1 Peter 2:9

You are a chosen race, a royal priesthood, a holy
    people.
Praise God who called you out of darkness and into
    his marvelous light.

GOSPELS

204. **Matthew 22:35-40** The first and most important
commandment.

205. **Matthew 28:18-20** Christ sends his apostles to teach
and baptize.

206. **Mark 1:9-11** The baptism of Jesus.

207. **Mark 10:13-16** Jesus loves children.

208. **Mark 12:28b-34 (longer) or 28b-31 (shorter)** Love God with all your heart.

209. **John 3:1-6** The meeting with Nicodemus.

210. **John 4:5-14** Jesus speaks with the Samaritan woman.

211. **John 6:44-47** Eternal life through belief in Jesus.

212. **John 7:37b-39a** Streams of living water.

213. **John 9:1-7** Jesus heals a blind man who believes in him.

214. **John 15:1-11** Union with Christ, the true vine.

215. **John 19:31-35** The death of Christ, the witness of John the apostle.

II. OTHER FORMS OF THE INTERCESSIONS (PRAYER OF THE FAITHFUL)

Any one of the following forms given in this baptismal ritual may be used for the prayer of the faithful. Petitions may be added or omitted at will, taking into consideration the special circumstances of each family. The prayer always concludes with the invocation of the saints.

216.
As given in no. 47.

217.
We have been called by the Lord to be a royal priesthood, a holy nation, a people he has acquired for himself. Let us ask him to show his mercy to these children, who are to receive the graces of baptism, to their parents and godparents, and to all the baptized everywhere.

Through baptism, bring these children into your Church.
℟. **Lord, hear our prayer.**

Throughout their lives, help them to be faithful witnesses to your Son, Jesus Christ, for they are being marked with his cross.
℟. Lord, hear our prayer.

As they are being buried in the likeness of Christ's death through baptism, may they also share in the glory of Christ's resurrection.
℟. Lord, hear our prayer.

Teach them by the words and example of their parents and godparents, and help them to grow strong as living members of the Church.
℟. Lord, hear our prayer.

Renew the grace of baptism in each of us here.
℟. Lord, hear our prayer.

May all Christ's followers, baptized into one body, always live united in faith and love.
℟. Lord, hear our prayer.

The invocation of the saints follows.

218.
My fellow Christians, let us ask the mercy of Jesus Christ our Lord for these children who will receive the gift of baptism, for their parents and godparents, and for all baptized persons.

Through baptism, make these children God's own sons and daughters.
℟. Lord, hear our prayer.

Help these tender branches grow to be more like you, the true vine, and be your faithful followers.
℟. Lord, hear our prayer.

May they always keep your commands, walk in your love, and proclaim your Good News to their fellow men.
℟. Lord, hear our prayer.

May they be counted as God's friends through your

saving work, Lord Jesus, and may they inherit eternal life.
R̝. Lord, hear our prayer.

Help their parents and godparents to lead them to know and love God.
R̝. Lord, hear our prayer.

Inspire all men to share in the new birth of baptism.
R̝. Lord, hear our prayer.

The invocation of the saints follows.

219.
We have been called by the Lord to be a royal priesthood, a holy nation, a people he has acquired for himself. Let us ask him to show his mercy to these children, who are to receive the graces of baptism, to their parents and godparents, and to all the baptized everywhere.

Through baptism may these children become God's own beloved sons and daughters. We pray to the Lord.
R̝. Lord, hear our prayer.

Once they are born again of water and the Holy Spirit, may they always live in that Spirit, and make their new life known to their fellow men. We pray to the Lord.
R̝. Lord, hear our prayer.

Help them to triumph over the deceits of the devil and the attractions of evil. We pray to the Lord.
R̝. Lord, hear our prayer.

May they love you, Lord, with all their heart, soul, mind and strength, and love their neighbor as themselves. We pray to the Lord.
R̝. Lord, hear our prayer.

Help all of us here to be models of faith for these children. We pray to the Lord.
R̝. Lord, hear our prayer.

May all Christ's faithful people, who receive the sign of the cross at baptism, always and everywhere give witness to him by the way they live. We pray to the Lord.
℟. Lord, hear our prayer.

The invocation of the saints follows.

220.
Let us ask Christ's mercy for these children, their parents and godparents, and all baptized Christians. Give them a new birth to eternal life through water and the Holy Spirit.
℟. Lord, hear our prayer.

Help them always to be living members of your Church.
℟. Lord, hear our prayer.

Inspire them to hear and follow your gospel, and to give witness to you by their lives. We ask this, Lord.
℟. Lord, hear our prayer.

May they come with joy to the table of your sacrifice.
℟. Lord, hear our prayer.

Help them to love God and neighbor as you have taught us.
℟. Lord, hear our prayer.

May they grow in holiness and wisdom by listening to their fellow Christians and by following their example.
℟. Lord, hear our prayer.

Let all your followers remain united in faith and love.
℟. Lord, hear our prayer.

The invocation of the saints follows.

III. ANOTHER FORM OF THE PRAYER OF EXORCISM

221.
**Almighty God,
you sent your only Son
to rescue us from the slavery of sin,
and to give us the freedom
only your sons and daughters enjoy.**

**We now pray for these children
who will have to face the world with its temptations,
and fight the devil in all his cunning.**

**Your Son died and rose again to save us.
By his victory over sin and death,
cleanse these children from the stain of original sin.
Strengthen them with the grace of Christ,
and watch over them at every step in life's journey.
We ask this through Christ our Lord.**
All: **Amen.**

IV. BLESSING AND INVOCATION OF GOD OVER BAPTISMAL WATER

222. See the formula in no. 54a.

223. Facing the font (or vessel) containing the water, the celebrant says the following.

**Praise to you, almighty God and Father,
for you have created water to cleanse and to give life.**

All sing or say the following or some other suitable acclamation.

Blessed be God.

Celebrant:
**Praised to you, Lord Jesus Christ, the Father's only
  Son,
for you offered yourself on the cross,
that in the blood and water flowing from your side**

and through your death and resurrection
the Church might be born.

All: **Blessed be God.**

Celebrant:
**Praise to you, God the Holy Spirit,
for you anointed Christ at his baptism in the waters
    of the Jordan,
that we might all be baptized in you.**

All: **Blessed be God.**

Celebrant:
**Come to us, Lord, Father of all,
and make holy this water which you have created,
so that all who are baptized in it may be washed
        clean of sin
and be born again to live as your children.**

All sing or say the following or some other suitable invocation.
Hear us, Lord.

Celebrant:
**Make this water holy, Lord,
so that all who are baptized into Christ's death and
        resurrection by this water
may become more perfectly like your Son.**

All: **Hear us, Lord.**

A

The celebrant touches the water with his right hand and
continues.

**Lord,
make holy this water which you have created,
so that all those whom you have chosen
may be born again by the power of the Holy Spirit
and may take their place among your holy people.**

All: **Hear us, Lord.**

B

During the Easter season, if there is baptismal water already blessed, the celebrant concludes with the following:

**You have called your children, N. and N.,
to this cleansing water,
that they may share in the faith of your Church and
have eternal life.
By the mystery of this consecrated water
lead them to a new and spiritual birth.**

We ask this through Christ our Lord.

All: Amen.

224. Facing the font (or vessel) containing the water, the celebrant says the following.

**Father, God of mercy,
through these waters of baptism
you have filled us with new life as your very own
children.**

All sing or say a suitable acclamation or the following.
Blessed be God.

Celebrant:
**From all who are baptized in water and the Holy
Spirit,
you have formed one people,
united in your Son, Jesus Christ.**

All: **Blessed be God.**

Celebrant:
**You have set us free and filled our hearts with the
Spirit of your love,
that we may live in your peace.**

All: **Blessed be God.**

Celebrant:
**You call those who have been baptized
to announce the Good News of Jesus Christ to
people everywhere.**

All: **Blessed be God.**

The celebrant concludes with the following.
You have called your children, N. and N.,
to this cleansing water and new birth,
that by sharing the faith of your Church they may
  have eternal life.
Bless ✛ this water in which they will be baptized.

We ask this in the name of Jesus the Lord.

All: **Amen.**

V. ACCLAMATIONS AND HYMNS

ACCLAMATIONS FROM SACRED SCRIPTURE

225. Exodus 15:11
Lord God, who is your equal?
Strong, majestic, and holy!
Worthy of praise, worker of wonders!

226. 1 John 1:5
God is light: in him there is no darkness.

227. 1 John 4:16
God is love: he who lives in love, lives in God.

228. Ephesians 4:6
There is one God, one Father of all:
he is over all, and through all:
he lives in all of us.

229. Psalm 34:6
Come to him and receive his light!

230. see Ephesians 1:4
Blessed be God who chose you in Christ.

231. Ephesians 2:10
You are God's work of art, created in Christ Jesus.

232. 1 John 3:2
You are now God's children, my dearest friends.
What you shall be in his glory has not yet been
revealed.

233. 1 John 3:1
Think of how God loves you!
He calls you his own children,
and that is what you are.

234. Revelation 22:14
Happy are those who have washed their robes clean:
washed in the blood of the Lamb!

235. Galatians 3:28
All of you are one:
united in Christ Jesus.

236. Ephesians 5:1-2
**Imitate God, walk in his love,
just as Christ loves us.**

HYMNS IN THE STYLE OF THE NEW TESTAMENT

237. 1 Peter 1:3-5
**Praised be the Father of our Lord Jesus Christ:
a God so merciful and kind!
He has given us a new birth, a living hope,
by raising Jesus his Son from death.
Salvation is our undying inheritance,
preserved for us in heaven,
salvation at the end of time.**

238.
**How great the sign of God's love for us,
Jesus Christ our Lord:
promised before all time began,
revealed in these last days.
He lived and suffered and died for us,
but the Spirit raised him to life.
People everywhere have heard his message
and placed their faith in him.
What wonderful blessings he gives his people:
living in the Father's glory,
he fills all creation
and guides it to perfection.**

SONGS FROM ANCIENT LITURGIES

239.
**We believe in you, Lord Jesus Christ.
Fill our hearts with your radiance,
and make us the children of light!**

240.
**We come to you, Lord Jesus.
Fill us with your life,
make us children of the Father,
and one in you.**

241.
Lord Jesus, from your wounded side
flowed streams of cleansing water:
the world was washed of all its sin,
all life made new again!

242.
The Father's voice calls us above the waters,
the glory of the Son shines on us,
the love of the Spirit fills us with life.

243.
Holy Church of God, stretch out your hand
and welcome your children
newborn of water
and of the Spirit of God.

244.
Rejoice, you newly baptized,
chosen members of the kingdom.
Buried with Christ in death,
you are reborn in him by faith.

245.
This is the fountain of life,
water made holy by the suffering of Christ,
washing all the world.
You who are washed in this water
have hope of heaven's kingdom.

VI. FORMS OF THE FINAL BLESSING

246. See the formula in the rite of baptism for several
children, no. 70.

247.
Celebrant:
May God the almighty Father, who filled the world
with joy by giving us his only Son, bless these
newly-baptized children. May they grow to be more
fully like Jesus Christ our Lord.
All: Amen.

Celebrant:

May almighty God, who gives life on earth and in heaven, bless the parents of these children. They thank him now for the gift he has given them. May they always show that gratitude in action by loving and caring for their children.
All: Amen.

Celebrant:

May almighty God, who has given us a new birth by water and the Holy Spirit, generously bless all of us who are his faithful children. May we always live as his people, and may he bless all here present with his peace.
All: Amen.

Celebrant:

May almighty God, the Father, and the Son, ✛ and the Holy Spirit, bless you.
All: Amen.

Celebrant: Go in peace.
All: Thanks be to God.

248.
Celebrant:

May God, the source of life and love, who fills the hearts of mothers with love for their children, bless the mothers of these newly-baptized children. As they thank God for a safe delivery, may they find joy in the love, growth, and holiness of their children.
All: Amen.

Celebrant:

May God, the Father and model of all fathers, help these fathers to give good example, so that their children will grow to be mature Christians in all the fullness of Jesus Christ.
All: Amen.

Celebrant:

May God, who loves all people, bless all the relatives and friends who are gathered here. In his mercy, may he guard them from evil and give them his abundant peace.
All: Amen.

Celebrant:

**And may almighty God, the Father, and the Son, ✛
and the Holy Spirit, bless you.**
All: **Amen.**

Celebrant: **Go in peace.**
All: **Thanks be to God.**

249.

Celebrant:

**My brothers and sisters, we entrust you all to the
mercy and help of God the almighty Father, his only
Son, and the Holy Spirit. May he watch over your
life, and may we all walk by the light of faith, and
attain the good things he has promised us.**

**Go in peace, and may almighty God, the Father, and
the Son, ✛ and the Holy Spirit, bless you.**
All: **Amen.**

Celebrant: **Go in peace.**
All: **Thanks be to God.**

APPENDIX

LITANY OF THE SAINTS

LITANY FOR SOLEMN INTERCESSIONS

In those sections which contain several sets of invocations marked by A and B, one or the other may be chosen as desired. The names of some saints may be added in the proper place such as the patron saint, title of the church, name of the founder, but in a different typeface. Some petitions adapted to the place and need may be added to the petitions for various needs.

I. PETITIONS TO GOD

A
Lord, have mercy
Lord, have mercy
Christ, have mercy
Christ, have mercy
Lord, have mercy
Lord, have mercy

B

God our Father in heaven	**have mercy on us**
God the Son, our redeemer	**have mercy on us**
God the Holy Spirit	**have mercy on us**
Holy Trinity, one God	**have mercy on us**

II. PETITIONS TO THE SAINTS

Holy Mary	**pray for us.**
Mother of God	**pray for us.**
Most honored of all virgins	**pray for us.**
Michael, Gabriel, and Raphael	**pray for us.**
Angels of God	**pray for us.**

Prophets and Fathers of our Faith

Abraham, Moses and Elijah	**pray for us.**
Saint John the Baptist	**pray for us.**
Saint Joseph	**pray for us.**

Holy patriarchs and prophets   **pray for us**

Apostles and Followers of Christ

Saint Peter and Saint Paul	**pray for us**
Saint Andrew	**pray for us**
Saint John and Saint James	**pray for us**
Saint Thomas	**pray for us**
Saint Matthew	**pray for us**
All holy apostles	**pray for us**
Saint Luke	**pray for us**
Saint Mark	**pray for us**
Saint Barnabas	**pray for us**
Saint Mary Magdalen	**pray for us**
All disciples of the Lord	**pray for us**

Martyrs

Saint Stephen	**pray for us**
Saint Ignatius	**pray for us**
Saint Polycarp	**pray for us**
Saint Justin	**pray for us**
Saint Lawrence	**pray for us**
Saint Cyprian	**pray for us**
Saint Boniface	**pray for us**
Saint Thomas Becket	**pray for us**
Saint John Fisher and Saint Thomas More	
	pray for us
Saint Paul Miki	**pray for us**
Saint Isaac Jogues and Saint John de Brebeuf	
	pray for us
Saint Peter Chanel	**pray for us**
Saint Charles Lwanga	**pray for us**
Saint Perpetua and Saint Felicity	**pray for us**
Saint Agnes	**pray for us**
Saint Maria Goretti	**pray for us**
All holy martyrs for Christ	**pray for us**

Bishops and Doctors

Saint Leo and Saint Gregory	**pray for us**
Saint Ambrose	**pray for us**

Saint Jerome	pray for us
Saint Augustine	pray for us
Saint Athanasius	pray for us
Saint Basil and Saint Gregory	pray for us
Saint John Chrysostom	pray for us
Saint Martin	pray for us
Saint Patrick	pray for us
Saint Cyril and Saint Methodius	pray for us
Saint Charles Borromeo	pray for us
Saint Francis de Sales	pray for us
Saint Pius	pray for us

Priests and Religious

Saint Anthony	pray for us
Saint Benedict	pray for us
Saint Bernard	pray for us
Saint Francis and Saint Dominic	pray for us
Saint Thomas Aquinas	pray for us
Saint Ignatius Loyola	pray for us
Saint Francis Xavier	pray for us
Saint Vincent de Paul	pray for us
Saint John Vianney	pray for us
Saint John Bosco	pray for us
Saint Catherine	pray for us
Saint Teresa	pray for us
Saint Rose	pray for us

Laity

Saint Louis	pray for us
Saint Monica	pray for us
Saint Elizabeth	pray for us
All holy men and women	pray for us

III. PETITIONS TO CHRIST

A

Lord, be merciful	Lord, save your people
From all evil	Lord, save your people
From every sin	Lord, save your people
From the snares of the devil	
	Lord, save your people

From anger and hatred	Lord, save your people
From every evil intention	Lord, save your people
From everlasting death	Lord, save your people
By your coming as man	Lord, save your people
By your birth	Lord, save your people
By your baptism and fasting	
	Lord, save your people
By your sufferings and cross	
	Lord, save your people
By your death and burial	Lord, save your people
By your rising to new life	Lord, save your people
By your return in glory to the Father	
	Lord, save your people
By your gift of the Holy Spirit	
	Lord, save your people
By your coming again in glory	
	Lord, save your people

B

Christ, Son of the living God	have mercy on us
You came into this world	have mercy on us
You suffered for us on the cross	have mercy on us
You died to save us	have mercy on us
You lay in the tomb	have mercy on us
You rose from the dead	have mercy on us
You returned in glory to the Father	
	have mercy on us
You sent the Holy Spirit upon your Apostles	
	have mercy on us
You are seated at the right hand of the Father	
	have mercy on us
You will come again to judge the living and the dead.	have mercy on us

IV. PETITIONS FOR VARIOUS NEEDS

A

Lord, be merciful to us	Lord, hear our prayer
Give us true repentance	Lord, hear our prayer
Strengthen us in your service	Lord, hear our prayer

Reward with eternal life all who do good to us
>Lord, hear our prayer

Bless the fruits of the earth and of man's labor
>Lord, hear our prayer

B

Lord, show us your kindness
>Lord, hear our prayer

Raise our thoughts and desires to you
>Lord, hear our prayer

Save us from final damnation
>Lord, hear our prayer

Save our friends and all who have helped us
>Lord, hear our prayer

Grant eternal rest to all who have died in the
faith
>Lord, hear our prayer

Spare us from disease, hunger, and war
>Lord, hear our prayer

Bring all peoples together in trust and peace
>Lord, hear our prayer

C — always used

Guide and protect your holy Church
>Lord, hear our prayer

Keep the pope and all the clergy in faithful service to
your Church
>Lord, hear our prayer

Bring all Christians together in unity
>Lord, hear our prayer

Lead all men to the light of the Gospel
>Lord, hear our prayer

V. CONCLUSION

A

Christ hear us
Christ hear us

Lord Jesus,
>Lord, hear our prayer

Lord Jesus,
>Lord, hear our prayer

B

Lamb of God, you take away the sins of the
world:
>have mercy on us

Lamb of God, you take away the sins of the
world: have mercy on us
Lamb of God, you take away the sins of the
world: have mercy on us

PRAYERS

God of love, our strength and protection,
hear the prayers of your Church.
Grant that when we come to you in faith,
our prayers may be answered:
through Christ our Lord.
Or:
Lord God, you know our weakness.
In your mercy
grant that the example of your Saints
may bring us back to love and serve you
through Christ our Lord.

LITANY FOR CONSECRATIONS AND SOLEMN
BLESSINGS

In any ceremony, the names of some saints may be added in
the proper place in the litany. This may include the patron
saint, the saints after whom the church is named, the
founder, patrons of those being consecrated, all the apostles
in the ordination of a bishop, and so on. Invocations which
are more appropriate for individual occasions may also be
added to the litany.

Lord, have mercy

                                    Lord, have mercy

Christ, have mercy

                                    Christ, have mercy

Lord, have mercy

                                    Lord, have mercy

Holy Mary, Mother of God   pray for us
Saint Michael   pray for us
Holy angels of God   pray for us
Saint John the Baptist   pray for us

Saint Joseph	pray for us
Saint Peter and Saint Paul	pray for us
Saint Andrew	pray for us
Saint John	pray for us
Saint Mary Magdalene	pray for us
Saint Stephen	pray for us
Saint Ignatius	pray for us
Saint Lawrence	pray for us
Saint Perpetua and Saint Felicity	pray for us
Saint Agnes	pray for us
Saint Gregory	pray for us
Saint Augustine	pray for us
Saint Athanasius	pray for us
Saint Basil	pray for us
Saint Martin	pray for us
Saint Benedict	pray for us
Saint Francis and Saint Dominic	pray for us
Saint Francis Xavier	pray for us
Saint John Vianney	pray for us
Saint Catherine	pray for us
Saint Teresa	pray for us
All holy men and women	Lord, save us
Lord, be merciful	Lord, save us
From all evil	Lord, save us
From every sin	Lord, save us
From everlasting death	Lord, save us
By your coming as man	Lord, save us
By your death and rising to new life	Lord, save us
By your gift of the Holy Spirit	Lord, save us
Be merciful to us sinners	Lord, hear our prayer

Guide and protect your holy Church

Lord, hear our prayer

Keep our pope and all the clergy in faithful service to
your Church   Lord, hear our prayer

Bring all peoples together in trust and peace

Lord, hear our prayer

Strengthen us in your service

Lord, hear our prayer

SPECIAL INVOCATIONS

WHEN THERE IS BAPTISM DURING THE EASTER VIGIL

Give new life to these chosen ones by the grace of baptism   Lord, hear our prayer

ORDINATIONS

Bless these chosen men   Lord, hear our prayer
Bless these chosen men and make them holy
                              Lord, hear our prayer
Bless these chosen men, make them holy, and consecrate them for their sacred duties
                              Lord, hear our prayer

Ordination of one person:

Bless this chosen man   Lord, hear our prayer
Bless this chosen man and make him holy
                              Lord, hear our prayer
Bless this chosen man, make him holy, and consecrate him for his sacred duties   Lord, hear our prayer

DEDICATION OF A CHURCH

Make this church holy and consecrate it to your worship   Lord, hear our prayer

Jesus, Son of the living God Lord, hear our prayer
Christ, hear us
                              Christ, hear us

Lord Jesus, hear our prayer
                              Lord Jesus, hear our prayer

RITE OF CONFIRMATION

RITE OF CONFIRMATION

Decree
Apostolic Constitution
Introduction (1-19)

CHAPTER I
RITE OF CONFIRMATION WITHIN MASS

Liturgy of the Word (20)

Sacrament of Confirmation
Presentation of the Candidates (21)
Homily or Instruction (22)
Renewal of Baptismal Promises (23)
The Laying on of Hands (24-25)
The Anointing with Chrism (26-29)
General Intercessions (30)

Liturgy of the Eucharist (31-32)
Blessing and Prayer over the People (33)

CHAPTER II
RITE OF CONFIRMATION OUTSIDE MASS

Entrance Rite
Entrance Song (34-35)
Opening Prayer

Celebration of the Word of God (36-37)

Sacrament of Confirmation
Presentation of the Candidates (38)
Homily or Instruction (39)
Renewal of Baptismal Promises (40)
The Laying on of Hands (41-42)
The Anointing with Chrism (43-46)
General Intercessions (47)
Lord's Prayer (48)
Blessing and Prayer over the People (49)

CHAPTER III
RITE OF CONFIRMATION BY A MINISTER WHO
IS NOT A BISHOP (50-51)

CHAPTER IV
CONFIRMATION OF A PERSON IN DANGER OF
DEATH (52-56)

CHAPTER V
TEXTS FOR THE CELEBRATION OF
CONFIRMATION (57-65)

SACRED CONGREGATION FOR DIVINE WORSHIP

Prot. n. 800/71

DECREE

In the sacrament of confirmation the apostles and the bishops, who are their successors, hand on to the baptized the special gift of the Holy Spirit, promised by Christ the Lord and poured out upon the apostles at Pentecost. Thus the initiation in the Christian life is completed so that believers are strengthened by power from heaven, made true witnesses of Christ in word and deed, and bound more closely to the Church.

To make "the intimate connection of this sacrament with the whole of Christian initiation" clearer, Vatican Council II decreed that the rite of confirmation was to be revised.[1]

Now that this work has been completed and approved by Pope Paul VI in the Apostolic Constitution *Divinae consortium naturae* of 15 August 1971, the Congregation for Divine Worship has published the new *Rite of Confirmation*. It is to replace the rite now in use in the Roman Pontifical and Ritual. The Congregation declares the present edition to be the *editio typica*.

All things to the contrary notwithstanding.

From the Office of the Congregation for Divine Worship, August 22, 1971.

Arturo Cardinal Tabera
Prefect

Annibale Bugnini
Secretary

---

[1] See SC art. 71 [DOL 1 no. 71].

APOSTOLIC CONSTITUTION ON THE SACRAMENT OF CONFIRMATION

PAUL, BISHOP
Servant of the Servants of God For an Everlasting Memorial

The sharing in the divine nature received through the grace of Christ bears a certain likeness to the origin, development, and nourishing of natural life. The faithful are born anew by baptism, strengthened by the sacrament of confirmation, and finally are sustained by the food of eternal life in the eucharist. By means of these sacraments of Christian initiation, they thus receive in increasing measure the treasures of divine life and advance toward the perfection of charity. It has rightly been written: "The body is washed, that the soul may be cleansed; the body is anointed, that the soul may be consecrated; the body is signed, that the soul too may be fortified; the body is overshadowed by the laying on of hands, that the soul may be enlightened by the Spirit; the body is fed on the body and blood of Christ, that the soul may be richly nourished by God."[1]

Conscious of its pastoral charge, the Second Vatican Ecumenical Council devoted special attention to these sacraments of initiation. It prescribed that the rites should be revised in a way that would make them more suited to the understanding of the faithful. Since the *Rite of Baptism for Children*, revised at the mandate of the Council and published at our command, is already in use, it is now fitting to publish a rite of confirmation, in order to show the unity of Christian initiation in its true light.

In fact, careful attention and application have been devoted in these last years to the task of revising the manner of celebrating this sacrament. The aim of this work has been that "the intimate connection of this sacrament with the whole of Christian initiation may stand out more clearly."[2] But the link between confirmation and the other sacraments of initiation is more easily perceived not simply from the fact that their rites have been more closely conjoined; the rite and words by which confirmation is conferred also make this link clear. As a result the rite and words of this

---

[1]Tertullian, *De resurrectione mortuorum* 8, 3: CCL 2, 931.
[2]SC art. 71.

sacrament "express more clearly the holy things they signify and the Christian people, as far as possible, are able to understand them with ease and take part in them fully, actively, and as befits a community."[3]

For that purpose, it has been our wish also to include in this revision what concerns the very essence of the rite of confirmation, through which the faithful receive the Holy Spirit as Gift.

The New Testament shows how the Holy Spirit was with Christ to bring the Messiah's mission to fulfillment. On receiving the baptism of John, Jesus saw the Spirit descending on him (see Mk 1:10) and remaining with him (see Jn 1:32). He was led by the Spirit to undertake his public ministry as the Messiah, relying on the Spirit's presence and assistance. Teaching the people of Nazareth, he showed by what he said that the words of Isaiah, "The Spirit of the Lord is upon me," referred to himself (see Lk 4:17–21).

He later promised his disciples that the Holy Spirit would help them also to bear fearless witness to their faith even before persecutors (see Lk 12:12). The day before he suffered, he assured his apostles that he would send the Spirit of truth from his Father (see Jn 15:26) to stay with them "for ever" (Jn 14:16) and help them to be his witnesses (see Jn 15:26). Finally, after his resurrection, Christ promised the coming descent of the Holy Spirit: "You will receive power when the Holy Spirit comes upon you; then you are to be my witnesses" (Acts 1:8; see Lk 24:49).

On the feast of Pentecost, the Holy Spirit did indeed come down in an extraordinary way on the apostles as they were gathered together with Mary the mother of Jesus and the group of disciples. They were so "filled with" the Holy Spirit (Acts 2:4) that by divine inspiration they began to proclaim "the mighty works of God." Peter regarded the Spirit who had thus come down upon the apostles as the gift of the Messianic age (see Acts 2:17–18). Then those who believed the apostles' preaching were baptized and they too received "the gift of the Holy Spirit" (Acts 2:38). From that time on the apostles, in fulfillment of Christ's wish, imparted to the newly baptized by the laying on of hands the gift of the Spirit that completes the grace of baptism. This is why the Letter to the Hebrews listed among the first ele-

[3]SC art. 21.

ments of Christian instruction the teaching about baptisms and the laying on of hands (Heb 6:2). This laying on of hands is rightly recognized by reason of Catholic tradition as the beginning of the sacrament of confirmation, which in a certain way perpetuates the grace of Pentecost in the Church.

This makes clear the specific importance of confirmation for sacramental initiation, by which the faithful "as members of the living Christ are incorporated into him and configured to him through baptism and through confirmation and the eucharist."[4] In baptism, the newly baptized receive forgiveness of sins, adoption as children of God, and the character of Christ by which they are made members of the Church and for the first time become sharers in the priesthood of their Savior (see 1 Pt 2:5, 9). Through the sacrament of confirmation those who have been born anew in baptism receive the inexpressible Gift, the Holy Spirit himself, by whom "they are endowed . . . with special strength."[5] Moreover, having been signed with the character of this sacrament, they are "more closely bound to the Church"[6] and "they are more strictly obliged to spread and defend the faith, both by word and by deed, as true witnesses of Christ."[7] Finally, confirmation is so closely linked with the holy eucharist[8] that the faithful, after being signed by baptism and confirmation, are incorporated fully into the Body of Christ by participation in the eucharist.[9]

From ancient times the conferring of the gift of the Holy Spirit has been carried out in the Church through various rites. These rites have undergone many changes in the East and the West, but always keeping as their meaning the conferring of the Holy Spirit.

In many Eastern rites it seems that from early times a rite of chrismation, not yet clearly distinguished from baptism,[10] prevailed for the conferring of the Holy Spirit. That rite continues in use today in the greater part of the Churches of the East.

[4]AG no. 36.
[5]LG no. 11.
[6]Ibid.
[7]Ibid. See also AG no. 11.
[8]See PO no. 5.
[9]See ibid.
[10]See Origen, *De principiis* 1, 3, 2: GCS 22, 49ff.; *Comm. in Ep. ad Rom.* 5, 8: PG 14, 1038. Cyril of Jerusalem, *Catech.* 16, 26; 21, 1–7, PG 33, 956; 1088–93.

In the West there are very ancient witnesses concerning the part of Christian initiation that was later distinctly recognized to be the sacrament of confirmation. There are directives for the performance of many rites after the baptismal washing and before the eucharistic meal—for example, anointing, the laying on of the hand, consignation[11]—contained both in liturgical documents[12] and in many testimonies of the Fathers. Consequently, in the course of the centuries, problems and doubts arose as to what belonged with certainty to the essence of the rite of confirmation. Worth mentioning, however, are at least some of the elements that, from the thirteenth century onward, in the ecumenical councils and in papal documents, cast considerable light on the importance of anointing, but at the same time did not allow the laying on of hands to be forgotten.

Our predecessor Innocent III wrote: "The anointing of the forehead with chrism signifies the laying on of the hand, the other name for which is confirmation, since through it the Holy Spirit is given for growth and strength."[13] Another of our predecessors, Innocent IV, mentions that the apostles conferred the Holy Spirit "through the laying on of the hand, which confirmation or the anointing of the forehead with chrism represents."[14] In the profession of faith of Emperor Michael Palaeologus read at the Council of Lyons II mention is made of the sacrament of confirmation, which "bishops confer by the laying on of hands, anointing with chrism those who have been baptized."[15] The Decree for the Armenians, issued by the Council of Florence, declares

---

[11]See Tertullian, *De Baptismo* 7–8: CCL 1, 282ff. B. Botte, ed., *La tradition apostolique de Saint Hippolyte: Liturgiewissenschaftliche Quellen und Forschungen* 39 (Münster, W., 1963) 52–54. Ambrose, *De Sacramentis* 2, 24; 3, 2, 8; 6, 2, 9; CSEL 73, 36; 42; 74–75; *De mysteriis* 7, 42; CSEL 73, 106.

[12]Mohlberg LibSacr 75, H. Lietzmann, ed., *Das Sacramentarium Gregorianum nach den Aachener Urexemplar: Liturgiegeschichtliche Quellen* 3 (Münster, W., 1921) 53ff. M. Ferotin, ed., *Liber Ordinum: Monumenta Ecclesiae Liturgica* V (Paris, 1904) 33ff. Mohlberg MissGall 67C. Vogel and R. Elze, *Le Pontifical Romano-Germanique du dixième siècle: Le Texte II; Studi e Testi* 227 (Vatican City, 1963) 109. M. Andrieu, *Le Pontifical Romaine du XIIe siecle* in *Le Pontifical Romain au Moyen-Age* v. 1: *Studi e Testi* 86 (Vatican City, 1938) 247ff., 289; *Le Pontifical de la Curie Romaine au XIIIe siècle*, ibid. v. 2: *Studi e Testi* 87 (Vatican City, 1940) 452ff.

[13]Innocent III, *Ep. "Cum venisset"*: PL 215, 285. The profession of faith that the same Pope imposed on the Waldenses has these words: "We regard confirmation by the bishop, that is, the laying on of hands, to be holy and to be received with reverence": PL 215, 1511.

[14]Innocent IV, *Ep. "Sub Catholicae professione"*: Mansi 23, 579.

[15]Council of Lyons II: Mansi 24, 71.

that the "matter" of the sacrament of confirmation is "chrism made of olive oil . . . and balsam"[16] and, quoting the words of the Acts of the Apostles concerning Peter and John, who gave the Holy Spirit through the laying on of hands (see Acts 8:17), it adds: "in the Church in place of that laying on of the hand, confirmation is given."[17] The Council of Trent, though it had no intention of defining the essential rite of confirmation, designated it simply by the term "the holy chrism of confirmation."[18] Benedict XIV made this declaration: "Therefore let this be said, which is beyond dispute: in the Latin Church the sacrament of confirmation is conferred by using the sacred chrism or olive oil mixed with balsam and blessed by the bishop, and by the sacramental minister's tracing the sign of the cross on the forehead of the recipient, while the same minister pronounces the words of the form."[19]

Taking account of these declarations and traditions, many theologians maintained that for valid administration of confirmation only the anointing with chrism, done by placing the hand on the forehead, was required. Nevertheless, in the rites of the Latin Church a laying of hands on those to be confirmed prior to anointing them with chrism was always prescribed.

With regard to the words of the rite by which the Holy Spirit is given, it should be noted that already in the primitive Church Peter and John, in order to complete the initiation of those baptized in Samaria, prayed that they might receive the Holy Spirit and then laid hands on them (see Acts 8:15–17). In the East the first traces of the expression *seal of the gift of the Holy Spirit* appeared in the fourth and fifth centuries.[20] The expression was quickly accepted by the Church of Constantinople and still is a use in Byzantine-Rite Churches.

---

[16]*Epistolae Pontificiae ad Concilium Florentinum spectantes:* G. Hofmann, ed., *Concilium Florentinum* v. 1, ser. A, part II (Rome, 1944) 128.
[17]Ibid, 129.
[18]CT 5, Act. II, 996.
[19]Benedict XIV, *Ep. "Ex quo primum tempore"* 52: *Benedicti XIV . . . Bullarium*, v. 3 (Prati, 1847) 320.
[20]Cyril of Jerusalem, *Catech.* 18, 33: PG 33, 1056. Asterius, Bishop of Amasea, *In parabolam de filio prodigo*, in the "Library of Photius," Cod. 271: PG 104, 213. See also *Epistola cuiusdam Patriarchae Constantinopolitani ad Martyrium, Episcopum Antiochenum:* PG 119, 900.

In the West, however, the words of the rite that completes baptism were less settled until the twelfth and thirteenth centuries. But in the twelfth-century Roman Pontifical the formulary that later became the common one first occurs: "I sign you with the sign of the cross and confirm you with the chrism of salvation. In the name of the Father and of the Son and of the Holy Spirit."[21]

From what we have recalled, it is clear that in the administration of confirmation in the East and the West, though in different ways, the most important place was occupied by the anointing, which in a certain way represents the apostolic laying on of hands. Since this anointing with chrism is an apt sign of the spiritual anointing of the Holy Spirit who is given to the faithful, we wish to confirm its existence and importance.

As regards the words pronounced in confirmation, we have examined with the consideration it deserves the dignity of the respected formulary used in the Latin Church, but we judge preferable the very ancient formulary belonging to the Byzantine Rite. This expresses the Gift of the Holy Spirit himself and calls to mind the outpouring of the Spirit on the day of Pentecost (see Acts 2:1–4, 38). We therefore adopt this formulary, rendering it almost word for word.

Therefore, in order that the revision of the rite of confirmation may, as is fitting, include even the essence of the sacramental rite, by our supreme apostolic authority we decree and lay down that in the Latin Church the following are to be observed for the future.

THE SACRAMENT OF CONFIRMATION IS CONFERRED THROUGH THE ANOINTING WITH CHRISM ON THE FOREHEAD, WHICH IS DONE BY THE LAYING ON OF THE HAND, AND THROUGH THE WORDS: BE SEALED WITH THE GIFT OF THE HOLY SPIRIT.[a]

But the laying of hands on the elect, carried out with the prescribed prayer before the anointing, is still to be regarded as very important, even if it is not of the essence of the sacramental rite: it contributes to the complete perfec-

---

[21]M. Andrieu, *Le Pontifical Romain du XIIe siècle* in *Le Pontifical Romain au Moyen-Age*, v. 1: *Studi e testi* 86 (Vatican City, 1938) 247.
[a]Latin: ACCIPE SIGNACULUM DONI SPIRITUS SANCTI.

tion of the rite and to a more thorough understanding of the sacrament. It is evident that this prior laying on of hands differs from the later laying on of the hand in the anointing of the forehead.

Having established and declared all these elements concerning the essential rite of the sacrament of confirmation, we also approve by our apostolic authority the rite for the same sacrament. This has been revised by the Congregation for Divine Worship, after consultation with the Congregations for the Doctrine of the Faith, for the Discipline of the Sacraments, and for the Evangelization of Peoples on the matters that are within their competence. The Latin edition of the rite containing the new sacramental form will come into effect as soon as it is published; the editions in the vernacular languages, prepared by the conferences of bishops and confirmed by the Apostolic See, will come into effect on the date to be laid down by each conference. The old rite may be used until the end of the year 1972. From 1 January 1973, however, only the new rite is to be used by those concerned.

We intend that everything that we have laid down and prescribed should be firm and effective in the Latin Church, notwithstanding, where relevant, the apostolic constitutions and ordinances issued by our predecessors, and other prescriptions, even those worthy of special mention.

INTRODUCTION

I. DIGNITY OF CONFIRMATION

1. Those who have been baptized continue on the path of Christian initiation through the sacrament of confirmation. In this sacrament they receive the Holy Spirit whom the Lord sent upon the apostles on Pentecost.

2. This giving of the Holy Spirit conforms believers more fully to Christ and strengthens them so that they may bear witness to Christ for the building up of his Body in faith and love. They are so marked with the character or seal of the Lord that the sacrament of confirmation cannot be repeated.

II. OFFICES AND MINISTRIES IN THE CELEBRATION OF CONFIRMATION

3. One of the highest responsibilities of the people of God is to prepare the baptized for confirmation. Pastors have the special responsibility to see that all the baptized reach the completion of Christian initiation and therefore that they are carefully prepared for confirmation.

Adult catechumens who are to be confirmed immediately after baptism have the help of the Christian community and, in particular, the formation that is given to them during the catechumenate. Catechists, sponsors, and members of the local Church participate in the catechumenate by means of catechesis and community celebrations of the rites of initiation. For those who were baptized in infancy and are confirmed only as adults the plan for the catechumenate is used with appropriate adaptations.

The initiation of children into the sacramental life is ordinarily the responsibility and concern of Christian parents. They are to form and gradually increase a spirit of faith in the children and, at times with the help of catechism classes, prepare them for the fruitful reception of the sacraments of confirmation and the eucharist. The role of the parents is also expressed by their active participation in the celebration of the sacraments.

4. Pains should be taken to give the liturgical service the festive and solemn character that its significance for the local Church requires. This will be achieved above all if the candidates are gathered together for a community celebration of the rites. All the people of God, represented by the families and friends of the candidates and by members of the local community, will be invited to take part in such a celebration and will endeavor to express their faith by means of the effects the Holy Spirit has produced in them.

5. As a rule there should be a sponsor for each of those to be confirmed. These sponsors bring the candidates to receive the sacrament, present them to the minister for the anointing, and will later help them to fulfill their baptismal promises faithfully under the influence of the Holy Spirit whom they have received.

In view of contemporary pastoral circumstances, it is desirable that the godparent at baptism, if available, also be the sponsor at confirmation. This change expresses more clearly the link between baptism and confirmation and also makes the function and responsibility of the sponsor more effective.

Nonetheless the option of choosing a special sponsor for confirmation is not excluded. Even the parents themselves may present their children for confirmation. It is for the local Ordinary to determine diocesan practice in the light of local conditions and circumstances.

6. Pastors will see that the sponsors, chosen by the candidates or their families, are spiritually fit to take on this responsibility and have these qualities:

a. sufficient maturity to fulfill their function;

b. membership in the Catholic Church and their own reception of Christian initiation through baptism, confirmation, and eucharist;

c. freedom from any impediment of law to their fulfilling the office of sponsor.

7. The ordinary minister of confirmation is the bishop. Normally a bishop administers the sacrament so that there will be a clearer reference to the first pouring forth of the Holy Spirit on Pentecost: after the apostles were filled with the

Holy Spirit, they themselves gave the Spirit to the faithful through the laying on of hands. Thus the reception of the Spirit through the ministry of the bishop shows the close bond that joins the confirmed to the Church and the mandate received from Christ to bear witness to him before all.

The law gives the faculty to confirm to the following besides the bishop:

a. territorial prelates and territorial abbots, vicars and prefects apostolic, apostolic administrators and diocesan administrators, within the limits of their territory and while they hold office;

b. in consideration of the person to be confirmed, priests who, in virtue of an office or the mandate of the diocesan bishop, baptize a person who is no longer an infant or receive a person who is already baptized into the full communion of the Catholic Church;

c. in consideration of those who are in danger of death, a pastor or in fact any priest.

8. The diocesan bishop is to administer confirmation himself or to ensure that it is administered by another bishop. But if necessity requires, he may grant to one or several, determinate priests the faculty to administer this sacrament.

For a serious reason, as sometimes is present because of the large number of those to be confirmed, the bishop and also a priest who, in virtue of the law or a particular concession by competent authority, has the faculty to confirm, may in individual cases associate priests with himself so that they may administer the sacrament.

It is preferable that the priests who are so invited:

a. either have a particular function or office in the diocese, being, namely, either vicars general, episcopal vicars, or district or regional vicars;

b. or be the pastors of the places where confirmation is conferred, pastors of the places where the candidates belong, or priests who have had a special part in the catechetical preparation of the candidates.

III. CELEBRATION OF THE SACRAMENT

9. The sacrament of confirmation is conferred through the anointing with chrism on the forehead, which is done by the laying on of the hand, and through the words: BE SEALED WITH THE GIFT OF THE HOLY SPIRIT.

The laying of hands on the candidates with the prayer, *All-powerful God*, does not pertain to the valid giving of the sacrament. But it is still to be regarded as very important: it contributes to the complete perfection of the rite and to a more thorough understanding of the sacrament.

The priests who may at times be associated with the principal minister in conferring the sacrament join him in the laying of hands on all the candidates, but say nothing.

The whole rite presents a twofold symbolism. The laying of hands on the candidates by the bishop and the concelebrating priest represents the biblical gesture by which the gift of the Holy Spirit is invoked and in a manner well suited to the understanding of the Christian people. The anointing with chrism and the accompanying words express clearly the effect of the giving of the Holy Spirit. Signed with the perfumed oil, the baptized receive the indelible character, the seal of the Lord, together with the gift of the Spirit that conforms them more closely to Christ and gives them the grace of spreading "the sweet odor of Christ."

10. The chrism is consecrated by the bishop in the Mass that is celebrated as a rule on Holy Thursday for this purpose.

11. Adult catechumens and children who are baptized at an age when they are old enough for catechesis should ordinarily be admitted to confirmation and the eucharist at the same time as they receive baptism. If this is impossible, they should receive confirmation at another community celebration (see no. 4). Similarly, adults who were baptized in infancy should, after suitable preparation, receive confirmation and the eucharist at a community celebration.

With regard to children, in the Latin Church the administration of confirmation is generally delayed until about the seventh year. For pastoral reasons, however, especially to implant deeply in the lives of the faithful complete obedience to Christ the Lord and a firm witnessing to him, the conferences of bishops may set an age that seems more suitable. This means that the sacrament is given, after the formation proper to it, when the recipients are more mature.

In this case every necessary precaution is to be taken to ensure that in the event of danger of death or serious problems of another kind children receive confirmation in good time, so that they are not left without the benefit of this sacrament.

12. Persons who are to receive confirmation must have already received baptism. Moreover, those possessing the use of reason must be in the state of grace, properly instructed, and capable of renewing the baptismal promises.

The conference of bishops has responsibility for determining more precisely the catechetical resources for the preparation of candidates for confirmation, especially children.

In the case of adults, those principles are to be followed, with the required adaptations, that apply in the individual dioceses to admitting catechumens to baptism and eucharist. Measures are to be taken especially for catechesis preceding confirmation and for the association of the candidates with the Christian community and with individual Christians. Such association is to be of a kind that is effective and sufficient as a practical help for the candidates to achieve formation toward both bearing witness by Christian living and carrying on the apostolate. It should also assist the candidates to have a genuine desire to share in the eucharist (see *Rite of Christian Initiation of Adults*, Introduction no. 19).

Sometimes the preparation of baptized adults for confirmation coincides with preparation for marriage. In such cases, if it is foreseen that the conditions for a fruitful reception of confirmation cannot be satisfied, the local Ordinary will judge whether it is better to defer confirmation until after the marriage.

If one who has the use of reason is confirmed in danger of death, there should, as far as possible, be some spiritual preparation beforehand, suited to the individual situation.

13. Confirmation takes place as a rule within Mass in order that the fundamental connection of this sacrament with all of Christian initiation may stand out in clearer light. Chris-

tian initiation reaches its culmination in the communion of the body and blood of Christ. The newly confirmed therefore participate in the eucharist, which completes their Christian initiation.

If the candidates for confirmation are children who have not received the eucharist and are not being admitted to first communion at this liturgical celebration or if there are other special circumstances, confirmation should be celebrated outside Mass. When this occurs, there is first to be a celebration of the word of God.

When confirmation is given during Mass, it is fitting that the minister of confirmation celebrate the Mass or, better, concelebrate it, especially with those priests who may be joining him in administering the sacrament.

If the Mass is celebrated by someone else, it is proper that the bishop preside over the liturgy of the word, doing all that the celebrant normally does, and that he give the blessing at the end of Mass.

Great emphasis should be placed on the celebration of the word of God that introduces the rite of confirmation. It is from the hearing of the word of God that the many-sided work of the Holy Spirit flows out upon the Church and upon each one of the baptized and confirmed. Through this hearing of his word God's will is made known in the life of Christians.

Great importance is likewise to be attached to the saying of the Lord's Prayer. Those to be confirmed will recite it together with the congregation—either during Mass before communion or outside Mass before the blessing—because it is the Spirit who prays in us and in the Spirit the Christian says, "Abba, Father."

14. The names of those confirmed, as well as the names of the minister, parents, and sponsors, and a notation of the place and date of the confirmation conferred, are to be entered into the registry of confirmations of the diocesan curia, or, where the conference of bishops or the diocesan bishop has so ordered, in a book to be kept in the parish archives. The pastor must inform the pastor of the recipient's place of baptism that confirmation has been conferred, so that this may be recorded in the baptismal register, according to the requirements of the law.

15. If the pastor of the place was not present, the minister should promptly inform him of the confirmation, either personally or through a representative.

IV. ADAPTATIONS PERMITTED IN THE RITE OF CONFIRMATION

16. By virtue of the Constitution of the Liturgy (art. 63 b), conferences of bishops have the right to prepare in particular rituals a section bearing the same title as the present title IV on confirmation in the Roman Pontifical. This is to be adapted to the needs of the individual parts of the world and it is to be used once the *acta* of the conference have been reviewed by the Apostolic See.[1]

17. The conference of bishops will consider whether, in view of local circumstances and the culture and traditions of the people, it is opportune:

a. to make suitable adaptations of the formularies for the renewal of baptismal promises and professions, either following the text in the rite of baptism or accommodating these formularies so that they are more in accord with the circumstances of the candidates for confirmation;

b. to introduce a different manner for the minister to give the sign of peace after the anointing, either to each individual or to all the newly confirmed together.

18. The minister of confirmation may introduce some explanations into the rite in individual cases in view of the capacity of the candidates for confirmation. He may also make appropriate accommodations in the existing texts, for example, by expressing these in a kind of dialogue, especially with children.

When confirmation is given by a minister who is not a bishop, whether by concession of the general law or by special indult of the Apostolic See, it is fitting for him to mention in the homily that the bishop is the original minister of the sacrament and to explain the reason why priests receive the

---

[1]See *Rite of Baptism for Children*, General Introduction to Christian Initiation nos. 30–33.

faculty to confirm from the law or by an indult of the Apostolic See.

V. PREPARATIONS

19. The following should be prepared for the administration of confirmation:

a. when confirmation is given within Mass, the vestments prescribed for the celebration of Mass both for the bishop and for any assisting priests who concelebrate with him. If the Mass is celebrated by someone else, the minister of confirmation as well as any priests joining him in administering the sacrament should take part in the Mass wearing the vestments prescribed for administering confirmation: alb, stole, and, for the minister, the cope; these also are the vestments worn when confirmation is given outside Mass;

b. chairs for the bishop and the priests assisting him;

c. vessel (or vessels) for the chrism;

d. Roman Pontifical or Roman Ritual;

e. when confirmation is given within Mass, the requisites for celebration of Mass and for communion under both kinds, if it is to be given;

f. the requisites for the washing of hands after the anointing of those to be confirmed.

CHAPTER I

RITE OF CONFIRMATION WITHIN MASS

LITURGY OF THE WORD

20. The liturgy of the word is celebrated in the ordinary way. The readings may be taken in whole or in part from the Mass of the day or from the texts for confirmation in the *Lectionary for Mass* (nos. 763-767) and listed below (nos. 61-65).

SACRAMENT OF CONFIRMATION

PRESENTATION OF THE CANDIDATES

21. After the gospel the bishop and the priests who will be ministers of the sacrament with him take their seats. The pastor or another priest, deacon, or catechist presents the candidates for confirmation, according to the custom of the region. If possible, each candidate is called by name and comes individually to the sanctuary. If the candidates are children, they are accompanied by one of their sponsors or parents and stand before the celebrant.

If there are very many candidates, they are not called by name, but simply take a suitable place before the bishop.

HOMILY OR INSTRUCTION

22. The bishop then gives a brief homily. He should explain the readings and so lead the candidates, their sponsors and parents, and the whole assembly to a deeper understanding of the mystery of confirmation.
He may use these or similar words:

On the day of Pentecost the apostles received the Holy Spirit as the Lord had promised. They also received the power of giving the Holy Spirit to others and so completing the work of baptism. This we read in the Acts of the Apostles. When Saint Paul placed his hands on those who had been baptized, the Holy Spirit came upon them, and they began to speak in

other languages and in prophetic words.

Bishops are successors of the apostles and have this power of giving the Holy Spirit to the baptized, either personally or through the priests they appoint.

In our day the coming of the Holy Spirit in confirmation is no longer marked by the gift of tongues, but we know his coming by faith. He fills our hearts with the love of God, brings us together in one faith but in different vocations, and works within us to make the Church one and holy.

The gift of the Holy Spirit which you are to receive will be a spiritual sign and seal to make you more like Christ and more perfect members of his Church. At his baptism by John, Christ himself was anointed by the Spirit and sent out on his public ministry to set the world on fire.

You have already been baptized into Christ and now you will receive the power of his Spirit and the sign of the cross on your forehead. You must be witnesses before all the world to his suffering, death, and resurrection; your way of life should at all times reflect the goodness of Christ. Christ gives varied gifts to his Church, and the Spirit distributes them among the members of Christ's body to build up the holy people of God in unity and love.

Be active members of the Church, alive in Jesus Christ. Under the guidance of the Holy Spirit give your lives completely in the service of all, as did Christ, who came not to be served but to serve.

So now, before you receive the Spirit, I ask you to renew the profession of faith you made in baptism or your parents and godparents made in union with the whole Church.

RENEWAL OF BAPTISMAL PROMISES

23. After the homily the candidates stand and the bishop questions them:

Do you reject Satan and all his works and all his empty promises?
The candidates respond together: **I do.**

Bishop:
Do you believe in God the Father almighty, creator of heaven and earth?
Candidates: **I do.**

Bishop:
Do you believe in Jesus Christ, his only Son, our Lord, who was born of the Virgin Mary, was crucified, died, and was buried, rose from the dead, and is now seated at the right hand of the Father?
Candidates: **I do.**

Bishop:
Do you believe in the Holy Spirit, the Lord, the giver of life, who came upon the apostles at Pentecost and today is given to you sacramentally in confirmation?
Candidates: **I do.**

Bishop:
Do you believe in the holy catholic Church, the communion of saints, the forgiveness of sins, the resurrection of the body, and life everlasting?
Candidates: **I do.**

The bishop confirms their profession of faith by proclaiming the faith of the Church:

This is our faith. This is the faith of the Church. We are proud to profess it in Christ Jesus our Lord.

The whole congregation responds: **Amen.**

For **This is our faith,** some other formula may be substituted, or the community may express its faith in a suitable song.

THE LAYING ON OF HANDS

24. The concelebrating priests stand near the bishop. He faces the people and with hands joined, sings or says:

My dear friends:
in baptism God our Father gave the new birth of
eternal life
to his chosen sons and daughters.
Let us pray to our Father
that he will pour out the Holy Spirit
to strengthen his sons and daughters with his gifts
and anoint them to be more like Christ the Son of
God.

All pray in silence for a short time.

25. The bishop and the priests who will minister the sacrament with him lay hands upon all the candidates (by extending their hands over them). The bishop alone sings or says:
All-powerful God, Father of our Lord Jesus Christ,
by water and the Holy Spirit
you freed your sons and daughters from sin
and gave them new life.
Send your Holy Spirit upon them
to be their Helper and Guide.
Give them the spirit of wisdom and understanding,
the spirit of right judgment and courage,
the spirit of knowledge and reverence.
Fill them with the spirit of wonder and awe in your
presence.
We ask this through Christ our Lord.
℞. **Amen.**

THE ANOINTING WITH CHRISM
26. The deacon brings the chrism to the bishop. Each candidate goes to the bishop, or the bishop may go to the individual candidates. The one who presented the candidate places his right hand on the latter's shoulder and gives the candidate's name to the bishop; or the candidate may give his own name.

27. The bishop dips his right thumb in the chrism and makes the sign of the cross on the forehead of the one to be confirmed, as he says:

N., be sealed with the Gift of the Holy Spirit.
The newly confirmed responds: **Amen.**

The bishop says:
Peace be with you.
The newly confirmed responds: **And also with you.**

28. If priests assist the bishop in conferring the sacrament, all the vessels of chrism are brought to the bishop by the deacon or by other ministers. Each of the priests comes to the bishop, who gives him a vessel of chrism.

The candidates go to the bishop or to the priests, or the bishop and priests may go to the candidates. The anointing is done as described above (no. 27).

29. During the anointing a suitable song may be sung. After the anointing the bishop and the priests wash their hands.

GENERAL INTERCESSIONS

30. The general intercessions follow, in this or a similar form determined by the competent authority.

Bishop:
My dear friends:
let us be one in prayer to God our Father
as we are one in the faith, hope, and love his Spirit
 gives.

Deacon or minister:
For these sons and daughters of God,
confirmed by the gift of the Spirit,
that they give witness to Christ
by lives built on faith and love:
let us pray to the Lord.
℟. Lord, hear our prayer.

Deacon or minister:
For their parents and godparents
who led them in faith,
that by word and example they may always encourage
 them
to follow the way of Jesus Christ:

let us pray to the Lord.
℟. Lord, hear our prayer.

Deacon or minister:
For the holy Church of God,
in union with N. our pope, N. our bishop, and all the
     bishops,
that God, who gathers us together by the Holy Spirit,
may help us grow in unity of faith and love
until his Son returns in glory:
let us pray to the Lord.
℟. Lord, hear our prayer.

Deacon or minister:
For all men,
of every race and nation,
that they may acknowledge the one God as Father,
and in the bond of common brotherhood
seek his kingdom,
which is peace and joy in the Holy Spirit:
let us pray to the Lord.
℟. Lord, hear our prayer.

Bishop:
God our Father,
you sent your Holy Spirit upon the apostles,
and through them and their successors
you give the Spirit to your people.
May his work begun at Pentecost
continue to grow in the hearts of all who believe.
We ask this through Christ our Lord.

LITURGY OF THE EUCHARIST

31. After the general intercessions the liturgy of the
eucharist is celebrated according to the *Order of Mass*, with
these exceptions:
  a) the profession of faith is omitted, since it has already
been made;
  b) some of the newly confirmed may join those who bring
the gifts to the altar;

c) when Euchaustic Prayer I is used, the special form of **Father, accept this offering** is said.

32. Adults who are confirmed, their sponsors, parents, wives and husbands, and catechists may receive communion under both kinds.

BLESSING

33. Instead of the usual blessing at the end of Mass, the following blessing or prayer over the people is used.

God our Father
made you his children by water and the Holy Spirit:
may he bless you
and watch over you with his fatherly love.
R̷. Amen.

Jesus Christ the Son of God
promised that the Spirit of truth
would be with his Church for ever:
may he bless you and give you courage
in professing the true faith.
R̷. Amen.

The Holy Spirit
came down upon the disciples
and set their hearts on fire with love:
may he bless you,
keep you one in faith and love
and bring you to the joy of God's kingdom.
R̷. Amen.

The bishop adds immediately:
May almighty God bless you,
the Father, and the Son, ✚ and the Holy Spirit.
R̷. Amen.

PRAYER OVER THE PEOPLE

Instead of the preceding blessing, the prayer over the people may be used.

The deacon or minister gives the invitation in these or similar words:

Bow your heads and pray for God's blessing.

The bishop extends his hands over the people and sings or says:

God our Father,
complete the work you have begun
and keep the gifts of your Holy Spirit
active in the hearts of your people.
Make them ready to live his Gospel
and eager to do his will.
May they never be ashamed
to proclaim to all the world Christ crucified
living and reigning for ever and ever.
R̷. Amen.

The bishop adds immediately:
And may the blessing of almighty God
the Father, and the Son, ✝ and the Holy Spirit
come upon you and remain with you
     for ever.
R̷. Amen.

CHAPTER II

RITE OF CONFIRMATION OUTSIDE MASS

INTRODUCTORY RITES

ENTRANCE SONG

34. When the candidates, their sponsors and parents, and the whole assembly of the faithful have gathered, the bishop goes to the sanctuary with the priests who assist him, one or more deacons, and the ministers. Meanwhile all may sing a psalm or appropriate song.

35. The bishop makes the usual reverence to the altar with the ministers and greets the people:

Peace be with you.
All: **And also with you.**

OPENING PRAYER
Let us pray.

God of power and mercy,
send your Holy Spirit
to live in our hearts
and make us temples of his glory.
We ask this through our Lord Jesus Christ, your
    Son,
who lives and reigns with you and the Holy Spirit,
one God, for ever and ever.
℟. **Amen.**

Or:
Lord,
fulfill your promise:
send your Holy Spirit to make us witnesses before the
    world

to the Good News proclaimed by Jesus Christ, our
    Lord,
who lives and reigns with you and the Holy Spirit,
one God, for ever and ever.
℟. Amen.

Or:
Lord,
send us your Holy Spirit
to help us walk in unity of faith
and grow in the strength of his love
to the full stature of Christ,
who lives and reigns with you and the Holy Spirit,
one God, for ever and ever.
℟. Amen.

Or:
Lord,
fulfill the promise given by your Son
and send the Holy Spirit
to enlighten our minds
and lead us to all truth. Grant this through our Lord
    Jesus Christ,
who lives and reigns with you and the Holy Spirit,
one God, for ever and ever.
℟. Amen.

CELEBRATION OF THE WORD OF GOD

36. The celebration of the word of God follows. At least one
of the readings suggested for the Mass of confirmation (see
nos. 61-65) is read.

37. If two or three readings are chosen, the traditional order
is followed, that is, the Old Testament, the Apostle, and the
Gospel. After the first and second reading there should be a
psalm or song, or a period of silence may be observed.

SACRAMENT OF CONFIRMATION

PRESENTATION OF THE CANDIDATES

38. After the readings the bishop and the priests who will be ministers of the sacrament with him take their seats. The pastor or another priest, deacon, or catechist presents the candidates for confirmation, according to the custom of the region. If possible, each candidate is called by name and comes individually to the sanctuary. If the candidates are children, they are accompanied by one of their sponsors or parents and stand before the celebrant.

If there are very many candidates, they are not called by name, but simply take a suitable place before the bishop.

HOMILY OR INSTRUCTION

39. The bishop then gives a brief homily. He should explain the readings and so lead the candidates, their sponsors and parents, and the whole assembly to a deeper understanding of the mystery of confirmation.

He may use these or similar words:

On the day of Pentecost the apostles received the Holy Spirit as the Lord had promised. They also received the power of giving the Holy Spirit to others and so completing the work of baptism. This we read in the Acts of the Apostles. When Saint Paul placed his hands on those who had been baptized, the Holy Spirit came upon them, and they began to speak in other languages and in prophetic words.

Bishops are successors of the apostles and have this power of giving the Holy Spirit to the baptized, either personally or through the priests they appoint.

In our day the coming of the Holy Spirit in confirmation is no longer marked by the gift of tongues, but we know his coming by faith. He fills our hearts with the love of God, brings us together in one faith but in different vocations, and works within us to make the Church one and holy.

The gift of the Holy Spirit which you are to receive

will be a spiritual sign and seal to make you more like Christ and more perfect members of his Church. At his baptism by John, Christ himself was anointed by the Spirit and sent out on his public ministry to set the world on fire.

You have already been baptized into Christ and now you will receive the power of his Spirit and the sign of the cross on your forehead. You must be witnesses before all the world to his suffering, death, and resurrection; your way of life should at all times reflect the goodness of Christ. Christ gives varied gifts to his Church, and the Spirit distributes them among the members of Christ's body to build up the holy people of God in unity and love.

Be active members of the Church, alive in Jesus Christ. Under the guidance of the Holy Spirit give your lives completely in the service of all, as did Christ, who came not to be served but to serve.

So now, before you receive the Spirit, I ask you to renew the profession of faith you made in baptism or your parents and godparents made in union with the whole Church.

RENEWAL OF BAPTISMAL PROMISES
40. After the homily the candidates stand and the bishop questions them:

Do you reject Satan and all his works and all his empty promises?
The candidates respond together: **I do.**

Bishop:
Do you believe in God the Father almighty, creator of heaven and earth?
Candidates: **I do.**

Bishop:
Do you believe in Jesus Christ, his only Son, our Lord, who was born of the Virgin Mary, was crucified, died, and was buried, rose from the dead,

and is now seated at the right hand of the Father?
Candidates: **I do.**

Bishop:
**Do you believe in the Holy Spirit,
the Lord, the giver of life,
who came upon the apostles at Pentecost
and today is given to you sacramentally in
    confirmation?**
Candidates: **I do.**

Bishop:
**Do you believe in the holy catholic Church,
the communion of saints, the forgiveness of sins,
the resurrection of the body, and life everlasting?**
Candidates: **I do.**

The bishop confirms their profession of faith by proclaiming
the faith of the Church:

**This is our faith. This is the faith of the Church.
We are proud to profess it in Christ Jesus our Lord.**
The whole congregation responds: **Amen.**

For **This is our faith,** some other formula may be substituted, or the community may express its faith in a suitable
song.

THE LAYING ON OF HANDS

41. The concelebrating priests stand near the bishop. He
faces the people and with hands joined, sings or says:

**My dear friends:
in baptism God our Father gave the new birth of
    eternal life
to his chosen sons and daughters.
Let us pray to our Father
that he will pour out the Holy Spirit
to strengthen his sons and daughters with his gifts
and anoint them to be more like Christ the Son of
    God.**

All pray in silence for a short time.

42. The bishop and the priests who will minister the sacrament with him lay hands upon all the candidates (by extending their hands over them). The bishop alone sings or says:

All-powerful God, Father of our Lord Jesus Christ,
by water and the Holy Spirit
you freed your sons and daughters from sin
and gave them new life.
Send your Holy Spirit upon them
to be their Helper and Guide.
Give them the spirit of wisdom and understanding,
the spirit of right judgment and courage,
the spirit of knowledge and reverence.
Fill them with the spirit of wonder and awe in your
    presence.
We ask this through Christ our Lord.
℞. **Amen.**

THE ANOINTING WITH CHRISM

43. The deacon brings the chrism to the bishop. Each candidate goes to the bishop, or the bishop may go to the individual candidates. The one who presented the candidate places his right hand on the latter's shoulder and gives the candidate's name to the bishop; or the candidate may give his own name.

44. The bishop dips his right thumb in the chrism and makes the sign of the cross on the forehead of the one to be confirmed, as he says:

N., be sealed with the Gift of the Holy Spirit.
The newly confirmed responds: **Amen.**

The bishop says:
Peace be with you.
The newly confirmed responds: **And also with you.**

45. If priests assist the bishop in conferring the sacrament, all the vessels of chrism are brought to the bishop by the deacon or by other ministers. Each of the priests comes to the bishop, who gives him a vessel of chrism.
The candidates go to the bishop or to the priests, or the bishop and priests may go to the candidates. The anointing is done as described above (no. 44).

46. During the anointing a suitable song may be sung. After the anointing the bishop and the priests wash their hands.

GENERAL INTERCESSIONS

47. The general intercessions follow, in this or a similar form determined by the competent authority.

Bishop:
My dear friends:
let us be one in prayer to God our Father
as we are one in the faith, hope, and love his Spirit
        gives.

Deacon or minister:
For these sons and daughters of God,
confirmed by the gift of the Spirit,
that they give witness to Christ
by lives built on faith and love:
let us pray to the Lord.
R̿. Lord, hear our prayer.

Deacon or minister:
For their parents and godparents
who led them in faith,
that by word and example they may always encourage
        them
to follow the way of Jesus Christ:
let us pray to the Lord.
R̿. Lord, hear our prayer.

Deacon or minister:
For the holy Church of God,
in union with N. our pope, N. our bishop, and all the
        bishops,
that God, who gathers us together by the Holy Spirit,
may help us grow in unity of faith and love
until his Son returns in glory:
let us pray to the Lord.
R̿. Lord, hear our prayer.

Deacon or minister:
For all men,
of every race and nation,

that they may acknowledge the one God as Father,
and in the bond of common brotherhood
seek his kingdom,
which is peace and joy in the Holy Spirit:
let us pray to the Lord.
R̂. Lord, hear our prayer.

Bishop:
God our Father,
you sent your Holy Spirit upon the apostles,
and through them and their successors
you give the Spirit to your people.
May his work begun at Pentecost
continue to grow in the hearts of all who believe.
We ask this through Christ our Lord.

LORD'S PRAYER

48. All then say the Lord's Prayer, which the bishop may
introduce in these or similar words:

Dear friends in Christ,
let us pray together
as the Lord Jesus Christ has taught.

All:
Our Father. . . .

49. After the Lord's Prayer the bishop blesses all present.
Instead of the usual blessing, the following blessing or
prayer over the people is used.

God our Father
made you his children by water and the Holy Spirit:
may he bless you
and watch over you with his fatherly love.
R̂. Amen.

Jesus Christ the Son of God
promised that the Spirit of truth
would be with his Church for ever:
may he bless you and give you courage
in professing the true faith.
R̂. Amen.

The Holy Spirit
came down upon the disciples
and set their hearts on fire with love:
may he bless you,
keep you one in faith and love
and bring you to the joy of God's kingdom.
℟. Amen.

The bishop adds immediately:

May almighty God bless you,
the Father, and the Son, ✝ and the Holy Spirit.
℟. Amen.

PRAYER OVER THE PEOPLE

Instead of the preceding blessing, the prayer over the people
may be used.
The deacon or minister gives the invitation in these or similar words:

Bow your heads and pray for God's blessing.

The bishop extends his hands over the people and sings or
says:

God our Father,
complete the work you have begun
and keep the gifts of your Holy Spirit
active in the hearts of your people.
Make them ready to live his Gospel
and eager to do his will.
May they never be ashamed
to proclaim to all the world Christ crucified
living and reigning for ever and ever.
℟. Amen.

The bishop adds immediately:

And may the blessing of almighty God
the Father, and the Son, ✝ and the Holy Spirit,
Come upon you and remain with you forever.
℟. Amen.

CHAPTER III

RITE OF CONFIRMATION BY A MINISTER WHO IS NOT A BISHOP

50. The minister of confirmation who is not a bishop and who confirms either by concession of the general law or by special indult of the Apostolic See observes the rite described above.

51. If, because of the large number of candidates, other priests join the celebrant in the administration of the sacrament, he chooses them in accord with no. 8 above. These priests should also concelebrate the Mass in which confirmation is conferred.

CHAPTER IV

CONFIRMATION OF A PERSON IN DANGER OF DEATH

52. It is of the greatest importance that the initiation of every baptized Christian be completed by the sacraments of confirmation and the eucharist. The sick person in danger of death who has reached the age of reason should therefore be strengthened by confirmation before he receives the eucharist as viaticum, after the necessary and possible catechesis.

Confirmation in danger of death and anointing of the sick are not ordinarily to be celebrated in a continuous rite.

In the case of a child who has not yet reached the age of reason, confirmation is given in accord with the same principles and norms as for baptism.

53. When circumstances permit, the entire rite described above is followed.

54. In case of urgent necessity, the minister of confirmation lays his hands upon the sick person as he says:

All-powerful God, Father of our Lord Jesus Christ,
by water and the Holy Spirit
you freed your son (daughter) from sin
and gave him (her) new life.
Send your Holy Spirit upon him (her)
to be his (her) Helper and Guide.
Give him (her) the spirit of wisdom and
understanding,
the spirit of right judgment and courage,
the spirit of knowledge and reverence.
Fill him (her) with the spirit of wonder and awe in
your presence.
We ask this through Christ our Lord.
R̶⁊. Amen.

55. Then the minister dips his right thumb in the chrism and makes the sign of the cross on the forehead of the one to be confirmed, as he says:

N., be sealed with the Gift of the Holy Spirit.

The newly confirmed responds, if he is able: **Amen.**

Other parts of the preparatory and concluding rites may be added in individual cases, depending on the circumstances.

56. In case of extreme necessity, it is sufficient that the anointing be done with the sacramental form:

N., be sealed with the Gift of the Holy Spirit.

CHAPTER V

TEXTS FOR THE CELEBRATION OF CONFIRMATION

I. MASS FOR THE CELEBRATION OF CONFIRMATION

57. One of the following Masses is celebrated where confirmation is given within Mass or immediately before or after it, except on the Sundays of Advent, Lent and Easter, Solemnities, Ash Wednesday, and the weekdays of Holy Week. Red or white vestments are worn.

A

58.

INTRODUCTORY RITES
Ezekiel 36:25-26
I will pour clean water on you and I will give you a new heart, a new spirit within you, says the Lord.

OPENING PRAYER

**God of power and mercy,
send your Holy Spirit
to live in our hearts
and make us temples of his glory.**

**We ask this through our Lord Jesus Christ, your Son,
who lives and reigns with you and the Holy Spirit,
one God, for ever and ever.**
℟. **Amen.**

Or:
**Lord,
fulfill your promise.
Send your Holy Spirit
to make us witnesses before the world
to the good news proclaimed by Jesus Christ, our
    Lord,**

who lives and reigns with you and the Holy Spirit,
one God, for ever and ever.
R̷. Amen.

Another prayer may be chosen from nos. 59, 60.
See Lectionary for Mass, nos. 763–767.

PRAYER OVER THE GIFTS
Pray, brethren ...

Lord,
we celebrate the memorial of our redemption
by which your Son won for us the gift of the Holy
      Spirit.
Accept our offerings,
and send us your Spirit
to make us more like Christ
in bearing witness to the world.

We ask this through Christ our Lord.
R̷. Amen.

When Eucharistic Prayer I is used, the special form of **Father,
accept this offering** is said.

Father,
accept this offering
from your whole family
and from those reborn in baptism
and confirmed by the coming of the Holy Spirit.
Protect them with your love and keep them close to
      you.
[Through Christ our Lord.   R̷. Amen.]

COMMUNION RITE
See Hebrews 6:4
All you who have been enlightened, who have experienced the gift of heaven and who have received
your share of the Holy Spirit: rejoice in the Lord.

PRAYER AFTER COMMUNION
Let us pray.

Pause for silent prayer, if this has not preceded.

Lord,
help those you have anointed by your Spirit
and fed with the body and blood of your Son.
Support them through every trial
and by their works of love.
build up the Church in holiness and joy.
Grant this through Christ our Lord.
R̷. Amen.

SOLEMN BLESSING
God our Father
made you his children by water and the Holy Spirit:
may he bless you
and watch over you with his fatherly love.
R̷. Amen.

Jesus Christ the Son of God
promised that the Spirit of truth
would be with his Church for ever:
may he bless you and give you courage
in professing the true faith.
R̷. Amen.

The Holy Spirit
came down upon the disciples
and set their hearts on fire with love:
may he bless you,
keep you one in faith and love
and bring you to the joy of God's kingdom.
R̷. Amen.

May almighty God bless you.
the Father, and the Son, ✝ and the Holy Spirit.
R̷. Amen.

Or:

PRAYER OVER THE PEOPLE
God our Father,
complete the work you have begun
and keep the gifts of your Holy Spirit
active in the hearts of your people.
Make them ready to live his gospel
and eager to do his will.

May they never be ashamed
to proclaim to all the world Christ crucified
living and reigning for ever and ever.
R�7. Amen.

And may the blessing of Almighty God,
the Father, and the Son, ✝ and the Holy Spirit,
come upon you and remain with you for ever.
R�7. Amen.

B
59.

INTRODUCTORY RITES
See Romans 5:5; 8:11
The love of God has been poured into our hearts by
his Spirit living in us.

OPENING PRAYER
Lord,
send us your Holy Spirit
to help us walk in unity of faith
and grow in the strength of his love
to the full stature of Christ,
who lives and reigns with you and the Holy Spirit,
one God, for ever and ever.
R�7. Amen.

Another prayer may be chosen from nos. 58, 60.
See Lectionary for Mass, nos. 763–767.

PRAYER OVER THE GIFTS
Pray, brethren ...

Lord,
you have signed our brothers and sisters
with the cross of your Son
and anointed them with the oil of salvation.
As they offer themselves with Christ,
continue to fill their hearts with your Spirit.
We ask this through Christ our Lord.
R̊. Amen.

When Eucharistic Prayer I is used, the special form of **Father, accept this offering** is said, as in the preceding Mass.

COMMUNION RITE
Psalm 34:6, 9
Look up at him with gladness and smile; taste and see the goodness of the Lord.

PRAYER AFTER COMMUNION
Let us pray.

Pause for silent prayer, if this has not preceded.

**Lord,
you give your Son as food
to those you anoint with your Spirit.
Help them to fulfill your law
by living in freedom as your children.
May they live in holiness
and be your witnesses to the world.**

**We ask this through Christ our Lord.
R̃. Amen.**

II. OTHER PRAYERS
60.

OPENING PRAYER
**Lord,
fulfill the promise given by your Son
and send the Holy Spirit
to enlighten our minds and lead us to all truth.
Grant this through our Lord Jesus Christ, your Son,
who lives and reigns with you and the Holy Spirit
one God, for ever and ever.
R̃. Amen.**

PRAYER OVER THE GIFTS
Pray, brethren ...

**Lord,
accept the offering of your family**

and help those who receive the gift of your Spirit
to keep him in their hearts
and come to the reward of eternal life.
We ask this in the name of Jesus the Lord.
R̸. Amen.

PRAYER AFTER COMMUNION

Let us pray.

Pause for silent prayer, if this has not preceded.

Lord,
we have shared the one bread of life.
Send the Spirit of your love
to keep us one in faith and peace.

R̸. Amen.

III. BIBLICAL READINGS

61. Readings from the Old Testament

1. Isaiah 11:1-4a
On him the Spirit of the Lord rests.

2. Isaiah 42:1-3
I have endowed my servant with my Spirit.

3. Isaiah 61:1-3a, 6a, 8b-9
The Lord God has anointed me and has sent me to bring
Good News to the poor, to give them the oil of gladness.

4. Ezekiel 36:24-28
I will place a new Spirit in your midst.

5. Joel 2:23a, 26-30a
(Hebrew 2:23a; 3:1-3a)
I will pour out my Spirit on all mankind.

62. Readings from the New Testament

1. Acts 1:3-8
You will receive the power of the Holy Spirit, and you will
be my witnesses.

2. Acts 2:1-6, 14, 22b-23, 32-33
They were all filled with the Holy Spirit, and began to speak.

3. Acts 8:1, 4, 14-17
They laid hands on them, and they received the Holy Spirit.

4. Acts 10:1, 33-34a, 37-44
The Holy Spirit came down on all those listening to the word of God.

5. Acts 19:1b-6a
Did you receive the Holy Spirit when you became believers?

6. Romans 5:1-2, 5-8
The love of God has been poured into our hearts by the Holy Spirit which has been given to us.

7. Romans 8:14-17
The Spirit himself and our spirit bear united witness that we are children of God.

8. Romans 8:26-27
The Spirit himself will express our plea in a way that could never be put to words.

9. 1 Corinthians 12:4-13
There is one and the same Spirit giving to each as he wills.

10. Galatians 5:16-17, 22-23a, 24-25
If we live in the Spirit, let us be directed by the Spirit.

11. Ephesians 1:3a, 4a, 13-19a
You have been signed with the seal of the Holy Spirit of the promise.

12. Ephesians 4:1-6
There is one body, one Spirit, and one baptism.

63. Responsorial Psalms

1. Psalm 22:23-24, 26-27, 28 and 31-32
R̊. (23): **I will proclaim your name to my brothers.**
or: (John 15:26-27):
When the Holy Spirit comes to you, you will be my witness.

2. Psalm 23:1-3a, 3b-4, 5-6
R̊. (1): **The Lord is my shepherd; there is nothing I shall want.**

3. Psalm 96:1-2a, 2b-3, 9-10a, 11-12

R̶. (3): **Proclaim his marvelous deeds to all the nations.**

4. Psalm 104:1ab and 24, 27-28, 30-31, 33-34

R̶. (30): **Lord, send out your Spirit, and renew the face of the earth.**

5. Psalm 117:1, 2

R̶. (Acts 1:8): **You will be my witnesses to all the world.**
or: **Alleluia.**

6. Psalm 145:2-3, 4-5, 8-9, 10-11, 15-16, 21

R̶. (1b): **I will praise your name for ever, Lord.**

64. Alleluia Verse and Verse before the Gospel

1. John 14:16

**The Father will send you the Holy Spirit, says the
    Lord,
to be with you for ever.**

2. John 15:26b, 27a

**The Spirit of truth will bear witness to me, says the
    Lord,
and you also will be my witnesses.**

3. John 16:13a; 14:26b

**When the Spirit of truth comes, he will teach you all
    truth
and bring to your mind all I have told you.**

4. Revelation 1:5a, 6

**Jesus Christ, you are the faithful witness, firstborn
    from the dead;
you have made us a kingdom of priests to serve our
    God and Father.**

**5. Come, Holy Spirit, fill the hearts of your faithful;
    and kindle in them the fire of your love.**

**6. Come, Holy Spirit;
    shine on us the radiance of your light.**

65. Gospel

1. Matthew 5:1-12a
Theirs is the kingdom of heaven.

2. Matthew 16:24-27
If anyone wishes to follow me, let him deny himself.

3. Matthew 25:14-30
Because you have been faithful in small matters, come into the joy of your master.

4. Mark 1:9-11
He saw the Spirit descending and remaining on him.

5. Luke 4:16-22a
The Spirit of the Lord is upon me.

6. Luke 8:4-10a, 11b-15
Some seed fell into rich soil. These are the people who receive the word and bear fruit in patience.

7. Luke 10:21-24
I bless you, Father, for revealing these things to children.

8. John 7:37b-39
From the heart of the Lord shall flow fountains of living water.

9. John 14:15-17
The Spirit of truth will be with you for ever.

10. John 14:23-26
The Holy Spirit will teach you everything.

11. John 15:18-21, 26-27
The Spirit of truth who issues from the Father, will be my witness.

12. John 16:5b-7, 12-13a (Greek 5-7, 12-13a)
The Spirit of truth will lead you to the complete truth.